PUNISHMENT AND INCLUSION

just ideas

transformative ideals of justice in ethical and political thought

series editors

Drucilla Cornell

Roger Berkowitz

PUNISHMENT AND INCLUSION

RACE, MEMBERSHIP, AND THE LIMITS OF AMERICAN LIBERALISM

Andrew Dilts

FORDHAM UNIVERSITY PRESS

NEW YORK   2014

Frontispiece: Metropolitan Correctional Center, Chicago, Illinois.
Photo by Markus Hardtmann

Fordham University Press has no responsibility for the persistence or accuracy of URLs for external or third-party Internet websites referred to in this publication and does not guarantee that any content on such websites is, or will remain, accurate or appropriate.

Fordham University Press also publishes its books in a variety of electronic formats. Some content that appears in print may not be available in electronic books.

Library of Congress Cataloging-in-Publication Data

Dilts, Andrew.
  Punishment and inclusion : race, membership, and the limits of American liberalism / Andrew Dilts.
      pages cm. — (Just ideas)
  Summary: "This book gives a theoretical and historical account of felon disenfranchisement, showing deep connections between punishment and citizenship practices in the United States. These connections are deployed quietly and yet perniciously as part of a political system of white supremacy, shaping contemporary regimes of punishment and governance" — Provided by publisher.
  Includes bibliographical references and index.
  ISBN 978-0-8232-6241-0 (hardback) — ISBN 978-0-8232-6242-7 (paper)
  1. Suffrage—United States.   2. Prisoners—Suffrage—United States.   3. Political rights, Loss of—United States.   4. Discrimination in criminal justice administration—United States.   5. Punishment—United States.   6. Citizenship—United States.
  7. Race—Political aspects—United States.   8. Liberalism—United States.   9. United States—Politics and government.   I. Title.
  JK1846.D55 2014
  324.6'20869270973—dc23

                                                            2014011964

Printed in the United States of America

16 15 14   5 4 3 2 1

First edition

for SK

Contents

Preface

The Los Angeles County jail system holds approximately twenty thousand inmates on any given day, and around a quarter of them are held in Men's Central Jail. By some counts, it holds more people in custody than any other single facility in the world. Like most jails, its original purpose was to house pretrial inmates who were either denied or could not post bail and sentenced inmates who are back in LA County for court dates. But as the California prison system swelled after the 1970s, Men's Central now also houses inmates serving long state sentences. There are more and more such inmates at Men's Central and at local jails throughout the state since the U.S. Supreme Court ordered California in 2011 to reduce unconstitutional levels of overcrowding in the state prisons.

During a recent visit to Men's Central with a group of students, a sergeant in the Los Angeles Sheriff's Department who works in the jail's Community Transition Unit spent a few hours showing us around the facility. He pointed out a set of color-coded lines painted along the floor. "It's just like in the hospital," he stated, showing how the different colored lines lead to different parts of the facility. Inmates walk single file along the lines, and many stop and turn to face the wall when visitors like us approach. This is not a firm rule any longer, the sergeant told us, but the men who have been here a while still turn away from us out of habit. Our guide told us that Men's Central is one of the largest jails in the "free world" and that across the street—in the Twin Towers Correctional Facility, also a part of the county jail system—is the largest mental health facility in the "free world."

Along the walls of the corridors of Men's Central Jail are murals painted by inmates (a project run by a retired sheriff's deputy who volunteers in the jail, but one which is constantly under threat of cancellation), stenciled rules and warnings to inmates, and contact information for the American Civil Liberties Union of Southern California for inmates with complaints about the conditions of their confinement. The ACLU currently acts as a court-appointed monitor of jail conditions in Los Angeles, following a series of successful lawsuits against the county for inhumane and illegal treatment of inmates. I asked the sergeant about the ACLU oversight as we entered a "recreation yard"—nothing more than a windowless room with several small tables bolted to the floor—and he replied that most of the complaints are about the food. Since we entered the jail, we had not been in a room that has direct natural light. The sergeant told us that they used to use the roof of the jail as an exercise yard but had to stop doing so because of "security concerns."

Along one of the corridors, a small flyer with a large American flag and the words "LA Votes!" caught my eye. It was from the Los Angeles County Registrar-Recorder's office informing inmates of their voting rights. Inmates jailed at Men's Central who are qualified California voters (i.e., citizens of the United States who will be at least eighteen years old at the time of the next election and have not been declared "mentally incompetent" by a court) may register to vote by mail if they are awaiting trial, are currently on trial, or are serving time for misdemeanor or traffic offenses. As defined in the California State Constitution, citizens are disenfranchised upon conviction of a felony until the completion of their sentences (including any time served on parole). California, like nearly every other state in the United States, disenfranchises convicted felons during the time of their punitive sentences as a collateral consequence of their conviction. Many other states disenfranchise felons long after their sentences are completed, and some for the rest of their lives, permanently barring felons from the franchise.

It is difficult to know how many inmates at Men's Central Jail vote, but a two-week-long voter-registration drive inside the jail organized by the Community Transition Unit registered more than twelve hundred new voters before the 2012 presidential election. Across the rest of California, there are over 130,000 inmates incarcerated for felony convictions: not all of them would otherwise be eligible voters, but all of them are definitively barred from the ballot box. These inmates are still counted in census figures for purposes of political representation and government funding. California recently became one of only a handful of states that count inmates as residing in their last place of residence (at least for purposes of representation). In contrast, the vast majority of states count inmates where they are incarcerated, a form of gerrymandering that gives localities with large prison populations increased political and economic power but does not require them to be electorally accountable to the prisoners they hold. Given the disproportionately nonwhite population of most state prisons and the relative whiteness of most prison towns, many of us who study and teach about mass incarceration in the United States point back to the original language of the U.S. Constitution to identify a precursor for the form of racial domination that felon disenfranchisement represents. In the United States today, felons appear analogous to the "three fifths of all other Persons" counted in addition to "free persons" in the antebellum period.

Men's Central Jail sits just north of downtown Los Angeles, and along with the Twin Towers complex next door, it looms over the busy freeways that crisscross the city. I do not know how many of the hundreds of thousands of people driving by each day know what it is, or if they give it much thought. But even if they do not, this jail, along with all the prisons throughout the United States (including those intentionally hidden from sight and out of mind), shapes the world we live in, giving meaning and form to our practices and ourselves. The jail is also visible from the windows of an elementary school in Boyle Heights, a largely immigrant neighborhood in East Los Angeles that is one of the most heavily policed neighborhoods in the city. My students and I spent the night there after our visit to the jail and meetings with several groups working to reduce gang violence, police brutality, and mass incarceration. One group we met with had posters up in its offices that read, "Build Schools, Not Jails." The group works to dismantle what has come to be called the "school-to-prison pipeline." That phrase, capturing the way in which the lives of marginalized youth are criminalized, tracked, and policed such that their life chances are shaped with incarceration as their destiny, takes on renewed force as I sit in the classroom and look at the jail—one of the largest houses of confinement in the "free world."

This book is about punishment and membership. It is about the meaning of the vote and the practice of voting under the conditions of felon disenfranchisement. It is about how we use punishment to both exclude and include people in the political body of the United States, and it is about how we use the rights of political membership to punish people. It is about how we violate deeply held public commitments to self-government, democratic equality, and liberal freedom and about how these violations nevertheless support those same commitments, operating through the pernicious and persistent history of white supremacy as a political system. It is about how we come to be the persons we are through these violations and how we police the boundaries of whiteness, masculinity, ability, and normality through institutions and practices that are supposed to be blind to ascriptive differences. To that end, this book is about how we think about justice, the politics of inclusion, and how we organize our political lives in relation to others. It calls for policy changes, to be sure, but it also demands a frank confrontation with the reasons that policy is so difficult to change. Doing so asks us to confront how what we do to others shapes ourselves. The final question, to echo the words of Simone de Beauvoir, is whether we will allow this state of affairs to continue.

Acknowledgments

As I learned from my friend and teacher Patchen Markell, acknowledgment is a difficult practice. Trying to account for all the ways in which this book is the product of many years of work is a powerful and happy reminder of how deeply and widely connected to others I am fortunate to be. But as with any appearance of a thing in public, I also cannot possibly account for everything that has gone into this book; and any list of debts I owe will be necessarily incomplete, and any expression of the gratitude that I feel to so many others who have helped me and challenged me will be insufficient.

Nevertheless, I must first thank the teachers at the University of Chicago who directly helped to shape this project: Patchen Markell, Robert Gooding-Williams, Bernard Harcourt, Cathy Cohen, and Iris Marion Young. This project began in their classrooms and their offices, and I am eternally grateful for their mentorship, guidance, and friendship.

Most of this book was written while I lived in Chicago. The "city on the make" and its people will always have a hold on me. I owe much to the Department of Political Science and the Society of Fellows in the Liberal Arts at the University of Chicago, which supported me materially and surrounded me with teachers, colleagues, and friends at the university and beyond its walls. Many of these people read pieces of this book and gave me frank and helpful advice. And everyone single one of them supported me with their thoughts and their patience. The argument of this book and my ability to make it is directly indebted to Bethany Albertson, Kathy Anderson, Greg Beckett, Jeremy Bell, John Brehm, Chris Buck, Zachary Callen, Rob Campbell, Craig Carson, Jon Caverley, Jamila Celestine-Michener, Anita Chari, Katie Chenoweth, Bertram Cohler, Gabriella Coleman, Chris Deis, John

Dobard, Marie Draz, Lauren Duquette, Erin Fehskens, Samantha Fenno, Joe Fischel, Andrea Frank, Emily Garcia, Dorit Geva, Loren Goldman, Marissa Guerrero, Dina Gusejnova, Melissa Harris-Perry, Anne Holthofer, Dilek Huseyinzadegan, Robin James, O'Donavan Johnson, Jenna Jordan, Reha Kadakal, Julia Klein, Andrew LaZella, Leigh Clare La Berge, Jacob Levy, Megan Luke, Chris Macintosh, Mara Marin, Jana McAulife, Kristin Mc-Cartney, John McCormick, J. J. McFadden, Ben McKean, Mona Mehta, Emily Meierding, Julie Merseth, Tim Michael, Tom Miles, Nuno Monteiro, Darell Moore, Holly Moore, Sankar Muthu, Victor Muñiz-Fraticelli, Emily Nacol, Michael Naas, Ian Needham, Patricia Nordeen, Eric Oliver, Nima Paidipaty, Jennifer Palmer, Jeff Pardikes, Amanda Parris, Jennifer Pitts, Heather Rakes, Neil Roberts, Gerry Rosenberg, Keven Ruby, Shalini Satkunanandan, Jade Schiff, Nitzan Shoshan, Ian Storey, Nathan Tarcov, Kevin Thompson, Neil Verma, Danielle Wallace, Christopher Warren, Richard Westerman, Rosa Williams, Deva Woodly, Anna Youatt, Rafi Youatt, and Perry Zurn.

I have been able to finish this book with the amazing support of new friends and colleagues at Loyola Marymount University in Los Angeles. The Department of Political Science, the dean's office of the Bellarmine College of Liberal Arts, and the Center for Service and Action each provided material support and the time to make necessary revisions. At LMU, my deepest thanks go to Feryal Cherif, Richard Fox, Michael Genovese, Bryan Kimoto, Gil Klein, Margarita Ochoa, Gene Park, John Parrish, Jennifer Ramos, Brad Stone, Jessica Viramontes, Jeffrey Wilson, and Chris Zepeda-Millán.

Earlier versions of most of the chapters in this book have been presented at conferences and workshopped, and I have benefited greatly from the feedback of fellow panelists, discussants, audiences, and many other careful readers. All remaining mistakes, errors, and confusions are entirely my own, of course, but I am deeply grateful to all those people who directly commented on parts of the book at various stages in its development. Thank you to Barbara Arneil, Anita Chari, George Ciccariello-Maher, Jennifer Culbert, Suzanne Dovi, Stefan Dolgert, Marie Draz, Alec Ewald, Lennie Feldman, Joe Fischel, Fred Lee, Stephanie Jenkins, Colin Koopman, Nancy Luxon, Keally McBride, Ladelle McWhorter, Emily Nacol, Michael Nordquist, John Parrish, Paul Passavant, Brian Pinaire, Michael Ralph, Claire Rasmussen, Alice Ristroph, Neil Roberts, Stephen Rosow, Jade Schiff, Molly Shanley, Jill Stauffer, Ian Storey, Shatema Threadcraft, Megan Wachspress, Michael Welch, and Deva Woodly.

Thank you to everyone at Fordham University Press, especially Helen Tartar, Thomas Lay, Andrew Katz, Loomis Mayer, Eric Newman, Kate O'Brien-Nicolson, and Kathleen Sweeney. And thank you so much to Roger Berkowitz and Drucilla Cornell for showing such interest in my work and inviting me to join the Just Ideas series. The excellent comments from reviewers of the manuscript challenged me to clarify my argument, and the resulting book is far improved thanks to their incredible work. Portions of Chapter 3 were originally published in "Michel Foucault Meets Gary Becker: Criminality Beyond *Discipline and Punish*," in *The Carceral Notebooks*, vol. 4 (2008). An earlier version of Chapter 4 appeared as "To Kill a Thief: Punishment, Proportionality, and Criminal Subjectivity in Locke's *Second Treatise*," *Political Theory* 40, no. 1 (February 2012). And portions of Chapters 7 and 8 were published as "Incurable Blackness: Collateral Consequences to Incarceration and Mental Disability," *Disability Studies Quarterly* 32, no. 3 (July 2012). Thank you to Bernard Harcourt, Sage Publications, and the Society for Disability Studies for allowing me to reprint this material here. Moreover, thank you to the editors and anonymous reviewers at these journals for helpful feedback and the opportunity to publish with them.

Several people deserve special and repeated thanks. Thank you to Chris Buck and Emily Meierding for their particular roles as cofounders of Harper House. Bethany Albertson and Deva Woodly have mentored me since I began graduate school, and I continue to aspire to be like them in everything that I do. Greg Beckett displayed the courage of a true friend throughout the editing of this book. Keally McBride (and her wonderful family) provided a physical space to finish revisions to this book, and she has been an incredible intellectual guide and friend throughout. Perry Zurn guided me through difficult questions of translation and interpretation, and his own work inspires me to try to write more like him. Anne and Jon Dilts have read every page of this book with a critical eye that only teachers and newspaper editors have and the patience only parents possess.

I cannot write these acknowledgments without reflecting on the loss of Iris Young and Joel Olson. I originally came to Chicago to study with Iris. I can only hope that these pages reflect a little bit of her wisdom, passion, and dedication to justice. She always asked the hardest questions, and I hope that I have begun to come up with answers for her. I was never close to Joel Olson, but reading his work and learning about his dedication to antiracist action changed how I think. Both Iris and Joel worked tirelessly inside and outside the classroom to fight for justice, putting their bodies on the line and always insisting on the connection between thought and action. Their thought runs through this book, and their deaths have left the world a far poorer place.

The final stages of preparing this book for publication were marked by the sudden and devastating loss of Helen Tartar. I am beyond fortunate to have been able to work with Helen as my editor, and I am honored to have been able to call her my friend. This book, like so many others, would never have come to be without her careful guidance and unfailing support. The depth of our loss is as immeasurable as the reach of her gifts to us all.

I close with the most difficult debt to acknowledge, because there are no words to express it. Sina Kramer is my first and last interlocutor. She is my partner in thought and life. I cannot imagine thinking or writing without her in mind, and I hope to someday be able to think and write as clearly and passionately as she does about philosophy, politics, and justice. This book is for her, and it is for us.

A Note About the Cover

The photograph on the cover of this book is a close-up of the windows of the Metropolitan Correctional Center, Chicago. This federal jail facility was built in 1975, at the very start of the era of mass incarceration. It is located in the middle of downtown Chicago, just around the corner from the Chicago Board of Trade, the Federal Reserve Bank of Chicago, and the Harold Washington Library. It is hyper-visible with its triangular shape and distinctive window slits (each window is without bars and measures 5 inches wide by 7 feet tall). But it is also a building that hides in plain sight. When I lived in Chicago, I often passed this building without a thought, not realizing at all what it is. And it is precisely for this quality that I find it to be a fitting image for the cover of this book. The U.S. punishment system is a part of our built environment, a constant force in the lives of those who reside in the United States, and yet typically also an afterthought. This detail view of MCC Chicago, made by Markus Hardtmann and used with his kind permission, captures for me the way in which what we "see" of this system is always a matter of perspective, and requires a multiplicity of views if we are to understand it, let alone if we hope to change it.

PUNISHMENT AND INCLUSION

A Productive Injustice

It might be helpful to start with some numbers. At the start of the twenty-first century, roughly 1 percent of the population of the United States is in jail or prison.[1] Roughly 3 percent of the population of the United States is "on paper," that is, on parole or probation.[2] In forty-eight states and the District of Columbia, incarcerated felons cannot cast a vote; in thirty-five states, parolees cannot vote; in thirty of these, felons on probation cannot vote. In nine states, disenfranchisement may be permanent for certain offenses. And in three states—Kentucky, Virginia, and Iowa—disenfranchisement is for life. There are an estimated 5.3 million adult Americans who cannot vote because of a felony-class criminal conviction. Of these, over 2 million have *completed* their sentences in their entirety, while only about 1.3 million are actually incarcerated.[3] In total, this is a little more than 2 percent of the voting-age population.[4] A full third of the disenfranchised are African American, effectively disenfranchising nearly 8 percent of all adult African Americans in the United States. In Alabama, Kentucky, and Florida, one in every five adult African Americans cannot vote.[5]

The constitutionality of these restrictions on the right to vote is largely a settled question. On October 7, 2010, the full Ninth Circuit Court of Appeals ruled that the Voting Rights Act of 1965 does not prohibit criminal disenfranchisement, absent a showing of discriminatory intent in the adoption of disenfranchisement provisions.[6] Should this case be appealed and heard by the Supreme Court, there is little reason to expect it to disagree. The 1974 standard set by the Court in *Richardson v. Ramirez* expressly rejected a similar Voting Rights Act claim, noting that Section 2 of the Fourteenth Amendment to the U.S. Constitution allows the abridgment of voting rights for "participation in rebellion, or other crime." Provided that a disenfranchisement provision was not drawn up with explicit discriminatory intent, the courts have routinely insisted that a technically "color-blind" provision is entirely constitutional.

It is difficult to speak in generalities about felon disenfranchisement in the United States, as each state sets its own voting qualifications, governed only by a few federal mandates.[7] As such, there is great variation among states as to which classes of persons (ex-felons, probationers, parolees) are allowed to vote. To an important degree, it is misleading to refer to this form of exclusion as specifically "felon disenfranchisement" as if it were a unified form of criminal disenfranchisement.[8] This has led Department of Justice officials to characterize the mix of state laws as a "crazy-quilt" of policies.[9] Nevertheless, a recent series of policy changes in Iowa is illustrative of how precarious the right to vote is for persons with felony convictions.

In 2005, former governor Thomas Vilsack of Iowa made national headlines when he issued Executive Order 42 on the Fourth of July that year. The order restored the voting rights of nearly eighty thousand Iowans who had completed criminal sentences. Prior to this moment, Iowa was one of only five states that permanently disenfranchised felons. The state's first constitution, enacted in 1846, barred any person convicted of a felony or an "infamous crime" from holding office or casting a ballot. Vilsack's order was heralded by voting rights activists and, in particular, was seen as a major advancement of African American voting rights. Iowa has one of the most racially disproportionate incarceration rates in the country. While constituting less than 3 percent of the state population, African Americans represent a full quarter of the state's prison population. Prior to Vilsack's order, the disenfranchisement rate for African Americans in the state was above 30 percent, the highest in the nation. What was perhaps more important was that Order 42 effectively ended ex-felon disenfranchisement in Iowa. The Iowa

Department of Corrections was ordered to submit monthly lists of persons completing their sentences to the governor's office for automatic and immediate voting rights restoration. As a result, an additional twenty thousand Iowans have regained their right to vote since then.

Yet within hours of Governor Terry Branstad's inauguration on January 14, 2011, he fulfilled a campaign promise by rescinding Order 42, effectively ending automatic rights restoration. The estimated one hundred thousand Iowans who had been reenfranchised will not be affected, and so-called ex-felons are still eligible to apply to have their rights restored on a case-by-case basis. Such applications, however, can only be filed after an individual has fully paid all court costs, fines, and fees owed to the state. Such debt can easily reach tens of thousands of dollars, leading the Iowa-Nebraska State Conference of the NAACP to liken the process to a "modern day poll tax."[10] It is not alone in making such a comparison. Civil rights lawyer and author Michelle Alexander recently pointed to felon disenfranchisement as a key component of the "New Jim Crow" in the United States. "We have not ended racial caste in America," she writes; "we have merely redesigned it."[11]

The central question motivating this book is deceptively simple: what is the meaning of all this? What does it mean that Americans have, largely since the colonial period and most expansively during the later half of the nineteenth century, insisted again and again that the right to participation in collective self-government should be limited to people without criminal convictions? What does it mean to cast a vote under such conditions? What, to borrow a turn of phrase from Frederick Douglass, does it mean to be an American under the terms of felon disenfranchisement?

When I ask, "what does all this mean?" it is necessary to be clear what I do not mean. I do not mean, first of all, that this is about whether felon disenfranchisement is just or unjust under some specific terms of normative evaluation, although this is necessarily a question with which we will have to grapple. I do not mean to ask what social, economic, or political variables predict which states are most likely to disenfranchise felons.[12] Nor do I mean to discover the estimated electoral effects of disenfranchisement provisions.[13] And while there is a great deal to be said about the recent developments in Iowa and Florida and at various levels of the U.S. appellate court system, I do not mean narrowly to explain why various governors have issued the orders that they have or why various courts have issued the opinions that they have.[14]

I mean something else, something that intentionally steps back from the expressly normative and empirical questions about felon disenfranchisement and asks what this practice tells us about American liberalism as an organizing public ideology and, in particular, what it reveals about the relationship between punishment and citizenship under the terms of American liberalism.[15] To ask the question in this way, focusing on the social and political meaning of felon disenfranchisement, is to ask about the *work* of felon disenfranchisement, for those whom it directly affects and also for the subterranean but no less important work it does for those who remain identified as free and upstanding citizens. In the end, it is necessarily a way of asking what the practice tells us about the American political condition generally and about the productive limits of American liberalism's reliance on specific understandings of justice, inclusion, punishment, and membership.

I argue that felon disenfranchisement does not tell us very good things about living in the United States in the early years of the twenty-first century. This kind of academic focus tells us (if we limit "us" to those persons who have not been barred from the ballot box) that we continue to live in a racial caste system, that we fail to live up to our liberal ideals, that we trip over our commitments to civic republicanism, that we criminalize others who are different, that we treat each other as means toward our own ends of social and political equality, and most troubling of all, that we do so through one of our most cherished and sacred institutions: the franchise. Yet the deeper paradox of disenfranchisement is that it is a *productive failure*, in that it is symptomatic of liberalism's typical refusal to address the foundational tension between state punishment and political membership. Both the standard normative and empirical approaches to disenfranchisement reflect this symptomatic blindness as well, as they are caught up in justificatory frameworks that inhibit a consideration of how disenfranchisement produces and maintains the same subjects that are excluded from the franchise. For all of our failings, we continue to restrict access to the ballot box not simply because we have fallen short of our ideals (which we may surely have) but also because such failings are productive of those ideals, offering a sense of identity, security, and meaning.

To this end, *Punishment and Inclusion* tells a peculiar story about felon disenfranchisement. This practice, rooted in the history of political thought, contemporary social theory, postslavery restrictions on suffrage, and the contemporaneous emergence of the modern American penal system, reveals the deep connections between two American political institutions often thought to be separate: the boundaries of membership and the terms of criminal justice. I treat disenfranchisement first and foremost as a symptom, rather than as the disease itself. In this case, it points us to a deep tension *and* interdependence that persists in democratic politics between who is considered a member of the polity and how that polity punishes persons who violate its laws. The account given here reveals the work of membership done quietly by our criminal justice system and, conversely, the work of punishment done by the electoral franchise.

The story of criminal disenfranchisement told in this book is also particular to the United States and, as such, grapples with the broader structure of white supremacy as a political system. I follow the philosopher Charles Mills's account of white supremacy as "*itself* a political system, a particular power structure of formal or informal rule, socioeconomic privilege, and norms for the differential distribution of material wealth and opportunities, benefits and burdens, rights and duties."[16] As Mills argues, white supremacy is the "unnamed political system" that has produced the world we live in and the United States in particular. Criminal disenfranchisement plays an important role as a productive technique of race-making in the United States. From at least the nineteenth century until today, criminal disenfranchisement has worked to establish and maintain the color line as a marker of domination and control. As historical and empirical studies have already documented, the adoption of criminal disenfranchisement provisions and their continued popular support cannot be explained without reference to the racial history of the United States.[17] But my claim goes further: at the core of the American liberal project, a system of racial subordination and domination is continually reestablished and maintained through the current electoral system that operates under the terms of felon disenfranchisement.

Ultimately, I want to tell a story about how legal techniques, punitive practices, and political discourses have been routinely deployed to manage this internal tension between punishment and membership by displacing it onto the bodies of criminalized others. Disenfranchisement helps to produce the figures of the innocent citizen and the dangerous felon that it is supposed to manage or constrain. In doing so, it attempts to alleviate a set of broader anxieties of living in a social world where harm may come from our own hands and our own failings, rather than simply from others. If liberal theories of justice rely on such displacements, we must rethink the meaning of justice itself, refiguring it in a way that is sensitive to the contingency of one's political and legal standing, the production and fabrication of criminal kinds, and the social, political, and epistemological work done by the very practices we seek to adjudicate.

I absolutely think the practice of felon disenfranchisement must end in this country. Yet it is also my worry that this will not be sufficient if we continue to miss the connections between punishment and political membership as they define the American polity. The quest for inclusion will necessarily be incomplete if we fail to acknowledge the mutual constitution of punishment and citizenship. To end the practice of felon disenfranchisement without attending to its roots may simply displace the problem, producing a new symptom at a different border. This process is arguably already under way in the expansion of new techniques of punitive control that mange real and imagined American borders, such as the expansion of criminal background checks for employment, sex-offender registration requirements, and the massive proliferation of immigration detention centers—that is, prisons. It is better for us to confront the overlap between punishment and citizenship than to disavow the work that "criminals" do for us.

This book takes it title, in part, from Iris Young's *Inclusion and Democracy*.[18] As will become clear throughout my argument, her work greatly influences my thinking about disenfranchisement in particular. More generally, Young's work shapes my thinking about the meaning of justice, inclusion, deep democracy, and the importance of critical theory for understanding our situation. Part of our collective difficulty, Young notes, is that when we think about the boundaries of civil society and its political associations, we tend to assume in advance who members are and what kinds of activities and actions are acceptable. When such assumptions take the form of exclusion—blocking or preventing persons from the self-determination of their social and political lives—we are usually right to call this injustice and turn to inclusion as an obvious remedy. But as Young reminds us, we must be very careful to think about the terms on which inclusion operates, such that it does not produce what she calls "internal exclusions." Young's analysis reminds us that it is necessary to account for forms of exclusion and domination that have become built into our political environment, our language, and our theories of justice. This is difficult work, but it is important if we want to do more than simply end an unjust practice but also address the underlying reasons that make it so difficult to end.

Ending disenfranchisement—and the conditions that allow it to be so productive—requires us to first frankly diagnose the work it does for us and to take seriously "radical" proposals such as prison abolition, an investment in politics far beyond the ballot box, or the complete political inclusion of all stakeholders in democratic processes.[19] It also calls for a reorientation of our everyday practices as political and ethical ones, as practices necessarily caught up in a shared life with others. There is therefore something perverse about this book. It reflects an obsession with voting rights and the meaning of voting, and yet it is ultimately a call to get past voting rights, to get past voting itself, and to push far beyond the limited—yet necessary—terms of political inclusion that voting represents.

THE "FAILURE" OF FELON DISENFRANCHISEMENT

There are clear predecessors for criminal disenfranchisement as far back as ancient Greece and Rome as well as medieval Europe.[20] From being given the status of *atimia* in ancient Greece to being deemed an "outlaw" in medieval Germany and England to the declaration of "civil death" in feudal law, there have been numerous ways that authorities have stripped individuals of political standing, protections, or rights.[21] Such practices, importantly, were understood as overtly punitive, based primarily on the logic of retribution. Criminal disenfranchisement in the United States, however, sits powerfully within two distinctively "modern" forces: the rise of the rehabilitative ideal and figuration of citizenship as a birthright. As sociologists Jeff Manza and Chris Uggen put it succinctly in their empirical study of disenfranchisement, "The problem [of dismissing political rights for criminal offenders] becomes fundamentally different in a world in which mass participation— and citizenship *rights* defined by birth—emerges alongside notions of the possibility of *rehabilitating* criminal offenders."[22] Under classical and medieval conditions, the notions of political and participatory rights were already dramatically limited by today's standards.[23] The shift toward the ideal of rehabilitation alongside ever-increasing franchise rights seems to give criminal disenfranchisement a new form, if not a new meaning.

This is largely to say that the *meaning* of disenfranchisement is always situated in relation to the historically specific and contingent basis of membership already established. Early American colonial law, for instance, carried over criminal political exclusions from English common law, primarily in the form of restrictions of participation in public deliberations, the ability to hold public or honorific office, and the eligibility to act as a public witness. But given how restricted suffrage was in the colonial and postrevolutionary periods before the Jacksonian-era expansion of the franchise, what we would understand as criminal restrictions—removal from the electorate—simply did not exist in the United States until the early nineteenth century. Only Kentucky and Vermont had constitutional provisions for the disenfranchisement of criminals before 1800.[24] By 1821, however, eleven states had added some form of restriction or had authorized their legislatures to draw up some restriction on criminals.[25] Property qualifications on the franchise in nearly all these states (including ten of the original thirteen colonies) had already reduced the actual electorate.[26] The two key periods of growth for disenfranchisement are the years leading up to about 1850 and the period following the Civil War. In each period, the meaning of criminal disenfranchisement was necessarily linked to broader expansions of the franchise: the inclusion of white workingmen and former slaves, respectively.

During this first period, most criminal disenfranchisement restrictions were implemented in the Northeast beginning in the 1840s, directly following white manhood suffrage.[27] Manza and Uggen argue that white workingmen's suffrage directly drove this first wave of criminal disenfranchisement and was maintained alongside persistent restrictions on women, African Americans, and immigrants as roughly coequal groups of "undesirable voters." That is, in addition to the continued denial of the vote from these groups *as groups*, criminal exclusions emerged to police the franchise among persons recently given voting rights. As Manza and Uggen note, "Between 1840 and 1865, all 16 states adopting felon disenfranchisement measures did so *after* establishing full white male suffrage by eliminating property tests."[28] The two driving factors were the expansion of a criminal justice system and workingmen's suffrage, revealing disenfranchisement as embedded within the social and political context.[29]

Provisions enacted during this period (like nearly all disenfranchisement provisions throughout U.S. history) made no explicit or overt mention of race. During the pre–Civil War period, suffrage was largely restricted to white men through separate eligibility requirements. Yet concern increased throughout northern and border states about the status of "free Negroes" within their jurisdictions. Free blacks were a source of anxiety, particularly in terms of labor competition with white and immigrant workers and the public standing of whites in relation to former slaves. The question of how to deal with the "Negro problem" prompted numerous proposed "solutions," including mass deportation. The same period in which white workingmen won the right to vote was also a period of increasing support of state funded and managed colonization efforts in Liberia to remove blacks from the United States. Moreover, to assume these restrictions were not racialized because they were seemingly color-blind does not mean they were not part of redefining what it meant to be both white and a citizen. In fact, criminal disenfranchisement provisions did not need to be explicitly racialized in order to maintain and support a white vision of citizenship and innocence.

The second wave of disenfranchisement, immediately following the end of the Civil War, was far more openly racialized and concentrated in southern states, with nineteen states increasing restrictions on criminal exclusions.[30] While the most pernicious voting rights exclusions that emerged during this period were not linked to criminal convictions (e.g., poll taxes, grandfather clauses, etc.), the use of criminal disenfranchisement directly assisted the widespread project in southern states to resist the effects of the Thirteenth, Fourteenth, and Fifteenth Amendments to the Constitution, which banned chattel slavery and extended citizenship, due process, and voting rights to (some) freed slaves.[31] Post-1870, the single strongest predictor of criminal disenfranchisement provisions has been the relative proportion of African Americans incarcerated in a given state.[32]

Following the massive expansion of disenfranchisement after Reconstruction, little movement occurred until the civil rights era brought with it a period of general liberalization during the 1960s and early 1970s, focused primarily on removing *lifetime* voting bans but leaving disenfranchisement itself intact.[33] The high point in liberalization came during the early 1970s, in which twenty-three states made some substantial reform to their disenfranchisement provisions.[34] Nevertheless, these reforms were focused on the specifics of disenfranchisement and did not reflect a challenge to the practice itself. Popular sentiment and the difficulty of amending state constitutions further hampered reform in this period.[35] This "reform" period was also the same period in which heated rhetoric regarding crime policy reached a fever pitch, indicated by calls at federal, state, and local levels for a "war on crime" and a "war on drugs," which perniciously targeted nonwhite persons and has exacerbated racial inequality in the United States.[36] While there was some liberalization in the harshness of disenfranchisement provisions, the sheer number of persons who became subject to these provisions began to expand dramatically because of the rise of mass incarceration.[37] According to David Garland, two features define mass incarceration (or mass imprisonment): first, the sheer number of persons imprisoned became identifiably large in historical or comparative terms, and second, there was a "social concentration of imprisonment's effects."[38] The United States has met these criteria since the early 1970s, when incarceration became normalized for young black men concentrated in urban areas.[39] In terms of the franchise, Alexander Keyssar nicely sums up the difficulties of reform in the face of mass incarceration:

> At the beginning of the twenty-first century, convicted felons constitute the largest single group of American citizens who are barred by law from participating in elections. . . . That this group remains disfranchised despite the transformation of voting laws in the 1960s and 1970s reflects not only its racial composition but also its utter lack of political leverage. Indeed, convicted felons—mostly minority males, many of them young—probably possess negative political leverage: it would be costly to any politician to embrace their cause.[40]

In the past two decades, however, a new wave of reform has taken shape, and disenfranchisement provisions remain in flux. This is in part due to the increased attention on the issue after the 2000 election and the highly publicized question of inaccurate felon lists in Florida.[41] Additionally, several social movement organizations have emerged in the past decade, alongside professional policy organizations (such as the Sentencing Project), that agitate on behalf of disenfranchised persons.[42] Between 1997 and 2006, sixteen states substantially reformed their disenfranchisement provisions, leaving far fewer states with permanent exclusions.[43]

At the same time as this reform, however, there have also been revealing reversals. Since 1998, Utah, Massachusetts, and Kansas each substantially restricted voting rights for felons. Utah and Massachusetts (which previously had no restrictions on felon voting whatsoever) disenfranchised inmates, and Kansas disenfranchised probationers.[44] Of the states where rights restoration has become automatic upon completion of sentence, many states routinely fail to provide this information to former inmates. In Florida, the state's executive clemency office established an automatic restoration process for nonviolent offenders in 2007, but this decision was reversed in 2011.[45] And in Iowa, as already noted, the sweeping clemency offered for released prisoners in 2005 was overturned by executive order in 2011. Perhaps most importantly, there is still a strong barrier to allowing currently incarcerated felons the right to vote.[46] Even some of the strongest critics of felon disenfranchisement continue to take the exclusion of incarcerated persons as self-evident.[47] To a great degree, the disenfranchisement reform movement has (either for strategic or substantive reasons) solidified support for the disenfranchisement of currently incarcerated felons, focusing campaigns primarily on reducing "ex-felon" restrictions. And given the sheer number of people incarcerated in the United States, this is not a trivial number of persons categorically barred from franchise. More important, however, is the question of what it means that the United States continues to be so willing to link a foundational right of political membership with the punishment of incarceration.

FAILING JUSTICE, FAILING NORMATIVE THEORY

The puzzle of disenfranchisement runs far deeper than its reach. The scale of its impact is what often draws attention to it, something only possible in the past forty years of extreme incarceration rates. For instance, criminal disenfranchisement has always been a staggering failure as a form of punishment. "As a penal measure," Keyssar notes, "disfranchisement did not seem to serve any of the four conventional purposes of punishment: there was no evidence that it deterred crimes; it was an ill-fitting form of retribution; it did not limit the capacity of criminals to commit further crimes; and it certainly did not further the cause of rehabilitation."[48] On its face, disenfranchisement is a violation of most justifications for punishment, in that it is fundamentally a disproportionate practice. It is a poor fit in the narrow sense, in that it is a paradigmatically "collateral" consequence to a criminal conviction, applied statutorily as an *addition* to a punitive sentence. And it has disproportionate aggregate effects, punishing predictable groups more than others. As noted already, a full third of those who are disenfranchised for a criminal conviction are African American, and also, as noted, in states with the most sweeping disenfranchisement provisions, one in three adult black men are unable to vote.[49] As I argue at greater length throughout this book, this racial character is neither accidental nor trivial.

Traditional theories of just punishment understand punitive action as a necessary harm requiring specific justification, often constrained by the limitation that it must not inflict more harm than is right, good, necessary, or prudent. The adage that punishment must in some sense "fit the crime" appears in most philosophical literature dealing with the subject. Retributivists, utilitarians, classical liberals, and contemporary legal theorists (despite their substantial differences) typically all insist on a version of this principle. Some substantive concern for the proportionality of punishment can be found in otherwise diverse thinkers as Hobbes, Beccaria, Locke, Bentham,

Mill, Kant, and Hegel.[50] While the frame of reference might be in dispute (e.g., as in Bentham, where punishment must be kept proportional to its usefulness, or Kant, where punishment is bounded by its ability to satisfactorily establish the moral standing of the criminal), there remains broad agreement that punishment must reflect the character or the quality of the crime in question. For legal theorists in the Anglo-American tradition, proportionality is a central concern of justifying punishment, and this basic premise is augmented with a distinction between actions and actors: punishment ought to fit the *crime* rather than the *criminal*.[51] While punishment is meted out *on* a person (and as such may require some adjustment for a particular person's situation), it is nevertheless meted out *for* a crime, requiring an additional justificatory step connecting the crime to the criminal in a way that proves the subject in question is deserving of punishment.[52]

But as disenfranchisement is practiced across the United States, it cannot reasonably be said to apply to a crime. It applies, rather, to the criminal. Individuals are disenfranchised with reference to their status as convicted felons or as currently incarcerated and not by virtue of their particular criminal transgressions. This is a relatively recent development. The earliest provisions for disenfranchisement targeted specific offenses (such as public drunkenness, voter fraud, and larceny) but quickly gave way to categorical forms of disenfranchisement (focused on crimes of "moral turpitude" and "infamy"). The movement to wider categories of disenfranchisement, notably, tracks both the widespread adoption of sentencing guidelines as well as the broader expansions of the franchise. As a categorical "punishment," disenfranchisement nevertheless focuses on the criminal rather than the crime. This is nowhere clearer then when disenfranchisement persists after a criminal sentence has been served, making its excessive character more visible. If it is a punishment, then, it is a definitive case of disproportionate and excessive punishment. From this perspective, there is wide agreement that disenfranchisement is not simply a punitive failure but also an overtly *unjust* practice.[53]

Not surprisingly, there are a growing number of scholars making forceful normative objections to disenfranchisement on a variety of grounds, including its racial disparity, its unconstitutionality, its incompatibility with traditional theories of citizenship, and its failure as a form of punishment. The manner and history of these critiques are themselves interesting and indicate the limited terms of debate that have been available. A first wave of these criticisms emerged in the legal studies literature during the 1970s, focusing primarily on the disproportionate character of felon disenfranchisement and the unsettled interplay between punishment, voting rights, and citizenship.[54] Construed narrowly as a constitutional question, these theorists asked if the Fourteenth Amendment, which provides an explicit exception for the protection of voting rights in the case of "treason and other crimes," trumps Section 2 of the Voting Rights Act of 1965, which states that a demonstration of racially discriminatory effect can overturn state-level restrictions.[55] The doctrine laid down by the Supreme Court in 1974 in *Richardson v. Ramirez* states that disenfranchisement is a viable exception to the Fourteenth Amendment's equal protection clause. So long as the Fourteenth Amendment remains as written, then, criminal disenfranchisement statutes are permissible unless it can be shown that they were devised with discriminatory *intent*.[56] The Supreme Court has only once invalidated a criminal disenfranchisement provision, and this was because the proceedings of the Alabama Constitutional Convention clearly demonstrated that the provision intended to disenfranchise African Americans specifically.[57] While a series of promising cases worked their way through the federal court system in recent years, cases that might have provided opportunities under the Voting Rights Act to overturn disenfranchisement provisions, courts have routinely denied them hearings.[58] Even as the courts have held that citizenship cannot be revoked as a part of criminal punishment and that voting is "essentially equivalent to citizenship," they have also allowed states to disenfranchise large groups of citizens as a result of their status upon conviction for crimes classed as felonies.[59] The legal studies literature of this period has not produced a major legal victory, but by expressing repeated concern that felon disenfranchisement is at best a troubling practice, linking such restrictions to archaic legal practices inherited from Roman law and English common law, it did lay the historical groundwork necessary to begin shifting the debate to more explicitly normative theorizing.

Through the 1980s and 1990s, the normative philosophical literature on disenfranchisement continued to develop primarily in legal journals, continuing to question the logic of the Court's ruling in *Richardson* (particularly by trying to assert that disproportionate effects provide the basis for a challenge on grounds of vote dilution).[60] Though still largely restricted to legal analysis, a conceptual shift began, framing the question in philosophical debates over punishment, citizenship, and justice. [61] This work draws primarily from social contract liberalism and civic republicanism, and nearly all of it reduces the question to one of *justification* under some set of ideal conditions.[62] In general, the question for liberals is whether felons should lose their rights because they have violated the social contract. For civic republicans, the concern is whether criminal actions indicate that an offender is unworthy of the rights and responsibilities incumbent on citizens, revealing the danger the offender poses to the so-called purity of the ballot box. Both of these justifications have been expressed in U.S. jurisprudence, most notably in *Green v. Board of Election*, in which the ruling states, "A man who breaks the laws he has authorized his agent to make for his own governance could fairly have been thought to have abandoned the right to participate in further administering the compact." [63] Earlier, in an 1884 Alabama Supreme Court decision, the court stated, "The presumption is, that one rendered infamous by conviction of felony, or other base offense indicative of great moral turpitude, is unfit to exercise the privilege of suffrage."[64] What unites both approaches, however, is a theory of the criminal subject as irredeemable and therefore unfit for political membership. This viewpoint, what some scholars call "liberal republicanism," is based on "the importance of *individual* virtue and moral character as the basis of a strong moral economy and stable polity."[65]

Not surprisingly, many arguments for and against disenfranchisement on these grounds often note that felon disenfranchisement cannot be justified as punishment (i.e., as a deterrent, rehabilitation, incapacitation, or retribution) and argue that it must therefore be evaluated on other terms, such as those involved in liberal or republican notions of citizenship or "public safety." Disenfranchisement, nevertheless, is and continues to be directly connected to the state's authority to punish individuals as well as its authority to exclude certain people from membership. It is a practice that sits at the intersection between these discourses, even if it is a failure of one or both of them. While the state derives its authority from particular liberal principles, it disregards these principles in order to punish a certain class of citizens with exile from the polity. This is done, so the argument goes, in order to protect the polity as it is constituted but not through the means which it has sanctioned for its constitution.

Even when theorists do take up felon disenfranchisement as a form of punishment, the approach tends to be strictly normative, following H. L. A Hart's insistence that questions about punishment are *necessarily* questions of its justification or R. A. Duff's assertion that justification is "the central question in philosophical discussions of punishment."[66] The central question posed (again and again) is whether disenfranchisement is justifiable under some set of agreed-on principles (typically the traditional retribution-versus-deterrence framework). And yet felon disenfranchisement routinely fails (again and again) to satisfy any standard justification for punishment. Versions of this argument repeat themselves so frequently that a standard form has emerged in the normative literature on felon disenfranchisement. First, it identifies a governing set of liberal or civic republican principles of membership or ideal justifications for a punishment. Second, it introduces the practice of felon disenfranchisement and demonstrates how it violates some or all of these principles. Finally, in light of our commitments to the stated principles, it concludes that we should abandon felon disenfranchisement. Felon disenfranchisement, the argument goes, should be eradicated by a renewed and deeper attachment to the liberal principles we all hold dear.[67]

There are several problems with this approach. First, the key quality of felon disenfranchisement—its excessive character—is both the driving reason why normative scholars tend to reject it as a practice and precisely what should make it such an interesting practice for political theory. As such, these analyses arrive at felon disenfranchisement's most important feature, and yet it is at this moment that the discussion ends. Second, while the relationship between punishment and citizenship is nowhere more obvious than in practices of felon disenfranchisement, these two discourses are rarely theorized together. When the practice is approached as a question of citizenship, its punitive character is ignored, and when it is approached as a form of punishment, its relationship to citizenship is deemphasized. Part of this problem stems from the lack of attention theorists have given to the documentary evidence of deliberations over criminal disenfranchisement.[68] Third, the persistent normative approach inhibits analysis of the practice. While it may be relatively easy to reject felon disenfranchisement under such justificatory frameworks, it is the frameworks themselves that have generally preempted a consideration of the meaning of the practice and its persistence.

Perhaps the most telling evidence of this preemption is that there has been little work questioning *felon* disenfranchisement itself. The standard form of the argument is limited to the case of *ex*-felons. Few theorists are willing to make the harder claim that currently incarcerated persons should be allowed to vote, largely because it would require a deeper analysis of the terms of justification.[69] Few theorists consider felon disenfranchisement from a theoretical point of view that departs from the terms of liberalism or civic republicanism and does not work within the standard justification framework, taking its disproportionate character as something meaningful in its own right.[70] Approaching disenfranchisement as a purely normative question has obscured what we can learn about American politics (and the principles governing it) from the fact that we do engage in a practice that looks like a prima facie contradiction of our principles, and moreover we are not sure if the normative question is properly about punishment, citizenship, or both.

PRODUCTIVE FAILURES

We need to collectively redirect our vision and learn to see how liberalism succeeds by failing the felon.[71] We need to understand how disenfranchisement is a *productive* failure. As Michel Foucault notes in *Discipline and Punish*, since the introduction of prisons in the early nineteenth century as a form of punishment, they have constantly been criticized as failures on their own terms: "The critique of the prison and its methods appeared very early on, in those same years 1820–45; indeed, it was embodied in a number of formulations which . . . are today repeated almost unchanged."[72] As long as prisons have been used to punish, not only have they failed in this charge, but the solution to the prison's failures has always been an improved version of the prison itself: "For a century and a half the prison had always been offered as its own remedy: the reactivation of the penitentiary techniques as the only means of overcoming their perpetual failure; the realization of the corrective project as the only method of overcoming the impossibility of implementing it."[73] Foucault notes that we are asking the wrong question when we inquire as to why we should keep the constantly failing prison. Rather we should "reverse the problem and ask . . . what is served by the failure of the prison."[74]

Likewise, versions of the standard argument have been appearing in law journals since the 1970s, since the beginning of the "reform" or "liberalization" period of disenfranchisement. Prior to this period, the documentary record reveals that for as long as disenfranchisement provisions have been written into state constitutions, opposition to them has been voiced claiming that we must be true to our founding principles of liberal proportionality, just punishment, and civic responsibility.[75] When disenfranchisement is posited as a failure of liberal, republican, or punitive principles, the solution has been to reassert these same principles. If the boundaries of political membership are actively produced and reproduced through the practice of punishment, and if this (re)production is particularly pronounced in the punishing of persons' characters by disenfranchisement rather than their crimes, then we must begin posing the question of disenfranchisement differently.

That is to say, this book takes the practice of felon disenfranchisement *and* the theoretical confusion surrounding it as symptoms and asks what they reveal about the significance of felon disenfranchisement as a real (and troubling) practice. Rather than "Is disenfranchisement justified?" we should ask, "What is served by disenfranchisement?" Instead of asking, "Was this practice applied to a particular racial group in violation of liberal norms of equality?" we should ask, "How does the practice of disenfranchisement help produce and manage the unstable and changing conception of this particular racial group?" Turning away from expressly normative questions and empirical questions that center on causal rather than interdependent relations, we must ask, what does this practice, which sits on the boundary between discourses of punishment and of citizenship, do for us theoretically? What tensions or assumptions does it reveal in the liberal theory of punishment? Ultimately, what does disenfranchisement tell us about the relationships between punishment, citizenship, and the American state?[76]

By changing the question, we can begin to provide answers that both explore the general logic of disenfranchisement in the United States and also point to its meaning as a practice of racial formation and domination. In particular, we can reformulate our questions in terms of the deployment of multiple discourses, of simultaneous exclusions, and we can move beyond causal models of explanation. To these ends, I center my analysis of felon and criminal disenfranchisement on questions of function and meaning, following the work of Nietzsche, Durkheim, Mead, and Foucault, each of whom eschews normative analysis in favor of a "social analysis" of punishment.[77] In this way, I situate my work within the tradition of critical theory, grounded in skepticism of a clean fact/value distinction traditionally held in positivist approaches. Iris Young succinctly defines critical theory as "socially and historically situated normative analysis and argument."[78] To understand a practice such as disenfranchisement and to evaluate it normatively requires that we first "reject as illusory the effort to construct a universal normative system insulated from a particular society."[79] To this end, both the "facts" of history and the normative terms applied to those facts must be in question. A critical theoretical approach provides us with a far greater possibility of both addressing the injustice of criminal disenfranchisement and making sense of why our current normative appeals for its end have both been repeated so frequently and failed so often. "A critical theory," Young argues, "does not derive such principles and ideals from philosophical premises about morality, human nature, or the good life. Instead, the method of critical theory . . . reflects on existing social relations and processes to identify what we experience as valuable in them, but as present only intermittently, partially, or potentially."[80]

From such a perspective, disenfranchisement and other seemingly punitive restrictions on freedom derived from status rather than action both produce and maintain the social order in ways we do not yet fully understand. As a practice, disenfranchisement reveals the liminal position that the felon occupies, defined and managed by both criminal and constitutional law. The emergence of the felon captures the intersection of theoretical discourses of punishment, law, identity, and race, ultimately revealing that the modern liberal state is formed and maintained through the joint punishment and exclusion of some of its own members and is not simply an aberrant departure from liberal principles.[81] If punishment is necessary in liberal systems because it is a foundational part of that liberal order, rather than simply being a response to "bad acts" or "bad characters," then any hope of arriving at "just" or "fitting" punishment requires facing the exclusions on which liberalism is founded.

If we understand the study of punishment as having two related methodological perspectives, an ideal typology on one side and an empirical or descriptive typology on the other, the goal of analysis about punishment seems to be (1) correctly specifying the ideal model with reference to some ethical principle and (2) identifying the way in which the "real world" instances of punishment either resemble or fail to resemble that model. This book traces an alternative perspective that seeks the implicit, unspoken, and disavowed characteristics of punishment that might be categorical violations of the ideal yet persist in punishment as it is practiced. In the case at hand, the implication is that if disenfranchisement is not rightly understood as punishment, it is not because it fails to live up to either an ideal or a descriptive sense of the term but instead because punishment as we have come to define and analyze it also fails to conform to either our theoretical or descriptive notions. I argue that excess is simultaneously integral to and in violation of the logic of punishment. The project of the state is subsequently to manage this excessive character.

Felon disenfranchisement, as a symptom, is enlightening because it brings this fact into relief and ultimately allows us to think more critically about the underlying conditions that give rise to that symptom. As such, before we can rightly *evaluate* felon disenfranchisement, we must *understand* it as an articulation of this problem: the inherent quality of excess that goes into punishment and how the management of that excess brings together the interdependence between civil membership and punitive justice.

Felon disenfranchisement is a practice that both reveals and helps maintain a triangular relationship among the felon, the innocent citizen, and the state. The practices of excessive punishment and selective exclusion/inclusion from the political order define these three figures. At the practical level, I argue that felon disenfranchisement is productive of the same figures it seeks to negotiate—the felon, the citizen, and the state. It helps to bring into existence an order that is presumed to be stable because it offloads that stabilizing work onto one of its figures, that of the criminal.[82] In the United States, it has done this in a racialized manner, and any critique of disenfranchisement (as with any critique of American punishment more generally) must directly grapple with its connections to white supremacy as a political system.[83] Disenfranchisement does something that "we" might need but that our political commitments *also* expressly exclude. At the discursive level, I argue against reading punishment and citizenship as distinct spheres. In order to make sense of punishment, we must attend to our conceptions of citizenship, and vice versa.[84] This deep connection is borne out in historical analysis through attention to the meaning of suffrage in the United States and its linkages to punitive institutions and practices.

This means that I necessarily must grapple with liberalism as arguably the central public philosophy in the United States.[85] Of course, liberalism (especially in the United States) cannot be said to operate in a single or simplistic way, and any discussion of the relationship between a practice such as felon disenfranchisement and liberalism will necessarily run a bit rough over its nuances and various forms. Yet, as Mary Katzenstein, Lelia Mohsen Ibrahim, and Katherine Rubin rightly note in their analysis of disenfranchisement and liberalism, "Liberal arguments are the mainstay of much debate and policy-making," and they figure most prominently in normative and policy arguments about disenfranchisement.[86] Liberalism is the primary language in which disenfranchisement is discussed, and with good reason. Katzenstein, Ibrahim, and Rubin identify felon disenfranchisement as a problem that is internal rather than external to American liberalism as its "dark side." Pushing beyond Rogers Smith's multiple traditions approach, they argue that felon disenfranchisement exposes the internal exclusionary logic at work within liberalism, writing otherwise illiberal theories of racial ascription, worthiness, and virtue into its conceptual core:

> The felony disenfranchisement debate points to the ways that liberalism *incorporates* both republicanism and ascription. It is the hybrid character of liberalism with its exclusionary liberal-republicanism and its liberal ascription rather than the "helix" (intertwined but independent) of the multiple traditions thesis which best characterizes the history of felony disenfranchisement. . . . American liberalism, despite serving as a vital source of challenges to ascription, has paradoxically also provided justification for continued exclusion.[87]

Rather than simply existing alongside or being sometimes complicit with illiberal accounts of the subject, criminal disenfranchisement points out that such ascriptive accounts exist at the core of liberalism. The deep racial dimension of liberalism (especially in its contractarian forms) has been well documented both at the level of unstated assumptions as well as outcomes in practices of colonialism, domination, and political subordination.[88] It is my contention that the "paradox" of liberalism's tension with racial ascription ceases to be paradoxical if we take into account its conception of punishment. The core of liberalism's exclusionary nature is observable in its use of punishment to manage the boundaries of political membership.[89] Importantly, it does this not only through overt forms of exclusion (i.e., punishment through death, exile, banishment, etc.) but also through punishment's *production* or *fabrication* of the liberal subject. This is apparent across multiple moments of liberalism: in the foundational exclusions of criminals in Lockean liberalism, in nineteenth- and twentieth-century forms of American liberalism driven by the practice and the legacy of chattel slavery, and in the ascendency of economic and social neoliberalism, focused on universal assumptions of rational agents and normative "color-blindness." And in the American context, this exclusionary nature has been linked to the formation of race and a racial caste system.

As an analysis of underlying political commitments, felon disenfranchisement ultimately exposes the foundations of liberalism itself, and a central part of my argument is that liberalism is insufficient to address the injustice of disenfranchisement. Jesse Furman writes in his critique of disenfranchisement, "The paradox of disenfranchisement . . . is a reflection of a much deeper inconsistency—an ambivalence deep within modern liberalism's normative ideals."[90] Furman is right to insist that the *kind* of problem disenfranchisement poses is not simply a failure to properly enact liberalism's ideal set of conditions but rather that disenfranchisement is a revelatory practice that lets us get at the heart of a deeper tension between consensus and exclusion. Liberalism may be used to reject disenfranchisement, but it is also enabled by it, leaving it, in a sense, as a remainder of foundational exclusion or disavowal.[91]

THE ARGUMENT OF THE BOOK AND ITS METHODS

As I noted earlier, a central goal of this book is to redirect our vision when we think about criminal disenfranchisement in particular and about punishment and political membership more generally. To this end, I rely on two methods throughout this book: textual interpretation and philosophical genealogy. These methods of reading social and political life are intertwined in my usage, and both point me to texts and archival sources as empirical artifacts of social and political meaning. I read such texts both contextually (attending to the specific conditions and situations in which they were written and problems which they sought to address) and rhetorically (attending to the way figures, tropes, and other literary devices are used to advance the author's arguments). In both these senses, I assume there is no such thing as a "definitive reading" of a text, but I do assume there are better or worse readings. I therefore read texts sympathetically (to better understand how they work as texts) but also directed toward specific ends (to better understand pragmatic social and political phenomena). Put differently, the criteria for a "better" reading is twofold. First, does the reading shed light on the internal meaning or coherence of the text itself by bringing it into relief through some external phenomena? Second, does the reading shed light on external phenomena in a way that could not be seen absent that reading?

My argument is an attempt to rethink the general relationship between political organization and punitive practices but also to account for the way in which *a particular political body* has constituted and reconstituted itself through *a specific punitive practice*, one that professes itself to be both punitive and not punitive (i.e., simply regulatory of a state's constitution and makeup). Felon disenfranchisement is read as an exemplary practice, as a political and social artifact of a broader discourse. The success of my analysis will hinge on its ability to provide a better understanding of this specific practice as historically contingent and also on its ability to reveal something of this practice's persistence within the American tradition of liberalism. Specifically, I seek to advance understandings of both the authors with whom I textually engage and the meaning and significance of felon disenfranchisement as a material practice. To be clear, an attention to the practice of criminal disenfranchisement and the attendant figures that are produced, managed, and simultaneously occluded by this same practice forces a harsh (yet also sympathetic) critique of American liberalism's professions of progress, color-blindness, and moral rectitude. The chapters of this book seek to demonstrate that there can be no simple separation between how to think about the American self-construction of a citizen and white supremacy as a political system. Moreover, this means we must recognize the limits of any proposals for "reform" that do not also directly challenge the system of white supremacy itself.

To demonstrate this more difficult claim, I turn to the work of genealogy, following Foucault's usage of the term.[92] The term "genealogy," as others have noted, is vastly overused and widely misused.[93] I make no claims of settling those debates or to being completely faithful in my own usage.[94] What I mean by it here is a method of material historical analysis that helps us to understand our present moment both by challenging the way we have arrived at this moment and by upsetting our confidence that this moment is transparent or known to us in advance. As Foucault puts it,

> To follow the complex course of descent is to maintain passing events
> in their proper dispersion; it is to identify the accidents, the minute
> deviations—or conversely, the complete reversal—the errors, the false
> appraisals, and the faulty calculations that gave birth to those things that
> continue to exist and have value for us; it is to discover that truth or
> being do not lie at the root of what we know and what we are, but the
> exteriority of accidents.[95]

This attention to contingency, to the exteriority of accidents, means, as Ladelle McWhorter puts it, "Genealogy is a critical redescription of a dominant description."[96] That is, it gives a history we already know but which we have ceased to interrogate. Pragmatically, this requires that the work be material and both geographically and temporally specific. As with the tradition of critical theory noted earlier, genealogical work must resist universalization. Some abstraction is nevertheless a part of genealogy, and, for my purposes, I turn to discursive "figures" as anchors within space and time.[97]

The figure of the felon, of the delinquent, of the thief, of the "free Negro laborer"—each of these figures will in the course of this book occupy the space between generality and specificity, in that each of them will direct our attention to the *way* in which they have been constructed and continue to shape our actions and thought.

Genealogical analysis at its best gives a disruptive history, pointing out the contingency of the world rather than its determinism. Colin Koopman succinctly notes the orthodox "standard answer" to what a genealogy does: "Genealogy denaturalizes, destabilizes, and renders (historically) contingent that which was assumed to be (metaphysically) necessary."[98] This answer, Koopman rightly continues, is correct yet insufficient and arguably misses the point. He writes, "The point of a genealogy is not just to denaturalize— though certainly it is that too. The more important point of a genealogy is to show *how* that which is so easily taken as natural was composed into the natural-seeming thing that it is."[99] What a good genealogy can do is not simply point out that the world might have been otherwise or that the world is filled with social constructions that shape our actions (something that is already widely accepted).[100] A good genealogy describes *how* the present came to be, with particular attention to the question of subject formation and what that means for the possibility of reshaping ourselves as different subjects. Koopman writes, "Foucault's primary aim is . . . to show *how* we have contingently formed ourselves so as to make available the materials we would need to constitute ourselves otherwise."[101] This means that insofar as this book takes itself to be within the tradition of critical theory and draws from a wide variety of texts, it does so ultimately with the aim of not simply rethinking the practice of disenfranchisement but rethinking ourselves, our ethical relations to others, and the politics entailed (and made possible) by that rethinking. In the case of the United States and its practice of restricting the rights of criminals to take part in self-government, this *how* entails confronting white supremacy as a political system and the complicity with which that system operates under "color-blind" liberalism.

Perhaps not surprisingly, this book continues by engaging Foucault's thought on punishment, subjectivity, and liberalism. Chapters 2 and 3 give an extended rereading of Foucault's analysis of two modern criminological figures, the delinquent and *homo œconomicus*. These chapters demonstrate how such figures come into existence in order to manage the tensions and contradictions between discursive spheres. The contemporary felon, by virtue of the practice of disenfranchisement, must be understood as such a figure, managing the tensions that emerge in the unacknowledged over-lap between discourses of punishment and citizenship. Yet the chapters also demonstrate the limits of Foucault's analysis for understanding disenfran-chisement and call for our own genealogy of felons, criminal disenfranchise-ment, and the phenomena of excess and proportionality.

Chapters 4 and 5 turn to the specific connection between punishment and political membership in liberal theory. First, in Chapter 4, I give a read-ing of John Locke's *Second Treatise of Civil Government*, demonstrating the depth of connection between punishment and membership in the Western tradition. As a founding text of Western liberal thought centrally concerned with the role of punishment in defining and maintaining a contractual body politic, Locke's account reveals the way in which punishment and member-ship are inextricably linked and shows that this connection has not always been disavowed. Focusing on Locke's usage of the "thief" as a central figure of his political thought, this chapter demonstrates how the origins of liberal political orders are soundly rooted in the terms of punishment. Moreover, it reveals how the difficulty and instability of punishing transgressors is man-aged by producing subjects who can be so punished to make the founda-tional violence of civil society palatable.

Chapter 5 continues this reading of liberal thought through a critique of Judith Shklar's theory of citizenship as standing, investigating the relation-ship between suffrage, slavery, and punishment in the United States. Shklar offers a powerful corrective to legal accounts of citizenship, arguing that citizenship is an expression of a relational public standing signified by the rights to work and vote, rather than a legal status. She does not acknowl-edge, however, that these rights are instrumental in producing the identi-ties of groups within a polity, causing her to insist that universal suffrage has been achieved in the United States despite the longstanding exclusion of criminals. This "blindness" to criminal exclusions is symptomatic of a larger liberal blindness to the discursive fabrication of criminological fig-ures. Through an examination of Shklar's wider body of work, I demon-strate her presumption of an underlying "truth" to the moral standing of criminals. Given Foucault's account of the discursive fabrication of crimi-nological figures and Chapter 4's reading of Locke, there is little reason to assume that categories of "guilty" and "innocent" are at all stable reflections of one's actions. The perverse outcome is that voting becomes not simply a demonstration of membership and political standing but an expression of innocence and of the "purity of the ballot box," both of which continue to be purchased on the backs of felons.

Chapters 6 and 7 work in concert and take up the specific genealogical work of the book. They trace the history of suffrage restrictions in Maryland. As a border state with a fraught history of slavery, manumission, and emancipation from the colonial period onward, Maryland serves as an exemplary case to unpack Chapter 5's account of labor, suffrage, and figures of black criminality. Most importantly, Maryland has held multiple constitutional conventions since becoming a state, including a series of conventions immediately before, during, and following the Civil War in 1851, 1864, and 1867. During these nineteenth-century conventions, the delegates debated the limits of political membership and the franchise in the context of a perceived crisis of "free Negro labor." The suffrage restrictions that emerged from these debates persisted through the twentieth century and have only recently become the object of electoral reform during the past decade. Using the transcripts of these constitutional debates, these chapters explore the discursive nexus of labor, disability, and the morally inflected status of white supremacy that continues to ground felon disenfranchisement in Maryland and throughout the United States.

Chapter 6 turns to the specific nexus of criminality and blackness posited by convention delegates. The figure of the "free Negro" was persistently invoked to do this work: free blacks were figured as inherently criminal, irrational, and dependent to reduce the threat that their new freedom imposed on the standing of white workingmen. Moreover, the chapter explains how the nineteenth-century understandings of penality and citizenship have been reconfigured in the twentieth century. As it became increasingly impossible for white supremacist discourses to openly manage the internal liberal tension of punishment and membership, the language of the nineteenth-century convention debates paved the way for a pair of discursive shifts in twentieth-century disenfranchisement provisions: first, a move from "infamy" to "felony" as the primary marker of criminal exclusions; second, the movement of all disenfranchisement provisions from the state constitution to election law. These discursive shifts were attempts to manage the instability of punishment and membership through separation. They were attempts to split the discourses of punishment, ability, and citizenship and ultimately to rationalize disenfranchisement provisions. The ultimate effect of these changes has not been to undo racialized conceptions of citizenship but rather to mask the continuing work of social and political differentiation performed by disenfranchisement: the maintenance of the ideal citizen as white and innocent. Chapter 7 focuses on the contradictory yet complementary logics of competence, responsibility, guilt, and dependency to show how civil and political disabilities have been constructed both within and against understandings of disability in general and mental disability in particular. I argue that the convention debates show that the delegates understood disenfranchisement as a practice that managed the boundaries of full citizenship through the courts' power to determine criminal guilt and mental competence.

Chapter 8 calls for a turn away from the relatively moribund literature in the study of justice and instead toward communicative and deliberative theories of democratic practice that begin by theorizing *in*justice, difference, and subjectivity. Drawing on the ethical theories of Iris Marion Young, Michel Foucault, and Simone de Beauvoir, I argue that our normative evaluation of felon disenfranchisement (as well as the entire regime of collateral consequences of mass incarceration) must *begin* by recognizing what it is as a practice and that it is successful in managing the liberal punishment/membership paradox precisely because it is a seeming failure. We must accept the relationship between punishment and the boundaries of political membership and instead rethink our practical and institutional articulations of exclusion and punishment. There is, sadly, no getting punishment or citizenship "right." Instead, we must confront the tension *as a tension* and manage it openly through a critical and self-reflective democratic practice.

2

Fabricating Figures

When taking up the question of felon disenfranchisement, we typically assume that the normative terms of the debate have already been settled, and we also often fail to appreciate that the practice of disenfranchisement might be performing some very useful work for us, even if that work is illiberal, unjust, or contradictory. As a result, not only do we fail to be the kind of liberals who attach ourselves to an ethic of inclusion, but also we attach ourselves to a specific assumption and way of thinking about punishment and citizenship generally and criminality and voting rights in particular: *the assumption of a stable and knowable subject on which voting restrictions are applied.*

That is, we often take it for granted that disenfranchisement is something that is *done to* or *applied to* some properly identified and known group of persons—in this case, duly convicted felons. Even when the term "felon" serves as a proxy for some other group of individuals in the popular imagination (such as African Americans, for example), we still nevertheless assume that we already know the stable markers of identification on which we will judge the fitness (or lack of fitness) of a sanction. This is arguably a subspecies of the broader identitarian logic typical of Western political thought: we presume that we already know who is or who is not black, female, working, or generally independent, prior to the assignment of the markers or emblems of political membership. We follow Aristotle and assume that politics is the domain of those whom we *already know* to be equal persons by some natural quality.

Any injustices that arise when we fail to include such persons in the franchise are due to incorrectly identifying those subjects as unworthy or unfit for full political membership. But this is to assume away the central political question of the subject, the question that should be at the heart of our analysis, rather than presumed at the outset. Instead, we should approach the question of the subject as itself a product of disenfranchisement. There is such a thing as a "felon," to be sure, and it is a thing that comes into existence, not something with an essential character. The *failure* of disenfranchisement as punishment produces an order of subjectivity that renders some persons as innocent members of a political community (at least provisionally) and at the same time gives us a way to know who is and who is not a member of that community. Yet in existing studies of felon disenfranchisement, the "felon" is at best taken to be a purely legal status category that exists in a technical universe of legal language. At worst, the figure of the felon is left entirely unexamined. Disenfranchisement is likewise at best dismissed as an obvious aberration of liberal commitments and at worst (and far more commonly) ignored altogether in conversations about both voting rights and punishment.

This chapter and the next are about redirecting our gaze, by investigating the felon as a *figure* and disenfranchisement as a productive practice. This approach stems directly from an engagement with the philosophy of Michel Foucault and his account of subject formation at the intersection of discourse, power, and knowledge.[1] From the middle to the late 1970s, Foucault's analyses of power, discipline, government, liberalism, and neoliberalism all made frequent reference to a series of "figures" tied to crime and punishment, including the delinquent, the convicted offender, the abnormal, the thief, and finally, *homo œconomicus* as the criminal. Each of these figures reflects the development of Foucault's own thinking about the exercises of power and the forms of knowledge (what Foucault typically denotes with the term "*savior*") associated with those exercises; attention to these figures also suggests instructive lessons about how to approach the "felon" and felon disenfranchisement, prioritizing the *practice* of disenfranchisement as constitutive of the subject position on which it is applied.

It seems odd that, in the existing theoretical approaches to felon disenfranchisement in the United States, there has been virtually no attention paid to Foucault's theorizing of punishment, discipline, and governmentality to help us understand disenfranchisement's function.[2] This is perhaps because Foucault has little to say about voting rights or because it is often difficult to extricate obvious normative statements from his analysis. Yet Foucault is an obvious place to turn for help in unpacking the relationship between the state, its subjects, and those it exiles from self-government, because the notion of subject formation and figure fabrication is found persistently throughout his works.[3] This is most explicit within the criminological context and in particular in the closing sections of *Discipline and Punish* and in his lecture course at the Collège de France titled *Abnormal*, given in the spring of 1975.[4] In these two texts, Foucault argues that through a process of discursive exchange between the power/knowledge regimes of the penitentiary technique, the judicial system, and the use of expert psychiatric opinion, the "delinquent" emerges in order to explain and enable the transformations that occur in each of these realms. Foucault seeks to explain how the prison came to be the de facto institution of punitive science, asking what kind of work the penitentiary does on the people both inside and outside its walls. Here, I briefly reconstruct Foucault's theory of how the delinquent is *created, produced, or fabricated* by the penitentiary technique in order to suggest a more general theory of discursive subject formation that may help us understand the relation between collateral consequences and felons in the contemporary United States.

This chapter begins with an exegesis of the fabrication of the delinquent in *Discipline and Punish* and *Abnormal*. The critical feature of my reading of these texts is to show how the figure being produced emerges in order to resolve tensions within and between different discourses of subjectivity. On the basis of the features of discursive subject formation given by this reconstruction, I reinterpret felon disenfranchisement within the analytic of discipline and the rehabilitative ideal, noting the striking similarity between the figures of the delinquent and the felon. But this application will be only partially satisfying because the felon is not a perfect analogue of the delinquent: the disenfranchised felon is a figure that cannot be rehabilitated and, as such, calls for continual (and possibly permanent) political exclusion. The next chapter complicates this analysis, turning to Foucault's analysis of the post-rehabilitative conception of criminality that he finds articulated in the neoliberalism of the "Chicago School" of economic thought.

FABRICATION OF THE DELINQUENT IN *DISCIPLINE AND PUNISH*

In the years following Foucault's appointment to the Collège de France in January 1971, his annual lectures showed his increasing interest in the question of punishment in the modern era. Building directly from his earlier interest in the discourses of medicine and mental illness, the lectures from 1971 to 1975 persistently focused on the connections between the ways of knowing individuals in clinical and psychiatric settings and the forms of criminological knowledge demonstrated in the courtroom and the penitentiary.[5] In particular, both the 1974 and 1975 lectures often focused on the phenomenon of expert psychiatric testimony in criminal trials. In this same period, Foucault also was increasingly involved in the *Groupe d'information sur les prisons* (GIP), a radical organization that sought to disseminate information on the conditions of French prisons.[6]

In the closing sections of *Discipline and Punish*, published in France in 1975, Foucault identifies a crucial side effect of the transformation of punishment under the terms of disciplinary techniques: the sudden historical emergence of the "delinquent." Foucault focuses his attention on this figure—an individual who is thoroughly associated with criminality, monstrosity, and dangerousness—as a specific discursive production of the modern period. While the penitentiary was publicly justified as a response to such persons, Foucault insists that this institution and this figure actually came into existence in the same historical moment.

Near the end of *Discipline and Punish*, Foucault writes, "The penitentiary technique and the delinquent are in a sense twin brothers."[7] The delinquent is not revealed as some kind of objectively real thing "that the abstraction and rigidity of the law were unable to perceive" but instead is fabricated by the institution that operated on it.[8] The one does not precede the other, but rather "they appeared together, the one extending from the other, as a technological ensemble that forms and fragments the object to which it applies its instruments."[9] The delinquent and the prison are both technological innovations, and they paradoxically work together to produce meaning and justification for each other. While the prison form and its technique of power comes into existence historically as a response to products of the judicial system (i.e., convicted offenders), it maintains and gives meaning to itself through the careful production and maintenance of the delinquent as its object. Throughout Foucault's work, there is an ambiguous relationship between subjects and objects. Generally, we take subjects as persons who *act*, while objects are things that are *acted on*. But central to Foucault's analysis is the recognition that individual bodies or persons always exist as both subject and object, and any distinction between the two is a product of one's viewpoint. As such, there is sometimes an intentional slippage between the terms in his thought, drawing attention to how subjects are figured as objects in specific practices and techniques of power.

This is apparent in Foucault's first mention of the delinquent in *Discipline and Punish*, where he writes,

> From the hands of justice, [the penitentiary apparatus] certainly receives a convicted person [*condamné*]; but what it must apply itself to is not, of course, the offence, nor even exactly the offender [*l'infracteur*], but a rather different object, one defined by variables which at the outset at least were not taken into account in the sentence, for they were relevant only for a corrective technology. This other character, whom the penitentiary apparatus substitutes for the convicted offender [*l'infracteur condamné*], is the *delinquent*.[10]

The court deals with responsible subjects who act and can be identified as responsible for specific crimes and, in doing so, produces a specific subject/object: the convicted offender. But the prison, as a system of techniques of disciplinary power, is only interested in the guilt of the offender insofar as it places him or her in the penitentiary as an object to be reformed. The penitentiary apparatus and its techniques of normalization do not operate on crimes but instead focus on individuals who are simultaneously responsible for that crime and of a kind that can (and must) be rehabilitated. The prison requires subjects who can bear the punishment for their bad acts but also, by virtue of their entire biographical characters, are rightly seen as objects to be reshaped through discipline. This is why the delinquent suddenly appears, substituted for the convicted offender. The delinquent is "fabricated" so that a penitentiary has a fitting object for its corrective future-oriented project of rehabilitation. Part of the trick, Foucault argues, is that the delinquent, as a fabricated object of disciplinary power to be reformed into some kind of innocent citizen, will never be successfully reformed. As I will take up in the next section, however, this future orientation is primarily justificatory, as the penitentiary system is actually obsessed with the biographical past of the offender and barely concerned with the crime itself. Moreover, this process of substitution (or doubling of the offender and the offense) actually begins in the courtroom, rather than simply at the doors of the prison.

Foucault distinguishes between the *convicted offender* and *delinquent* in two domains, first in reference to the institution that establishes them and second in their relation to the criminal act. The *convicted offender* is a product of the penal justice system, whereas the *delinquent* is the product of the prison. Foucault writes, "The correlative of penal justice may well be the offender, but the correlative of the penitentiary apparatus is someone other; this is the delinquent, a biographical unity, a kernel of danger, representing a type of anomaly."[11] The prison receives the convicted person "from the hands of justice," but the prison "substitutes" the *delinquent* for this *offender*. It appears, at least in *Discipline and Punish*, that Foucault implies a distinct border between the juridical discourse and the punitive discourse. We will see later, however, that this border is (significantly) permeable. Neither discourse has complete authority over one or the other character.

The two figures are distinguished also by the relationship each has to the criminal action. Foucault writes, "The delinquent is to be distinguished from the offender by the fact that it is not so much his act as his life that is relevant in characterizing him."[12] In the penal justice system, the offender is linked to the crime as an individual being held responsible for a singular legal offense, established in terms of causal responsibility as guilty for a specific criminal action. The delinquent, on the other hand, is a "biographical" entity in whom the offense and the offender are united as a character who is not simply responsible for a crime but whose entire conduct and status is itself criminal.

This differentiation can be characterized in both spatial and temporal terms by paying attention to the direction and object of the gaze of both the court and the prison. The court, in its work of establishing guilt and pronouncing a punitive sentence, must look backward to the harmful act. While the punitive technique also looks backward to ground that punishment, it does so in order to establish an entire order of knowledge with which to determine that person's future and to justify its harsh treatment of the offender. The legal system's application of punishment focuses on the past act, while the punitive technique itself focuses on the subject as a future actor: "The legal punishment bears upon an act; the punitive technique on a life; it falls to the punitive technique, therefore, to reconstitute all the sordid detail of a life in the form of knowledge [*la forme du savoir*]."[13] The

punitive technique, despite our inclination to think of it as purely retributive and tied specifically to the action, necessarily operates on a transgressor
rather than a transgression, requiring an order of knowledge that is certain
of the kind of person the transgressor was and must become. This is why
Foucault writes, "The penitentiary technique bears not on the relation between author and crime, but on the criminal's affinity with his crime."[14] This
is a shift of attention from acts to actors and, more importantly, from free
subjects to determinate objects. It is, Foucault argues, a shift required in the
historical movement from punishment to discipline as a project of liberal
reform. The simultaneous substitutability and differentiation between these
figures marks an internal working out of (sometimes) contradictory notions
of liberal subjectivity between and across discourses.

While it is probably true that the delinquent could not exist without a
logically prior category of offender, Foucault is not simply telling a story
about how we once punished criminals and we now discipline delinquents.
It is incorrect to think the distinction between offender and delinquent is
perfectly discrete. Rather, he is pointing to the way the fabrication of the
delinquent enables the historical transformation of state punishment *and*
that this transformation redefines both punishment and criminality, making
criminology possible as a form of knowledge:

> Thus a "positive" knowledge of the delinquents and their species, very
> different from the juridical definition of offences and their circum-
> stances, is gradually established; but this knowledge is also distinct from
> the medical knowledge that makes it possible to introduce the insanity
> of the individual and, consequently, to efface the criminal character of
> the act. . . . The task of this new knowledge is to define the act "scientifi-
> cally" *qua* offence and above all the individual *qua* delinquent. Crimi-
> nology is thus made possible.[15]

The importance of the delinquent is that this character does both practical
work in bringing together various techniques of juridical power that operate on individuals caught up in the justice system and theoretical work in
altering the discourse of crime and punishment, in turn changing our understandings of actions and actors:

> At the point that marks the disappearance of the branded, dismembered,
> burnt, annihilated body of the tortured criminal, there appeared the
> body of the prisoner, duplicated by the individuality of the "delinquent,"

by the little soul of the criminal, which the very apparatus of punishment fabricated as a point of application of the power to punish and as the object of what is still called today penitentiary science.[16]

The fabrication, as David Garland notes, is real in two specific senses: "First of all, [the prison] 'made' delinquents in a literal sense by creating the conditions for recidivism. . . . Secondly, the prison produced the delinquent in a categorical or epistemological sense, by creating in the course of its practices, the category of 'the individual criminal.'"[17] In this first sense, the fabrication is real in that the delinquent is very likely to end up back in prison because of the ways in which the delinquent has been formed, and in the second sense, it is real in that it has brought into being a kind of person that did not exist before. Foucault notes this first sense, writing, "It is said that the prison fabricated delinquents; it is true that it brings back, almost inevitably, before the courts those who have been sent there."[18] This is the twice-told story of recidivism and of the failure of the prison system to succeed in its goal of rehabilitation. Foucault continues to identify specific ways in which this is the case, insisting that the prison is causally responsible for recidivism: "Those leaving prison have more chance than before of going back to it; convicts are, in a very high proportion, former inmates."[19] This is because, Foucault notes, "the conditions to which the free inmates are subjected necessarily condemn them to recidivism: they are under the surveillance of the police; they are assigned to a particular residence; . . . they are unable to find work," and it is because "the prison indirectly produces delinquents by throwing the inmate's family into destitution."[20] But something else is more important: "But it [the prison] also fabricates them in the sense that it has introduced into the operation of the law and the offence, the judge and the offender, the condemned man and the executioner, the non-corporal reality of the delinquency that links them together and, for a century and a half, has caught them in the same trap."[21]

The delinquent unites the multiple functions and endless justifications of punishment in a single body. The liberal legal system developing throughout the eighteenth and nineteenth centuries was designed to operate on crimes, to establish the identity of the offender, and subsequently to establish the offender's eligibility for punishment in a retributive response to the offender's action and in accordance with a broadly utilitarian justification for punishment in general. But, as Foucault has attempted to establish in his history of the emergence of discipline, the penitentiary came into existence to work on the soul of the offender rather than the body. The penitentiary technique guided by the rehabilitative ideal required not something identified by past action but something merely related to the crime, so as to define the dangerous individual who requires handling and transformation. It is not the monstrosity of the crime that the penitentiary responds to but the monster itself, largely independent of the crime.[22] The crime has passed and can do no additional harm, but the monster remains present as a future threat. The forward-looking justifications of punishment for deterrence or incapacitation rest on the possibility of there being a threat that calls for such a response. The delinquent becomes this object of discipline, uniting the criminal monster and the possibility of a rehabilitated subject:

> The penal justice defined in the eighteenth century by the reformers traced two possible but divergent lines of objectification of the criminal: the first was the series of "monsters," moral or political, who had fallen outside the social pact; the second was that of the juridical subject rehabilitated by punishment. Now the "delinquent" makes it possible to join the two lines and to constitute under the authority of medicine, psychology, or criminology, an individual in whom the offender of the law and the object of a scientific technique are superimposed—or almost—one upon the other.[23]

This new figure is one that exists temporally before and spatially outside the crime. As such, it calls for a particular handling that cannot be understood as part of the criminal sentence. This is possible due to a specific shift that occurs in the formation of the "biographical" subject: the possibility of prefiguring the criminal before the crime through focusing the penitentiary technique on the individual as a "biographical" person:

> The delinquent is to be distinguished from the offender by the fact that it is not so much his act as his life that is relevant in characterizing him. The penitentiary operation, if it is to be a genuine re-education, must become the sum total existence of the delinquent, making of the prison a sort of artificial and coercive theatre in which his life will be examined from top to bottom. The legal punishment bears upon an act; the punitive technique on a life; it falls to this punitive technique, therefore, to reconstitute all the sordid detail of a life in the form of knowledge. . . . It is a biographical knowledge and a technique for correcting individual lives.[24]

This distinction is accomplished by turning from the single action that brings the offender before the court to the sum of actions that led up to that act. The action that made him or her an "offender" rather than a suspect (in concert with the actions of investigation, prosecution, and conviction) becomes a type of conduct that characterizes the entire individual. If it were only the individual *act* that remained relevant, then the entire penitentiary technique would be unnecessary—only simple punishment would be called for. The penitentiary technique expects a coherent life to be reformed, not the punishment of a single crime, so it produces the delinquent to solve the problem. But the necessary side effect of this solution is the presumption that the "criminal" is not *necessarily* related to any specific crime. One's criminality can therefore exist independent of transgression. This directly undermines the notions of responsibility that brought the accused before the power of the law, such as the presumption that the accused could have done otherwise. What should be seen as a contradiction, however, only serves as support for the expansion of the penitentiary system:

> Because it [the introduction of the biographical] establishes the "crimi-
> nal" as existing before the crime and even outside it. And, for this
> reason, a psychological causality, duplicating the juridical attribution of
> responsibility, confuses its effects. At this point one enters the "crimi-
> nological" labyrinth from which we have certainly not yet emerged: any
> determining cause, because it reduces responsibility, marks the author
> of the offence with a criminality all the more formidable and demands
> penitentiary measures that are all the more strict.[25]

CONVERSATION BETWEEN DISCOURSES IN *ABNORMAL*

A more detailed treatment of this phenomenon of subject formation and substitution is given during Foucault's lectures at the Collège de France in the spring of 1975, *Les anormaux* (published in English under the title *Abnormal*), in which he sought to explore "the large, ill-defined, and confused family of 'abnormal individuals,' the fear of which haunts the end of the nineteenth century."[26] The lecture course—during which *Discipline and Punish* appeared in print—develops themes found in his other works and lays out foundational work dealing with discursive exchanges that occur between domains of knowledge.[27] The opening lectures provide deeper insight into how the formation of the delinquent enables the transformation of the convicted offender into a doubled subject/object whose criminality exists before the commission of the crime, unifying the multiple functions of punishment in a single body. We find in *Abnormal* that the logic of discursive subject generation exists outside the penitentiary technique in the prior juridical process of determining guilt. There is, at first glance, an inconsistency in that it seems in *Abnormal* that the delinquent comes into existence partly in the juridical sphere and not exclusively as a production of the penitentiary technique, as it seems to do in *Discipline and Punish*.

Foucault argues that the transformation of the convicted offender into the delinquent was made possible by the introduction of expert psychiatric opinion in the trial as required by Article 64 of the nineteenth-century French penal code, which excused the insane from criminal prosecution.[28] The provision was introduced to reduce an individual's responsibility for a crime, but it also gave rise to a discourse of knowledge in which individuals could be understood as criminals before the commission of a crime. In this first lecture, Foucault describes three "doublings" that occur because of this expert testimony: a doubling of the offense, of the offender, and of the judge.

First is the doubling of the offense. The specific offense is linked with any manner of other activities that become associated with the offense. The actual offense is doubled with "a whole series of other things that are not the offense itself but a series of forms of conduct, of ways of being that are, of course, presented in the discourse of the psychiatric expert as the cause, origin motivation, and starting point of the offense."[29] There are two important functions of this doubling. First is a shift from action to ways of being: "Its function is to repeat the offense tautologically in order to register it and constitute it as an individual trait. Expert psychiatric opinion allows one to pass from action to conduct, from an offense to a way of being, and to make this way of being appear as nothing other than the offense itself, but in general form, as it were, in the individual's conduct."[30] Second, ways of being that are not crimes subsequently take on a criminal character: "The function of this series of notions is to shift the level of reality of the offense, since these forms of conduct do not break the law."[31] The doubling of the offense thus has the effect of extending the law's reach beyond the action that has brought the offender before the court.

The actual offense is taken off the table, and in its place a biographical narrative of the individual is substituted. A series of nonoffenses become the evidence of the criminal before the crime to explain the subsequent real offense. Foucault says of psychiatric experts, "When they are asked to assess a delinquent, psychiatrists say, 'After all, if he has stolen, it is basically because he is a thief.'"[32] This odd inversion of causality (that the thief was already a thief before stealing anything) is troubling because this logic does not, Foucault insists, actually explain the crime but rather explains "the thing itself to be punished that the judicial system must bite on and get hold of."[33] It is an explanation of the criminal subject, not the criminal act. This explanation serves "to legitimize, in the form of scientific knowledge, the extension of punitive power to something that is not a breach of the law," namely, any prior conduct of the "criminal" before an actual crime has been committed.[34] The judge does not condemn an offender for the crime but for being a criminal who already existed as such. In the extreme form of this doubling, there need not be any crime at all but only one that must be invented to justify criminal prosecution and punitive sanction.[35]

This leads Foucault to invoke the emergence of the delinquent as the second doubling. The offender becomes both the "author of the offense" and a delinquent, someone characterized by criminal conduct. Recall the line in *Discipline and Punish* quoted earlier describing the delinquent as "an individual in whom the offender of the law and the object of a scientific technique are superimposed—or almost—one upon the other."[36] At this stage, while still in the grasp of the court, the accused is both a responsible subject and an object suitable for correction. This doubling occurs because Article 64 requires the expert to "determine whether a state of dementia allows us to consider the author of the action as someone who is no longer a juridical subject responsible for his actions."[37] But once expert opinion is included, this is not what happens at all. According to Foucault, the expert instead works to "show how the individual already resembles his crime before he has committed it."[38] Obviously related to the first doubling, in which past actions that are possibly deviant or improper but not illegal become evidence of the preexisting criminality of the offender, the offender is now revealed to have been a criminal long before having been brought before the court as some kind of unconvicted criminal.[39] "The purpose of describing his delinquent character, the basis of his criminal or paracriminal conduct since childhood," Foucault states, "is clearly to facilitate transition from being accused to being convicted."[40]

The judge is thus able to see the offender not as a subject characterized by free agency, responsible for a specific criminal offense, but as a determinate object characterized by need for the penitentiary technique. "Magistrates and jurors no longer face a legal subject," Foucault states, "but an object: the object of a technology and knowledge of rectification, readaptation, reinsertion, and correction. In short, the function of the expert opinion is to double the author of the crime, whether responsible or not, with a delinquent who is the object of a specific technology."[41] This is the condition of possibility that connects the juridical discourse and the penitentiary discourse described in *Discipline and Punish*. Legal subjects responsible for a specific transgression call for punishment in a purely retributive sense, in relation only to the criminal action. But delinquents, as a class of dangerous persons, must be handled differently as the objects of the penitentiary technique.

The third doubling occurs on the level of this judgment, between the judge and the doctor. There is a doubling of their roles in that "the psychiatrist really becomes a judge; he really undertakes an investigation, and not at the level of an individual's legal responsibility, but of his or her real guilt."[42] The doctor/judge begins the biographical project that will be completed in the hands of the penitentiary apparatus and by the punitive technique, which take up the offender as the delinquent with his "sordid details of a life in the form of knowledge."[43]

Perhaps it is at this stage that we begin to understand why the kind of criminal that is handed over to the penitentiary apparatus is not suitable simply to be punished but must be reformed and rehabilitated:

> Penal sanction will not be brought to bear on a legal subject who is
> recognized as being responsible but on an element that is the correlate
> of a technique that consists in singling out dangerous individuals and
> of taking responsibility for those who are accessible to penal sanction
> in order to cure them or reform them. In other words, from now on, a
> technique of normalization will take responsibility for the delinquent
> individual. Along with other processes, expert psychiatric opinion
> brought about this transformation in which the legally responsible
> individual is replaced by an element that is the correlate of a technique
> of normalization.[44]

The all-important shift that occurs in the fabrication of the delinquent is from understanding the individual as responsible in relation to a specific action to understanding the individual as someone the state needs to take responsibility for. The elaboration in *Abnormal* makes clear why the offender, at least in the world of expert opinion, must be handed over to the penitentiary apparatus, rather than to the executioner. This shift from subject to object shows how the delinquent comes into existence and also how the previous category of criminal offender is linked to this new character as a predetermined object of juridical power under the gaze of the doctor/ judge.

If at first there seemed to be a conflict between the description of how the delinquent emerges between *Discipline and Punish* and *Abnormal*, in terms of where the delinquent is fabricated (does it emerge in the juridical setting, the prison setting, or both?), the resolution comes from recognizing the more complicated way in which discourses interact through these liminal figures. First, it is important to note that the argument in *Abnormal* operates on a different level of analysis, taking the delinquent as only one subset of abnormal figures generated by modern regimes of power/knowledge. Second, it illustrates the way in which the formation of a new discursive subject (the delinquent) reflects backward and redefines prior categories (the convicted offender). It is incorrect to assume a chronological temporality in unpacking the emergence of the modern criminal subject in relation to the delinquent (that one comes before the other in time). There are important moments (such as the adoption of Article 64) that enable changes in a discourse and a transformation of meanings, but we should not be surprised to find the current meaning of concepts to be both radically distinct from and also deeply tied to past meaning. These changes in the juridical discourse may enable the fabrication of the delinquent, but they are not sufficient to bring it into existence. The same is true of the penitentiary. Discursive changes and emerging institutions are independently necessary, but they are only jointly sufficient to fabricate the delinquent. The new liminal figure subsequently bleeds across both discourses (the juridical and the penitentiary), infecting each with the logic of delinquency.

Both of these explanations are given by Foucault in response to a query from the audience asking why it was that Foucault spoke only about the changes in medico-juridical discourses rather than about abnormality as promised. He states first that it is true these are not the same thing but that in referring to Article 64, he was showing "that starting from the problem of expert medico-legal opinion" he would "come to the problem of abnormal individuals."[45] That is, although *Abnormal* and *Discipline and Punish* can be read as complementary texts, with roughly similar methodologies and subjects of inquiry, there is an important difference of emphasis. *Discipline and Punish* seeks to explain the emergence of a particular technique of normalization, while *Abnormal* focuses more generally on normalized subjects—that is, on practices and figures, respectively.

Second, he goes on to explain that it is in this example of the double medical and juridical forms of knowing the subject that we can see the possibility of "an exchange between juridical categories defined by the penal code."[46] The terms of medical discourse and juridical discourse become implicated in each other, infecting, informing, and redefining both. The prison and the hospital can no longer be neatly distinguished, and what emerges instead is "a sort of protective continuum throughout the social body ranging from the medical level of treatment to the penal institution."[47] This is the new punitive structure exemplified by the prison that Foucault seeks to explain in *Discipline and Punish*. The formation of the delinquent occurs at the intersection of these discourses, both enabling and resulting from a discursive exchange between different orders of knowledge. On the one hand, there is a juridical order of knowledge establishing causal responsibility for a particular bad act. On the other hand, there is a psychological order of knowledge establishing a biographical narrative of the individual as having an affinity with criminal conduct, as criminal before the crime. The delinquent carries the burden of hosting this conversation, manages what would otherwise be contradictory, and occupies a unique position that enables an analysis of this transformation.

Discursive subject formation of this sort has four important factors. First, the delinquent *is a genuine fabrication*—a socially produced category that is used in the world—taking on the status of an essentialized or naturalized subject. Second, the delinquent *does material work in the world*. Foucault notes that under the conditions of modern capitalism, the delinquent enables the organization of other illegalities, aids in the control of the margins of society, controls lesser forms of disorder, aids in colonization of the periphery, and allows the illegality of dominant groups (e.g., enabling political and economically powerful persons to escape punishment for crimes).[48] These are, Foucault insists, empirically verifiable functions enabled by the existence of delinquents in the world. Third, the delinquent *does theoretical work*. In this case, the delinquent resolves a tension between the responsible offender and the penitentiary system to which the delinquent is subjected. Is the subject a causal agent in respect to a specific crime or in relation to the specter of crime, with merely an "affinity" to the crime? Should this individual be punished or corrected? The doubling of the delinquent and the offender enables the response to this individual looking backward to punish the bad act and looking forward to either reform or constrain the dangerous individual. Fourth, the *fabrication of this figure occurs at the intersection of discourses*, bringing them together in order to solve potentially real problems and enabling these discourses to alter and change their terms and meanings.

PRODUCING FELONS AND CITIZENS

It is possible to simply subsume the figure of the felon into Foucault's genealogy of the prison and the fabrication of the delinquent. Foucault makes almost direct reference to the idea of collateral effects to incarceration as a part of this fabrication and as a part of the "success" of the prison's obvious failure. He writes,

> Perhaps one should look for what is hidden beneath the apparent cynicism of the penal institutions, which after purging convicts by means of their sentence, continues to follow them by a whole series of "brandings" . . . and which thus pursues as a "delinquent" someone who has acquitted himself of his punishment as an offender? Can we not see here a consequence rather than a contradiction? If so, one would be forced to suppose that the prison, and no doubt punishment in general, is not intended to eliminate offences, but rather to distinguish them, to distribute them, to use them; that it is not so much that they render docile those who are liable to transgress the law, but that they tend to assimilate the transgression of the laws in a general tactics of subjection.[49]

Delinquents are branded, marked, and followed by the state long after they cease to be offenders, remaining criminal objects for all time and thus justifying continued discipline and surveillance. The felon, on this account, is perhaps just another word for the delinquent, and collateral consequences (including disenfranchisement) are just a part of this formation.

There is also reason to directly link the felon to a restriction of expression of democratic ideals of liberty and representation. Foucault notes that the prison has a "'self-evident' character" because it is "based first of all on the simple form of 'deprivation of liberty.' How could prison not be the penalty *par excellence* in a society in which liberty is a good that belongs to all in the same way to which each individual is attached . . . by a 'universal and constant' feeling?"[50] Just as incarceration expresses the value of liberty, disenfranchisement expresses the value of self-rule. There are those who are fit for self-rule and those who are not, and what better way to identify both groups than by identifying those who fail to govern their own lives accordingly? Foucault shows why we should not be surprised at restricting voting rights, since the notion of criminals as a separate class itself indicates a realization that the law is not made for all but for some, just as suffrage is not for all but only for some: "It would be more prudent to recognize that it [the law] was made for the few and that it was brought to bear upon others."[51] While it is possible to simply subsume the figure of the felon and the practice of disenfranchisement into the depiction of carceral society described in *Discipline and Punish*, to do so obscures some important features particular to the figure of the felon.

A more compelling reading would attend to both the similarities and the differences between disenfranchisement and the felon, on the one hand, and the prison and the delinquent, on the other. The similarities are reasonably clear. Just as the prison fabricates the delinquent so that the penitentiary technique is given meaning and justification, operating on an object of its own creation, disenfranchisement operates on the felon at the same time that it fabricates "the felon" as a category justifying exclusion from political voice. Disenfranchisement is to the penitentiary technique as the felon is to the delinquent. The felon is, like the delinquent, a fabrication, and the technique that is central to this creation is disenfranchisement. Disenfranchisement is, on this account, not just another source of delinquency but rather caught up in a productive process of its own.

Like the use of the prison, disenfranchisement is not just punitive but is a technique producing the kind of subject that requires disenfranchisement. Following Foucault's analysis of how the prison substitutes the delinquent for the offender, disenfranchisement extends this subject generation, substituting the felon for the particular offense, impressing on the public that such a person must not be allowed to exercise political voice. Such persons must be marked not only as social outsiders but as political ones as well. Fabricating the felon gives society a kind of subject/object who is essentially flawed, who is the source of criminality. The source of the evil done to "innocent" members of society comes not from within the community of innocents but from the outside, by those felons who are essentially different from us. Foucault writes about the delinquent, "One should not see in delinquency the most intense, most harmful form of illegality, the form that the penal apparatus must try to eliminate through imprisonment because of the danger it represents; it is rather an effect of penality (and of the penality of detention) that makes it possible to differentiate, accommodate and supervise illegalities."[52] The failure of the prison to stamp out criminals is in fact its success: it "brings out a form of illegality that seems to sum up symbolically all the others, but which makes it possible to leave in the shade those that one wishes to—or must—tolerate."[53] In the same way, disenfranchised felons give security and comfort to nonfelons, not through their actual removal from social life but by identifying them as scapegoats for social and political harm.

All political states may have use for the category of delinquency, but the democratic state has the additional need of identifying those persons who are specifically unfit for self-government. Defining who will be members of a community might logically require identifying those who are not members through some form of differentiation, those who must be excluded in order to include others. As Andrew Shapiro puts it, "When society strips an offender of his rights of citizenship, it labels him irredeemably different and dangerous."[54] It is notable in this analysis that labeling of offenders as irredeemable stems not from their criminal guilt but from their disenfranchisement. If the known guilt of the delinquent establishes a community of those who are known as innocent, it is specifically the stripping of rights through disenfranchisement of guilty persons that these innocent members are marked not merely as innocent but as full *citizens*. Those who retain their voting rights (nonfelons) are established as normal, harmless, and above all, true citizens. The felon thus is not only the source of criminality and evil; the felon has the dubious honor of comforting us nonfelons by showing us that we—by contrast to those others—surely are capable of self-government.

The practice of disenfranchisement thus produces such normalization, fabricating the felon through three mechanisms: (1) placing the subject outside the imagined *demos*, changing the status of incarceration from physical to political, (2) maintaining a substitution of felon for offense through the continued effects of the practice, and (3) serving as the logical political foundation for other forms of social exclusion faced by felons.

First, if we imagine a democratic society as existing in both a physical and imagined sense, incarceration removes the felon from the physical society, while disenfranchisement removes the felon from the imagined one. The physical society is what we commonly think of as the real world: the places and people with whom we interact, the jobs we hold, the places we visit, our families, our neighborhoods, our clubs, our friends, and the countless other social forms we physically take part in. Felons are removed from this physical world through incarceration, placed "outside" by being locked up "inside" prisons. But while they are physically "exiled" in this way, they remain inside the imagined political boundaries of the nation (unlike ancient practices of exile which removed offenders from both physical and imagined societies). To remove them from the imagined community, to ensure that they are truly outsiders not only physically but also ideally, disenfranchisement removes them from the *demos*, from those members of society who take part in collective self-government. Incarceration would therefore be an incomplete disciplinary technology in the democratic context. Disenfranchisement, in addition to incarceration (or perhaps even instead of incarceration), ensures that the felon, as a particular *kind* of delinquent, is exiled from the imagined political community as well as from the physical community.

Second, voting is an annual, repeated practice and as such continually remakes and reminds criminal subjects that they are and continue to be felons. Disenfranchisement becomes the annual reminder that the felon is constituted as an object with an affinity to a crime rather than a responsible subject. Every year, when the felon is denied a political voice, an act-identity substitution occurs. Disenfranchisement, more than the retributive or protective punishment of incarceration, conflates past action and future identity, determining subjects as things outside their own control or determining the subject as merely an object. The act-identity substitution works in the reverse, as well. We can argue that the act of voting substitutes for an identity of citizen: while not a necessary condition of citizenship (one can be a citizen without voting), it is a sufficient one (if one does vote, we are certain of the voter's citizenship, at least within that jurisdiction). With the exception of children and persons determined as mentally incompetent, those who are barred from the vote surely cannot be considered full citizens. In this way, two actions, criminal behavior on the one hand and voting on the other, serve both to identify who is a felon and to indicate that the felon is necessarily not a full citizen. In those states where disenfranchisement extends beyond physical incarceration, the identity of felon is persistent in conflating act and identity.

Third, the right to vote is in many ways a foundational right in procedural democratic regimes such as the United States. Being a felon in the United States makes one ineligible for a wide variety of other political rights (such as jury service or holding public office), social services, jobs, and educational opportunities.[55] Arguably, these broader and immediate effects of felon "identity" are much more relevant than voting rights for felons trying to reintegrate themselves into society postincarceration. Felons are socially and politically exiled in more ways than just their voting rights, but voting rights restrictions act as a foundation for these other forms of disenfranchisement. While political activity or political participation is surely not limited to the ballot box, and voting is surely not a wholly sufficient form of political participation, it is a necessary form of political participation given the representative structure of the United States. How are the interests of formerly incarcerated persons expressed without the vote? How can we expect legal barriers to employment, education, or housing to be contested when those who have the most interest in contesting those barriers cannot vote? This is especially true given the phenomenon of mass incarceration and the scale of its effects: a full 1 percent of the population in the United States.[56] Voting rights become the simplest signification of membership and standing in the political community: while not sufficient, they are surely necessary in a representative democracy.[57]

The payoff of disenfranchisement policies, whether intentional or not, is not simply that felons become persons who have an affinity with transgression but that they are placed outside democratic society, being marked in a persistent way as political outsiders. Having accepted that physical exile is no longer practical, symbolic exile takes its place—and given the necessary status of voting in the context of the United States, this exile is performed through revocation of the necessary symbol: the franchise. "Felon" assumes its distinction as not simply a technical category of criminal classification but a kind of person who does not belong, who lives outside the bounds of society in large part because we signal outsider status by the stripping of voting rights.

Note the circular move present in felon disenfranchisement. The felon, in losing the vote, is placed outside the *demos*. In turn, this is used as the proof of why the felon should be, in classic republican terms of protecting the *demos*, prevented from taking part in the collective decision making of the state. Shapiro again puts it nicely:

> Disenfranchisement is based not upon what we believe but upon what it allows us to believe. The notions that felons have freely chosen to renege on a social contract or are morally defective outsiders lacking the neces-

sary virtues for political citizenship follow from, rather than explain, a pre-existing sense that ex-felons cannot be members of the community. This deep impulse contributes to a self-perpetuating, self-congratulatory belief system that shapes our conceptions of citizenship and criminality, and that forms the basis of ex-felon disenfranchisement.[58]

In this way, we can see how disenfranchisement operates to construct the felon and the citizen, bringing into existence a kind of character who can and must be excluded from the process of democratic decision making, in contrast to the innocent citizen.

Foucault's analysis of the delinquent and the frameworks of discipline and normalization is responsive to a specific set of conditions and practices, meaning that we must attend to several important differences between felons and delinquents that limit the analogy between the two figures. First, while the fabrication of the delinquent occurs as a substitution (or doubling) in relation to the character of the convicted offender—the penitentiary apparatus creates the delinquent so it has an appropriate object to operate on, to deal with the shortcomings of the convicted offender—disenfranchisement, as a historical practice, operates on a criminological figure that already exists. While we can track the creation of the delinquent through its sudden emergence in the eighteenth century, the "felon" has a much longer history and has not always been the subject of political exclusion. To the degree that disenfranchisement fabricates the felon, then, it does so by changing the meaning and significance of the felon rather than conjuring up an entirely new character. Still, this is very much a process of fabrication. In the case of the delinquent and its relation to the convicted offender, we find that an integral part of the fabrication is the substitution of one character for another. But as explained in *Abnormal*, this new character redefines the other as well. The doubling of offender and delinquent occurs, importantly, in the same body before the court and is passed along to the penitentiary apparatus. Accordingly, we should not be surprised to find that felons are brought into being in the same place that they stood before but as a distinctly new kind of thing. This is a refabrication of the figure, and as such, we must attend to how the existing category of the felon is deployed in its own redefinition.

That disenfranchisement can do this work is in large part because it sits, as a practice, at the intersection of civil, constitutional, and criminal law. That is, the figures and practices that straddle discursive formations are of particular importance for understanding those respective formations. Insofar as Foucault argues that the *prison* gives rise to an entire regime of governmentality characterized by the carceral form—a carceral society—this is not simply because disciplinary techniques have been adopted outside the penitentiary. Rather, it is because these disciplinary practices already and always engage *multiple* discourses in their work, and figures such as the delinquent or the abnormal exist between and beyond their boundaries. Disenfranchisement, by this account, is likewise already engaged in subject formation at the intersection of founding and punishing. When contemporary legal theorists attempt to address a practice such as disenfranchisement, the tendency to separate those domains of law (criminal, constitutional, criminal) also prevents capturing the practice fully. The felon and the practice of disenfranchisement become important sites to investigate *because* they straddle these legal discourses, ultimately revealing the work they do for each other and masking the tensions between them.

In the cases Foucault takes up in *Discipline and Punish* and *Abnormal*, there is an exchange between the juridical discourse (which establishes the guilt of individuals in a way that possibly reflects their entire character rather than their bad act) and the penitentiary discourse (which substitutes the delinquent for the convicted offender as required by the modified juridical discourse while at the same time enabling that modification). The delinquent is the evidence or artifact of this exchange: it is through this figure that Foucault shows how these two discourses transformed and produced this offspring, redefining themselves. The convicted offender gives way to the delinquent and in the process becomes redefined in relation to the delinquent, in a circular movement.

In the case of the felon, we see a similar process occurring within a singular term by way of extending seemingly punitive collateral consequences to a technical category of offender, giving it a subjective content that justifies its use as an exclusionary marker for the polity. The felon *as we know them* only comes into existence when the civil and criminal law come together, when the felon ceases to be simply a technical classification and becomes a reality of its own. That is, felon disenfranchisement substitutes this seemingly technical classification based on the severity of a criminal action (the felony) for a subject that requires formal exclusion from the symbolically most important form of political participation (the felon). The technique both rests on and gives meaning to the content of the felon as a figure, character, or human kind. But rather than creating a subject identifiable by an original nomenclature (in the way that the delinquent comes into being as a new figure), we observe, in the case of the felon, a permutation of terms (e.g., the ex-felon, ex-convict, former felon, ex-offender).

Finally—and most importantly—the logic of delinquency is intimately tied to the rehabilitative ideal expressed by the penitentiary technique: the delinquent is managed within the context of proportional punishment and disciplinary practices. Even if the delinquent represents a productive failure of the penitentiary technique, the rehabilitative ideal is still publicly maintained. The felon, however, is figured especially as a political outsider who seems to call for excessive or disproportionate handling, confounding the possibility of rehabilitation and reintegration. While the delinquent (as an abstract figure) is a permanent criminological fixture, individual delinquents seem to retain the possibility of being reformed or rehabilitated. But the felon, both as a category and in individual cases, seems to figure the unredeemable, the unreformable, and the persistent criminal other. The felon and the delinquent surely have distinct genealogies. While the delinquency/disciplinary framework is helpful in understanding the figure of the felon and the practice of disenfranchisement, its utility turns out to be quite limited. A chief characteristic of disenfranchisement is its excessive character, a quality that has a far greater affinity with juridical forms of corporal punishment than with the emblematic regime of discipline and "soul-work" that characterizes the history of delinquency. The felon, as a creature that cannot be reformed and must be exiled from politics, cannot adequately be explained by the economy of power that Foucault presents in *Discipline and Punish* or *Abnormal.*

Contemporary practices of the carceral society as well as criminological analysis have surely not dispensed with the notion of delinquency or departed from an attachment to think of some individuals as a distinct human kind imbued with a deep affinity with crime or as persons who are criminal before the crime. But the sway held by this conception of criminal subjectivity has waned over the course of the twentieth century, most explicitly in criminology and legal theory. It is a simple but often unstated point that *Discipline and Punish*, while surely a project engaged in the theorizing of the present, is also the genealogy of the penitentiary form and the carceral society and as such is dated primarily in the modern rather than the contemporary period, as well as being driven by the analysis of European rather than American punitive practices.[59] *Discipline and Punish* often seems clumsy when applied to contemporary punitive practices and out of step with current criminology, especially as contemporary practices are further and further detached from the rehabilitative ideal and focus far more on the management of danger and risk at the level of protecting a population. This is also true of contemporary manifestations of felon disenfranchisement. It is not simply a disciplinary technique but also draws expressly on a logic of excessive punishment and operates at a far more theoretical than physical or corporeal level on the convicted offender.

Felons in the United States are not simply analogous to delinquents. That is to say, my roughly Foucauldian analysis of felon disenfranchisement is complicated by at least three factors: (1) the analyses of *Discipline and Punish* and *Abnormal* are rooted in a different time (the eighteenth, nineteenth, and early twentieth centuries) and location (France rather than the United States); (2) the importance of race and the legacy of chattel slavery is almost entirely ignored here; and (3) in the 1978 and 1979 lectures at the Collège de France, Foucault himself turned his attention away from his established understanding of the criminological discourse of disciplinary power under liberalism and toward the emergence of "governmentality" and "biopolitics" associated with neoliberalism.[60] To overcome these shortcomings, we cannot simply bring Foucault's analysis across the Atlantic Ocean: this would both do a disservice to Foucault's analysis and ignore his own methodological commitments, as genealogical investigations must be specific to temporal and geographic particularities of the objects in question. Instead we must conduct our *own* genealogical analysis of punishment and citizenship in the United States, one that is especially attentive to our own temporal and geographic particularities as well as to the complication that Foucault himself introduced in his lectures: the (re)emergence of *homo œconomicus* as the central figure of criminal subjectivity as a direct challenge to the pathologies of the delinquent. The next chapter continues to define what it means to talk about a "discursive production" or a "figure" that does "work." Specifically, it interrogates the terms of subjectivity at the core of liberalism and its more contemporary reworking in the United States and Europe under the framework of neoliberalism.

3

Neoliberal Penality and the Biopolitics of *Homo Œconomicus*

Figures—such as those described in the previous chapter—are fabricated for largely strategic purposes, resolving or managing the tensions and outright contradictions that occur between the exercises of power by various actors, institutions, practices, and ways of knowing that form entire social and political bodies. In a sense, we are what we do, solidified in a time and place contingently but nevertheless materially. The figure of the felon and the practice of disenfranchisement are no exceptions, as they come into being over time and in a specific place and they change in their form and their practice as actors, institutions, and ways of knowing likewise change.

The previous chapter mapped a logic of subject formation that is specific to a time and place in which the rehabilitative ideal was ascendant and the liberal way of punishing focused on the reformation of the offender through the disciplinary model. It is fair to say that the latter half of the twentieth century was a time in which prison populations expanded beyond this form dramatically and any collective faith in the rehabilitative ideal was dramatically shaken but not abandoned. Prisons have always been tightly linked with economic rationalities, but it is telling that the economic metaphor for prisons today has largely shifted to "warehouses" rather than "workshops."[1] It is true that there continues to be a great deal of disciplinary power exercised in prisons and throughout carceral society more generally, but it is also the case that criminological concepts, legal practices, and entire ways of thinking about politics have changed.

Tracing how the felon is fabricated requires attending to the ways in which the practice of criminal disenfranchisement and the policing of the boundaries of political membership have likewise changed over time. The work of genealogy, as noted in the first chapter, is importantly about *how* the contemporary moment has come into being and less about simply noting that our present is contingent, that practices morph over time, or that figures and identities are not timeless. If my concern here were limited to the initial introduction of criminal disenfranchisement provisions in the eighteenth and nineteenth centuries, then the framework described in the previous chapter would arguably be sufficient to that task. But as noted, felons are not simply analogous to delinquents, and the twentieth-century reforms of disenfranchisement are themselves a part of the fabrication of the felon as a figure today.

I continue to engage with Foucault in this chapter in part because he was keenly aware of such discursive changes, and during his lectures at the Collège de France in the late 1970s, he repeatedly returned to the question of punishment and the configuration of criminal offenders as a site to explain the changing forms of political rationality in the modern period.[2] A crucial part of this analysis was Foucault's interest in the American neoliberal economic thought of the so-called Chicago School, exemplified in the economist Gary Becker's foundational work in the theory of human capital and the economic analysis of crime and punishment.[3] And the central feature of this analysis is the reintroduction (and critical redescription) of the figure of *homo œconomicus*—economic man—to the criminological conversation. In the hands of the American neoliberals, a universal model of rational agency has emerged alongside a reorganization of the state and the market (what Foucault identifies as a part of neoliberal governmentality), and this model and this reorganization is firmly connected to contemporary punishment and political membership.

In this chapter, I turn to the genealogy of *homo œconomicus* as a figure through Foucault's theorization of it in order to better understand how the logic of fabrication discussed in the previous chapter shifts and changes over the course of time and under different locations. Insofar as *homo œconomicus* expresses the theory of subjectivity of neoliberal governmentality, according to Foucault, it points us to a better understanding of how various modes of power operate on others and ourselves.[4] Neoliberalism and its paradigmatic figure define the implicit framework of subjectivity that marks the conditions of possibility for the late-twentieth-century "reforms" of criminal disenfranchisement. Nineteenth-century conceptions of criminality and membership, which saw disenfranchisement as expressly punitive, ultimately give way to more "regulatory" conceptions that enable and support the operation of white supremacy in the contemporary United States.

To that end, the work of this chapter is multiple and responds to the shortcomings identified at the end of the previous chapter. First, because criminal and felon disenfranchisement is anything but a relic of a previous time, it is necessary to move beyond the nineteenth century. Foucault's public lectures from the late 1970s are some of the only places where he directly took up twentieth-century formations of power/knowledge. Second, insofar as neoliberalism has become an important scholarly and popular framework for understating the current moment, punishment scholars have rightly identified ways this framework directly implicates punitive concerns. Theorists of neoliberal penality (as it is sometime called) have pointed out the ways in which harsh punitive sanctions and the paternalistic governance of poverty and race support rather than undermine neoliberal economic policy. We would do well, however, to go deeper into these connections and attend to the particular kinds of subjects formed by and through neoliberalism and, by extension, to the policing of political membership that relies on such subjects. If the relationship between the economic and the political is called into question by neoliberalism, then, as I argue in this chapter, this relationship is managed by a theory of subjectivity riddled with criminological assumptions. Lastly, this chapter sets up a turn back to the terms of liberalism in the American tradition (taken up in subsequent chapters) by showing the way in which race, punishment, and political membership are tied together in the neoliberal account of subjectivity.

NEOLIBERALISM AND NEOLIBERAL PENALITY

Analyzing social policy through the lens of "neoliberalism" has become both commonplace and contentious, given its widespread usage as well as diffusion of the concept.[5] Generally, the idea of neoliberalism has been used to refer to ideologically driven free-market policies deployed in Western nations in the late twentieth century and, in particular, to note how the embrace of such policies easily cut across traditional American and European left/right political distinctions. When neoliberalism functions as state policy, according to David Harvey, it represents a basic redefinition of the fundamental conception of freedom, one that "reflects the interests of private property owners, businesses, multinational corporations, and financial capital."[6] As such, it reflects the ideological capture of the basic terms of egalitarian liberalism that successfully redirects the benefits of freedom toward the owners of capital. For Marxist critics such as Harvey, neoliberalism represents an *intensified* form of liberalism that ultimately exposes the ripening contradiction that liberal freedom is in fact nothing more than bourgeois freedom. Such freedom relies on the excesses and instability inherent in financial capital and economic colonialism. That neoliberalism is said to dominate the entire left/right political landscape in countries such as the United States or the United Kingdom reflects its pervasive power to reshape the grounds of all economic policy questions, taking hold in those countries as a "distinctive political-economic philosophy" since the 1970s.[7]

Broadly speaking, a second interpretation of neoliberalism comes out of political theory. For political theorists, neoliberalism runs deeper into our ways of thinking and has a longer history, with commentators noting its emergence as a distinct form of liberal thought as early as the mid 1950s.[8] Specifically, neoliberalism not only operates at the level of public policy and through ideological capture of the terms of liberal freedom, but it also fundamentally alters those terms and changes the way politics, economics, and the self are *thought* and *practiced*. As Wendy Brown explains, "In order to comprehend neoliberalism's political and cultural effects, it must be conceived of as more than a set of free market economic policies that dismantle welfare states and privatize public services. . . . Certainly neoliberalism comprises these effects, but as a political rationality, it also involves a specific and consequential organization of the social, the subject, and the state."[9] For Brown, who is building directly on Foucault's reading of all forms of liberalism as "political rationalities," neoliberalism operates most importantly as a way of knowing, spanning epistemological as well as political ground. To this end, it is a deployment of power/knowledge that reflects a basic reorganization of liberalism's core tenets and opens up new ways of thinking and doing. This is to say that referring to neoliberalism as a "bundle of economic policies" misunderstands what is specifically "neo-" about neoliberalism.[10]

In contrast to more Marxist understandings, neoliberalism must not be thought of as simply an intensification of classical liberalism under new material conditions of capital or as a condition of heightened contradiction. Its distinctive form can be found in the insistence that economic analysis be extended to noneconomic questions. "Neo-liberal rationality," Brown writes, "is not only or even primarily focused on the economy; rather it involves *extending and disseminating market values to all institutions and social action*, even as the market itself remains a distinctive player."[11] As such, this approach explains why neoliberalism can so easily cut across the left/right spectrum in "liberal democratic" societies: it reshapes the terms under which left/right conflicts are conceptualized to such a degree that conflict between "sides" nevertheless operates within the terms of neoliberal rationality. It can do this because neoliberalism operates at the level of grounding assumptions of subjectivity, agency, and reason itself. Neoliberalism does not simply say, "We can apply market principles to nonmarket activities," but instead says something more like, "There are no activities that are strictly speaking nonmarket activities." It is at the level of such assumptions that neoliberalism can rightly be said to be distinct from previous forms of liberalism, while still deeply indebted and connected to those earlier forms.

What unites various approaches to the analytics of neoliberalism is that the term is almost exclusively used in a negative sense in academic and popular circles.[12] For Brown, neoliberalism is a particularly pernicious and overarching political rationality, undercutting the basic tenets of social democracy and subsuming all accounts of agency under those of narrow economic rationality. Insofar as it signals a rejection of the public/private divide (in favor of seeing all actions as inherently private or at least possible to privatize), it necessarily impoverishes the space of the public as one of political action, such critics argue. To this end, supporters of distinctly political forms of freedom are right to worry about neoliberal rationality's departure from classical liberalism, because it insists there is no proper political space outside market reason. "While liberal thought has often proposed an intimate relationship between political and market freedoms," Joe Soss, Richard Fording, and Sanford Schram write, "neoliberalism goes further by treating market liberties as a model (and substitute) for political freedoms."[13] Or as Pierre Bourdieu puts it bluntly, "This tutelary theory is a pure mathematical fiction. From the start it has been founded on a formidable abstraction. For, in the name of a narrow and strict conception of rationality as individual rationality, it brackets the economic and social conditions of rational orientations and the economic and social structures that are the condition of their application."[14] At its core, Bourdieu argues, neoliberalism's "essential" character is the radical displacement of the "collective" with the "individual." As such, it asserts the logic of narrow rational self-interest not in service of solving collective-action problems (as we might imagine a Hobbesian account could give) but only to serve the interests of those who are already powerful, already wealthy, and in control of both material and fictitious resources. It represents a complete rewriting of liberal thought, and its economic, political, and social effects have arguably been profound and far-reaching.

Yet, even if neoliberalism is not quite so hegemonic or authoritative, it has surely had an effect on how we think about punishment in the United States and the kinds of persons subjected to punishment. Scholars have rightly noted that when neoliberal principles have been applied to the penal sphere, something openly contradictory has appeared in a form of distinctively "neoliberal penality." According to theorists such as Loïc Wacquant and Bernard Harcourt, during the same periods of massive deregulation and privatization that occurred in the United States, the size and scope of the penal sphere also sharply increased.[15] For Wacquant and Harcourt, this particular manifestation of neoliberal penality seems (at first glance) to be contradictory to neoliberal prescriptions for radical deregulation of markets and a withdrawal of state power from all social and political institutions. This is especially the case for the key architects of neoliberal thought, whose zeal for deregulation typically extends to every political institution that liberalism considers sacred. Yet the techniques and discourses of policing that characterize the same period since the late 1970s intensify state involvement: endemic "urban violence," zero-tolerance policing, increased forms of electronic and human surveillance, the increased criminalization of vagrancy and homelessness, and the phenomenon of mass incarceration.[16]

While this seeming contradiction is often dismissed as the result of a failure to take neoliberal principles far enough, such "failure" is arguably a part of how neoliberalism rewrites political thinking. As Wacquant puts it, the "distinctive paradox" of neoliberalism is that "the state stridently reasserts its responsibility, potency, and efficiency in the narrow register of crime management at the very moment when it proclaims and organizes its own impotence on the economic front, thereby revitalizing the twin historical-cum-scholarly myths of the efficient police and the free market."[17] This paradox, Jamie Peck and Adam Tickell note, is not limited to the penal domain but runs throughout neoliberal policymaking as a "series of paradoxical and contradictory 'double-movements.' . . . Only rhetorically does neoliberalism mean 'less state'; in reality, it entails a thoroughgoing *reorganization* of governmental systems and state–economy relations."[18] In their account, neoliberalism (especially in the form embraced by the United Kingdom during the Thatcher years) operates by "rolling back" older forms of state regulation while simultaneously "rolling out" neoliberal forms that only *appear* to reflect the laissez-faire principles of traditional liberalism.

State punishment, however, remains a particularly pernicious form of this paradoxical double movement. The "new punitive commonsense" that has taken hold in recent decades is arguably not in tension or contradiction with neoliberal economic theory but directly maintains and supports it. In the United States, Wacquant argues, neoliberal penality emerged "alongside the neoliberal economic ideology that it translates and applies in the realm of 'justice.'"[19] The resolution of this seeming contradiction relies, in Wacquant's account, on the retrenchment of existing cleavages of difference (especially class and race) which ought to be ignored by neoliberal rationality but which are central to its deployment. This is partly a tactic used to support the reconstruction of the welfare state on the "workfare" model, using punitive sanction to keep "clients" in place. As Lester Spence puts it, "Punitive and increasingly bureaucratic techniques of government are used to deal with non-white populations deemed incapable of exercising freedom."[20] In this sense, policing the "free" neoliberal state takes on a distinctive form that is, according to Wacquant, "(neo)liberal and noninterventionist at the top, in matters of taxation and employment; intrusive and intolerant at the bottom, for everything to do with the public behaviors of the members of the lower class caught in a pincer movement by the generalization of underemployment and precarious wage labor, on the one side, and the retrenchment of social protection and profligacy of services, on the other."[21] To maintain this order, the poor are disproportionately policed, and the conditions of poverty are criminalized:

Far from contradicting the neoliberal project of deregulation and decay of the public sector, the irresistible rise of America's penal state constitutes, as it were, its negative—in the sense of obverse but also of revelator—as it manifests the implementation of a *policy of criminalization of poverty that is the indispensable complement to the imposition of precarious and underpaid wage labor* as civic obligation from those locked at the bottom of the class and ethnic structure, as well as the redeployment of social-welfare programs in a restrictive and punitive sense that is concomitant with it.[22]

While the economistic readings of subjectivity at the core of neoliberal human capital theory may be applied to the people at the top of the socio‑economic distribution, far more regulatory and brutal forms of management continue to apply to those at its lower rungs, increasingly exposed to erratic (and yet also endogenous) fluctuations of capital. In the United States (and increasingly in European states), this exposure cannot be simply analyzed through the realm of class but must also include other forms of difference, including (but not at all limited to) race, gender, ability, and sexuality.

There is no disjunction, therefore, between the demands of neoliberal economic policy and its public ideology of state austerity, market deregulation, and "free" capital movements and the fact of a massively increasing police state. There is no contradiction at all once one realizes that neoliberal ideology, at least partly (if not totally), rests on and operates through preexisting categories of difference such as class or race. The form of neoliberal thinking that Wacquant identifies as the "American model" exported to the rest of the world is *founded on* and *maintained through* a racial divide. Moreover, this model remains "devoted to buttressing the discipline of the market" through the use of a penal system that is "in step with the deployment . . . of neoliberal ideology and policies it inspires, in matters of labor as well as criminal justice."[23] For example, Soss, Fording, and Schram have demonstrated that poverty governance in the United States has taken on a distinctly neoliberal form since the late 1960s, combining with a racialized conception of paternalism that treats social welfare clients as entirely responsible for their social and economic positions. In the context of U.S. welfare reform since the 1960s, the authors document a powerful relationship between race and poverty governance that functions in mutually supporting ways. Racialized understandings of class, gender, and civic membership helped to drive the "new poverty regime" of neoliberal paternalism, while at the same time, "this regime generates systematic racial disparities. . . . Race provides a key cultural resource for the production of poverty governance. But poverty governance is also, in its own right, a site where racial meanings and inequalities get produced."[24] This is to say that race is central to the deployment of neoliberal policy in the United States in that it operates *on and through* the existing social and political cleavages. Not surprisingly, racial politics themselves are easily rewritten through neoliberal policy.[25] But more importantly and also more difficult to trace, race and racial disparities are at the heart of the theoretical claims of neoliberalism as well.

In this way, my interest in neoliberalism necessarily goes beyond the aforementioned accounts of neoliberalism and neoliberal penality. Instead I am exploring how neoliberalism functions specifically in relation to race and the formation of subjects who can be punished and refused political membership—persons who are rendered as both morally unfit for self-government and radically responsible for their exclusion. I turn to Foucault to help examine neoliberalism because of his notably early attention to neo-liberal economists' theory of crime and of punishment specifically. One of the earliest "nonmarket" domains to which neoliberal thinkers applied their analysis was the economics of crime and the law.

The foundation of this analysis, as Foucault rightly noted in 1979, is the figure of *homo œconomicus* and the theory of human capital that redescribes all activity as investments in the self. *Homo œconomicus*—figured as the ra-tional, responsible, and governable figure of the late-liberal state—allows for the persistence of a deep criminal subjectivity (the felon as a figure) while at the same time providing a plausible deniability that such subjectivity exists (the insistence that disenfranchisement is collateral). As such, at the mo-ment when neoliberalism opposes subjectivizing punitive practices, it allows those practices to operate more effectively and silently. Most importantly, *homo œconomicus* acts as the historical bridge between the eighteenth- and nineteenth-century conceptions of "the felon" (who appears much more like "the delinquent") and contemporary conceptions of "the felon." This enables a reconfiguration of criminological thought that allows for the felon to be figured as a person who not only can bear the weight of a disproportionate punitive response but seemingly calls for it by being figured as completely responsible for all outcomes. What we will find is that eighteenth- and nineteenth-century conceptions of criminal subjectivity, which map more to forms of liberal governmentality (relying on techniques of disciplinary power and conceptions of the criminal subject as pathological, deviant, and abnormal), give way to twentieth- and twenty-first-century conceptions of neoliberal governmentality (which approach the criminal subject as a deeply responsible rational agent). This conception of the subject produces the felon as a deeply responsible and yet also pathologically monstrous figure.

Understanding neoliberal subjectivity in this way points our attention to how "life" (and collections of "lives") is captured, arrested, and constrained by the state. For Foucault, this means that we must reorient our understanding of liberalism within the broader context of biopolitics, a mode of governing that focuses not simply on the body of the criminal but on the entire population. Liberalism in its various forms defines the conditions of knowing—the *savoir*—for this form of power over life. Why insist on this connection? First, biopolitics for Foucault emerges historically alongside liberalism. Second, biopolitics reconfigures itself through the ascendency of neoliberalism, adopting new techniques of power. And third, the emergence of biopolitics also marks the historical appearance of modern racism as a form of state racism.

LIBERALISM(S) AS THE *SAVOIR* OF BIOPOLITICS

Put succinctly by Thomas Lemke, "The notion of biopolitics refers to the emergence of a specific political knowledge and new disciplines such as statistics, demography, epidemiology, and biology. These disciplines make it possible to analyze processes of life on the level of populations and to 'govern' individuals and collectives by practices of correction, exclusion, normalization, discipline, therapeutics, and optimization."[26] This way of thinking about the relationship between "life" and "politics" was not founded in Foucault's thought, but his conception is arguably one of the most influential in circulation today. For Foucault, the term "biopolitics" operates alongside what he later calls "governmentality," which he defines as the techniques of power exercised at the level of "life" and the "conducting of conducts" that support and shape these techniques.[27]

Biopolitics should be understood as a technique of power (hence biopower; Foucault does not cleanly differentiate between these terms) that emerges when the question of politics shifts to the level of the entire population (hence the interest in not simply the conduct of subjects but the conduct of conducts).[28] Lemke identifies three distinct but related forms of biopower/biopolitics in Foucault's usage: (1) as a contrast to other forms of power, in particular, sovereign power or juridical power, (2) as a central feature in the emergence of modern (i.e., state) racism, and (3) as a mode of power coincident with liberalism. In each of these uses, the unifying principles for Foucault are a sensitivity to the changing way that subjects are formed (and form themselves) through mechanisms of power and a resistance to simplistic or archaic understandings of how power operates.

The terms are introduced into his lexicon in 1976, in the closing section of the first volume of *The History of Sexuality* and in his lecture course that year at the Collège de France.[29] "It seems to me," he states in the final lecture of *Society Must Be Defended*, "that one of the basic phenomena of the nineteenth century was what might be called power's hold over life. What I mean is the acquisition of power over man insofar as man is a living being, that the biological came under State control."[30] This form of power is identified as distinct from disciplinary and juridical power and yet is importantly related. As he argues earlier in *The History of Sexuality*, a new "analytics of power" must be developed that will move us beyond its traditional form in which power is collapsed into notions of sovereignty and linked to the language of law and prohibition and, more generally, to a "juridico-discursive" representation.[31] In its place, Foucault insists, we must make sure our accounts of power reflect a "strategical model" that emphasizes the "multiple and mobile field of force relations."[32] In both the lecture course and *The History of Sexuality*, Foucault looks at the exercise of the death penalty to demonstrate how force relations have changed in the West: "Together with war it [the death penalty] was for a long time the other form of the right of the sword; it constituted the reply of the sovereign to those who attacked his will, his law, or his person."[33] But while sovereignty had traditionally been defined in Hobbesian terms as that body (collective or singular) that possesses an exclusive right over life and death—to "take life or let live"—the "very profound transformation" of force relations in the West means that "the right of the sovereign is now manifested as simply the reverse of the right of the social body to ensure, maintain, or develop its life."[34] As such, the state and other nonstate actors exercise power increasingly focused on life itself and, in particular, at the level of the population rather than simply at the level of the individual.

The effect of this transformation can be traced in the corresponding shift in the logic of the death penalty in this same period: "As soon as power gave itself the function of administering life, its reason for being and the logic of its exercise . . . made it more and more difficult to apply the death penalty. How could power exercise its highest prerogatives by putting people to death, when its main role was to ensure, sustain, and multiply life, to put this life in order?"[35] Whereas the death penalty of the classical age operated through a public execution and the spectacle of the scaffold, in a world of the disciplinary system, to resort to execution would signal a failure to reform a delinquent and thus a failure of power. As an exercise of biopower in the administration of life itself, an execution would appear as a contradiction of the "new" *raison d'état*: taking life rather than making live. The transformation would be to both shun execution (but without completely abolishing it) and, at the same time, give it a new justification: "For such a power [i.e., biopower], execution was at the same time a limit, a scandal, and a contradiction. Hence capital punishment could not be maintained except by invoking less the enormity of the crime itself than the monstrosity of the criminal, his incorrigibility, and the safeguard of society. One had the right to kill those who represented a kind of biological danger to others."[36] This transformation—which does not ban the death penalty but reconfigures it as a technique for the promotion of some life at the necessary expense of those lives seen as a threat—provides the conceptual footing for the bloodiest and most horrific executions of the twentieth century.[37]

In *The History of Sexuality*, biopolitics and biopower are distinguished primarily from juridical forms of power as well as from disciplinary power. Foucault specifically identifies biopower as having "two basic forms" that have emerged since the seventeenth century. First, biopower appears as disciplinary power through an *"anatomo-politics of the human body*," focused on the life of the individual through the body that could be made, formed, and reformed as a normal subject. Second, biopower appears in the *"biopolitics of the population*," focused on the life of the entire population, through *"regulatory controls"* that would respond to these "events" through mechanisms of security to produce optimal rates and levels throughout the broader body politic.[38] As Lemke notes, these two forms do not stand in opposition to or independent from each other, but rather they mutually implicate and define each other.[39] They remain conceptually distinct, however, as Foucault explains in the lectures. The second technique "does not exclude . . . disciplinary technology, but it does dovetail into it, integrate it, modify it to some extent, and above all, use it by sort of infiltrating it. . . . [It] does not simply do away with the disciplinary technique, because it exists on a different level, on a different scale, and because it has a different bearing area, and makes use of very different instruments."[40] Unlike disciplinary power, biopower is "directed not at man-as-body but at man-as-species," taking the population as a whole as its object and taking as its domain the "control over the relations between the human race . . . and their environment, the milieu in which they live."[41] In this way, biopower responds not primarily to persons but to "events" within the population of persons, employing mechanisms that are distinct from disciplinary techniques of power, including "forecasts, statistical estimates, and overall measures," whose purposes are not to "modify any given phenomenon as such . . . [but to] intervene at the level of their generality."[42] Or as he puts it in the *History of Sexuality*, "One would have to speak of *bio-power* to designate what brought life and its mechanisms into the realm of explicit calculations and made knowledge-power an agent of transformation of human life. It is not that life has been totally integrated into techniques that govern and administer it; it constantly escapes them."[43]

Foucault both complicates and clarifies this account of biopower in his Collège de France lecture in the following years.[44] In his opening lecture of *Security, Territory, Population* (given in the spring of 1978), Foucault states that he wants to pick up where he left off: "I would like to begin studying something that I have called, somewhat vaguely, bio-power."[45] Here, he follows his previous argument of 1976, tracing how this new form of power has become prevalent in the modern period and continues to characterize the contemporary moment. His method of delineating this new form of power is through examples, and in the first three lectures of *Security, Territory, Population*, Foucault renames the second form of biopower described previously—that which operates through regulatory controls on the population—as "mechanisms of security." As Mariana Valverde notes, the meaning of the English "security" is not directly equivalent to the French "*sécurité.*" She writes, "*Sécurité* is the future-oriented management of risks; by contrast, national security and security forces would fall under the rubric of *sûreté* [safety]."[46] In this way, biopower becomes associated with at least two distinct techniques of power—disciplinary and security—but with a stronger association with the latter, in that biopower seeks to manage the future life of the species, fostering its growth and health.

The delineation between these modulations of power is made clearer through Foucault's concrete examples, the first of which is drawn from the penal context: theft. In an economy of power primarily characterized by juridical power, the paradigmatic response to theft has the form of a prohibition: "Take a completely simple penal law in the form of a prohibition like, say, 'you must not kill, you must not steal' along with its punishment, hanging, or banishment, or a fine."[47] Under an economy of power characterized by a primarily disciplinary power (the regime explicated at length in *Discipline and Punish*, becoming dominant in the modern period), the paradigmatic response to the same crime builds on the first juridical punishment: "In the second modulation [of power] it is still the same penal law,

'you must not steal.' And it is still accompanied by certain punishments
if one breaks this law, but now everything is framed by, on the one hand,
a series of supervisions, checks, inspections and varied controls that, even
before the thief has stolen, makes it possible to identify whether or not he
is going to steal."[48] Importantly, the rise of disciplinary power does not ban-
ish the law or the punishment but dramatically expands and reconfigures
how power is exercised over the criminal, such that the criminal can be
thought of, identified, and managed in the absence of the crime itself. This
is the fundamentally important work of fabrication described in the previous chapter: the thief as a *delinquent* comes into being from and through
such knowledge. And insofar as the *life* of the thief is captured, such capture
extends beyond the body of a criminal itself and into the biographical and
anthropological life of the criminal, through normalizing techniques such
as training, measurement, and surveillance (in addition to the ever-present
threat of bodily punishment).

But there is a "third modulation" of power that is now on the table, which
is exercised through these mechanisms of "security" and which responds to
"theft" and the "thief" quite differently:

> The third modulation is based on the same matrix, with the same penal
> law, the same punishment, and the same type of framework of surveil-
> lance on one side and correction on the other, but now, the application
> of this penal law, the development of preventative measures, and the
> organization of corrective punishment will be governed by the following
> kind of questions. For example: What is the average rate of criminality
> for this [type]? How can we predict statistically the number of thefts at a
> given moment, in a given society, in a given town, in the town or in the
> country, in a given social stratum, and so on?"[49]

The relevant questions for "security" become those that operate at the level
of the population more generally, relying on aggregate forms of knowledge,
eschewing the management of individuals qua individual. This notion of
the "population" is instrumental to the emergence of Foucault's third modulation of power, both operated on and brought into existence by the mechanisms of security that function here.

Foucault's delineation of this third modulation of power from juridical/
legal and disciplinary forms is most clear in the way mechanisms of security
respond to threats through what he calls a form of internal self-cancellation.[50]
Foucault states,

The law prohibits and discipline prescribes, and the essential function of security, without prohibiting or prescribing, but possibly making use of some instruments of prescription and prohibition, is to respond to a reality in such a way that this response cancels out the reality to which it responds—nullifies it, or limits, checks, or regulates it.[51]

For criminological discourse, this means giving priority to the management of crime rates over punishing or rehabilitating offenders. Juridical and disciplinary techniques will continue to be used but are subsumed under a political rationality that seeks to manage crime through self-regulating mechanisms of security. Such a deployment of power manages and controls a population through the manipulation of the social environment, primarily in a way that will appear as having little or no direct intervention at all, at least in comparison to the more "visible" forms of juridical and disciplinary power Foucault previously diagnosed.

Interestingly, this shift toward the level of the population and the manipulation of the environment sets up a new possibility of outcome in the exercise of power. Foucault states, "These mechanisms [of security] do not tend to a nullification of phenomena in the form of the prohibition, 'you will not do this,' nor even, 'this will not happen,' but in the form of a progressive self-cancellation of phenomena by the phenomena themselves. In a way, they involve the delimitation of phenomena within acceptable limits, rather than the imposition of a law that says no to them."[52] This is to say that there is no a priori assumption that the phenomena in question will have their rate be reduced to zero. Instead, the goal is to discover some acceptable "natural" or "efficient" rate, one that is conducive to the flourishing of the *life* of the population. As in the case with the biopolitical justification of the death penalty (where one might still kill but only for the *sake* of the survival of the population), the exercise of power over criminals is justified for public safety, rather than simply as punishment of a morally responsible actor.

Neoliberal penality, as diagnosed by Harcourt and Wacquant, is eminently biopolitical in that it manages the seeming paradox between a discourse of individual responsibility and rights and a dominating and heavy-handed punitive response. And in particular, given that biopower *includes* the exercise of juridical and disciplinary power, we should not be surprised by the seeming contradictions that arise under widespread neoliberalism: that at a time when all persons are assumed to be rational agents, we find a proliferation of paternalism or that seemingly race-neutral market logics applied to the political domain exacerbate racial inequalities and support white supremacy. This, of course, should be no surprise to readers of Foucault, for whom one of the key ways biopower is exercised is in the emergence of modern racism, specifically a state-based form of racial distinction that always borders on genocidal and exterminatory logics. As Lemke notes, "The idea of society as a biological whole assumes the provision of a central authority that governs and controls it, watches over its purity, and is strong enough to confront 'enemies' within its borders and beyond: the modern state. Foucault argues that, from the end of the nineteenth century, at the latest, racism guided the rationality of state actions; it finds form in its political instruments and concrete policies as 'State racism.'"[53] As will become clearer in subsequent chapters, the development of criminal exclusions to the franchise in the nineteenth century in the United States hinged on a conception of race that conforms with this notion of biopower and governmentality.

The last piece of the puzzle for us, however, is how to link together this notion of biopower with the notion of neoliberalism, specifically with its economistic approach to social phenomena. For Foucault, the linkage is obvious: the "new" *raison d'état* that is expressed by this organization of biopolitical power which takes hold in the modern period is grounded in liberal political economy.[54] That is, if we are interested in *government* and *governing*, if we are interested in the way this third modulation of power functions in practice, then we also must take up liberal and neoliberal political economy to understand its functioning. After describing the mechanisms of security as a third modality of power, Foucault shifts his language, introducing the term "governmentality" as,

> first, . . . the ensemble formed by institutions, procedures, analyses and reflections, calculations, and tactics that allow the exercise of this very specific, albeit very complex, power that has the population as its target, political economy as its major form of knowledge, and apparatuses of security as its essential technical instrument. Second, by "governmentality" I understand the tendency, the line of force, that for a long time, and throughout the West [*l'Occident*], has constantly led towards the pre-eminence over all other types of power—sovereignty, discipline, and so on—of the type of power that we can call "government" and which has led to the development of a series of specific governmental appara-

tuses (*appareils*) on the one hand [and, on the other] to the development of a series of knowledges (*saviors*).[55]

The key point of this passage is to note the three dimensions of any modulation of power: its target, its form of knowledge (*savoir*), and its techniques (or instruments). These dimensions can be applied as a rubric for each modality of power (sovereign/juridical, disciplinary, etc.) as a mode of analysis, and, in general, they call for two lines of historical inquiry: first, along practices of governance (i.e., the governmental apparatuses) rather than institutions and, second, along the forms of knowledge (*savoirs*) which support these practices.[56] With this schema in mind, *Security, Territory, Population* can be read as an extended study of the practices of governance (covering the targets and the techniques of biopower) but not its *savoir*. This is where Foucault next turns his attention: to the forms of knowledge of biopolitics in its liberal and neoliberal forms. And notably, this is also where Foucault returns to criminological figures and the kinds of penal practices that fabricate them, focusing in part on the American neoliberal approach to crime and punishment and on the emergence of *homo œconomicus* as a new kind of criminological (non)figure.

BEYOND THE REHABILITATIVE IDEAL

Foucault reflected on the lectures he had given the following spring in 1979—*The Birth of Biopolitics*—stating, "This year's course was devoted entirely to what should have been only its introduction."[57] Giving a proper "introduction" to biopolitics—what he succinctly refers to in the course summary as the endeavor "to rationalize the problems posed to governmental practice by phenomena characteristic of a set of living beings forming a population"—required Foucault to dwell on "the framework of political rationality within which they appeared and took on their intensity."[58] This framework can be broadly understood as liberalism, and the lectures take the form of an extended analysis of classical liberalism, German *ordo*-liberalism, and American *neo*-liberalism.[59] As Duncan Ivison puts it, "What intrigues Foucault is that liberalism problematizes the very notion of government and at the same time develops its own distinctive form of governmentality—its own form of the liberal 'conduct of conduct.'"[60]

Having spent the previous year's lecture describing in detail the target (the population) and the techniques (mechanisms of *sécurité*), Foucault is self-consciously turning to the question of political economy as the *savoir* of governmentality, insisting that the liberal and neoliberal forms of political economy are the most relevant forms for thinking about biopower. American neoliberalism differed from both classical liberalism and German *ordo-liberalism* by rethinking the fundamental relationship between the state and the economy. Classical liberalism (specifically the expression of liberalism that was inherited by Americans from British and French sources and that defined the terms of the American Revolution) was driven by an understanding of laissez-faire economic polices as the basis of individual liberty. Proponents of individual liberty, on this account, should look to the state as a protector of a sphere of noninterference for the individual. For the German *ordo*-liberals, as Lemke explains, the "starting point was their idea of a 'social market economy,' in other words from a notion of a market that was constantly supported by political regulations and had to be flanked by social intervention."[61] Both conceptions presupposed the existence of the state (or at least take the state to be necessarily contingent) to the functioning of the market. Classical liberals and *ordo*-liberals, while primarily concerned with the market, still take the state for granted and theorize the market as an external limit to politics, delimiting the reach of policy from the outside.

In contrast to American neoliberals' classical and German counterparts, their radical innovation was to insist that the market form is *prior* to the political sphere, placing the market at the center of analysis and subsuming all political questions within it. Foucault describes this as a basic reversal of the relationship between state and market, in which the market itself becomes the foundation of the state. He says, "The demand for liberalism founds the state rather than the state limiting itself through liberalism."[62] As Lemke glosses, "For the neo-liberals the state does not define and monitor market freedom, for the market is itself the organizing and regulative principle underlying the state. . . . Neo-liberalism removes the limiting, external principle and puts a regulatory and inner principle in its place: it is the market form which serves as the organizational principle for the state and society."[63] Under such a rearticulation of state and economy, the traditional understanding of laissez-faire itself undergoes a similar transformation. The theory of state and economy does not call for a retraction of the state in order to secure a space of negative liberty in which one can act freely. Rather, it becomes the purpose for government itself and a "permanent economic tribunal" against which all governmental activity is judged.[64]

Foucault demonstrates this reversal by reconstructing two areas of study in American neoliberal scholarship: the theory of human capital and the analysis of crime and punishment.[65] What connects these two for Foucault is the reinvocation and subsequent redefinition of the figure of *homo œconomicus*. Traditionally understood as that individual who interacts with the market, *homo œconomicus* is "an economic man, . . . the man of exchange, the partner, one of two partners in the process of exchange."[66] Becker, building on the work of Theodore Schultz, theorizes human capital as a form of personal investment, reframing consumption as productive activity.[67] Under Becker's neoliberal theory of human capital, the person is something that can be *invested* in, and *homo œconomicus* becomes "not at all a partner in exchange. *Homo œconomicus* is an entrepreneur, an entrepreneur of himself."[68] As Lemke explains, this theory of human capital redescribes the factors of production such that "wage labourers are no longer the employees dependent on a company, but are autonomous entrepreneurs with full responsibility for their own investment decisions and endeavoring to produce surplus value."[69] Individuals are to be understood not as traditional factors of production but as themselves a site of productive activity through personal self-development.

Foucault attributes this development directly to Becker's theory of consumption as production: "The man of consumption, insofar as he consumes, is a producer. What does he produce? Well, quite simply, he produces his own satisfaction."[70] Whereas, in the classic liberal conception, *homo œconomicus* was not the total perspective of analysis for the individual but merely one perspective among others, under neoliberal analysis, *homo œconomicus* is taken to be able to account for the human subject in its entirety, and the presumption of this universal figure underlies the neoliberal approach to extending economic analysis to all spheres of social life.[71] This disciplinary extension of economic analysis is driven by the new concept of *homo œconomicus* and is exemplified in its starkest clarity, Foucault argues, in the work of Becker, George Stigler, and Isaac Ehrlich on crime. Their approach to the question of crime and punishment demonstrates all the hallmarks of the neoliberal shift in analysis and, most importantly, represents a complete rejection of the multiple figures of *homo legalis*, *homo penalis*, and *homo criminalis* in favor of a universal *homo œconomicus*.

Foucault contrasts the classic liberal and neoliberal conceptions of crime by briefly rearticulating some of his analysis from *Discipline and Punish*. The early liberal theorists of punishment (Beccaria and Bentham, specifically) developed an understanding of law in economic terms that linked penalties in proportion to the severity of crimes, such that *homo penalis* was coincident with *homo œconomicus*. The penal law that built on Beccaria's plan of reform and that was schematized by Bentham used the law to dispatch the most economical regime of punishment, in the sense that the amount and kind of punishment satisfied utilitarian concerns. Punishment is "economical" insofar as (1) a crime is defined in the law, (2) penalties are fixed in law, (3) the same law fixes those penalties in proportion to the severity of the crime, and (4) the criminal court will be the location that applies this law, determining the specific penalty undergone by the criminal in relation to the severity of the crime.[72] What these principles produce is the "least costly and most effective form of obtaining punishment and the elimination of conducts harmful to society."[73] Under this classical sense, the individual who can be punished is the same as the economic individual, and in this sense, it is the law that brings together the penal and the economic: "*Homo penalis*, the man that can legally be punished, the man exposed to the law and who can be punished by the law is," Foucault argues, "strictly speaking, *homo œconomicus*. And it is precisely the law which enables the problem of penal practice to be connected to the problem of the economy."[74]

The central paradox of this economy of punishment is that the rationalized application of the law requires a criminal anthropology, the ability to identify the criminal before the crime. Prohibitive law is defined in terms of bad actions but cannot be applied to actions themselves. It can only be applied to those actors who are rightly called offenders. But insofar as the punishment can serve as a deterrent to other possible offenders, and insofar as the punishment's severity lets the offender make amends, it becomes necessary to delve into the life of the offender. The economical requirements of the classical liberal system call forth *criminology* and give rise to the figure of *homo criminalis* directly out of *homo penalis*. It is in this sense that the classical liberals, insofar as they may have sought to rationalize their criminal law, enable and support the notion of an economy of punishment in which some individuals are of a criminal kind, even if they are, in a sense, also *homo œconomicus*.

Foucault focuses on Becker's 1968 article "Crime and Punishment: An Economic Approach" to identify the neoliberal analytic shift.[75] By Foucault's account, Becker wants to return to Bentham and Beccaria's insistence on economy and reformist impulse but to somehow escape the "problem of history" and, most importantly, to place the principle of utility *within* the juridical structure. Insofar as Bentham and Beccaria understood punishment through an economic approach, it was to subject punishment to economics. Foucault notes that the slide from *homo legalis* to *homo penalis* and finally to *homo criminalis* was a process of subjecting the law to economic constraints, to making it align with an external principle of utility. The neoliberal approach, however, starts with *homo œconomicus* and refuses any slippage toward a pathologized criminal kind. The problem of crime, in this approach, begins and ends with economic analysis as an interior logic, prior to the use of any legal framework. It is not that the application of the law should be economical but that economics should dictate the law.

On Foucault's account, Becker begins by noting that the proper definition of a crime is not found in the law but in its cost: punishment as price.[76] Foucault states that crime is, according to Becker, simply that which exposes an individual to punishment. What matters is the double move of (1) placing *homo œconomicus* at the center of the analysis and (2) recognizing that this figure is in fact already oneself. When I, as *homo œconomicus*, determine whether an action is a crime, I ponder whether it is something that would expose me to punishment. The perspective of the law is exchanged for the perspective of the subject. Foucault insists, "It is the same definition, . . . but the point of view has simply changed. . . . We ask: What is the crime for him, that is to say, for the subject of an action, for the subject of a form of conduct or behavior? Well, it is whatever it is that puts him at risk of punishment."[77]

The effect of this move is enormous: if we "move over to the side of the individual subject by considering him as *homo œconomicus*" and take the definition of crime as "that action an individual commits by taking the risk of being punished by the law," we arrive at Becker's famous claim that there is no difference between a traffic violation and premeditated murder.[78] As Becker puts it, "Some persons become 'criminals' . . . not because their basic motivation differs from that of other persons, but because their benefits and costs differ. . . . A crime is apparently not so different analytically from any other activity that produces external harm and when crimes are punishable by fines, the analytical differences virtually vanish."[79]

Becker's stance, Foucault states, "also means that in this perspective, the criminal is not distinguished in any way by or interrogated on the basis of moral or anthropological traits. The criminal is nothing other than absolutely anyone whomsoever. That criminal, any person, is treated only as anyone whomsoever who invests in an action, expects a profit from it, and who accepts the risk of a loss."[80] There is no such thing as a moral or anthropological "criminal" kind but only individuals who function in a market of possible profits and losses. But from Foucault's viewpoint, the sharp distinction from the logic of the delinquent is most important: "You can see that in view of this the penal system will no longer have to concern itself with that split reality of the crime and the criminal."[81] There is no doubling of criminal and crime, since there is, strictly speaking, no such thing as a *criminal*. There is only one kind of human, *homo œconomicus*, and only one kind of social interaction: exchange. This shift renders the question of crime and punishment as one of supply and demand, subject to standard economic analysis. Borrowing specifically from welfare economics, crime is taken as a market with strong negative externalities, and as such, punishment should be thought of in the same way that taxation is used by the state to adjust costs associated with any market activities that produce negative externalities. The deployment of this *savoir* would call for radically different practices of the policing, punishment, and management of offenders. It would (as Becker himself insists) call for a complete reworking of criminal law, focusing on the "rules of the game" rather than on the "players" themselves. Such a revised approach to the law parallels (if not directly matches) what Foucault means by biopower operating on the level of generality.

This analytic shift opens up a split between the law and its enforcement. Rather than operating directly on the body (as the sovereign law does, through a direct application of force), the law becomes reduced (or perhaps revealed) as nothing other than a command, "*a speech act*."[82] The law has a linguistic reality of its own and yet already calls into question its own force as merely speech. This in turn calls into question its "enforcement" as something more than its mere application. It matters, in other words, that a prohibition need not always be carried out in fact. The enforcement of law, like all forms of intervention from the neoliberal point of view, is a question separate from the law itself and will have an equilibrium point not necessarily (or at all likely) to be equal to zero. As with all things under a neoliberal regime, this means that the level of enforcement is subject to an efficiency test. The neoliberal approach to crime need not seek the complete elimination of crime—a goal which, however difficult, was still a chief motivation for classical liberal thinkers about crime. The complete elimination of crime is not just practically difficult; it is undesirable insofar as it would impose diminishing utility costs beyond positive returns. Foucault quotes

George Stigler, who writes, "The goal of enforcement, let us assume, is to achieve that degree of compliance with the rule of prescribed (or proscribed) behavior that the society believes it can afford. There is only one reason why the society must forgo 'complete' enforcement of the rule: enforcement is costly."[83] "Consequently," Foucault says,

> good penal policy does not aim at the extinction of crime, but at a balance [*un équilibre*] between the curves of the supply of crime and negative demand. Or again: society does not have a limitless need for compliance. Society does not need to conform to an exhaustive disciplinary system. A society finds that it has a certain level of illegality and it would find it very difficult to have this rate indefinitely reduced. This amounts to posing as the essential question of penal policy, not, how should crimes be punished, nor even, what actions should be seen as crimes, but what crime should we tolerate? Or again: what would it be intolerable to tolerate? This is Becker's definition in "Crime and Punishment." There are two questions, he [Becker] says: "How many offences should be permitted? Second, how many offenders should go unpunished?" This is the question of penal practice.[84]

Under neoliberalism, we are no longer concerned about the eradication of crime, nor are we concerned about individual criminals. The only relevant questions are those that operate at the general level of the population: the crime rate. Further, in drawing on the assumptions of neoliberal economic theory, the equilibrium point is determined by market conditions and never assumed to be equal to zero. As with other market phenomena (e.g., employment, inflation), there is some nonzero level of crime that can be called a "natural" rate. Such an approach to law enforcement has reshaped American policing strategy, with varied effects and its own pathologies.[85] More important for our purposes is the effect this approach has on the notion of the criminal as a figure.

TOWARD A CRIMINOLOGY OF *HOMO ŒCONOMICUS*

Foucault draws out two key consequences of this approach to crime and punishment as an example of how the market form extends to encompass a nonmarket sphere of activity. First, there is the "*gommage anthropologique du criminel*," an "erasure" of the anthropological understanding of criminality and of the psychological criminal and the delinquent as particular human kinds.[86] *Homo œconomicus* is deployed as the foundational concept of the human agent, an individual whose only activity is consumption, differing from others only through revealed preferences and, perhaps, through an aversion to risk. This "*gommage*" does not, Foucault insists, eliminate all techniques of power that influence an individual's behavior, but rather "an element, dimension, or level of behavior can be postulated which can be interpreted as economic behavior and controlled as such."[87] Even the most monstrous of criminals can be understood in terms of that individual's sensitivity or responsiveness to punishment. Foucault directly quotes the neoliberal economist Isaac Ehrlich, saying, "There is no reason a priori to expect that persons who hate or love others are less *responsive* to changes in costs and gains associated with activities they may wish to pursue than persons indifferent towards the well-being of others."[88] If we cling to the notions of criminality from an earlier period and see murderers as monstrous, all that matters is that even such a monster is more or less a "responsive" individual. Foucault states,

> All the distinctions that have been made between born criminals, occasional criminals, the perverse and the not perverse, and recidivists are not important. We must be prepared to accept that, in any case, however pathological the subject may be at a certain level and when seen from a certain angle, he is nevertheless, "responsive" to some extent to possible gains and losses, which means that penal action must act on the interplay [*le jeu*] of gains and losses or, in other words, on the environment.[89]

There are two subsidiary effects from this erasure. First, even if we do not completely relinquish the terms of the disciplinary age, the neoliberal approach states that any offender has a responsive quality—that even the most pathological are at least in some sense responsive to changes in penal policy. This, in turn, means that changing penal policy is about altering the rules of the game rather than acting on the player of that game. Penal policy, under this framework, is a form of environmental policy, that is, a policy concerning the field of play in which players find themselves. As Lemke puts it, "[Neoliberal penal policy] focuses not on the players, but on the rules of the game, not on the (inner) subjection of individuals, but on defining and controlling their (outer) environment."[90]

The second effect is that, in rejecting the effort to shape the deep subjectivity of an offender involved in disciplinary or normalizing penal policy, the neoliberal approach claims to leave behind the techniques of discipline and normalization:

> What appears on the horizon of this kind of analysis is not at all the ideal or project of an exhaustively disciplinary society in which the legal network hemming in individuals is taken over and extended internally by, let's say, normative mechanisms. Nor is it a society in which a mechanism of general normalization and the exclusion of those who cannot be normalized is needed. On the horizon of this analysis we see instead the image, idea, or theme-program of a society in which there is an optimization of systems of difference, in which the field is left open to fluctuating processes, in which minority individuals and practices are tolerated, in which action is brought to bear on the rules of the game rather than on the players, and finally in which there is an environmental type of intervention instead of the internal subjugation of individuals.[91]

The internal contradiction of the classical liberal position, in which the need to tailor punishment to each specific offense gave rise to normalizing discourses and the biographical doubling of the criminal with the crime, now gives way to a market structure that sees difference as a resource to be "optimized" and understands the role of government to be "environmental" rather than focusing its attention on a specific organism within that environment. Under neoliberalism, the analyst of crime policy (as well as all social policy) ought to be less attentive to those policies that operate on the bodies of offenders and instead focus primarily on frameworks that establish the milieu in which those offenders find themselves, bringing together multiple forms of biopolitical administration.

Foucault characterizes this horizon of neoliberalism as a system in which the byproducts of the disciplinary regime, the forces of normalization and the exclusion of the radically abnormal, give way to a society in which difference becomes a market virtue and the work of the state is centered on the individual and on the conditions in which the individual (hopefully) thrives. Yet most telling is the idea of a tolerance between individuals and minority practices. Does this mean that the neoliberal conception of society allows the flourishing of activities that, under the disciplinary regime, are excluded? What exactly does "tolerance" of such practices entail? Given that a central principle of the neoliberal regime is the extension of the market form to all spheres of social life, it must be the case that "tolerance" refers to those activities that can express themselves under that form. That is, such differences continue to operate and function as differences. And ideally, there would be no set limit to what these practices are. Yet it is here that Foucault, in invoking what seems to be a rather positive appraisal of the neoliberal view, calls attention to its hidden underside.

If we read Foucault's analysis of neoliberalism as continuous with his longstanding project of tracing and identifying the ways in which power transforms its configuration under different contexts and in different institutional and intersubjective relations, what we should see in his description of neoliberalism is not a glowing appraisal but a map of where one should look for the particular exercise of power under such a regime. If the lesson of *Discipline and Punish* is to recognize the way in which power continued to be exercised through discipline, albeit in a more efficient form, the lesson of the governmentality lectures of 1978 and 1979 is to recognize how power is now exercised through the management of the "rules of the game" and the "environment."

"Minority" practices, like crimes, for example, are tolerated in the sense that they are not in and of themselves taken as morally inappropriate actions. But insofar as a minority practice might generate a negative externality (as a crime most likely would be thought to do), what is meant by toleration becomes more clear: an associated tax or penalty attached to the activity in order to bring the supply of these activities more in line with the socially optimal level. Toleration, in market terms, in no way needs to mean flourishing. Foucault once famously noted that his point was "not that everything is bad, but that everything is dangerous."[92] Neoliberalism, in this sense, is neither good or bad, but rather, like everything, it is *dangerous* insofar as discourses, especially those which try to function with a universalized subject at their base, disavow their internal problems and seek to mask their contingencies and contradictions.

Certainly, Foucault gives credit to the neoliberals where it is due: a theory of criminal subjectivity in which there is no difference among murderers, traffic violators, and professors of economics certainly throws a much-needed wrench in the criminological works. It is a deeply refreshing move and one that, as Foucault notes and as Becker himself is aware, has deep roots in classical liberalism. Becker closes the famous 1968 article writing,

> Lest the reader be repelled by the apparent novelty of an "economic"
> framework for illegal behavior, let him recall that two important con-

tributors to criminology during the eighteenth and nineteenth centuries, Beccaria and Bentham, explicitly applied an economic calculus. Unfortunately, such an approach has lost favor during the last hundred years, and my efforts can be viewed as a resurrection, modernization, and thereby I hope improvement on these much earlier pioneering studies.[93]

Becker and company see themselves as rational reformers of punishment, just as Bentham and Beccaria did, refusing to pathologize and dehumanize criminal offenders. Yet, as Foucault's *Discipline and Punish* illustrates, the liberal reformers once paved the way for the penitentiary apparatus to undo their work, leading directly to the fabrication of the delinquent. Foucault argues that this new articulation of liberalism, placing *homo œconomicus* at its center and subjecting the entire basis of government to the market form, might be able to avoid the old trap of doubling the criminal and the crime. After all, it does not, by its definition, fabricate the category of delinquents in order to solve the discursive tension between the court of law and the penitentiary. To the reform-minded individual, neoliberalism's rationalism and purity are both its greatest virtues and its most seductive qualities. But this seduction rests on the reintroduction of the universal and depoliticizing figure of *homo œconomicus* into the criminal justice context, and it is with this figure that we find the danger.

Under neoliberalism, individuals become radically and fully "responsible" for their actions. *Homo œconomicus*, under the terms of human capital theory, is no longer merely a partner of exchange (the classical conception of the figure) but also is an entrepreneur of the self. Individuals are people who work on themselves for a future return, acting as consumer-investors in order to increase their value on the labor market. This shift in perspective (to see one's consumption choices as investments in the self) reconfigures the individual to bear the responsibility for good *and* bad investments in the self. That is, entrepreneurs are rewarded for taking risks that achieve high returns, while they are "punished" if the risks they take turn out to be poor investments. They bear the *entire* burden of their investments. Individuals, as *homo œconomicus*, bear full responsibility, in the market sense, for their actions.[94]

This *homo œconomicus*, the responsible "interface between government and the individual," is "someone who is eminently governable. From being the intangible partner of *laissez-faire, homo œconomicus* now becomes the correlate of a governmentality which will act on the environment (milieu) and systematically modify its variables."[95] An era in which mechanisms of security (e.g., risk management) come to have "preeminence" over other forms of power (e.g., disciplinary and juridical) is one characterized by intervention at the level of the population, meaning that this organization of power takes the population as a whole as its object. This is not to say that individuals cease to exist from the point of view of the state but rather that they only articulate themselves as *homo œconomicus*, governable because they are, to borrow directly from Ehrlich's language, "responsive" to changes in the milieu. At this moment, as Colin Gordon puts it, "Economic government here joins hands with behaviourism."[96] Neoliberal political economy, centered on the responsive *homo œconomicus*, gives mechanisms of security as exercises of biopower their conceptual footing.

The reemergence of *homo œconomicus* demonstrates how the discursive production of criminological features has proceeded following the end of an era in which the rehabilitative ideal was dominant. Part of the reason liberal theorists have failed to understand the meaning and significance of disenfranchisement is because they have not attended to the discursive exchanges that produce these figures. Nor have they attended to how these discourses have altered over time. To understand the felon and voting rights restrictions today, it is necessary to understand that this figure has been discursively fabricated within the context of changing discourses of law, citizenship, crime, and punishment, with its sequence of criminological figures, from the delinquent to *homo œconomicus*. Foucault's analyses give us a conceptual framework, a set of starting points, and most importantly, the proper orientation to the kinds of questions we should be asking. Foucault points us in the direction we must attend to first: a critique of classical liberalism as a doctrine that is founded on punishment and of the contemporary and neoliberal move to disavow that history.

THE FELON, DISENFRANCHISEMENT, AND THE FIELD
OF NEOLIBERAL PLAY

Foucault only points out the relatively hidden dangers of the neoliberal way of thinking. He does not take an explicitly normative position on these dangers. If we are interested in analyzing biopower, biopolitics, or governmentality, we must understand its conceptual framework, its way of knowing, its *savoir*. Moreover, if we read his subsequent interest in the care of the self as an ethical version of the economic entrepreneurship of the self, it seems that Foucault was indebted to this line of thought.[97] But here it is our job to make more explicit the work that this figure of *homo œconomicus* does in enabling practices, hiding assumptions, and managing contradictions among (and within) discourses. Neoliberal theories of crime and punishment have left us with real problems.

First, *homo œconomicus*, by implying a form of complete responsibility for criminal behavior, combined with existing attachments to criminals, delinquents, ne'er-do-wells, gangsters, and so on, actually enables a new meaning of criminality. The monstrous individual, the criminally insane, the incorrigible offender, and the recidivist each persist as recognizable figures, yet they become fully responsible despite their "known" condition of fundamental irresponsibility. Central to the disciplinary conception of these forms of otherness implied by the disciplinary form was that (1) they could be changed or reformed and (2) the same qualities that demonstrated their difference also diminished their culpability. What emerges is a conception of the irresponsible individual being held responsible for all the harm that individual has committed.[98] In the reality of the neoliberal world, the felon is always both a disciplinary and a biopolitical object. The most extreme form of disenfranchisement, being barred from the vote permanently, reflects this confused image of the felon as irresponsible and yet responsible.

What we will see, however, is a split between two forms of how the felon appears in different periods. As will be shown in detail in subsequent chapters, the nineteenth-century conception of the criminal who must be excluded from the ballot box will look more like the delinquent: dangerous, pathological, and monstrously associated with crime, blackness, and unworthiness. Here, the logic of fabrication dominates. By the late twentieth century, however, this figure will recede to the background, and in its place, the felon must be excluded purely as a collateral effect, as a public safety concern, and as figure who remains dangerous but is fully responsible for that danger as a rational (and therefore predictable) actor. Here, the logic of responsibilitization dominates. What will be important to keep in mind is the way these two forms of biopolitical management are united through the single figure of the felon and the practice of disenfranchisement. The specifically "American" tradition of liberalism brings these forms together, in that they are both biopolitical in practice: focused on the *racialized* bodies of (non)members of the polity.

Second, a new concept of "dangerousness" emerges as a result of *homo œconomicus* taking center stage. A standard justification for incarceration is that some individuals, regardless of their culpability, are permanent sources of danger and potential harm. While the figure of *homo œconomicus* proclaims that there is no fundamental difference between the murderer and the traffic violator, neoliberalism still allows these differences to assert themselves, albeit in a different venue or on a different level. While the neoliberal regime says we cannot refer to any form of deep subjectivity of these individuals, it still allows and encourages the prediction of harm and the assessment of risk on the basis of past actions and descriptive characteristics. While the neoliberal position might reject the clinical assessment of dangerousness, it wholly embraces an actuarial assessment of dangerousness.[99] What we see emerging in these first two problems are the contradictions produced in the space between biopower and disciplinary power, as one form shifts into preeminence over the other without complete displacement. In fact, Foucault is careful to remind us that we should never assume that modalities of power operate in isolation. Rather, juridical power, disciplinary power, and biopower each support and maintain each other, even as they remain in tension. What is necessary is an account of the *strategic* practices that allow for them to exist together.[100]

This fact of discursive overlap is especially problematic because, third, neoliberalism's insistence that a single discursive regime covers all social life blocks the analysis of "interdiscursive dependencies."[101] Under classical forms of liberalism, analysis gives priority to economic exchange and insists on a sphere of noninterference in the market, but it does so while maintaining distinctions among the market, the family, and the state. The viewpoint of neoliberal analysis, however, focuses on a unitary interface between the individual and all social life, *homo œconomicus*, and as such refuses any analysis, however productive, insightful, or empirically accurate, about what happens when discourses interact with each other.

Lastly, asserting a universal grid of intelligibility as a form of (reduced) subjectivity, which admittedly purports to optimize difference rather than to exclude or normalize it, is ultimately a way to disavow difference altogether, especially along lines of race, gender, sexuality, and disability. These forms of difference do not disappear but are left to reassert themselves without recourse to a political redress.[102] In this sense, Marx's early critique of liberalism continues to be apt:

> The state abolishes . . . the distinctions established by *birth, social rank, education, occupation,* when it decrees that birth, social rank, educa-

tion, occupation are *non-political* distinctions; when it proclaims, without regard to these distinctions, that every member of society is an *equal* partner in popular sovereignty, and treats all the elements which compose the real life of the nation from the standpoint of the state. But the state, none the less, allows private property, education, occupation, to *act* after *their* own fashion, namely as private property, education, occupation, and to manifest their *particular* nature. Far from abolishing these *effective* differences, it only exists so far as they are presupposed; it is conscious of being a *political state* and it manifests its *universality* only in opposition to these elements.[103]

Insofar as the neoliberal "state" operates through and is subordinated to the market, the same presupposition of difference can be said to be at work in the establishment of *homo œconomicus* as an *equal* condition and the market as the universal sphere of activity. As a universality, this assertion logically presupposes difference in order to assert itself as the universal arbiter of that difference. The only location for difference to assert itself is under the form of "tastes" or "revealed preferences." In economic analysis, such preferences are typically taken as exogenous and given. If they are to be questioned, they can only be questioned insofar as they can be modeled in terms of a utility function, granting the assumption of rationality or at least responsiveness.[104] And yet, at the same time, in the experience of the United States, it is increasingly clear that "winners" and "losers" on neoliberal terms are raced and racialized. As Spence puts it, "The neoliberal turn itself is made possible because of racial politics. The ideological discourse of neoliberalism naturalizes these effects by 'racing' the winners and the losers in a range of policy contexts."[105]

In this light, the contemporary felon, much like the discursive figures of the delinquent or *homo œconomicus* identified by Foucault, comes into existence for a reason that is neither intentional nor accidental. The delinquent came into existence as a discursive figure to do the important work of bridging the gap between the competing yet mutually enabling demands of two fields of play: the rise of the penitentiary apparatus and the rationalization of criminal law. The court needed a figure to carry responsibility for the monstrosity of crime, and the penitentiary needed a body to be reformed, manipulated, and (maybe) returned to society. That the delinquent comes into existence is due to the spillover, the remainder, the leftover consequence of (arguably) good intentions. In Foucault's account of delinquency, he attends to the effects of discursive exchanges, to those moments when the juridical collides with the disciplinary: something must come into existence to manage that collision. Likewise, the neoliberal proposal to radically reconceive the human subject as the rational actor represents yet another well-intentioned attempt to reform and perfect the liberal ideal of an unencumbered, atomistic, and universal subject before the law. The only relevant difference between professor and murderer is to be found in their respective tastes, in their indifference curves and budget lines. Neoliberalism rejects the dangerous effects of discursive exchanges by insisting there are no such exchanges because there is only one discursive sphere: the market form. No specifically "criminological" figures are necessary to smooth over these tensions; no monsters really exist, as the only monstrosity out there is a tyrannical and inefficient legal system that is ignorant of the universal character placed before the law: *homo œconomicus*. As such, it is first and foremost on the level of the law that reform must take place, rationalizing, purifying, and simplifying it so that players might more readily know the "rules of the game."

Like the delinquent, the felon, defined as the convicted criminal who loses standing as a citizen, carries the burden of the demands of both a punitive discourse and a membership discourse (specifically the terms of participatory U.S. citizenship that developed through the mutually reinforcing terms of patriarchy, heteronormativity, ableism, and white supremacy). As in the case of poverty governance, in which such cleavages of difference both allow neoliberalism to take hold and also exacerbate inequalities and injustices across those cleavages, neoliberal penality, when viewed through the lens of subject formation, does not offer an elimination of difference but rather exacerbates difference-based injustices. Remaining citizens do not have to think about punishment as a part of membership, and when they punish others, they are afforded the right to avoid what this means in terms of membership. The felon stands in this overlap and lets us see it as a gap, as a separation. But the resurgence of *homo œconomicus* as the basis of criminality forces us to hold individuals fully responsible for their actions in a way that should have been impossible in our previous understanding of some individuals as criminals before the commission of the crime. We all become nothing more than our revealed market preferences, nothing more than our actions, and thus radically responsible for the "choices" we make between parking legally or illegally, between abiding by the law and violating its prohibitions. Contemporary felons are, on this account, nothing more than individuals whose actions burden other citizens too much, who "consume" more than they "pay for" and whose "costs" must be adjusted. But what we have trouble seeing, what is missing from this picture, is the foundational and constitutive exclusions, the sacrifices that allow for such a "universal" *homo œconomicus* to come into existence.[106]

The felon and disenfranchisement challenge Foucault's frameworks just as much as they follow them. The felon is constituted by an uneasy relationship between excess and proportionality. What makes felons uniquely the subjects they are is that they can and must carry the burden of an excessive punishment on their physical bodies as well as on their abstract selves as members of a political community. Following the lesson from Foucault about the process of discursive exchanges, the *terms* of political membership, proportionality and excess, and legitimacy are brought into existence as they are exercised. Disenfranchisement thus cannot simply be read as an aberration to the liberal order, not when it is also a (re)founding practice of the terms on which such an aberration can be understood.

Homo œconomicus turns our sights toward the foundation of liberal theory, questioning the structure of liberalism and the limits of excess and proportionality. One expected response to this assertion is that the problem is not with liberalism per se but with a failure to properly enact liberalism or to truly act as liberals. If we were actually the liberals we claim to be, if we followed Becker's advice to the letter (or Bentham's or Rawls's, for that matter), these problems would resolve themselves. That is, the problems I cite here are not failures of liberalism but failures of being properly liberal.[107] A second kind of response insists either that the purity of liberalism is sullied by being intimately connected to antiliberal discourses or that liberalism contains within it contradictory principles which are actively disavowed.[108]

But these responses are insufficient. Rather, we must entertain a response that has affinities with these two but looks to a different level of the problem. It might true that in liberalism, if some ideal form were actually to be practiced, the troubling assertions made earlier would cease to be problems, and *homo œconomicus* would cease to generate these effects. But this kind of purity is impossible, not necessarily because of an *internal* contradiction within liberalism but because the conditions of possibility for liberalism's coherence, for its terms of legitimacy and analysis to have meaning, are predicated on a prior antiliberal foundation. It is within the conditions of possibility of liberalism that the trouble is found. The ruptures and fissures that emerge are symptoms of prior foundational work that has been disavowed or forgotten.[109] In this context, the question becomes, "Who or what has to be sacrificed in order to posit the conditions of *homo œconomicus?*" Once we have answered this question, will we not have a better understanding of what sacrifice, what exclusion, what disavowal the felon represents?

In order to try to answer these questions, I turn to John Locke in the next chapter. Locke helps us understand (1) how a foundational inclusion/exclusion works and (2) how such a foundational inclusion/exclusion occurs in order to determine who gets punished and who gets to be a member. Locke, in this sense, acts as a father-confessor for liberalism, setting out the problem (we cannot know the terms of liberalism, proportionality, and right without forcing those terms into existence) and the solution (someone or something has to do that foundational work of settling the terms for the rest of us) such that we find it hard to acknowledge anymore, even when its descendant is right before our eyes. The disenfranchised felon thus allows us to (re)found the political community over and over again, as a remainder of an imagined foundational violence that brought about the very terms of contractarian liberalism and that established the order of excess and proportion that the disenfranchised felon continues to confuse.

4

To Kill a Thief

Whereas Robberies upon the high-ways, and Burglaries have been more frequently committed of late . . . [offenders] are deprived of the benefit of Clergy, in case of Robberies on the high-ways, and Burglaries, and the party robbed, for his encouragement to make resistance, is not to forfeit any thing, if he kill the Robber.

—CHARLES II, 1661[1]

It is difficult to overstate John Locke's influence on the American project and the formative effects his thought has had on our thinking about rights, liberties, and self-government. Beyond the obvious debt to Locke that is identifiable in Thomas Jefferson's careful choice of words in the Declaration of Independence, the Lockean social contract framework continues to hold the attention of the public imagination in the United States and serves as what Michael Sandel has called a public philosophy.[2] In the specific context of the legal and philosophical debates over criminal disenfranchisement, the specter of Locke and his contractarian thought have been brought to the stage both for and against the practice.[3] Criminals have broken the social contract, supporters argue, and thus have lost their right to self-representation and are no longer properly considered members of society. But Locke also forbids excessive and disproportionate punishment, detractors rightly note, and disenfranchisement as a collateral sanction is an obvious breach of liberal proportionality. As political theorist Jeffrey Reiman puts it succinctly in Lockean terms,

To continue to deprive ex-felons of the right to vote is, to use Locke's words, to continue the state of war against them. Since a criminal who has served his punishment has paid his debt to society and has been restored to normal liberty, neither self-defense nor continued punishment is justified against him, and thus it is wrong to continue the state of war with him.[4]

Such a reliance on Locke is not merely theoretical but also jurisprudential. When confronted with the constitutionality of disenfranchisement, U.S. courts have turned to Locke to guide their decisions, often quoting directly from the *Second Treatise of Government*.[5] As expressed in a ruling upholding felon disenfranchisement by a federal district court in 1997, "The rationale for felon disenfranchisement is based upon John Locke's social contract theory. According to Locke's theory . . . those individuals who do not abide by society's rules cannot participate in their promulgation."[6] As in this case, Locke's account of the social contract is typically used to normatively test a proposition or policy, to provide justification for a practice, or to find a language with which to condemn it. But Locke's social contract theory is not simply applicable in a normative or justificatory sense to questions of punishment. Rather, Locke's account of the social contract is *driven* by his account of punishment as a natural yet deeply unstable right.

Locke shows us just how deep the relationship between punishment and membership runs. Liberal political membership, as defined by Locke and as embraced in the court opinion just quoted, does not precede punishment but rather is brought into being through punishment's excessive character. As political theorist Keally McBride describes it more generally, liberalism *relies* on punishment to establish itself as a political order: "Because liberalism is based upon abstractions such as the social contract, natural rights, and even personhood that have no empirical referent, it has from the start relied upon practices of punishment to make these terms operable."[7] A careful reading of Locke through the lens of punishment can show us the critical set of discursive exchanges at work in liberal theory in particular and shed light on the meaning of the terms of punishment and political membership more generally. While Foucault helps us understand *how* stigmatized and excluded figures come into being at the intersection of different discourses, Locke shows us *which* discourses are most relevant for understanding punishments that seem "excessive" in the way that disenfranchisement does.

This chapter reconstructs the *Second Treatise*'s understanding of punishment by taking up an apparent instance of an excessive and disproportionate punishment: the insistence that thieves may be put to death. To understand Locke's argument for this claim, we must see how the meaning of the terms of proportionality, freedom, and self-rule are at stake. For Locke, the right to kill the thief is a proportional punishment because, albeit paradoxically, the limits of proportionality can be infinite and unbounded under certain conditions. The question for Locke is not how to make proportionality itself possible but how to establish a set of conditions that would allow it to meaningfully constrain punishment. Punishment's internal "excess" is thus always bound up in the terms of political membership, the motivation for persons to form and enter into a civil society, and the right for its members to rebel.

Typically, readers of Locke take up punishment only as a subset of his broader account of natural law or natural rights, often characterizing it as one specific "right" derived from the existence of natural law.[8] Such accounts read punishment as a concept subordinate to right or law or see it as merely exemplary of other key terms in Locke's lexicon (such as freedom or equality). In these standard accounts, punishment is looked to, at best, as illustrative of these terms or, at worst, as a deeply confusing mess to be either resolved or ignored.[9] Even readers of Locke who do locate punishment as central or integral in his thought nevertheless still strive to reduce the problematic character of punishment in Locke's thought as much as possible.[10] Collectively, they give short attention to how the idea of proportionality plays out in Locke's account of punishment and even less attention to the key criminological figure in Locke's rhetoric: the thief. In those rare occasions when the thief is specifically invoked by readers of Locke, this figure typically serves as an example of Locke's "confusion" over the demands of retributive versus utilitarian bases for the justification of punishment or, alternately, as a means of questioning the justification of the death penalty.[11]

My reading of Locke, in contrast, takes punishment to be an integral and indispensable part of his political theory and the figure of the thief to be an important rhetorical device for his argument. By tracing the discursive fabrication of the "thief" and the work that this figure does for the internal coherence of Locke's work, we can better consider the boundaries between punishment and membership in liberal thought more generally. Importantly, I am uninterested in settling punishment or getting it "right," normatively or conceptually. Nor am I interested in turning to Locke for an account of what we *should* be doing. Instead I turn to Locke to better understand what we are already doing but which we have difficulty acknowledging.

For Locke, punishment is a deeply unstable power that is put to productive use, offering a motivation for the formation of the commonwealth and a justification for the right of rebellion. Punishment always carries with it an excessive quality, and the purpose of founding a civil society is not to eradicate this excess but rather to manage and use it productively. That punishment can do this foundational and definitional work for political communities is due to its excess and instability, not to its perfection as a practice. Locke uses punishment to produce relatively stable subjects as a means of managing punishment's excess and instability. The creation of a subject that is capable of entering into a social compact and for whom full membership is possible requires the production of a different figure that carries the burden of danger and irrationality.

The argument of *The Second Treatise* relies on the figuration of criminal kinds as a source of physical and ontological threat and constructs them as a category of persons who, along with the "savages" of North America, generate a space between animals and "reasonable" persons. Locke's account of the foundation of the commonwealth and the right to rebellion are driven by the liminal figures that haunt the boundaries of membership and the border between the law of reason and the law of beasts, the human and the animal. And the traces of this work are visible throughout the text in the terms of animality and existential threat that pervade Locke's descriptions of tyrants, criminals, and all those persons who are degenerates, those *homini sacri* who manage the inside and outside by simultaneously marking and obscuring its boundary.[12] That this distinction could (and would) map so easily throughout the history of the American colonies, the Jacksonian United States, and especially in the post–Civil War period to racial and gender-based cleavages is not at all surprising, as these figures were produced as part of the production of what Shannon Winnubst identifies as "phallicized whiteness."[13] As she notes, "Many of the modern categories that we see at work in Locke's texts emerged in the post-bellum United States with a defensive tenacity that bred political, cultural, psychic, and physical violence."[14] That such violence is directed along racial cleavages is no accident.[15] If we want to understand a practice such as disenfranchisement, a punitive exclusion of membership that spills over itself in every moment, producing and reproducing the forms of difference it seeks to manage, a return to Locke's arguably foundational account of punishment shows how this quality might be built into the logic of liberalism itself.

PUNISHING THIEVES

In *The Second Treatise of Government*, Locke presents what he refers to as a "strange" doctrine of punishment.[16] Individuals, he asserts, possess a natural right to punish transgressors of the Law of Nature. Locke insists that the fundamental moral equality of persons in the State of Nature means that it is not simply wrong but *unlawful* to harm another person. Locke writes, "The *State of Nature* has a Law of Nature to govern it, which obliges everyone: And Reason, which is that Law, teaches all Mankind, who will but consult it, that being all equal and independent, no one ought to harm another in his Life, Health, Liberty, or Possessions" (§6). If there were no right to punish, Locke insists, the Law of Nature would be "in vain" (§7). Punishment is, in this sense, a part of the law and the essence of political power.[17] This natural right to punish, derived from the existence of natural law, is held in common by all persons in the State of Nature to "preserve the innocent and restrain offenders" (§7), yet it is also explicitly a limited right. Locke writes,

> In the State of Nature, *one Man comes by a Power over another*; but yet no Absolute or Arbitrary Power, to use a Criminal when he has got him in his hands, according to the passionate heats, or boundless extravagancy of his own Will, but only to retribute him, so far as calm reason and conscience dictates, what is proportionate to his Transgression, which is so much as may serve for *Reparation* and *Restraint*. (§8)

This "strong principle of limitation" means that punishment is constrained in reference to the specific transgression of the law in both the terms of retributive justice and utilitarian deterrence theory, limited in effect by its purposes (deterrence, recompense, and incapacitation) and its extent (only so much as to satisfy these purposes).[18] The proportionality requirement seems on its face to be a strong constraint, directly limiting the punitive response even though the criminal has, according to Locke, revealed himself[19] to be so radically dangerous as to be no longer a fully rational human (§8). Locke argues in favor of the death penalty not because of a simple symmetry between the crime and the punishment (akin to the *lex talionis*) but because there is no possibility of recompense for death, and a murderer continues to be dangerous to others (§11).

Immediately after opening the door to the death penalty, Locke restates the proportionality requirement in even stronger terms:

> By the same reason, may a Man in the State of Nature *punish the lesser breaches* of that Law? It will perhaps be demanded, with death? I answer, Each Transgression may be *punished* to that *degree*, and with so much *Severity* as will suffice to make it an ill bargain to the Offender, give him cause to repent, and terrifie others from doing the like. (§12)

This articulation of punishment—proportional, based in natural right, justified by retribution (in the sense of reparation and recompense) and deterrence, and rooted in claims of a natural moral universe in which justice and right exist in full force even prior to the presence of a political order—characterizes both Locke's view and the bulk of commentary about Lockean punishment. If punishment can include the death penalty, it only extends to the most egregious crimes, since Locke goes out of his way (in §12) to insist that punishment must be proportionate to some specific quality about the offender's assessment of the relative gains of crime, his desire to repent, and the fears of others in society.

The rearticulation of a limited right to punish in §12 begins to shift the measure of proportion from transgression to transgressor. What will count as sufficient reparation and restraint for a transgression, given the rephrasing quoted earlier in §12, cannot be determined without reference to what fits a particular transgressor. This determination requires a certain kind of knowledge about the transgressor, a knowledge that will be especially suspect in the absence of a commonwealth and that is grounded only through the attempt to stabilize the unstable right to punish. Jeremy Waldron echoes this reading of the text, noting that the moral calculus of proportionality specifically requires that we attend to "the violator . . . as a focus of concern."[20] Locke's logic of proportion is meant to impose a meaningful constraint on punishment, and this constraint is "founded on the Law of Nature" and therefore knowable through reason.[21]

Within only a few sections of his statement of proportionality, Locke nevertheless insists that it is "Lawful for a Man to *kill a Thief*, who has not in the least hurt him, nor declared any design upon his Life, any farther then by the use of Force, so to get him in his Power, as to take away his Money, or what he pleases from him" (§18). In §19, he affirms this right: "Thus a *Thief*, whom I cannot harm but by appeal to the Law, for having stolen all that I am worth, I may kill, when he sets on me to rob me."[22]

Is theft not a "lesser breach" of the law than murder? Perhaps not, given what Locke says later, in defining one's property to include "life, liberty, and estate," in §87 and §123. Locke's immediate purpose in the text, however, is not to define theft as a general form of crime (he is careful to note in §207 that not all theft by fraud is punishable by death) but rather to mark the "difference between the State of Nature, and the State of War" (§19).[23] Theft and its proportional punishment both define the boundary between these states and underscore the necessity of leaving the State of Nature. Locke places punishment squarely within a constellation of conceptions and practices that necessarily complicate a straightforward understanding of proportionality: war and slavery.

An aggressive word or action begins the State of War as a state of enmity and destruction (§16), because, Locke famously insists, "he who would get me into his Power without my consent, would use me as he pleased . . . and destroy me too when he had a fancy to it: for no body can desire to have me in his Absolute Power, unless it be to compel me by force to that which is against the Right of my Freedom, i.e. make me a Slave" (§17). The only imaginable purpose for placing another person under one's power is to revoke entirely the subject's freedom. Any transgression of this magnitude is also presumed to be an attempt to take away the freedom of everyone else as well (as stated earlier in §11). If the fundamental Law of Nature includes a right to self-preservation, then "the safety of the Innocent is to be preferred," meaning that "one may destroy a Man who makes War upon him, or has discovered an Enmity to his being, for the same Reason, that he may kill a Wolf or a Lyon" (§16).

The thief, by placing me under his power, opens the door to the possibility of ultimate destruction. Locke writes, "I have no reason to suppose that he, who would take away my Liberty, would not when he had me in his Power, take away every thing else" (§18). To be held under force, even for the purpose of robbery, is to be vulnerable to more than just losing one's "Horse or Coat" (§19). When the thief sets on me, he puts the entire Law into question by his use of force to put me into his power. This opens the possibility that not just my estate but also my entire property, my life and my liberty, are no longer protected by the law. The only rational response to the unjust use of force is to respond with equal force or else risk giving up my life.

The paradigmatic thief throughout the *Second Treatise* is the highway-man. In addition to the reference to one's "Horse or Coat" in §19, Locke refers in §182 to the "Thief that sets on me in the Highway," and again in §207, while likening tyranny to theft, he refers to "A Man with a Sword in his Hand [who] demands my Purse in the High-way." The image would have easily invoked the popular and well-known conception of the highway bandit, the exemplary seventeenth-century "outlaw" who preys on victims where there is, as Locke puts it, "no common Superior on Earth to appeal to for relief" (§19).[24]

Further, the figure of the highwayman reminds the reader that the essential aspect of the crime is the use of force, which can occur inside a duly constituted commonwealth as well as outside it. That is, the figure underscores how a State of War can emerge both within the State of Nature and within civil society, because the use of force without appeal to a common judge distinguishes war from peace. The moment of the robbery is one in which "the Law, which was made for my Preservation, where it cannot interpose to secure my Life from present force, which if lost, is capable of no reparation, permits me my own Defence, and the Right of War, a liberty to kill the aggressor, because the aggressor allows not the time to appeal to our common Judge, nor the decision of the Law" (§19). The thief's use of force has closed off the possibility of an appeal to a judge or the law, closing off any possible remedy in the case and making clear that war (and all its corresponding rights) is deployed during that moment and within that space.

Locke makes this point explicit throughout the text (most strongly in §§19 and 207), insisting that it is force without right that triggers a State of War between persons. A thief who does not use force (but instead steals through fraud or deception) is not to be punished with death. The reason, Locke writes, "is plain; because the one using *force*, which threatned my Life, I could not have *time to appeal* to the Law to secure it: And when it was gone, 'twas too late to appeal. . . . But in the other case, my Life not being in danger, I may have the *benefit of appealing* to the Law" (§207). That is, what the thief/highwayman conveys is an *immediate* moment of force, demanding action. When I am caught in the moment of uncertainty over the thief's intentions, I am necessarily caught outside the aid of the law. Even a duly constituted civil society is interrupted by the outbreak of a relation of war between the thief and his victim.[25]

The right to kill a forceful thief, thus, is not simply a right to self-defense but is also the execution of the Law of Nature: a proportional punishment, grounded in natural right and justified by the use of force where there is no right. Because Locke provides no conceptual distinction between crime and war in these early chapters, the response to theft is still rightly called punishment and the constraint of proportionality continues to apply, although without any moderating effect. Even when Locke does eventually introduce a distinction between crime and war in Chapter 16, his account of just and unjust conquest relies on the continued figuration of the State of War and the rights of the aggrieved as instances of crimes of robbery, burglary, or theft.[26]

The heart of the problem is temporal: during the crime, the thief has yet to become only a thief. A threat made against me during a highway robbery extends the aggression beyond my estate to include my liberty and, potentially, my life. If I am unable to flee for fear of further violence, to refuse to hand over my coat and horse is to risk death. The thief is in this moment indistinguishable from the murderer. Were he not indistinguishable in this way, he would be unable to bring me under his power and successfully take away my property. The temporal problem of the robbery shows how simple crime and open war overlap, giving me the justified right to respond in kind, striking down the aggressor. The aggressor only becomes a "thief" in retrospect, when it turns out that his design was not my death but merely the appropriation of my horse and coat.

So long as the State of War persists (i.e., during the crime), proportionality continues to exist formally but fails to impose effective limits. The question is to determine when the crime ends and the proportional response becomes something other than death. It is not that proportionality is required in one state and not in another but rather that the practical meaning of proportionality is different in these two states. In the condition of civil society (i.e., where there exists a "Common Superior on Earth"), we can expect a proportional punishment less than death: "When the actual force is over, the State of War ceases between those that are in Society, and are equally on both sides Subjected to the fair determination of the Law; because then there lies open the remedy of appeal for the past injury, and to prevent future harm" (§20). When the thief escapes with my property, and I am under civil society, the moment of actual force has ended, and the thief has finally turned out to be just a thief and not a murderer.

In the State of Nature, however, where there continues to be no possibility of appeal, where there are no "positive laws," the State of War "once begun, continues, with a right to the innocent Party, to destroy the other whenever he can, until the aggressor offers Peace" (§20). The State of War, triggered by a crime and continued in the punishment, does not come to an end even after the thief has fled. Even though the thief has turned out "only" to be a thief, the relation of force between him and his victim has not ceased. The only way to end this State of War, since there is no appeal to a common judge, is for the aggrieved either to accept an offer of peace or to punish the thief, that is, with death.

The problem, however, is that neither way of ending the State of War is feasible in the State of Nature. The thief, once tracked down and caught, faces a choice between compliance and resistance, but both options are futile. If the thief complies by offering peace, makes amends, and tries to bring a close to the State of War in hopes that he can accept punishment and potentially be restored to the realm of rational humanity, at least two problems emerge. First, it is unclear what an acceptable punishment would be. Because the State of War continues, the Law of Nature means that death is still an acceptable response. But something surely has changed from the moment of the crime itself: the thief has (at least in some common sense) turned out to be less than a murderer, especially since he is, in this case, offering to make amends. Something less than the justified proportional response of death seems called for, since the crime seems to have turned out to be of a different character, and what would be necessary for reparation and restraint is also likely to be lower. Even while being fully aware that the natural law requires proportional punishment, determining what would actually be proportional is a separate question. Locke seems to realize that there are easily multiple measures of proportion and no naturally given way to fix on the correct measure. He goes out of his way to avoid articulating what proportionality would require in the State of Nature: "Every Offence that can be committed in the State of Nature, may, in the State of Nature be also punished, equally, and as far forth as it may, in a Common-wealth; for though it would be besides my present purpose, to enter here into the particulars of the Law of Nature, or its measures of punishment; yet, it is certain there is such a Law" (§12).

Second, even if a precise measure could be established, there is no reasonable expectation that it would work. If death is the correct measure, then how could we expect the thief to concede? But even if the proportional punishment is less than death, Locke has already conceded that we cannot expect the aggrieved to execute the Law of Nature correctly, as "Ill Nature, Passion and Revenge" will surely "carry [him] too far in punishing others"

(§13). Such personal bias is not the sole reason why natural punishment might produce disproportionate responses, since even proportionate punishment is unlikely to bring the State of War to a close. For either reason, the State of War is expected to continue indefinitely, and the boundary between aggrieved and aggressor becomes increasingly indistinct. The thief is thus probably wise not to relent at all but openly to resist punishment.

What happens when we fail to punish because the aggressor refuses to make amends? In this case, the outcome turns on who is stronger. If the thief is able to overpower me, then it becomes likely that before I have a chance to punish, the State of War will end in death, and the thief will become a murderer, free to be killed by anybody else, beginning the punishment cycle again. If I am stronger and am able to prevail, the situation becomes even more complicated with the possibility that death and disorder might give way to a perpetual continuance of the State of War through institutionalized slavery. If I am justified in killing a person and demonstrate my ability to do so by bringing that person to the point of death, I am at liberty, Locke tells us, to delay the actual execution of sentence and leave the transgressor under my absolute power (§23). In this way, the State of War continues indefinitely. While spared a physical death (for at least the time being), such a slave is rendered radically unfree and completely subject to his conqueror under despotical power (§§23–24).

As explained by James Farr, Locke's commitment to equality is visible in this account of slavery and, as such, strongly departs from naturalistic accounts of slavery.[27] Locke's "just-war" theory of slavery, by having an "emphasis on unjust action," is consistent with his account of natural rights because a justly enslaved aggressor has violated the Law of Nature in a way that deserves death.[28] Slavery is Locke's other "strange doctrine" (§180) and is directly linked—structurally, rhetorically, and logically—to the natural right to punish. The difficulties in executing this right in the State of Nature lead persons not only to the threshold of death but into a living death subject to absolute and arbitrary power.

Because "life is essentially freedom," Andrew Norris notes, slavery is a form of living death, without the "rights and powers of the living."[29] Norris is careful to note that the slave is in fact "biologically alive" but by Locke's account is no longer characterized by the essential rights and powers of humanity established in the opening pages of the *Second Treatise*: equality and freedom. This description echoes Rousseau's gloss on slavery: "In taking an equivalent of his life, the victor did not spare it: instead of killing him unprofitably, he killed him usefully."[30] While Norris's account relies heavily on Agamben's distinction between bare life and human life,[31] the figuration of the slave as "living dead" can also be read through Orlando Patterson's language of slavery as a form of "social death."[32] The living death of slavery can be the direct product of the execution of the right of punishment.[33] Because the use of force against one's freedom can justify the death penalty as well as slavery, slavery is rightly figured as a kind of death itself, serving as fundamental antithesis of freedom.

To have even justified slavery is nevertheless destabilizing in the State of Nature. First, slaves are the only persons to posses a right to commit suicide by "resisting the Will of his Master" and "draw[ing] on himself the Death he desires" (§23). This paradoxical right of resistance is permitted to no other persons, and it is a right that ensures that the condition of slavery (as a continuation of the State of War) is anything but a stalemate or stable condition but is rather a continuing conflict. In a now-justified right of "resistance," though, an original aggressor gains the right to fight back. Second, justified slavery, as an extension of the right to punish, is likewise subject to a series of limitations outlined in Chapter 16 on conquest. But the specific danger Locke highlights in these passages (especially in §182) is the ease with which a lawful conqueror becomes an unlawful one, when a punishment would "be Robbery on my side" (§182). As David Bates puts it artfully, glossing on the instability of the categories of criminal and victim, "Real human bodies shift in position to their relationship with rationality."[34]

Once we grasp this connection between punishment and the perpetual continuation of the State of War in slavery, it should be no wonder how the State of Nature spirals into "Confusion and Disorder." The relationship between the guilty and the innocent is easily reversed or at least increasingly hard to distinguish because of human passions, the nearly unlimited scope of proportionality, or the perpetual State of War in slavery. In any case, what is crucial to note is that failure to end the State of War in this case is not solely or primarily based in the original crime itself but in its punishment. The problem, in the State of Nature at least, is less an existential fear of crime than a fear that punishment, even rightly carried out, is nothing more than the continuation of the State of War, where the crime persists, where proportionality is at best unclear and at worst potentially infinite, and where the only certain outcomes are death itself or the living death of slavery.

The key failure is that at the single moment when it would be possible to end the State of War peacefully, the natural law's requirement of proportionality does not actually limit punishment. Killing the highwayman, something that seems like an excessive punishment for robbery, is entirely consistent with Locke's binding requirement that punishment be constrained in proportion to the severity of the crime. In a sense, it allows the excessive to also be the proportional.[35] In the State of Nature, acts of theft and attempts at murder are indistinguishable, making the proper proportional response to any crime of force an unlimited one. The distinction, if one can be made at all, turns only on a nascent distinction between innocent and guilty, itself a distinction fraught by the difficulty in judging our own cases. A logic of justice focused on the transgressor rather than the transgression typically emerges and produces a violent and seemingly illiberal response that is at least legally permissible, if not guaranteed. Proportional punishment, on these terms, has no boundaries and generates the disorder and chaos that characterizes the State of Nature. While the possibility of crime might make the State of Nature unstable and dangerous, the practice of punishment makes it unacceptable.

PUNISHING, FOUNDING, AND REBELLING IN THE LIBERAL STATE

If we read Locke from this perspective that attends to the role that punishment plays in the *Second Treatise* and his larger political thought, we can reorient ourselves to the role that punishment plays more generally in producing, founding, and giving meaning to the terms of liberalism, our own political order, and ourselves as political subjects. That is to say, reading political theory and our own practices from the perspective of punishment works as a powerful lens for understanding how it is built into the structures that it relies on for its just and fair execution. Narrowly, the utility of reading the *Second Treatise* in this way, prioritizing Locke's account of punishment and the case of the thief, is in understanding the necessity of two of Locke's most important normative claims: the need to leave the State of Nature and enter into a civil society and the right to rebellion, which continues to be held by members of civil society after founding that society.

The instability of punishment in the State of Nature is neither an accident nor a slip in Locke's argument but rather helps reframe the usual question about punishment that we ask of Locke. Rather than ask how to make punishment just or possible, the question is more narrowly how to make the proportionality required by the Law of Nature an effective limit and what work punishment does for a political body.[36] Specifically, proportionality must be given a content that allows it to avoid the "Confusion and Disorder" that it caused in the State of Nature. That we can and must kill the thief is proportional in the State of Nature because the necessary set of conditions that make proportionality an effective limit have not yet been achieved.[37]

Locke is explicit that the difficulty of punishing according to the Law of Nature drives humans toward civil government. The "Confusion and Disorder" following excessive punishment and the spiral into permanent war, death, and slavery is the primary reason humans accept the social contract and is the chief reason "God hath certainly appointed Government to restrain the partiality and violence of Men" (§13). Locke twice refers to his doctrine of punishment as "strange" (§§9, 13); Wolfgang Von Leyden explains that what is truly "strange" about his doctrine is that such a doctrine seems foolish.[38] Pointing directly to §13, Von Leyden writes that this natural law theory of punishment "is strange in that the policy of putting the execution of the Law of Nature into everybody's hands (as though this were what the supposed equality of all men demanded) is unreasonable, wrong, and unsafe. Locke therefore 'easily' grants that the 'God appointed' alternative is life in political society and under civil government."[39] While the chief reason for the "inconveniences" of nature can be characterized by the lack of a neutral arbiter in cases of dispute, the driving force for government is to restrain the "partiality and violence" of *punishing* in those cases.

War and slavery emerge in the State of Nature not just easily but frequently if the cause stems not only from another person (i.e., the thief) but also from within (i.e., our own right to punish). This makes the demand to flee from the State of Nature in favor of civil government even stronger. Locke writes decisively that "to avoid this State of War (wherein there is no appeal but to Heaven, and wherein every the least difference is apt to end, where there is no Authority to decide between the Contenders) is one great reason of *Mens putting themselves into Society*, and quitting the State of Nature" (§21). Understanding slavery as "*the State of War continued*" underscores the imperative for founding civil government (§24). To return to Von Leyden: "One could say that the necessity of men's uniting into commonwealths is proportionate to the unacceptability of the doctrine that each man has by nature the power of punishing the transgressions of others."[40] It is not simply that the state is a preferable alternative to the difficulty in executing the law of justice. Rather, recognizing the near certainty that any crime will be met with extreme (but justified) violence and that the only likely resolution is death or slavery lets us see more clearly that civil government is necessary. That is, the "inconveniences" of nature are far more traumatic than is often understood.[41]

It is no wonder, then, that for Locke the natural right to punish is the basis of political power. The chief characteristic of a commonwealth is that it "comes by a power to set down, what punishment shall belong to the several transgressions which they think worthy of it, committed amongst the Members of that Society" (§88). More important, however, it is the transfer of executive power from the "members" to the government that is the only source of power held by the state. An individual "who has enter'd into civil Society, and is become a member of any Commonwealth, has thereby quitted his power to punish Offences against the Law of Nature" (§88). He has turned this power over to the government to wield on his behalf, giving "a right to the Commonwealth to imploy his force" (§88). This transfer, Locke declares, is the fundamental source of political power: "Herein we have the original of the *Legislative and Executive Power* of Civil Society, which is to judge by standing Laws how far Offences are to be punished . . . and . . . imploy all the force of all the Members when there shall be need" (§88). The people become a public, individuals become members, and the commonwealth comes into existence when the individual right to judge and execute the law is invested in the government. The ongoing relationship between the people and the government is entirely based on the transfer of the right to punish, and that this transfer becomes necessary or beneficial is because punishment needs to be bounded through the creation of a political order.

Once civil society is established, the rhetorical work of the thief is, however, not yet finished for Locke. The thief returns to show how the right to punish is not permanently alienated from members but can be reasserted after the foundation of a commonwealth and the establishment of a government. Joining together into a political society requires individuals to agree to transfer their right to punish in exchange for a government that can and will protect one's life, liberty, and property. The power given to that government "can never be suppos'd to extend farther than the common good; but is obliged to secure every ones Property by providing against those . . . defects . . . that made the State of Nature so unsafe and uneasie" (§131). If the government violates this condition, it puts itself into a State of War with its subjects both in the immediate moment and beyond that moment because it has ceased to function as a judge on the earth. The government thus becomes an aggressor itself and is liable to be punished according to the natural right possessed by the public. What characterizes a robbery in the State of Nature is that (1) I cannot know the ultimate intent of persons who place me under their power and (2) I have nowhere to appeal except to heaven. These are the same conditions that Locke identifies as the characteristics of despotic or tyrannical power.

As both Richard Ashcraft and John Dunn explain in their readings of the *Second Treatise*, the right to rebellion is grounded by the natural right to execute the Law of Nature and by the figuration of tyranny as the exercise of force without right, as a form of criminal action.[42] For Ashcraft in particular, Locke's revolutionary politics are connected to developing a "language" figuring kings as criminals and therefore subject to punishment for their crimes. Locke's "phraseology . . . links the concept of tyranny with Locke's definition of a state of war," which in turn allows him to "show under what circumstances a prince becomes a tyrant in order to justify resistance to the latter as an act of self-defense."[43] Self-defense is grounded on the right to use force as an execution of the Law of Nature, that is, of the right to punish forceful thieves for their unjust use of force. Ashcraft makes this link explicit, noting that "Locke specifically lumps together the actions of a thief, a pirate, a conqueror, a usurper, a tyrant and so forth, none of whom can be counted as members of political society, even if, like the thief or usurper, they began as members of that society and may still, empirically speaking, exist within its territorial boundaries."[44]

Being able to clearly substitute a king for a criminal is at the heart of Locke's justification for the prosecution and execution of actual English monarchs. Ashcraft plays out this linguistic substitution in Locke's implied case against Charles II:

> The "injury" and the "crime" committed by an "aggressor" or one who exercises "despotical power" is a crime chargeable to Charles II in his "illegal" use of power against the people. . . . The "injury" is . . . the loss of the people's "legislative power," a loss that automatically dissolves the government. This loss can only be "recovered" when the legislature has been "reinstated" and the aggressor "punished."[45]

This substitution relies on the equivalence established in the final four chapters of the *Second Treatise*, between unjust conquest, usurpation, and tyranny. "The Injury [of unlawful Force] and the Crime is equal," Locke insists, "whether committed by the wearer of a Crown, or some petty Villain. The Title of the Offender, and the Number of his Followers make no difference in the Offense" (§176). Such conquerors are figured in sections 181 and 182 as "beasts" and "thieves." The right to oppose a tyrant who lives outside the law is the same as that which opposes "a Thief and a Robber" (§202). And finally, the people are justified in rebelling against a tyrannical government because, as when being robbed in the street, they cannot know what the tyrant has in mind for them, nor do they have anywhere to appeal except heaven (§§228, 235, 243). The original political power that "reverts to the Society" (§243) is the same unstable (and productive) right to execute the Law of Nature, to punish those who use force where there is no right, and to resist despotical power. Even slaves are able to justly resist their masters, after all. In the moment of rebellion, it is from the basis of our foundational right to exercise the Law of Nature, including its otherwise disproportionate effects, that we can justify not only a new legislative or executive power but, if necessary, the killing of the king as a thief. In this moment, the people do nothing more than exercise a natural right to punish a criminal.

MEMBERSHIP AND REASON

Punishment is thus unstable not simply because it produces bad outcomes but because it is intimately tied up with the production of the civil commonwealth as well as the boundaries of political membership in the commonwealth. It stabilizes through its seeming instability, and as such, there is a persistent displacement of stability from one domain to the other. Ashcraft's otherwise illuminating reading assumes that one is a thief, a robber, or even a tyrant merely through one's own actions. Such a notion generally coheres with our own understandings of what makes a criminal a criminal: the authorship of a bad action that is necessarily and causally tied to an individual. Moreover, that authorship is presumed to be at least somewhat *intentional* rather than random, echoing a theory of criminality that assumes agency as a necessary grounds for responsibility, barring important exceptions for cases of strict liability. That is, thieves, by such an account, have *chosen* to place themselves outside society.[46] This wrongly assumes, however, that the boundaries of society are fixed prior to punishment and that the attribution of thief (or tyrant, pirate, robber, or member) is fixed entirely by one's own actions. Yet because proportional punishment is *also a temporal problem*, the case is necessarily more complicated.

Locke's political order comes into being in part to give proportionality acceptable limits and to find a way to deflect the temporal problem of knowing who is actually an aggressor and who is not. The necessary counterpart in all this is a conception of the criminal as distinctively and identifiably other. In Locke, this is accomplished through the production of the criminal (emblematically the thief) as necessarily beyond reason, as animalistic and dangerous, and constitutively defining the obedient subject as rational, innocent, and above all, free. The founding of the Lockean contract, therefore, *is also already about the production of subjects.* It is necessary, on Locke's own terms, to discern a way of knowing who is and who is not a rational agent, to distinguish between subjects capable of entering into a social compact and those who remain outside its reach. This question of judgment is only possible, however, through the performance of the practice that depends on this distinction or through punishment itself. That it to say, it is through both the injunction to punish and the practice of punishing that the categories of knowledge and responsibility on which that injunction and that practice relies come into being.

This is to say that the powerfully motivating force to form and join civil society is based not simply on an anxiety about punishment's instability but also on an anxiety about transgressors and punishers. Proportionality finally succeeds in becoming a constraining force through the formation of the twin figures of "thief" and "member."[47] The thief becomes the symbol of irrationality and unpredictability, importantly distinct from all those who lack reason by virtue of Nature (a partial list appears in §60, including "Lunaticks and Ideots," children, "Innocents," and "Madmen"). Locke tells us that punishment (especially in its most unlimited moments) is a response to the criminal as a human kind rather than the crime as an event. The criminal is one who "declares himself to live by another Rule, than that of Reason and common Equity, which is that measure God has set to the actions of Men, for their mutual security: and so he becomes dangerous to Mankind, the tye which is to secure them from injury and violence, being slighted and broken by him" (§8). The transgression is a rejection of God's gift of rational thought as well as a rejection of the Law of Nature's binding quality, leaving these men dangerous to all of humanity, not just the person whom they have harmed.[48] This character is so deviant that the transgressor "becomes degenerate, and declares himself to quit the Principles of Human Nature, and to be a noxious Creature" (§10). A "noxious creature" is dangerous by nature, predestined to attack us, and expecting it to be tame would be to expect it to be something other than it is. This is most clear in Locke's forceful statement on the matter:

A Criminal, who having renounced Reason, the common Rule and Measure, God hath given to Mankind, hath by the unjust Violence and Slaughter he hath committed upon one, declared War against all Mankind, and therefore may be destroyed as a Lyon or a Tyger, one of those wild Savage Beasts, with whom Men can have no Society nor Security. (§11)

The dual effect of the criminal's animal-like nature is captured perfectly in the last part of this passage. There is no possibility of building a social contract with such animals, nor is there any way to handle them other than to destroy them.

The other side of this description, of course, is to reinscribe the qualities that mark the executor of the Law of Nature, the individuals who ultimately join together for safety and security and appoint a civil government. These individuals are defined through their adherence to rationality, their lack of inherent dangerousness, and their demonstrated humanity. Nowhere are these qualities better demonstrated than by the fact that such individuals possess a natural right to execute the Law of Nature independent of the state. Surely, those who punish must be definitively innocent of crime, secure in their humanity, and right in their cause. Locke knows that punishment is foundational to the meaningful existence of natural law, but he also knows even rational humans run the nearly certain risk of going too far and becoming criminal aggressors themselves. The stability between member and criminal is upset (and thus the source of particular anxiety) because the line between them is so indistinct in the State of Nature. Kirstie McClure writes,

It [the right to punish] is a morally precarious power, for its distinctive means, the use of force, must conform to the rule of virtue to sustain the ordained separation between properly human agents and beasts of prey. To exceed this boundary, to punish wrongly or in excess, is itself an injury that renders its perpetrator beastlike and subject to punishment in turn. But to recognize this requirement is only to acknowledge that in Locke's view the exercise of this right, like all other forms of properly human liberty in the architecture of order, must conform to the imperatives of law and virtue.[49]

Such instability makes the motivation for quitting the State of Nature all the stronger and more pressing: it is not only the physical security of nature that is in question but also the security of the subject's identity as rational and fully human, eligible for full membership in civil society. It is through the formation and maintenance of the state—as the political invention that will manage punishment's potentially unlimited character—that the innocent can remain so. The foundation of the commonwealth and the possibility of being a rational individual (one with whom there can be "Security and Society") both rest on determining who is rightly punished and who is right to execute that punishment.

The act of punishing negotiates the boundary between the member and the criminal by fixing the criminal as a distinct kind of dangerous thing. It is the act by which the question of who is inside and who is outside is answered. Attention to how the thief is treated during the moment of the crime lets us see that the categories of "the guilty" and "the innocent" come into existence during the moment of punishment as much as (if not more than) in the act of crime itself. This continues to be the case in the period after the founding of the state, in that it provides for the dual justifications Locke offers for punishing. Recall that he establishes that the only purposes that can justify punishment are retributive notions of "reparation and restraint," bringing forward- and backward-looking perspectives together. Locke can hold these two positions simultaneously because he understands that while the criminal is certainly a radical other, this identity is in flux during this key moment.

Locke is particularly attuned to the way in which crime and punishment are caught between temporal perspectives. In the moment of the robbery, being able to call the transgressor a "thief" serves a dual function. The attribution of "thief" captures the backward-looking element in that a thief has committed a crime against one's property and therefore deserves punishment for that crime. But in the same moment, the identity of "thief" points forward, resolving some part of the future's uncertainty. We know in this moment that this person—the thief—is a character who will rob us in the future (or, during the moment of the crime, do anything to us while he has us in his power) and must be restrained. The use of a single name (thief) solves two distinct temporal problems, calling for separate reactions (or in the language of contemporary liberal theory, reflects different and possibly incompatible justifications for punishment). The backward-looking function concerns itself with retributive punishment, while the forward-looking function opens the grounds for the continued handling of thieves as types of individuals who, like animals, are known to us as kinds of people who will rob from us, who will kill us if they have to, and most importantly, who are by definition threats to our life, liberty, and estate and thus must be excluded, enslaved, or destroyed entirely.

Getting punishment "right" through the establishment of civil government is imperative for determining what it means to be rational, to be a true member of civil society. The foundation of the state and two key categories of subjectivity (criminal and member) are what make proportional punishment (as we would know it) possible. The inability to punish properly is, on these terms, a productive failure. Killing the thief, the highwayman, and even the king/tyrant become founding (and possibly refounding) moments of sovereignty that secure the identities of those who punish—politically, epistemologically, and ontologically—as full members, innocent subjects, and truly rational humans. Punishment is, as McBride puts it succinctly, "the midwife in the birth of the social contract."[50] It is the midwife of contracting subjects as well.[51]

RETHINKING THE CONTRACT

On this reading of Locke, through the figure of the thief and the punishment proportional to him, we can see how the foundational moment of the social contract is driven by the "inconveniences" of punishment. While a more typical reading of Locke sees the motivation as located in the already known figure of the irrational thief, it should now be clear that this knowledge is produced by the *punishment* of a crime, rather than by the crime itself. We tend to conflate a temporal order (crime, then punishment) with a logical priority between the two. As such, we misunderstand the source of meaning for the terms presumed to organize our political world. Thus, we also misunderstand the "solution" that Locke provides as well. We typically think that the problem of punishment is that we will do it badly and, thus, that civil society protects us against this mistake by establishing a third party to take on the burden of judgment. This keeps us from getting carried away, from punishing too far or too much. But this is simply not the central problem of the State of Nature: getting carried away and going too far makes sense under the conditions of the State of Nature as Locke has laid them out, because punishment is always already excessive when it is unclear (or unknowable) who is the aggressor and who is the aggrieved.

The first moment of genius in Locke's contract is not that a third party judge is appointed but rather that a distinction is created between insiders and outsiders, between those who are part of the contract (and therefore understood as reasonable) and those who remain outside it (who are irrational and who can justly be treated with what would otherwise be excessive punishment). It is this boundary of political membership that does the work, revealing the deep connection between what otherwise could be distinct discourses. The second moment of genius in Locke's account is that he does not make the mistake of thinking that this distinction solves the problem: the possibility of an otherwise rational member becoming a criminal (either of the petty sort or the grandest tyrant) remains. The State of War persists as a possibility even after the foundation of civil society and the appointment of a government. Locke makes use of persistent instability to ground the right to rebellion.

Not surprisingly, this Lockean account of punishment is by no means a complete theory of punishment, an explanation for how and why we punish the way we do; nor is it satisfying on normative grounds. It is possible to understand punishment as a phenomenon that cannot be perfected, but that remains immensely useful for understanding the social order under which we live. The Lockean account as an analysis of punishment lets us see how both the state and its subjects (the guilty and the innocent) come into existence simultaneously through the management of an excessiveness that must be disavowed as such. Taking seriously the fact that punishment always carries with it the possibility of being unconstrained and unstable and understanding what this instability produces gives us a different picture of the liberal order and may call that order into question. We should understand punishment not as practice with a measure or given proportionality dictated by the natural law but as practice that, in its continual failure to miss the mark, in its constant ability to renegotiate its limits, in its possibility of being infinitely proportional, produces the social order under which we live and is the basis of sovereign power that we often claim for ourselves.

This forces us to rethink both Locke's abstractions and those with which we organize, analyze, and understand our own political lives. For instance, while "war" and "slavery" are often thought to mark the boundaries of civil society, Locke reminds us of their longstanding persistence within civil society. Locke blurs conceptual distinctions between crimes and acts of war, both subsumed under the idea of force without right, and makes it clear in Chapter 16 ("Of Conquest") that they differ only in terms of degree.[52] While the language of warfare is routinely employed in the present day within a criminal justice context (and likewise, the language of justice and law is readily employed in the discourse about war), it is seldom the case that policymakers or political theorists allow crime and war to occupy such a close proximity without a great deal of discomfort.[53] Recent political and legal debates in the United States over prosecuting "enemy combatants" in criminal courts reflect an insistence that the two spheres are meaningfully separate and call for different procedures and standards of judgment, even as there remains great disagreement over who is rightfully a "criminal" and who is a "terrorist."

Moreover, slavery and the slavelike conditions of despotic rule exist not only in the memories of liberal states but continue in practice and in law. The theoretical, historical, and empirical connections between punitive systems and slave systems, especially in the United States, are perhaps more understandable if we read chattel slavery in relationship to practices of punishment. Slavery and involuntary servitude were not, strictly speaking, abolished by the Thirteenth Amendment to the U.S. Constitution but are preserved as punishment for crimes. We should hardly be surprised to find contemporary criminal justice theory at a loss in understanding the persistence of illiberal punitive practices. This might be because we have jettisoned some of the key terms required by the debate while they have nevertheless persisted in altered but no less meaningful forms.[54]

Political foundings and the maintenance of political bodies are not simply questions of contracts and institutional arrangements but assertions of subjectivity through acts of internal exclusion that are anything but final or definitive.[55] This is not to justify such violence but rather to question the limits of the conceptual distinctions that emerge in this moment. While there is an important distinction within Locke between the limited, proportional ideal of punishment (a system that restores balance on consequentialist grounds) and the possibility of a state of affairs that institutionalizes the imbalance caused by criminal transgression, he refuses to naively separate these two projects. This connection is the motivating factor for the erection of the commonwealth, foreclosing the possibility of war and slavery, solidifying punishment as the only legitimate response to transgression of right. At the very least, the commonwealth will limit such states of warfare and slavery to the margins of a society. Seemingly secure distinctions between war and crime, slavery and punishment, might be far less secure than we might like to think, and Locke is a paradigmatic thinker of the thresholds between these states.

It is noteworthy that the illustrative example Locke returns to repeatedly throughout the *Second Treatise* is neither the bloodthirsty murderer nor the conquering warlord but the thief. Locke recognizes that simple criminal actions are an exemplary form of war and, reciprocally, that all warfare is the outgrowth of the violation of law, that is, crime. As such, the forms of response and the methods by which individuals and societies respond to such transgressions are likewise understood as fundamentally similar. We are able to slide easily from punishment to death to slavery on his terms, recognizing that it is the existence of the state, and only the state, that allows for a limited proportional response of punishment to be realized. The failure to punish justly, which results in continuing the states of war through institutional forms of slavery, is an important motivating factor in the generation of the commonwealth.

Put differently, Locke's thief makes the multiple functions of punishment more visible. In the moment of identification as a criminal, an individual simultaneously becomes responsible for a specific transgression and becomes a kind of person who embodies transgression itself. We discover that the thief comes to be marked as such because he is responsible for a particular act and is therefore eligible for retributive punishment for that specific action. But he is also marked as the bad actor who must be handled and managed, not simply for criminal actions but for a way of being. This subjectivization serves as a basis for the conception of constraining proportionality under civil society and continues to exist as a process long after the foundation of the commonwealth, within the walls of the city that this process helped to build.

As a purely justificatory analysis, punishment theory presumes a straightforward relationship between the identity of the criminal and the punishment that is applied. The "problem" of punishment in this case is to determine, on one level, if punishment can be justified as an institutional response to criminals and, on another level, if an individual punishment can be justified in a particular case. But if we pay attention to the work that punishment does in the generation, fabrication, or production of the "criminal" or "felon" as an order of knowledge concerning criminal actions and identities, if we realize that the foundational "problem" of punishment is determining what work punishment does in the formation of a political order, we will necessarily see the justificatory question in a new light. Such a shift in focus lets us see that the identification process at work might include techniques of discipline and exclusion that we would not normally consider to be part of punishment yet that are inherent parts of identifying the criminal subject.

Locke's political thought does not settle the case, but it should disrupt any notion that questions of punishment and membership are distinct in what has become the dominant liberal tradition in the United States. One's "criminality" is always already a question of political membership, even in Locke, a thinker not typically read as interested in the problems of discursive subject formation. As such, we should now be able to see more clearly what disenfranchisement does for us: it maintains the *terms* of social contractarian liberalism. This, perhaps, explains the difficulty in successfully marshaling liberal normative theory against disenfranchisement. It is true that, as a nation, the United States fails to be properly liberal, but more deeply there is something possibly illiberal about liberalism's foundation and maintenance.

But questions nevertheless remain: To what degree has this complexity carried itself into contemporary liberal theory? To what degree do accounts of political membership still rely on the subject-formation work performed by prevailing discourses of criminality? Moreover, why is it so difficult to see the productive instability of punishment and the status of political subjects as members? If punishment and membership have been tied together so deeply in the terms by which they operate, and the terms we have inherited from figures such as Locke are so deeply implicated in this messiness, then why is it so hard to see these connections, specifically within the liberal tradition of the United States? I turn to these questions of our "blind spots" in the next chapter and argue that our lack of attention to the dual work of punishment and membership runs deep and is intimately connected with the political system of white supremacy and racial domination in the United States.

5

Innocent Citizens, Guilty Subjects

If any slave, in the darkness of midnight, looks down upon himself, feeling his limbs and thinking himself a man, and entitled to the rights of a man, shall steal away from his hovel or quarter, snap the chain that bound his leg, break the fetter that linked him to slavery, and seek refuge from the free institutions of a democracy, within the boundary of a monarchy, that that slave, in all his windings by night and by day, in his way from the land of slavery to the abode of freedom, shall be liable to be hunted down like a felon, and dragged back to the hopeless bondage from which he was endeavouring to escape.

—FREDRICK DOUGLASS, "Farewell Speech to the British People," March 30, 1847[1]

As Angela Davis put it during an interview with the philosopher Eduardo Mendieta in *Abolition Democracy*,

> Why has the disenfranchisement of people convicted of felonies become so much a part of the common sense thought structures of people in this country? I believe that this also has its roots in slavery. A white contemporary of slavery might have remarked: "Of course slaves weren't supposed to vote. They weren't full citizens." In the same way people think today, "Of course prisoners aren't supposed to vote. They aren't really citizens any more. They are in prison."[2]

The analogy Davis draws works so well because the notions of punishment and citizenship in the United States are deeply connected and cannot be explained without reference to the pernicious history and continued presence of white supremacy as a political and social system. Yet understanding criminal disenfranchisement as a practice that exposes this connection between who makes up the *demos* and who (and how) it *punishes* requires a broader analysis of "American" discourses of citizenship. The reading of Locke given in the previous chapter points our attention to the deep theoretical interconnection between the founding of political societies and their attempts to make punishment an acceptable expression of natural right, to the specific discourses that matter for liberal theory.

Yet it is significant that even someone as important to the "American" founding as Locke does not speak much about voting or even deploy the term "citizen" in the *Second Treatise*. Citizenship, the franchise, and the various systems of electoral representation that drive the central empirical puzzle of this book are not Locke's terms or objects of analysis, and despite the fact that jurists, analysts, and theorists of disenfranchisement have frequently turned to Locke's political lexicon to justify or decry disenfranchisement, it is not obvious that these readings of Locke, my own included, are able to properly speak to our particular situation. Most importantly, the domain of ideal theory (if we can categorize Locke as such) necessarily neglects the contingencies of history that have shaped and formed the discursive terrain on which we find ourselves today. As we have seen, Foucault reminds us to be attentive to the particular material practices and concrete discourses of our space and time in order to understand how those stigmatized and excluded figures are produced by these very practices that appear only to refer to them. For those of us in the contemporary United States, there is perhaps no more important historical legacy that has shaped American institutions of political representation, suffrage, and punishment than the practice of chattel slavery and its aftermaths.

But equally surprising, few scholars, when turning to the "American" experience of these excluded figures, to the history of political founding, or to the canonical expressions of membership in the political sphere of the United States, are attentive to these connections.[3] This would require being attentive to the specific nexus of race, citizenship, labor, and punishment in the United States and in particular how this nexus informs both popular and academic political thought. This chapter explores these concerns through the work of perhaps one of the most important and subtle defenders of contemporary liberalism, the late political theorist Judith Shklar. In particular, I focus my attention on Shklar's understanding of citizenship and her analysis of voting through a close engagement with her text *American Citizenship: The Quest for Inclusion.*[4]

Shklar's historical account of citizenship provides a useful framework for understanding the connection between suffrage and political membership in the United States. It gives us a compelling but ultimately incomplete theory for understanding how disenfranchisement performs the useful work of establishing or confirming political standing. One salient feature of American citizenship drives Shklar's analysis: the primary social significance of citizenship is the conferral of higher public standing on some individuals at the expense of others. In this chapter, I identify and reconstruct three central aspects of her analysis: (1) that citizenship-as-standing is based on the American history of slavery and its connection to suffrage and labor, (2) that public standing is conferred through denial of equal rights, and (3) that the right to vote, rather than voting itself, is where that conferral of status occurs. I argue that her analysis is insightful but does not go far enough, leaving unanswered questions regarding contemporary exclusions. Despite her noteworthy attention to the history of chattel slavery, Shklar does not account for its role in the social construction of race and its historical and functional connections to state punishment and in particular to the political economy of forced labor. Shklar states that there are no longer any remaining barriers for adults to vote in the United States, an omission symptomatic of how liberal theory more generally ignores how citizenship continues to be defined through the discourse of crime and punishment as well as missing the performative nature of voting itself.

To be clear, Shklar's analysis of the vote is useful because it is attentive to the connection between slavery and voting, something far too many theorists of suffrage and citizenship ignore. Yet, in overlooking the connection between slavery (as a system of labor exploitation) and punishment in the American experience (arguably as a labor system itself, especially following the Civil War), her account also misses the importance of continuing criminal exclusions to the franchise. She turns to nineteenth- and twentieth-century analysts of slavery, the franchise, and labor but does not turn to writing by theorists and philosophers who specifically identify the convict-lease system as a reconfiguration of the slave system as an institution of state punishment. This omission is illustrative of the more general trend in liberal theory to rely on essentialist notions of identity, not just of race, gender, or sexuality but also of the even more difficult constructions of good and bad persons, of criminals and innocents.

A perverse outcome of these omissions is that felon disenfranchisement—and the work it does of social and moral differentiation—reinforces a fetishistic attachment to suffrage. Not only does voting become prioritized above other forms of political and civic engagement; it becomes far more useful for the work of moral and political self-differentiation than for self-governance. That is, voting and vote choice are inscribed with antidemocratic force, used as tools for self-expression of superior standing at the same time they are held up as markers of democratic equality.

CITIZENSHIP, THE VOTE, AND PUBLIC STANDING

Shklar argues that American citizenship is characterized by persistent declarations of equality "in the accepted presence of its absolute denial."[5] The meaning of American citizenship is primarily a matter of "social standing," an admittedly "vague" notion that Shklar insists both resonates with the American people and that they also realize is essentially at odds with democratic commitments to equality.[6] Her account rightly drives home the point that the American commitment to citizenship as an expression of equality derives its meaning from the persistent denial of equal standing to large groups of persons. To have standing is to be recognized as having a place within a hierarchical society, and, in the American context, the standing conferred by citizenship is that of equality with those other citizens around you. Unlike social markers such as income, occupation, and education, which can confer numerous levels of hierarchical standing, American citizenship, understood as a form of standing, operates in a binary. Most simply, either one is a citizen or one is not.

"The two great emblems of public standing, the vote and the opportunity to earn," Shklar argues, confer this status.[7] Shklar analyzes the rights to vote and earn because they have defined "what was unique about American citizenship."[8] What distinguishes these two rights as such effective markers of standing is that they are thoroughly steeped in the pernicious history of American slavery. Shklar does not mean to say that voting or earning do not mark other contexts of citizenship (i.e., outside the American experience) but rather that these two practices have historically defined the boundaries of American citizenship as standing through their limited availability to large swaths of the population. Insofar as their exclusive quality has driven the desire for these rights, they reveal the meaning of American citizenship as a marker of public standing. Shklar insists that the "years of denial have left their paradoxical marks upon this constitutional right."[9] Because citizenship is revealed to be about the conferral of social standing, its chief markers are misunderstood if they are not analyzed with attention to *how* they have been used to confer such standing.

Referring to the "four great expansions of suffrage" by colonists, white workingmen, blacks, and women, Shklar writes,

> Only one thing was absolutely clear to everyone who used the word *citizen* in any of these early disputes about the vote: no slave was a citizen. Even before Justice Taney announced that no black person had any rights that white people needed to respect, *black chattel slavery stood at the opposite social pole from full citizenship and so defined it.* The importance of what I call citizenship as standing emerges out of this basic fact of our political history. *The value of citizenship was derived primarily from its denial to slaves, to some white men, and to all women.*[10]

This passage captures the two central points of Shklar's analysis: (1) citizenship, in the American context, has been articulated both literally and figuratively through *slavery*, and (2) citizenship's meaning for some people rests expressly on its *denial* to others.

The right to vote has value only insofar as it is able to confer standing by distancing those who possess the right from "slaves," who cannot possibly have it. Each group that struggled for the expansion of suffrage explicitly made its claim to equal standing in these terms, in contradistinction to some other group that could not make such a claim, persistently figured as slaves of some kind. Shklar writes,

> In the four great expansions of the suffrage, slavery was always a presence in the language of political argument. The Colonists rebelling against English rule, the white males disenfranchised by property and tax qualifications, the freedmen after the Civil War, and finally women all protested that they were reduced to the level of slaves if they did not have the vote and equal representation.[11]

In each of these historical moments, the figure of the slave stands as the paradigmatic outsider to freedom, as the antithesis of the American citizen who takes part in self-rule. The outright rejection of the idea of a citizen as a mere subject of the state defines the American citizen as a participant in rule and links the practice of voting for one's magistrates inseparably to being a citizen. This dual commitment to an ideal of political equality and to some procedure of self-government makes the vote fertile ground for conferring social standing. Shklar simply draws our attention to the fact that the struggle for equal standing has routinely been fought over the right to vote.

Shklar notes that "Americans were very quick to complain that if the British government did not meet their demands, they were little better than slaves."[12] While the language used by the American revolutionaries drew on the terms of political argument inherited from British sources, the very real existence of slavery in the colonies underscored their claims:

> The meaning of the word *slave* in America was not a mere metaphor for reduced political independence. It meant something far more concrete: the actual condition of most American blacks. And that this was a nightmare, though not a probability, for whites in America was at least in part due to the condition of indentured servants, who though far better off than black slaves were close enough to them to engrave the terror of enslavement upon many minds.[13]

If the American Revolution was about representation and securing rights of self-determination and independence from British rule, then it is no surprise that slavery, as a condition of complete dependence and despotic rule, would be the referent for these claims. In the early nineteenth century, when disenfranchised white workingmen made their claim of standing, they too drew on the language and practice of slavery to make their claims. The Jacksonian movement, Shklar claims, was driven by a central contention that all workingmen must be granted the right to vote or else they would be no different from that other class of laborers that filled the country: slaves.[14]

For actual slaves, of course, the connection between the right to vote and their condition as property was self-evident: "The freedmen saw the vote as a mark of social standing. It was, after all, *the* public sign that their years of servitude were over, and that they were citizens at last."[15] Drawing on Fredrick Douglass's insistence for the right to vote, Shklar writes, "No clearer statement of the idea of citizenship as standing could be imagined. This is hardly surprising, since the fear of slavery had always been at the very core of this particular conception of citizenship. *Who should express it better than an American ex-slave?*"[16]

For women, Shklar argues, the link between suffrage and slavery is more problematic. The Fifteenth Amendment, she writes, "did nothing at all for women. And the result was bitter resentment."[17] The women's suffrage movement reveals what Shklar calls "the darker side of citizenship as standing."[18] On her account, the women's suffrage movement demonstrates how appeals to standing need not be made in the terms of equality but can easily be made in terms of superiority. The problem for middle-class white suffragists was that what they took to be a clearly inferior group had been granted the rights and that they surely deserved more:

> It is . . . always possible to make a claim for the vote on grounds of superior, not equal, standing, as the advocates of property qualifications had done in the past. Women demanding the suffrage found that their cause might be better served by treating voting as a privilege limited to the educated and respectable, such as their own middle-class selves. It was in vain that Douglass, their supporter, pointed out the greater needs of the freedmen, compared to the many advantages enjoyed by these women. They did not see the difference between someone who can exercise all the privileges of legal citizenship except the vote, and someone who had no rights that a white man need respect.[19]

The language of slavery even figures into the opposition to women's suffrage, Shklar argues. The rejection of the Equal Rights Amendment (ERA) can be partly understood by how many women chafed under the implication that, absent explicit protection of their right to vote, they could be considered little more than slaves. "It is the imputation of slavery," Shklar writes, "the very word *slave* when applied to homemakers, that arouses the deepest resentment on the part of conservative female opponents of the ERA."[20] From both sides of the argument, the figure of slavery is central. For those in support of the ERA, to be denied explicit standing is to be considered a slave. For those opposed to the ERA, the invocation of slavery was to call their current standing a form of slavery, a condition emphatically rejected by women who understand their position in life to be anything but slave-like. "In either case," Shklar writes, "the dreaded memory [of slavery] still lingers."[21]

What Shklar hopes to show with her gloss on the history of the vote is that slavery, both as a real institution of the American experience and as a conceptual bulwark, was central to every instance of the expansion of voting rights in the United States.[22] Slavery, as the literal and figurative antithesis to freedom and independence, was also the antithesis of citizenship. While there might be space between full membership and slavery, some form of second-class citizenship, there is surely no doubt that to be a slave was to be definitively *not a citizen*. Conversely, to be secure in one's standing as a citizen had value because it meant that one was definitively *not a slave*, an impossible condition to accept.

The utility of these terms, "citizen" and "slave," is based on the denial of the vote in the face of a deeply held public commitment to equality. This is what invests the vote with such deep meaning: "What gave citizenship as standing its historical significance," Shklar writes, "is not that it was denied for so long to so many, but that this exclusion occurred in a republic that was overtly committed to political equality, and whose citizens believed that theirs was a free and fair society."[23] The claims made by the colonists, by white workingmen, by former slaves, and by women were not that the republic should be re-created with their interests included as well but that the republic, *as it was defined*, must respect that they too had equal standing in it. Denial of full citizenship under the claims of equality for members means that a denial to a group is not simply about difference but about difference that indicates lower social standing. In the absence of this ideological attachment to equality, it could be the case that those who are not included are simply not members, and one could make a good-faith claim that this denial does not imply reduced standing. But in the face of a public commitment to equality, exclusion necessarily reveals a hierarchical relationship of some kind.

Through each successive claim for the expansion of suffrage, the core injustice that colonists, workingmen, blacks, and women identified was that their denial of the vote represented a public admission that they were being denied equality. Moreover, each successive claim for inclusion continues to be predicated on the denial of complete equality to some other group. As each struggle for inclusion has demonstrated, it is no accident that the claims have persistently had recourse to a "darker side," maintaining an other whose continued exclusion demonstrates the true standing of those who are brought into the fold.

The history of the franchise reflects this tension between denial and equality, and as such, it has been the case that when claims of standing have been advanced, they have typically been made along existing cleavages of difference as claims of superiority. Shklar argues that it is entirely predictable, given the tension between equality and standing, that the classic boundaries between members and nonmembers are drawn along existing lines of difference taken as markers of superiority:

No historically significant form of government or of citizenship is in principle incompatible with the exclusion of large groups of people, but natural-rights theory makes it very difficult to find good reasons for excluding anyone from full political membership in a modern republic. To be sure, Americans have always found plenty of ideological reasons, from racism to social Darwinism, from religious bigotry to nativism, to justify exclusionary and discriminatory policies. Racism and sexism generally did most of this work of repudiation, and they did it very successfully for a very long time. Nor did they ever disappear. When eventually they did give way to political reality, the barriers to citizenship, piece by piece, had to come down.[24]

The *meaning* of the vote (and in turn, the value of citizenship itself) is defined on the basis of such denials, exclusions, and refusals to recognize some persons as possessing equal standing.

The obvious danger of defining citizenship as a form of standing, even when that standing is explicitly stated in terms of the equality among members, is that there is no reason why this necessarily prevents claims over the vote to be made in decidedly inegalitarian terms. "There is nothing equal about social standing in general," Shklar writes. "Nothing is more unequally distributed than social respect and prestige. It is only citizenship perceived as a natural right that bears a promise of equal political standing in a democracy."[25] The challenge that citizenship-as-standing faces is how to bridge the conflicting attachments to equality with the socially productive work of exclusion. What makes this problem a uniquely *American* problem is its unavoidable tie to the history and practice of slavery in the United States. "It was this juxtaposition of slavery and constitutional democracy," she writes, "above all else, that set America apart from other modern states."[26]

The central historical lesson that Shklar derives from this analysis is that we misunderstand the practice of voting itself. Social standing, as established through its denial to some people, is attached not to the practice of voting or its instrumental function (i.e., an ability to alter the outcome of electoral races or to register interest through its aggregative function) but to the right to vote itself. *The vote*, rather than *voting*, confers standing:

> It was the denial of the suffrage to large groups of Americans that made the right to vote such a mark of social standing. To be refused the right was to be almost a slave, but once one possessed the right, it conferred no other personal advantages. *Not the exercise, only the right, signified deeply.* Without the right one was less than a citizen. Once the right was

achieved, it had fulfilled its function in distancing the citizen from his inferiors, especially slaves and women.[27]

The vote as a *right* has been the site of struggles for enfranchisement and inclusion because the dignity and standing conferred by being *allowed* to vote confirms group membership in the polity. The exercise of the vote does not signify this standing and, as such, is not what carries voting's meaning. Recognizing this distinction, Shklar contends, helps make sense of the low voter-turnout rates and captures the degree to which the vote itself, even legally secured, is meaningless unless it also represents a shift in the standing of the group in question. In this sense, having the vote is the meaningful end (so long as it successfully confers standing) rather than a means to some other end:

> The right is not fundamental because it secures benefits or other rights directly for the individual voter acting alone; it does so only if he or she votes as a member of a group. . . . Voting is the necessary first step, but in itself it is not enough; additional forms of social and political action are required to promote and protect the interests and rights of ordinary citizens. The deepest impulse for demanding the suffrage arises from the recognition that it is the characteristic, the identifying feature of democratic citizenship in America, not a means to other ends.[28]

The difficulty in successfully conferring this standing, Shklar argues, is that the vote is not the only marker of standing in the American context. The right to achieve independence through work and earning also does this social work and is the remaining battleground for realizing the terms of political equality.

SLAVERY, RACE, AND PUNISHMENT

As Seyla Benhabib notes, Shklar was dedicated to theorizing politics "from the standpoint of the margins, from the standpoint of those who did not have a voice easily representable at the center [of public life]."[29] Benhabib argues that Shklar's analysis of citizenship is itself a response to Hannah Arendt's study of the American Revolution: "Instead of marginalizing and rendering invisible the plight of African-American slaves in the new republic as Arendt had done, Shklar places the injustice of slavery and the wounds it has inflicted on the meaning of American citizenship at the very center of her analysis."[30] This is, indeed, one of the most moving aspects of Shklar's work: unlike many twentieth-century liberal theorists, she demonstrates a specific concern for the excluded, the marginalized, and the exiled, placing questions about *injustice* squarely at the center of political theory. The history of struggle for suffrage is, in Shklar's analysis, a demonstration of the importance of understanding citizenship's meaning through material and historical terms, prioritizing those persons who made claims for their own inclusion over those already included in the polity.

Yet Shklar's account is characterized by a set of omissions that limits its ability to account for the continuing forms of exclusion that characterize the American practices of citizenship and punishment. These exclusions are important on her own terms, because of her otherwise convincing argument that we must pay close attention to the work that citizenship does in conferring differential social standing among groups of people. Building on each of the central features of her theory identified in the preceding section—the importance of slavery and the difference between *the vote* and *voting*—in this section I consider how American citizenship, along each of these terms, is inflected with the discourse of racialized punishment. I argue first that Shklar underplays the relationship between slavery and the formation of race and the racialized figure of the "white citizen." Second, I argue that Shklar misses the historical and functional connections between the institution of slavery and the discourse of punishment. If slavery's "dreaded memory still lingers" in contemporary citizenship, it is because slavery's institutions and practices were so easily taken up into punitive forms that outlived it.

In *The Abolition of White Democracy*, the late Joel Olson argues that Shklar, while attentive to race-based exclusions and the history of slavery, misses that the American citizen comes into existence as a necessarily *white* citizen.[31] Olson argues that Shklar does not "complete the thread" connecting slavery to blackness to citizenship: "Citizenship was not just standing, as Shklar argues, but *racialized* standing."[32] While Shklar persuasively shows how the legacy of slavery persists even in the contemporary conception of citizenship, it does so under racialized terms. On the basis of the historical exclusion of blacks, by virtue not only of overt racism but of their role as chattel slaves as the antithesis of the citizen, Olson argues that there is no escaping the fact that the "abstract" citizen is in fact the *white citizen*. Olson reinterprets the claims of immigrant groups, laborers, and women for equal standing and full citizenship as struggles for inclusion in whiteness. Their successes reflect not simply an expansion of standing to these groups but a remaking of the racial category of *white* to be relatively less nativist, class specific, or gendered. While these cleavages continue to exist, he argues, they do so within the terms of overall white supremacy.

The primary reason for Shklar's omission of the connection between slavery and blackness and the subsequent construction of the citizen as white, Olson claims in a footnote, is due to her racial essentialism. He writes, "One possible reason why Shklar does not make this connection between whiteness and citizenship is because she holds a biological conception of race."[33] While I agree that Shklar does tend toward conceptions of race and gender that assume them to be immutable ascriptive characteristics, she nevertheless is somewhat attentive to the mutability of where the lines of difference are drawn between groups. For instance, she notes that white workingmen fighting for the vote knew that the struggle for political exclusion was tied to their self-concept. "The vote was so important to these men," she writes, "because it meant that they were citizens, unlike women and slaves, as they repeated over and over again. Their very identity as free males was at stake."[34]

Nevertheless, Shklar repeatedly demonstrates that the heart of the citizenship "problem" is the exploitation of lines of stable difference in opposition to the American commitment to equal standing and the principle of inclusion. The questions of continued racial or gender domination even after inclusion and the social construction of identity are largely off the table in her account.[35] The only concern about "identity" that Shklar demonstrates is that white men find their social standing threatened in opposition to what they know to be true about themselves (i.e., that they are full members with higher standing than "other" groups). Olson's point is to demonstrate how this self-understanding comes into existence *through* the exclusion of women and blacks, rather than prior to it. Shklar's analysis is limited, according to Olson, because the question of American citizenship is about more than just settling the boundaries of membership. Settling these boundaries produces the characteristics that serve as the basis for exclusion. She does not appear to see citizenship struggles as constitutive in the formation of race and gender in the American context, and in turn, this leaves her theory of democratic inclusion in jeopardy:

> What Shklar implies but fails to elaborate, then, is that citizenship as standing links democracy to race. Standing not only reconciles equality and freedom with slavery; it builds white domination into democracy.

Thus, the democratic problem is not simply the legacy of slavery and racial exclusion or the failure of American democratic practices to live up to American democratic ideals. The democratic problem lies in the white citizen itself.[36]

Shklar's failing is that she does not seem to realize the extent to which the history of slavery has shaped not just the practices and problems of democratic citizenship but the very terms of abstract equality it relies on. In a classic reversal, Olson writes, "One did not receive the rights of American citizenship because one was white but rather the reverse: one was white because one possessed such rights."[37] The struggle for voting rights as a marker of citizenship-as-standing is importantly a struggle over the normalized conception of whiteness. This is most true in the context of the Jacksonian-era struggles for voting and working rights, Olson argues: "It was so important to become a citizen in the Jacksonian era in part because it was so important to become white. Once conjoined, the two identities were practically interchangeable."[38] In a later essay, Shklar herself comes close to this same reversal, writing, "To be a white male meant that one had to be a citizen."[39] This subsequent phrasing suggests a similar priority of political rights to the one Olson emphasizes and that the stakes of citizenship in the United States have always already been about becoming normatively white.[40]

While in the Jacksonian era, the homology between whiteness and citizenship was produced by black slavery, neither Olson nor Shklar traces how this connection was maintained in large part through punitive institutions in the postbellum period. Shklar is rightly drawn to the Civil War–era constitutional amendments to explain how extensions of suffrage signify extensions of political standing. She fails to note, however, that both the Thirteenth and Fourteenth Amendments carve out exceptions to the elimination of slavery and the right to vote. As Davis notes, there was actually no explicit mention of slavery in the U.S. Constitution until its abolition, and yet it is at this point that slavery is expressly linked to punishment.[41] In full, Section 1 of the Thirteenth Amendment states, "Neither slavery nor involuntary servitude, except as a punishment for crime whereof the party shall have been duly convicted, shall exist within the United States, or any place subject to their jurisdiction."

The language of the amendment was the subject of contentious debate during the first part of 1864, especially over the "except as a punishment for crime" clause.[42] This language's insertion into the amendment was driven by slaveholding interests in the Senate and laid the basis for the development of the Black Codes used in the South to maintain not only the continued restrictions of the suffrage to freedmen but the economic labor system of slavery, most perniciously through the convict-lease system.[43] As Davis puts it, "The abolition of slavery thus corresponded to the authorization of slavery as punishment."[44] Perversely, perhaps, it is finally at this moment that the U.S. legal system mirrors Locke's account of slavery as a form of punishment. These constitutional clauses formalize the Lockean connections described in the previous chapter between punishment, slavery, and political membership. This connection is solidified through free labor (as evidence of reason) and property (as evidence of independence). As Keally McBride notes, "At the time Locke was developing his theory of the social contract he perceived that linking citizenship to labor was one way to ensure the stability of liberal forms of government."[45] Private property creates the conditions of possibility for civil society as well as the motivation to enter into it voluntarily, she argues. And on this account, to be in a condition of slavery *even as a form of punishment*, renders one's labor alien and therefore leaves one categorically "ineligible for citizenship."[46] Insofar as chattel slavery operated through a property system, freed slaves would suddenly be able to make the most essential claim of liberal rights: the ability to own both oneself and the product of one's labor. Such holdings would ground blacks as eligible for participation in government, *unless* that eligibility was called into question by linking black labor itself with criminality.

THE IMPOSSIBILITY OF FREE NEGRO LABOR

This connection between forced labor, political membership, and punishment is as historical as it is theoretical. Drawing on Adam Hirsch's history of the penitentiary in the United States, Davis argues that "both institutions [slavery and the penitentiary] deployed similar forms of punishment, and prison regulations were, in fact, very similar to the Slave Codes—the laws that deprived enslaved human beings of virtually all rights."[47] Davis argues that any history of American punishment begins with the institution of slavery, which was dramatically altered by the language of the Thirteenth Amendment:

> After the abolition of slavery, former slave states passed new legislation revising the Slave Codes in order to regulate the behavior of free blacks

in ways similar to those that had existed during slavery. The new Black Codes proscribed a range of actions—such as vagrancy, absence from work, breach of job contracts, the possession of firearms, and insulting gestures or acts—that were criminalized only when the person charged was black. . . . According to the Black Codes, there were crimes defined by state law for which only black people could be "duly convicted."

Thus, former slaves, who had recently been extricated from a condition of hard labor for life, could be legally sentenced to penal servitude.[48]

This link between slavery and punishment was driven by the twofold interest in maintaining the economic structure of the slave economy and the social and political structures of white supremacy. As Alex Lichtenstein argues, the convict-lease system "operated not merely as a corrupt and unjust penal system, but as a system of labor recruitment, control, and exploitation particularly suited to the political economy of a post-emancipation society. . . . It stood as a system of forced labor in an age of emancipation."[49] Lichtenstein carefully demonstrates, however, that the convict-lease system was not simply a reintroduction of slavery but was itself a transformation of the American economy on the basis of the political terms established after the war.

This novel forced-labor system took advantage of the existing nexus between labor and race and redefined them through the language of criminality and the penal system, not simply through the expansion of criminal codes targeting former slaves. The language of the Thirteenth and Fourteenth Amendments themselves opened the door for the redefinition of criminality as blackness, and blackness as a mark of inherent criminality. Early Black Codes and the broader Jim Crow legal system seized on the space carved out in the amendments' exceptions. Prevailing notions of crime and punishment centered on the management of populations considered not fit for freedom, known through their affinity or relation to the now-forbidden system of chattel slavery. Davis notes, "Black people were imprisoned under the laws assembled in the various Black Codes of the southern states, which, because they were rearticulations of the Slave Codes, tended to racialize penality and link it closely with previous regimes of slavery."[50] That is to say, slavery and the physical, social, and political degradation that it inflicted on racialized bodies simply did not disappear with the Civil War but were displaced and "rearticulated" into a different location: the overlapping postbellum penal and labor systems. The effect would be both to dramatically alter the racial makeup of "criminals" in the United States and to dramatically alter the kind of work that an association with "crime" would do to social standing. Davis summarizes this nicely:

> If . . . the early incarnations of the U.S. Penitentiary in the North tended to mirror the institution of slavery in many important respects, the post–Civil War evolution of the punishment system was in very literal ways the continuation of a slave system, which was no longer legal in the "free" world. The population of convicts, whose racial composition was dramatically transformed by the abolition of slavery, could be subjected to such intense exploitation and to such horrendous modes of punishment precisely because they continued to be perceived as slaves.[51]

The ability to maintain this perception rested on ensuring that the twin markers of standing (earning and suffrage) would not be altered in fact by the end of slavery in the South. Wholesale political disenfranchisement through poll taxes, grandfather clauses, and especially criminal exclusions emerged immediately following the end of Reconstruction. Slave-labor extraction was maintained by directing the resources of the criminal justice system to continue the management of former slave laborers.

The way that the convict-lease system united discourses of race, membership, labor, and punishment was hardly lost on nineteenth-century theorists of race, including Ida B. Wells and W. E. B. Du Bois, who both identified the practice as instrumental to the postbellum maintenance of white supremacy. Writing in an 1893 pamphlet titled "The Reason Why the Colored American Is Not in the World's Columbian Exposition," Wells pointed to the convict-lease system and lynch law as "twin infamies" that "are the two great outgrowths and results of the class legislation under which our people suffer to-day."[52] On the basis of reports from the period, she noted two reasons why nine-tenths of the state convicts leased out to railways, mining companies, and plantation farms were "Negroes." First, former slaves had been systematically denied the resources, training, and skills necessary to "good" citizenship: "The white Christian and moral influences have not only done little to prevent the Negro becoming a criminal, but they have deliberately shut him out of everything which tends to make for good citizenship."[53] Second, the administration of justice was itself entirely skewed toward the interests of white men: "The judges, juries and other officials of course are white men. . . . They also make the laws. It is wholly in their power to extend clemency to white criminals and mete severe punishments to black criminals for the same or lesser crimes."[54] To be a black "free laborer" in the postslavery era was in effect to be marked for conviction and reassigned to forced labor through conviction (often on the very same plantations former slaves had worked before). Such a fate, Wells notes, not only was driven by powerful agricultural and industrial interests in virtually free labor but was also directly linked to the question of political power: "Every Negro so sentenced not only means able-bodied men to swell the state's number of slaves, but every Negro so convicted is thereby *disfranchised*."[55]

W. E. B. Du Bois echoes this account a decade later, stating simply, "A new slavery and slave-trade was established" with the convict-lease system.[56] Du Bois argues that the rise in "Negro Crime" in the South following the end of the Civil War had to be explained by the rise of the convict-lease system in addition to the same factors identified by Wells: openly racist courts, lynch law, and segregation.[57] Convict leasing was a perfect solution to the fact that, following the war, the southern states had no institutions to deal with either free black labor or increasing levels of "crime." Du Bois goes so far as to make the claim that a key reason crime rates increased following the emancipation was because "under a strict slave system there can scarcely be such a thing as crime."[58] Du Bois explicitly links the question of political status with rising crime rates among freed slaves, but he insists that this increase is a direct result of freed blacks now being called criminals rather than errant slaves and because "the police system of the South was primarily designed to control slaves."[59] The structure of the police system is, Du Bois argues, little more than an expression of the color line itself, as whites automatically assume the role of law enforcement and blacks are automatically seen as criminals:

> For such dealing with Criminals, white or black, the South had no
> machinery, no adequate jails or reformatories; its police system was arranged to deal with blacks alone, and tacitly assumed that every white
> man was *ipso facto* a member of that police. . . . The police system of the
> South was originally designed to keep track of all Negroes, not simply
> of criminals; and when the Negroes were freed and the whole South was
> convinced of the impossibility of free Negro labor, the first and almost
> universal device was to use the courts as a means of reënslaving the
> blacks. It was not then a question of crime, but rather one of color, that
> settled a man's conviction on almost any charge.[60]

On Du Bois's analysis, the convict-lease system solved numerous "problems" facing whites following emancipation. It maintained an economic system predicated on forced labor, radically undermining any political standing that was opened by the Reconstruction Amendments, and converted every white man in the South into a de facto police force (absorbing former plantation overseers as officers). In *Black Reconstruction*, Du Bois extends this analysis, writing,

> In Georgia, at the outbreak of the Civil War, there were about 200
> white felons confined at Milledgeville. There were no Negro convicts,
> since under the discipline of slavery, Negroes were punished on the
> plantation. The white convicts were released to fight in the Confederate
> armies. The whole criminal system came to be used as a method of keep-
> ing Negroes at work and intimidating them. Consequently there began
> to be a demand for jails and penitentiaries beyond the natural demand
> due to the rise of crime.[61]

This demand was driven, at least in part, by the beginning of the convict-lease system, which, as Du Bois notes, was in full swing by the mid 1870s, at the direction of Democrats in southern statehouses.[62]

The closing chapter of *Black Reconstruction* chronicles the countless devices employed by whites in the South to maintain the racial caste system, and Du Bois draws special attention to the connection between crime, punishment, and the perpetuation of slavery and slavelike conditions. He quotes an "English traveler" writing in 1877: "I confess I am more and more suspicious about the criminal justice of these Southern states. In Georgia there is no regular penitentiary at all, but an organized system of letting out the prisoners for profit. . . . This does seem simply a return to another form of slavery."[63] Du Bois offers this commentary: "In no part of the modern world has there been so open and conscious a traffic in crime for deliberate social degradation and private profit as in the South since slavery."[64] The same observation could continue to be made today but applied to the entire United States.

More recently, the sociological analysis of Loïc Wacquant provides a more structuralist account of this trajectory from slavery to punishment. Wacquant argues that slavery and the prison are tied together through a genealogy of the "four peculiar institutions" of race-making in the United Sates. He writes,

The task of *defining, confining, and controlling* African Americans in the United States has been successively shouldered by four "peculiar institutions": slavery, the Jim Crow system, the urban ghetto, and the novel organizational compound formed by the vestiges of the ghetto and the expanding carceral system.[65]

These four systems align through a set of goals that remain perpetually in tension with one another: labor extraction and social ostracism. That is, each of these systems attempts to simultaneously manage a labor pool while also ensuring a social separation between groups. Wacquant argues that beyond the historical connection, slavery and incarceration are linked through a "triple relationship of functional equivalency, structural homology, and cultural fusion."[66] The final point of his analysis, however, is not simply to indicate these connections but to demonstrate how these connections shed light on the contemporary carceral regime's role in

> the ongoing *reconstruction* of the *"imagined community" of Americans* around the polar opposition between praiseworthy "working families"— implicitly white, suburban, and deserving—and the despicable "underclass" of criminals, loafers, and leeches, a two-headed antisocial hydra personified by the dissolute teenage "welfare mother" on the female side and the dangerous street "gang banger" on the male side—by definition dark-skinned, urban, and undeserving.[67]

What brings this distinction into effect are the collateral consequences of being incarcerated in the United States. Wacquant notes the "triple-exclusion" experienced by criminals in the denial of cultural capital (labor-market and educational restrictions), social redistribution (e.g., denial of welfare benefits), and political participation (e.g., felon disenfranchisement), amounting to a modern form of *social death*, the term Orlando Patterson famously employed to capture the meaning of slavery.[68]

Complementing this structural account, Asatar Bair shows in his economic analysis of prison labor how the current conditions of convict labor are, quite simply, structured as a slave economy:

> Slavery exists in U.S. prisons, although it is of a different form than our common conception of slavery in such sites as the Caribbean or the American south during the Antebellum period. Inmates are enslaved due to the unique structure of the production and appropriation of

surplus labor, including the cultural, political, economic, and physical forces which overdetermine this class process.[69]

From an economic analysis of labor, Bair argues, there is simply no other way to describe the contemporary structure of prison labor than as a slave economy. Drawing on Patterson's analysis of the formation of slave identity, Bair notes that each of the key elements involved in the formation of slave identity are carefully attended to within the prison context: naming (exchanging one's name for a number), physical marking (exchanging ones own clothes for a prison uniform), and the severing of familial and community ties (incarceration, by definition, removes convicts from their social worlds and makes maintenance of those ties extremely difficult).[70] The creation of a "slave identity" forms the basis of surplus labor extraction through the form of prison labor, Bair argues. That is, the slavery-prison connection exists both through symbolic processes that directly echo slave societies as well as the surplus labor extraction directly modeled on slave economies.

What these accounts indicate, beyond simply pointing out the striking similarity in practice between chattel slavery and convict leasing in both form and function, is that the entire criminal justice system that emerged following the Civil War was expressly racialized in its conception of crime, in its system of policing, and in the forms of punishment employed. American punishment was increasingly racialized following the Civil War, and even as modern penal law becomes increasingly "color-blind," this has done little to correct this racialized character of punishment. This point is ultimately what Olson's account also misses: the construction of white citizenship is tied not just to black slavery but to the racialized practice of punishment. To speak of blackness in the postslavery period was necessarily also to speak of crime and punishment. To complete Olson's argument that the abstract citizen is raced as white, we must also note that the abstract criminal is figured both as a noncitizen and as nonwhite.[71]

Moreover, my critique of Shklar self-consciously echoes and seeks to build on Shklar's approach: we cannot rightly understand the meaning of American citizenship without attention to the exclusions that define it. She is correct to point us to the realization that slavery is *the* driving practice in the formation of the American polity. While her account focuses our attention on slavery, it does not recognize the extent to which slavery *continues* to shape the terms of social groupings constituted through exclusionary punitive practices that followed from the end of the chattel system of slavery. Attention to these factors extends her analysis of citizenship-as-standing and, more importantly, allows us to attend to those exclusions that continue to define American citizenship.

LOOKING BUT NOT SEEING: THE PROBLEM OF "UNIVERSAL" SUFFRAGE

Shklar's interest in the vote is ultimately in service of drawing attention to the second "emblem" of American citizenship: the independence conferred through the right to work in order to earn. To be a citizen is to carry both of these "emblems" and thus to be seen publicly as equal and worthy of participation in self-government. The historical connection, of course, between working and voting is the shared history of slavery. Just as the suffrage movement explicitly understood its achievement as a distancing from metaphorical slavery (and in the case of freed blacks, literal slavery), the ability to earn from one's labor is an explicit rejection of the economic position of the slave. The widespread practice of convict leasing (or alternately sharecropping and debt-peonage) might well have served to make clear just how deeply linked slavery and the ideology of independent earning are in the American context for shoring up the worth of a citizen.[72]

Shklar's primary practical concern in *American Citizenship* is not with suffrage but rather with the unrealized right to earn that persists in the post-civil-rights era, and she pivots her analysis to this "second emblem" on the claim that "the last barriers to universal adult suffrage" have fallen.[73] She writes,

> In spite of all the obstacles thrown in its way by injustice and discrimination in all its many forms, the vote was won, but not that other emblem of equal citizenship, the opportunity to earn one's livelihood. The Great Society was a triumph for voting, but its struggle against poverty and unemployment was not a success. All adult Americans are now constituents, equal voters in their districts, but they are not equally independent, and too many do not earn anything.[74]

Shklar is quite right to assert that the vote it not the sole "emblem" of equal standing in the United States and that the right to earn has also been a central battleground in the struggle for full membership in the American polity. And she is quite right to link together labor and suffrage in this way as twin markers that have always been deeply embedded and linked to each other. The problem, however, is that Shklar's shift from the vote to the right to earn is predicated on the incorrect claim that universal adult suffrage has been achieved.

Foreigners, children, the mentally incapacitated, and felons are all excluded from the right to vote. Shklar mentions the exclusion of children, but only to chide the "utter indifference of the young," who were granted the right to vote in the Twenty-Sixth Amendment and then failed to turn out to vote en masse. The exclusion of children is arguably defensible since their lower standing is, by definition, "not a permanent physical or social condition."[75] Foreigners, who are not taken up explicitly by Shklar, can shed their foreignness through some reasonably open process of naturalization (in theory at least). In contrast to these two exclusions, however, the mentally deficient or infirm present a different problem in that their exclusion appears to be permanent. Shklar is, unfortunately, in keeping with the broad company of political theorists who likewise fail to explicitly examine questions of ability and disability as central to political thought. More sympathetically, it is true that there has been limited historical struggle among the disabled to secure their right to vote compared to the scale of other suffrage movements.[76]

The omission of criminal exclusions, however, poses a different problem for Shklar's account since the history of such exclusions in the United States has a far longer history than does any other omitted exclusion. There are two notable moments in *American Citizenship* that seem to support the exclusions of criminals from equal standing and, by inference, the rights to vote and earn. First, in discussing the Rousseauian conception of the citizen, she notes that the relationship between membership in the polity characterized by moral freedom, that state in which one understands the law as given to oneself, includes even the acceptance of capital punishment: "And when he [the citizen] fails to obey the laws he has given himself, he is only 'forced to be free,' even in receiving capital punishment, since it is no more than a legal requirement which he agreed to impose on all citizens alike. *The lawbreaking citizen is really a traitor.*"[77] Second, in the closing lines of the text, while referring to the possibility of some limited conception of a right to earn, Shklar states, "*Like any right*, the right to earn can be forfeited, but that does not render it worthless."[78] What might signal the forfeiture of the right to earn and, by implication, a right to vote is left unstated. Nevertheless, Shklar's conception of "universal suffrage" seems open to the possibility of some restrictions given this language. Notwithstanding these two moments, Shklar simply does not address the question of criminal exclusions directly. And yet it was during these same historical periods, and in relation to the same historical struggles over standing that Shklar unpacks so carefully, that criminal exclusions to the elective franchise took hold across the United States. As noted earlier, criminal exclusions saw their first wave of expansion in northern states in the period following widespread adoption of white male suffrage and a second wave across the South and West following the Civil War.

In the face of these "basic facts of political history," to borrow Shklar's language, what is the meaning of the vote? And what, moreover, is the meaning of Shklar's omission of criminal disenfranchisement? By her own account, we should be extraordinarily sensitive to the public standing conveyed by the denial of the right to vote, to exclusions that map "existing cleavages" of difference, that fall disproportionately on persons of color, and to those practices that are directly tied to the history of chattel slavery. We are already primed by Shklar to tackle the question of criminal disenfranchisement in all its forms. What should we make of this omission, of this seeming blindness to the work of punishment in conferring equal standing through the vote?[79]

At one level, this puzzle can be asked in terms of Shklar's larger body of work. Her omission is all the more striking since Shklar, in this broader work, is particularly attentive to the danger of being branded a "criminal" by the state. Comparing herself to the first of the great liberal "reformers" of punishment, Caesare Beccaria, she argues in *The Liberalism of Fear* that a primary state cruelty that must be guarded against is the state's abuse of the criminal justice system.[80] A grounding principle of liberalism is this persistent fear of state power, captured nowhere better than in the extensive set of rights elaborated in the Bill of Rights for the protection of "the accused in criminal trials."[81] Arguably, the ultimate power of the state is its ability to rightfully punish individuals, and as such, the greatest protections must be afforded to individuals to preserve themselves in the face of power. "Without well-defined procedures, honest judges, opportunities for counsel and for appeals, no one has a chance. Nor should we allow more acts to be criminalized than is necessary for our mutual safety," she writes.[82] But her concern (oddly, given her self-avowed debt to Beccaria) is less with the treatment of those who are truly guilty of transgression than with those who have been treated *unjustly*, who are, it turns out, *innocent*. In the very next line, her concern pivots from the accused to the victimized: "Finally, nothing speaks better for a liberal state than legal efforts to compensate the victims of crime rather than merely to punish the criminal for having violated the law. For he did injure, terrify, and abuse a human being first and foremost."[83] The relevant point is that there seems to be a distinction in Shklar's mind between "true" criminals and those who are criminals only by virtue of state prosecution.

The same inflection, between true and false criminals, can be seen in the essay "Obligation, Loyalty, Exile." Shklar turns to the problem of exiles to help understand the terms of obligation and loyalty. While exile is historically a form of punishment, Shklar takes exiles as criminals due to some political transgression rather than a "real" crime (i.e., because some conflicting set of loyalties or obligations leads individuals to unjustly be expelled from their home nation). Her concern for such people, echoing Arendt, is that they are left without citizenship in any nation. She considers these exiles not truly criminals but instead victims of the abuse of political power. The mistake of "making political obligation dependent on group membership and loyalty both national and ethnic" has created the "refugee crisis" as a distinctly modern form of exile. Refugees excluded from their homes by virtue of their existing obligations to a kinship, ethnic, or linguistic group are, expressly, "people who would obey the law."[84] As such, Shklar argues that the "plight of the dispersed and excluded is unbearable."[85] Exile presumes that obedience to the law is grounds to be considered a citizen of at least some state. Persons who *would not* obey the law must lose this claim.

It matters whether one is guilty or not. But the power of Shklar's analysis is that regardless of whether we think persons *should* be excluded even for "good" reasons, her account demands that we reflect on the fact that citizenship derives its meaning, and voting its value, *from these exclusions*. Just as Shklar charges her readers to take seriously the very real history of American slavery and discrimination against workingmen, blacks, and women, we must also take up those exclusions which persist despite her incorrect claim that suffrage is universal.

Citizenship-as-standing implies that felons (like women, black men, and white workingmen before them) continue to be marked as having lower standing. In terms of American inclusion, they are not full citizens. Of course, it could be argued that this is exactly the point: to be a criminal is to have at least forfeited one's rights or, more precisely, to have *demonstrated* that one is not in the same position as others. But we should be troubled that the persons who find themselves in this position of lower standing, given the history of slavery (to which Shklar draws our attention) and its extension through the criminal justice system, are disproportionately black. Given this history, we should ask ourselves whether this idea of "real" criminals does more work than we recognize, preventing us from confronting disproportionate effects on some segments of the population.

On a different level, however, we can read Shklar's omission as symptomatic of the larger twentieth-century separation between the discourse of punishment and the discourse of citizenship. This split between domains, this symptomatic omission, creates a productive blind spot for us, produced to do crucial work for how we punish, how we vote, and how we understand ourselves as citizens. Such discursive separation of punishment and citizenship has at least two forms, conceptual and normative. On one hand, making a conceptual separation between punishment and citizenship assumes that each domain addresses a different set of political questions. For example, this conceptual distinction implies that punishment and citizenship must have different aims and purposes or that citizenship has a temporal or logical priority before punishment or that they each have fundamentally different grounds of justification (where citizenship is conferred according to ascriptive characteristics while punishment is meted out because of one's bad actions). To think about punishment and citizenship together would therefore amount to a conceptual error and confusion of two distinct kinds.

On the other hand, the normative separation recognizes connections between punishment and citizenship but identifies this as the problem to overcome, as a danger that must be addressed through the intentional separation of two discourses that ought not be mixed. This view makes strong claims that we must not punish wrongdoing by stripping an offender of one's citizenship, that we must not confuse the criminal and the civil codes, or that we must rationalize, liberalize, and clarify our legislation and establish one part of law for questions of membership and one part of law for questions of crime and punishment. To think about punishment and citizenship together, on this account, would therefore amount to a normative failure because we ought to keep them apart.

Whether on the conceptual level or the normative level, separating these discourses has multiple effects. First, we tend to forget that questions of punishment have already been figured as questions of membership *throughout* the history of political thought, and we neglect the central role that punishment plays in theories of political membership, in Sophocles or Plato, in Aquinas or Augustine, in the height of the republican tradition of Rousseau and Hegel, and above all for our purposes, in the foundational texts of liberal thought in Locke, Hobbes, Mill, or Bentham. Second, we neglect the centrality of *actual* punishment in the *actual* establishment of political communities and in the policing of both internal and external boundaries of political states throughout history. Third, because of the insistence that we must separate punishment from citizenship, we are left unable to account for felon disenfranchisement, since it is a practice that straddles these two discourses. And we are left unable to account for a seemingly contradictory practice. Surely, we think it is a relic of some past period, but it is neverthe-less a practice that has expanded more quickly and more quietly in our own lifetimes than for those before us. Surely it has been dramatically reformed in the past decade, with many states finally eliminating lifetime bans on felon voters, but in the same period, it has expanded into states that previ-ously had no criminal restrictions whatsoever on voting rights.

Shklar's own omission can be read as a symptom of a productive blind spot that is at the root of the reproduction of a systematically racialized criminal punishment system and of a conception of liberal political mem-bership that continues to be a violation of democratic equality. We use the vote as a signifier of our equality and our finally realized liberality, and at the same time it expresses our unearned and deeply illiberal desire for stand-ing, distinction, and hierarchy. Within this blind spot, we are able to re-assure both our liberal equality and our privilege. Here, we are able to look but not see.

As is clear in Shklar's account, the nineteenth and early twentieth centuries are periods in which public standing was expressly purchased through exist-ing social cleavages such as class, race, and gender. The twentieth-century story, a distinctly *liberal* story, is one in which these public expressions of superiority could no longer be sustained in the face of the outward promise of equality. And if we follow Shklar's historical method but also always at-tend to state punishment as one of the central mechanisms by which each of these expansions of political standing was managed, then we must conclude that, in the face of felon exclusions, the right to vote marks today's holders as continuing to possess higher political standing, purchasing equality through its denial to others.

But at the same time, we proclaim our great progress in finally achieving a color-blind, gender-blind, and class-blind electoral process, where we can and do find that the ballot box and the highest elective office in the country include persons who would have been previously excluded from that standing. The blind spot that comes from separating the discourses of citizenship and punishment is productive of a continued notion of citizenship as innocent and as free from our own pernicious past, while in point of fact, it continues to rely on a racially disproportionate and expansive disenfranchised population that is not only behind bars but outside the polity.

THE FETISH OF VOTING

Taken together, these critiques of Shklar's analysis, the limited analysis of the race-making and punitive dimensions of the history of slavery and the seemingly acceptable exclusion of criminals from full membership, can be explained by a deeper problem in her analysis: an attachment to an essentialist notion of identity and an attendant discounting of the performative work of voting.[86] The exclusions of white workingmen, women, and African Americans are taken to be unjust because they are grounded in identity categories that Shklar takes to be given. One effect of this is to discount the importance of *voting practices* as a part of the vote's meaning as well as the production and maintenance of these same identity categories. The *practice* of voting itself is crucial for the *maintenance* and reproduction of public standing, and under the conditions of felon disenfranchisement, this practice becomes a performance of innocence as well as political membership. Moreover, because voting is already a performance of political standing tied to action-based exclusions (i.e., felon disenfranchisement), voting becomes a practice that stands in for any number of political commitments, statements, or demonstrations of superiority that have weak grounding in democratic theory. That is, voting is infused with countless different meanings, all of which purport to demonstrate one's superior standing.

Shklar does not argue that the act of voting itself does not matter or is not important but that insofar as being allowed to vote is a marker of public standing, it is the *right* which confers this standing rather than its exercise. She uses this distinction to explain the low voter-turnout rates that plague the United States: given that suffrage has been extended, it is no longer a ground on which to contest standing, and its significance is thus diminished. That is, given that the question of suffrage is relatively settled (unlike, she asserts, the grounds of labor), we should not be surprised that the actual voting does not happen as much as we might prefer. Voting itself might matter, she asserts, but it simply does not do the work of conferring standing. Insofar as her analysis of citizenship as standing is attentive to the way in which the *meaning* of citizenship is the product of historical struggles, we can surmise that she likewise takes the meaning and content of the *citizen* as a figure to be similarly produced through these struggles. But because of her essentialist conception of identity, she argues that once a battle is over, once standing has been defined, the productive work has ended. Even if fewer and fewer people go to the polls each year, those who do are necessarily engaging in a performance of their full membership in the polity.

But as Olson's critique of Shklar demonstrates, political membership and the content of "identity categories" were already linked in American democracy. During times when workingmen were excluded from the polls, performing membership by voting also expressed property ownership. When all blacks are excluded from the franchise (as Olson notes), voting becomes a performance of whiteness. When women are excluded, masculinity is performed as a part of casting one's vote. And in the contemporary setting, when I walk into the polling place, find my name on the list of eligible voters, and cast my vote, among the many things that I publicly declare in that moment, one surely must be that I am not a felon. What is most striking about this performance is that I have no control over this utterance of innocence. It is implied by my participation whether I approve or not. It is not even predicated on my intentions or knowledge when I enter the voting booth. The common complaint made in response to this reading is, "But I didn't even know that felons can't vote. How could I be expressing my innocence?" This position, while perhaps true in a narrow and abstract sense, is largely irrelevant to the *meaning* of the vote because my knowledge and intentions are only one part of performativity. The more relevant question to ask oneself is whether one would feel any differently about voting or would be more or less likely to vote given the knowledge of criminal exclusions.

What must it mean to take seriously that citizenship is a form of public standing *and* to recognize that individuals convicted of crimes cannot vote? Both that criminals are, deductively, not full citizens *and* that my standing as demonstrated by my voting (and working) is purchased on their backs.[87] Shklar instructs us to look carefully at whose exclusion carries the burden of membership for those who are included. What she leaves open, however, is a structured blindness to the fact that these burdens continue to be carried, even if they are "guilty" and "criminal." It is true that, as Shklar argues, the vote is not really about self-government as much as it is about distinguishing oneself from one's inferiors. However, she wrongly concludes that the vote largely no longer does this work for us, as she wrongly concludes that universal suffrage has been achieved. The practice of voting and the practice of disenfranchisement together continually reproduce the figures of "innocent citizens" who rule over "guilty subjects."

This is a second (and perhaps stranger) result of citizenship-as-standing and its ties to the performative logic of casting a vote. Voting necessarily becomes expressive of far more than one's articulated choice between options on the ballot. First, the fact of voting itself becomes as expression of superiority through innocence as opposed to guilt. Second, the content of one's interest easily becomes an expression of superiority as well. Voting becomes about one's claim of being a progressive ("I'm voting green!"), antiracist ("I'm voting for the black candidate!"), or feminist ("I'm voting for the female candidate!"). There is nothing wrong with such claims in and of themselves, but insofar as voting derives its meaning from the *higher* social standing it confers, these expressions of what would otherwise be private preferences easily become expressions of those preferences as *superior* preferences. Voting (and vote choice) becomes a vessel through which to articulate superior standing, hardly a democratic expression of membership. It is in this way that the vote and voting take on a fetishlike property.[88]

The root of this obscuring of what voting signifies is not that we have misunderstood the vote but rather that we have failed to confront that voting is more than just a system of self-government but is also a practice of self-formation. Shklar's analysis of the meaning of suffrage is a first step to realizing this and critiquing the ideology of white citizenship. In the American context, the vote is deeply intertwined with the pernicious history of racial domination. Shklar's argument is that we should not be so surprised to discover that after having achieved "universal adult suffrage," there still remain so many persons living as second-class citizens. Participation in electoral politics is not sufficient to ensure that everyone is granted equal standing, and so she directs our attention to what she sees as the more pressing concern: the right to earn a living.

But if we are willing to look deeper than Shklar does and pay attention to the continued exclusions that exist in the United States today, we must reckon with the *kind* of social standing that they confer. Voting under the conditions of felon disenfranchisement expresses social standing necessarily within the terms of a criminal justice system historically implicated in the maintenance of white supremacy. That this is the case might be a travesty, but it should be apparent to us if we are attentive to the historical connections and structural similarity between institutions such as slavery and the penitentiary technique. In the American experience, the projects of punishing and of marking citizens are deeply intertwined, and if we are to make normative claims about who should and should not be included in the polity as citizens, it is imperative that we pay attention to these deep connections. The overlap between punishment and citizenship may well be unavoidable, but better that we bring them to the surface, acknowledge them, and be willing to own them than to continue to disavow them, letting the exclusion of criminals continue to do work for us without paying them any mind. We render citizens as worthy by marking them as innocent and independent and render any persons associated with criminality and dependence as unworthy. That felons and persons presumed to be felons before the fact are so easily degraded and disregarded should thus be no surprise. But perhaps the fact that we use arguably the most cherished form of political participation to do such work—ultimately the work of maintaining white supremacy—should shock us.

Across the United States, "eligible" voters go to the ballot box in full knowledge that we have arrived, as Shklar notes, in an era of "universal adult suffrage." And we know this because we know the history of the struggles over the vote and because we can look around ourselves and see other equal citizens casting their votes, persons who are no longer *categorically* denied the vote. We get to take pride in our liberalizing successes, in our achievements. We get to turn to the next great task at hand, as Shklar tells us, and focus on income inequality and the denial of independence for so many people who cannot earn. We get to turn ourselves to the next task, because the work of suffrage is over. And we get to claim the same righteous sense of confidence held by previous generations, who also *knew* with certainty that "universal" suffrage had *finally* been achieved.

The difference between our current blind spot and previous ones is not that the vote has lost its value and has stopped conferring political standing, because it surely continues to do this work, through the exclusion of not just criminals but also children, foreigners, and in thirty-nine states, persons under guardianship or otherwise deemed as mentally incompetent. The difference is that we have, through both an assumed and a performed separation between citizenship and punishment under the terms of American liberalism, found a way to deny that we are doing so. How, specifically, we have found this way is the subject of the next two chapters.

6

Punishing at the Ballot Box

Regarding the elective franchise as of inestimable value, [I] would watch over it and protect it as [I] would virgin chastity.

—DELEGATE JAMES U. DENNIS, 1851[1]

If we follow Judith Shklar's lead and take up the history of suffrage but this time with an eye toward the exclusion of criminals from the franchise, we see *how* this exclusion has figured "American" political membership as normatively white and innocent, linking them closely together. We can trace how the vote and the practice of voting have performed the work of social differentiation and how it continues to do so today. The vote does this work so effectively, especially in a period of de jure color-blindness—in which overtly racist justifications have become publicly untenable—because the vote has been historically linked to punitive discourses that themselves are connected to the production of citizenship as "purified" and the figure of the citizen as "responsible" and "worthy" in racially loaded ways.

This alternate story of suffrage told through the history of criminal disenfranchisement is a story of the production and maintenance of figures of innocence and guilt, of giving the "white citizen" its content through the punishment of moral failure through reduced standing of some members.

Here I follow Angela Davis's insistence that we do more than simply import Foucault's analysis of punishment to the context of the United States but instead conduct a historical and geographically specific analysis of how the practices in question have come into being.[2] I follow both Shklar and Foucault methodologically, turning to the specific history of criminal disenfranchisement in the United States and constructing a genealogy of the practice. If we want to understand the current meaning of disenfranchisement, we must understand its conditions of possibility and place it in the context of the broader struggles over political membership out of which it emerged.

Specifically, this chapter and the next narrow their focus to disenfranchisement provisions in the state of Maryland since the colonial period. I rely on available transcriptions of debates during several constitutional conventions in the state spanning two centuries. As such, it is primarily a discursive history, and I do not present Maryland or its history of disenfranchisement as a general case but rather as an exemplary or paradigmatic one.[3] Maryland serves this purpose nicely because (1) it is one of the original American colonies, (2) it was originally a slave state, (3) it remained in the Union during the Civil War but as a border state was deeply involved in the war and in conflict over manumission and abolition, (4) it has recently been praised for reforming its criminal disenfranchisement provisions during the past decade, and (5) it kept verbatim records of the constitutional conventions in which criminal disenfranchisement was debated at length (1851, 1864, and 1967). These records capture the arguments and political thought of elected delegates who were directly involved self-consciously in the reconstitution of a body politic.

The debates over disenfranchisement in Maryland reflect paradigmatic concerns over suffrage and are ripe for exploring the social and political meaning of the practice as a *discursive and historical object*. My reading of this object, however, does not offer mechanistic causes of disenfranchisement. It is not my goal here to use the Maryland debates as a test of what happened or to identify the specific sources of troubling constitutional practices. I read the debates over criminal disenfranchisement *rhetorically* rather than *definitively*.[4] I take them as expressions of public discourse on the meaning of the interrelated concepts of punishment and proportionality and race—terms that have run throughout this book so far. What we find is documentary evidence of a series of exchanges among the discourses of citizenship and punishment and the fabrication and management of figures of criminality through those exchanges. Reading the debates in this light reveals significant things about the discursive relations among citizenship, criminality, labor, and state authority.

The transcripts of the constitutional convention debates of 1851, 1864, and 1967 weigh in at thousands of pages each, covering a massive array of topics and concerns. Even narrowing my attention to those specific moments when delegates discussed criminal exclusions alone is too unwieldy for the scope of my argument.[5] In this chapter, therefore, I set up the broad sweep of disenfranchisement provisions in Maryland and focus on three claims that set up the key terms of the debates over disenfranchisement.

First, the discourses of punishment and political membership are intimately connected. The delegates at both the 1851 and 1864 conventions explicitly understood disenfranchisement both as a form of punishment, subject to the constraints of proportionality, and as fundamentally related to citizenship. They understood both that such a franchise restriction was expressly punitive in design, driven by the functional "objects" or "purposes" that punishment should have, and that it was necessary under a concept of citizenship requiring a trustworthy moral character. That is, to think about disenfranchisement as *either* punishment *or* citizenship simply did not occur to the delegates, unlike twentieth-century delegates and contemporary accounts of disenfranchisement more generally. The nineteenth-century delegates regarded punishment and membership as deeply related, tied together by the certainty that criminality implied dishonesty and that dishonesty implied an unworthiness to take part in the project of collective self-rule. Felons and infamous criminals required excessive treatment precisely because of the kind of threat they represented to the polity.

Second, this connection between punishment and membership is intimately tied to the politics of race and the production of a dichotomy between "innocent citizens" and "guilty others." While race was not invoked even once during the debates about criminal exclusions (making it simple to dismiss charges that racial animus drove the adoption of disenfranchisement provisions), concern over the "Negro problem" dominated both the 1851 and 1864 conventions before and during the Civil War. More importantly, the specific nature of this problem is expressed in two sets of terms: "free Negroes" are a danger to "free labor" and are explicitly linked to inherent criminal propensity. While the delegates may not have discussed race while debating criminal disenfranchisement provisions, when debating the presence of "free Negroes" in the workforce, they trade almost exclusively in the language of criminal threat. A tight nexus was established between race and criminality (especially through the crime of larceny), ensuring that delegates could exclude not simply blacks from the ballot box but also the idea of blackness carried by degenerate whites or any others who failed to maintain their political and racial membership. That is to say, part of what we see in these transcripts is the simultaneous redefinition of both citizenship and racial caste, mediated by the language of criminality.

Third, criminality and trustworthy character were linked in the minds of the delegates through technical and vernacular understandings of "infamy," "infamous crimes," and "felony." By tracing the debates over what specific classifications of crimes should be included in disenfranchisement, we see how the same features qualified individuals for both punishment and disenfranchisement, marking criminal figures as deceitful and corrupt. The attempt in recent years to link disenfranchisement solely with incarceration and with the commission of a felony as a purely technical distinction of law obscures the fact that felons had historically been (and continue to be) constructed as a criminal kind whose public standing *must* be diminished through voting restrictions. It was only in the latter half of the twentieth century that the punitive justification for disenfranchisement was rejected and discomfort with constitutional exclusions of this sort began to be expressed (albeit in a very limited fashion). But the effect of these two moves, from infamy to felony and from punishing to regulating the franchise, has been to hide the work that "felony" continues to do in expressly punitive and disproportionate terms. "Felony" is purported to be only a technical legal classification of criminal actions, but it carries with it the nineteenth-century distinction between citizens and noncitizens. The modern citizen *continues* to be figured as innocent, but the work of disenfranchisement has been hidden.

In tracing out these claims, an important periodization also emerges between the nineteenth- and twentieth-century understandings of disenfranchisement that figure the felon. These periods map roughly to the two forms of biopolitical governance described earlier in Chapter 3. The delegates in both centuries are eminently concerned with the security and health of the body politic—the life of the population—during times of political and social upheaval, and their language throughout reflects this overarching biopolitical concern. But the nineteenth-century delegates address this concern in largely disciplinary ways, tightly linking together the purposes of punishment, the management of racialized bodies, and the boundaries of suffrage. The twentieth-century delegates did so through a more neoliberal conception of governmentality, operating at the level of the law as a technical and environmental instrument and taking particular zeal in rationalizing and separating the discourses of punishment and membership. As I noted earlier, the ultimate effects of such neoliberal reform has been to produce not only fully responsible citizens but also fully responsible monsters, and recent reforms have left substantive concerns about disenfranchisement unaddressed while also maintaining the nineteenth-century notions of monstrosity and inherent criminality under new terms.

THE BOUNDARIES OF SUFFRAGE IN MARYLAND

Before turning to the debates themselves, it is helpful to begin with a broad overview of the constitutional history of the franchise in Maryland. Not only does this help set the context of my readings of the debates, but it is illustrative of the national trend as well: Maryland's policies track national trends in the various expansions and contractions of suffrage from the colonial period to present day.[6] Despite beginning with very restrictive voter eligibility, the franchise in Maryland was quickly expanded to included white workingmen early in the nineteenth century. In the years leading up to the Civil War, Maryland introduced its first (and most sweeping) criminal disenfranchisement rule, which was solidified and maintained during the Reconstruction era. Attempts at reform were made during the 1960s but with only marginal success. A reform movement that emerged in late 1990s through the first decade of this century has managed to successfully redraw the boundaries of felon disenfranchisement. As of this writing, Maryland now only excludes individuals automatically during incarceration.

During the colonial period, suffrage was limited both by the structure of Maryland's government and by a strict property qualification. Under colonial law, the only disenfranchiseable offense was a third conviction for public drunkenness, an offense that marked a person a "infamous."[7] The first Maryland state constitution, adopted after a long series of revolutionary and "martial" conventions spanning 1774 to 1776, provided little improvement in terms of expanding suffrage beyond a very restricted group of white landowners. It was, even according to official state accounts, "what came later to be recognized as a most undemocratic form of government."[8] Suffrage rights were limited by a stiff property qualification of fifty acres of land or thirty pounds.[9] There was no provision in the 1776 constitution for subsequent conventions, and the governing document underwent massive revision over the next seventy-five years through amendments. In 1801, the franchise was expressly limited to white men,[10] and the property qualifications were eventually removed through amendment by 1810.[11]

None other than Alexis de Tocqueville praised Maryland for this early embrace of "universal" suffrage (enshrining the political rights of only white laborers in the state), protecting the right to vote for "every free white male Citizen of this State above twenty-one years of age" who could establish his residency.[12] Yet, as Lisa Duggan succinctly critiques, relying on whiteness and maleness to establish political rights "is often interpreted as an expansion of democracy, because many propertyless white men were newly enfranchised. But the enactment of white male suffrage also constricted democracy. Some propertied women and free black people were newly disenfranchised by the new legislation."[13] Present from 1776 on, however, was a permanent exclusion from officeholding, though not from voting, of individuals convicted of giving any "bribe, present, or reward, or any promise, or any security for the payment or delivery of any money, or any other thing, to obtain or procure a vote."[14] That is, until 1851, no *categorical* criminal disenfranchisement provision was in effect. Only specific offenses were disenfranchised: repeated public drunkenness during the colonial period and offenses directly related to election fraud during the early years of statehood.

The constitution of 1776 became cumbersome quickly and failed to reflect the rapid demographic and industrial changes taking place in the state by the early part of the nineteenth century.[15] The system of representation designed in the original founding document and modified throughout the years ensured that the General Assembly was controlled by Whigs, primarily farmers from southern parts of the state, along with plantation-based interests along the eastern shore of the Chesapeake Bay. Baltimore City, rapidly growing in size and wealth, was underrepresented in the General Assembly by the mid 1850s.[16] Holding a new constitutional convention was difficult, since the 1776 constitution did not provide any automatic means for calling one. By 1845, after a series of "reform conventions" throughout the state, a statewide campaign was launched, and within five years, a convention was finally called by popular referendum in May 1850. The issue of representation was front and center throughout the debates, underscored by the re-markable *lack* of conversation about slavery. One of the first actions of the convention was to pass an order taking that question off the table.[17]

As noted, the state's first sweeping restrictions on criminal suffrage emerged in the 1851 convention. Three specific groups of offenders were identified. First, modifying the language of the 1776 provision on bribery, Section 2 of Article 1 of the 1851 constitution permanently disenfranchised anyone duly convicted of either offering or receiving any form of bribe, present, reward or promise in exchange for voting or refraining from voting. Second, Section 5 of Article 1 permanently stripped the voting rights of any person "convicted of larceny or other infamous crime, unless he shall be par-doned by the Executive." Third, the same section also held that no persons "under guardianship as a lunatic or as a person *non compos mentis*" would be allowed to vote. It is this basic form of the criminal restriction that has persisted until today, placing criminals in the same company as the mentally infirm (a connection that I take up in detail in the next chapter).

These categories have been remarkably durable. The constitutions of 1864 and 1867 made only minor changes to these two provisions.[18] While the 1864 constitutional convention was notable for abolishing slavery in Maryland, the delegates never even considered extending the franchise to women or nonwhites. The words "male" and "white" both remained in the 1867 con-stitution as well and were not formally removed from the constitution until 1971.[19] As noted in the Annotations to the Maryland Code, it was simply assumed that the Fifteenth and Nineteenth Amendments to the U.S. Con-stitution had removed these restrictions automatically. Maryland did not ratify the Fourteenth Amendment until 1959, and the state rejected both the Fifteenth and Nineteenth Amendments outright in 1870 and 1920, re-spectively. The rejection of the Fifteenth Amendment was overturned three years later, while the Nineteenth Amendment remains formally unratified by the state to this day. This does not mean that the state did not recognize the authority of the amendments. Citing *Neal v. Delaware*, Alfred Niles writes, "The word 'white,' . . . is assumed to have been stricken out *ipso facto* by the adoption of the Fifteenth Amendment to the Federal Constitution. In the Codes of 1888 and Bagby's Code of 1912, the article is printed with-out the word 'white,' which word a 'note' states to have been 'expunged,' or 'omitted' under the Fifteenth Amendment, and in several cases our court has quoted the article as if the word 'white' had never appeared therein."[20] This was still the case as late as the 1960s. In the study documents prepared for delegates at the 1967 convention, the text of the "present constitution" includes the words "white" and "male" with footnotes indicating that they are "now ineffective" in light of the federal Constitution.[21]

The major restriction of the franchise introduced in 1864, however, focused on the coming end of the Civil War. All persons who had served in the "so-called Confederate States of America" or who had given "aid, comfort, countenance or support to those engaged in hostility to the United States" were stripped of the vote. Election judges were empowered to demand that any prospective voter give an oath that he had been loyal to the Union during hostilities. The only substantive alteration to the elective franchise made in the 1867 constitution was to remove this provision, which had effectively disenfranchised most Democrats in the state.[22] Absent this change, the only mechanisms for rights restoration of rebels were either service in the U.S. Army or a two-thirds vote by the General Assembly.[23] As with the question of mental competency, I return to the meaning of the "rebel" exclusions in the next chapter.

Constitutional exclusions for persons convicted of "larceny or other infamous crime, unless pardoned," remained in effect until 1972, when by constitutional amendment, Article I, Section 2, was removed. In its place, on the basis of the recommendations of the 1967 constitutional convention (which produced a constitution but was rejected by popular vote), the General Assembly was empowered to "regulate or prohibit the right to vote of a person convicted of infamous or other serious crime or under care of guardianship for mental disability."[24] Like many other states during this period, Maryland began to remove all restrictions on the franchise from constitutional law and to place them under the election code as part of a broader rationalization of state legal systems.[25] Likewise, under current law, election fraud is no longer a specified punishment in the constitution but is handled in the election code.[26]

Until recently, §3–102 of the Maryland election code permanently disenfranchised any person twice convicted of a felony. In 1999, 2000, and 2001, attempts were made in both houses of the Maryland General Assembly to alter the existing rules on criminal exclusions.[27] None of these bills made it to a full vote in the Assembly. In 2001, HB 495, which originally began as a disenfranchisement reform bill, was redrafted to instead call for a "Task Force to Study Repealing the Disenfranchisement of Convicted Felons in Maryland." While the resulting report made no specific legislative recommendations, it concluded that criminal disenfranchisement seemed to be compatible with federal law, highlighted the racially disproportionate impact of such policies, and noted a high level of administrative difficultly in the practice. Specifically, the report noted that there existed no automatic system for election boards to have accurate and consistent access to criminal records (especially important since permanent disenfranchisement required two convictions for "infamous crimes"). "As a result of the lack of information regarding the felony status of would-be voters," the report concluded, "the quality and integrity of the voter registration rolls may be compromised."[28]

During the 2002 session, new legislation was passed that allowed first-time offenders to apply for restoration at the end of their sentences and two-time nonviolent offenders to apply after a three-year waiting period.[29] The success of the bill was largely the result of grassroots organizing and lobbying efforts, inspired by the fallout of the 2000 presidential election and the highly inaccurate felon lists used in Florida.[30] A second round of reform was attempted in 2005 and 2006 with the aim of dropping the waiting period for two-time felons and the restriction on violent crime. The proposed bills over these years were criticized as partisan attempts by Democrats to expand their electoral base and failed during both the 2005 and 2006 legislative sessions (in large part under the threat of the Republican governor's veto). Finally, in 2007 (and, not incidentally, with a newly elected Democratic governor in office), a reform bill was passed, amending the election code to restrict the suffrage of three groups: (1) persons convicted of a felony and currently serving a sentence of imprisonment, parole, or probation, (2) persons under guardianship for mental disability, and (3) persons convicted of buying or selling votes. This is the current state of the franchise in Maryland, bringing it in line with the majority of states' disenfranchisement statutes.

PROPORTIONAL PUNISHMENT AND MORAL MEMBERSHIP

When the 1851 convention delegates debated introducing a categorical disenfranchisement provision, they did so in the language of punishment. In contrast to the contemporary language used to describe disenfranchisement, which speaks of "collateral" consequences and focuses on the technical definitions of such terms as "felony" and "guardianship," the delegates at the 1851 convention took it for granted that disenfranchisement was justifiable as a form of punishment for a very distinctive criminal quality. In contrast to twentieth-century views of disenfranchisement that presume punishment and membership are distinct spheres, the nineteenth-century convention delegates who drafted Maryland's disenfranchisement provisions simply did not see such a separation. At least with respect to disenfranchisement, the two domains not only overlapped, but there was little to no distinction between them. Disenfranchisement was discussed as a form of punishment explicitly linked to a conception of full citizenship marking the boundary of broader political membership.

One after another, the delegates to the convention cited the "objects" and "purposes" of punishment to bolster and defend their claims about disenfranchisement, insisting that a restriction on suffrage for persons convicted of voter bribery, larceny, and "other infamous crimes" merits disenfranchisement in addition to any punishment imposed by a court.[31] The debate focused almost exclusively on the crime of vote bribery as the exemplary case, and a consensus emerged that criminal disenfranchisement is a fitting and necessary consequence to being convicted of voter bribery, larceny, or infamous crimes.[32]

The limited disagreement between delegates was over whether the period of disenfranchisement should be permanent or limited. On this question, they debated almost entirely within the language of liberal proportionality, despite the obvious fact that disenfranchisement is imposed in addition to the sentence already determined by the court and is thus prima facie disproportionate to the offense. For the delegates, disenfranchisement was subject to the language of proportionality in at least two distinct senses. First, it could be proportionate because the crimes in question are of such severity. This is especially the case for the provision against voter bribery. One delegate insisted that "murder, arson, burglary, [and] theft were venial offences in comparison" to voter bribery.[33] Bribing a voter is, from this perspective, so severe an offense to society that it should be punished with permanent expulsion from the electorate. For at least the case of voter bribery, that is, disenfranchisement was identified as the only fitting punishment available. Second, and more importantly, disenfranchisement was proportionate *to the danger presented by such persons*. Here, we can see the commonality between bribery and "infamous" crimes: they are marked by deceit, fraud, and corruption. Persons who have committed such crimes must be dealt with using extreme punishment, not simply because their offense is so horrible but because they themselves are unfit to take part in elections by virtue of the particular kind of criminal character they possess: deceit.

As I argued in Chapter 4, the logic of liberal proportionality is flexible both in terms of the transgression and the character of the transgressor. And the move from specific criminal actions (bribery and larceny) to character traits (infamy and deceit) is notable in the delegates' application of the idea of proportionality not solely to the relationship between the severity of the crime and the severity of the offense but also to the ratio between the punishment and moral character of the convicted person. At this point, we can see the delegates' conception of moral citizenship appear. To be a citizen in the nineteenth century, that is, to have *independent and equal public standing*, was to be free of this sort of illegality. The discourses of citizenship and punishment were, in this sense, indistinguishable because part of what it *meant* to be a citizen was to be innocent of the moral blemish associated with deceit. While this expressly moral understanding of punishment might be out of step with contemporary understandings, Delegate William D. Merrick, arguing for permanent disenfranchisement for offenders, made this conception clear:

> The great object of punishment was its example upon society—its effect in purifying and elevating the moral tone of that society. All punishments should be so framed as to have the greatest effect upon that moral tone; to preserve it pure, if it could be so, and to punish with a heavy hand all those who would attempt to pollute it.[34]

In the minds of the delegates, it is the offenders' moral failure as persons that demands the "additional" punishment of disenfranchisement. And their moral failure is revealed by their conviction and punishment for a crime of moral turpitude.

Even though there was some disagreement over whether disenfranchisement should be for life, the delegates uniformly agreed that the only fitting punishment for someone who has tried to tamper with the purity of an election was to be barred from voting.[35] In this sense, therefore, the delegates did not misunderstand proportionality or the terms of citizenship, but rather they used disenfranchisement to maintain the purity of the electorate exactly as a proportional punishment. The 1851 obsession over voter bribery most clearly reflected this impulse, and insofar as the debate centered on it, voter bribery was the paradigmatic crime that grounded all other criminal exclusions (i.e., other "infamous" crimes). Voter bribery was considered infamous because it produced "false" or "fraudulent" votes. The harm of this crime is that it diminishes the "truth" of an electoral outcome being reflective of popular sentiment. Ideally, the ballot box is a useful instrument of self-governance only insofar as it conveys the popular will.[36] Thus, the specific "danger" the delegates had in mind, at least if we accept their understanding of the problem of "infamy," is that some persons cannot be trusted at the ballot box. As historians of the franchise have noted, citizenship qualifications during this period were driven by the idea of capability, and one of those crucial capabilities was to be trustworthy.[37] Persons convicted of certain crimes who could be labeled through their guilt as *deceitful* thus demonstrated a lack of capability that was dangerous to the purity of the electorate.

This idea is made clearer in relation to additional categories of exclusion established in 1851. The same provision that excluded larceny and infamous crimes also excluded persons under the age of twenty-one and persons "under guardianship as a lunatic, or as a person *non compos mentis*." These are qualifications based on status that derive their justification expressly from a diminished *ability* to cast an independent vote. Criminals in this period are understood as essentially *incapable* of casting an independent and honest vote.[38] This is a form of criminal subjectivity of the sort Foucault identifies with the delinquent as a person who has some kind of natural affinity with crime rather than simply being guilty. "Men who would deliberately inflict a stab on the purity of the ballot-box," insisted Delegate James U. Dennis, "I would mark with the brand of Cain, and drive them with the lash of scorpions from the pale of free institutions."[39] Disenfranchisement serves as punishment for the moral character flaw exposed by the crime, a punishment deserved by offenders because of some kind of moral defect that they possess and continue to possess even after finishing their sentences.

While the delegates thought of these criminals as a distinct kind of person, there was also a telling hesitancy that emerged when boundaries were erected between full citizens and criminals. Some delegates cautioned about the possibility of being "mistaken" for a criminal. Delegate Levin L. Dirickson argued that the proponents of permanent disenfranchisement for voter bribery had forgotten the

> hustlings and mingling in the exciting scenes that ever, from the very nature of our government, surround the polls. Then under the influence of intense party feeling and in the midst of great strugglings, men with the most unblemished moral character and the most spotless integrity, might almost imperceptibly be hurried into the commission of deeds, which, however improper, could scarcely under all the circumstances, be denominated even by the strictest moralist as highly criminal.[40]

Even the "strictest moralist" runs the risk of being mistakenly seen as a criminal given the chaos of the polls.[41] The delegate was keenly aware that disenfranchisement might confer standing "incorrectly" if it was not carefully designed. Even more alarming was the possibility that the provision could be used to disenfranchise gentlemen farmers/politicians who during the harvest give a portion of their crops to the poor in their counties. Delegate Joseph T. Mitchell stated,

> It was well known that in all the counties there was a large proportion of poor men. Poor men have very large families generally. (Laughter.) It is the practice among those who desire to help this class, and to stand well in their neighborhood, to give out corn about the months of June and July. I know that about that time the corn-houses are thrown open, and as the natural effect is to give them popularity at home, if they should chance to be candidates for office, the people of that neighborhood would usually vote for them. Now, if any malicious individual should lay hold of this circumstance, he might bring these gentlemen into Court, and by a jury picked by political opponents, they might, notwithstanding their known popularity would have elected them, without any such act of liberality, be convicted under this section . . . and be forever disfranchised.[42]

At this point, the delegate said that he could no longer continue to make a speech, as he was "getting frightened here." The source of fear was that at least some of the delegates could *imagine themselves* becoming criminals under the bribery provisions. This fear of being mistakenly or maliciously punished with disenfranchisement is so powerful because it is a punishment associated with a loss of political standing, with a loss of citizenship. Perhaps most tellingly, one delegate noted that disenfranchisement itself refigured the individual as a person fundamentally outside the polity. To bar a person from the ballot box for life, Delegate Robert J. Brent argued, would be to "render it impossible for reformation to restore him to his forfeited rights as a freeman. . . . It makes him an unforgivable offender."[43] This connection between the franchise and public standing, made painstakingly clear by Shklar, drives the entire the nineteenth-century debate over the disenfranchisement of criminals. This connection is the starting point for Maryland's disenfranchisement provisions: an implicit understanding that it is a punishment that marks unqualified persons and therefore can manage a key boundary between citizens and noncitizens. The precise location of that boundary was all that was in question.

Because the nineteenth-century delegates simply did not distinguish between the domains of citizenship and punishment, they saw disenfranchisement as being perfectly in proportion to the "crime" of being unfit for citizenship. What seems so odd to us about this use of the conception of proportionality is that it seems to defy proportionality's modern meaning by endorsing a disproportionately extreme punishment, a punishment "in addition to" the one handed down by a criminal court. But this is only because it is easy to forget that to the nineteenth-century delegates, disenfranchisement was less a punishment for the harm done by an infamous crime than punishment for the fact of infamy, deceit, and moral turpitude of the offender. Since individuals either are or are not marked by such infamy, they either do or do not have equal standing; the proportional response *is* to be excessive. Liberal proportionality, in this context, yields only all-or-nothing outcomes.

THE "PROBLEM OF THE FREE NEGRO"

Nowhere in either the 1851 or 1864 debates on criminal disenfranchisement is there any explicit mention to either race or slavery.[44] Some historians of disenfranchisement have concluded on this basis that it is impossible to prove that racial animus played a part in the adoption of most criminal disenfranchisement provisions across the United States. For instance, John Dinan's comparative study of state convention debates found only one instance in which a delegate made an explicit connection between criminal disenfranchisement and racial discrimination or animus, and this was in the state of Alabama.[45] While Dinan is careful to note that this finding cannot disprove the claim that racial animus drove disenfranchisement provisions, he argues, given the frequency with which delegates were willing to speak in openly racist terms elsewhere in the debates, that it cannot be concluded that racialized politics played a decisive role in the formation of criminal exclusions. He writes, "The absence of racially discriminatory comments regarding *criminal* disenfranchisement provisions in the extant convention debates in states other than Alabama is not without significance."[46] Criminal exclusions, at least during this period, were produced as racially neutral, as "color-blind."

While Dinan notes that there are limits to his study, he speculates that racial animus is more likely to have taken advantage of existing provisions from the antebellum period by adding disqualifying offenses "assumed to be more associated with African Americans" during Reconstruction and the following decades.[47] This was most certainly the case, especially in southern states, where legislators routinely reclassified many forms of petty theft as disenfranchiseable larcenies and felonies. As historian Pippa Holloway has shown, in the Reconstruction-era South, a great deal of legislative attention turned to the issue of "livestock theft."[48] Holloway's careful study demonstrates how seemingly "color-blind" provisions can easily be abused by people with racial animus, but more importantly, it helps us to recast the way we ask the question about how race functions. In her analysis, the ability of the figure of the "chicken thief" to motivate legislative action was predicated on the social and racial meaning of criminality and citizenship in the South. As Holloway notes, the debates between southern Republicans and Democrats over the voting rights of convicted "chicken-stealers" was in truth a debate over African Americans' qualifications for citizenship. On the one hand, Holloway argues, Democrats could point to the crime as an instance of African Americans' innate criminality and inability to control themselves. Republicans, on the other hand, could rationalize chicken theft as a crime of desperation and, in fact, a marker of qualification for full citizenship, in that the crime itself was a way to provide for a family, a traditional masculine bourgeois value distorted by poverty.[49] In either case, however, two things were clear: first, a general acceptance by both supporters and opponents of disenfranchisement that African Americans were inclined (either by nature or circumstance) to theft and, second, that criminality and citizenship were indelibly linked.

In the case of Maryland, we can account for the absence of expressly racially motivated arguments for or against disenfranchisement in the 1851 or the 1864 conventions in several ways. First, the question of restricting black suffrage through criminal exclusions was largely unnecessary because other provisions excluded those persons. Suffrage was explicitly restricted to white men in the Maryland constitution until the passage of the Fifteenth Amendment. Second, and more importantly, because Dinan's study focuses *only* on the portions of debates where disenfranchisement was the question at hand, he fails to note the way in which blacks were routinely constructed as *inherently criminal* throughout the broader debates. Much like Shklar before him, Dinan seems to assume that race is a static variable rather than a socially produced attribute, negotiated in multiple discourses at once. Beyond the disenfranchisement discussion, the debates persistently figured "free Negroes" in terms of crime and deviance while whites were figured as productive laborers and the exclusive victims of black crime. The delegates at both the 1851 and 1864 conventions were thus overwhelmingly anxious about the increasing numbers of "free Negroes" as a result of manumission.

In the years leading up to the 1851 convention, Maryland saw a notable rise in the number of free blacks due to high rates of manumission. The resulting geographical splits drove questions of representation in the state legislature that were directly tied to geographical distribution of slaves (in the state's southern region and the eastern shore) and free blacks (in the state's western region, along the Pennsylvania border, and most importantly, in Baltimore and along the western shore).[50] This meant that a large group of free blacks would count toward representation but not have political franchise, potentially giving white Baltimore a far greater share of representation. Insofar as the 1851 convention was a response to the increasingly unbalanced system of representation in the state, the presence of free blacks (and their concentration in Baltimore and neighboring Washington, D.C.) was of particular concern to the Whigs in power in the legislature at the time.[51] Attempts had already been made during the 1830s to enable (and possibly force) the migration of free blacks out of the state, and the State Colonization Society was established by the legislature "to employ the funds collected in Maryland for the removal of the free negro population."[52] Throughout the 1850s and early 1860s, the General Assembly passed numerous bills regulating both slaves and "free Negroes," including restricting them from assembling for religious purposes and owning dogs or guns, prohibiting their education, restricting their physical movement and their job prospects, and ordering, finally, a census of all "free Negroes in this State."[53] By 1860, there were more free blacks in Maryland than in any other state in the Union, largely by virtue of manumission.[54]

Both the 1851 and 1864 conventions were conducted against the backdrop of the slavery question, but they moved in opposite directions. In 1851, the demographic shift of the state's population toward industrial Baltimore (where slave labor was not economically viable) pitted the agricultural and more culturally southern Whigs against underrepresented Democrats on the western shore, and the issue was taken off the table. There would be no attempt made during the convention to end "the relation of Master and Slave."[55] But by 1864, following a Unionist takeover of the General Assembly in the 1863 elections, the emancipation of slaves was settled relatively early. Passed through a strict party-line vote, Article 24 of the Declaration of Rights of 1864 categorically prohibited slavery in the state. But even though the prohibition of slavery was passed early in the first months of the convention and its passage was a foregone conclusion by virtue of the 1863 elections, it was nevertheless deeply contentions. As Charles Wagandt notes, "The decision on this clause was predetermined and the subject thoroughly exhausted, but the delegates would not let it pass without unleashing a verbal torrent. It was like a theatrical performance. All the players knew the outcome of the drama but eagerly awaited their turn on the stage."[56] The debate over Article 24 lasted for six days and had no set agenda. Its topics ranged widely and were generally unfocused, driven by long-winded speeches by delegates on slavery's morality, its legality in both British common law and U.S. constitutional traditions, its consistency with biblical teachings, and its economic and social effects, but most frequently, the question arose of monetary compensation for former slaveholders. This last question, on monetary compensation, was the most fraught. Ultimately, any form of compensation from the state was expressly prohibited, and the General Assembly was banned from providing for any such compensation in the future. This was in part a compromise to ensure that the slaveholders would be eligible for federal compensation if made available. Federal compensation never occurred, and three years later, the 1867 constitution included an exhortation to the federal government to compensate former slaveholders.[57]

But the question of "free Negroes" persisted. Nowhere in the debate throughout any of the three conventions in 1851, 1864, or 1867 was there any consideration of extending the franchise to black men. In 1851, the central question was to find a way to ensure that "Negroes" could be removed from the state, while ensuring that free whites would not likewise be removed. While the convention never explicitly took up the question of forced migration, the delegates took great care to ensure that Article 21 of the Declaration of Rights, which prohibited imprisonment, forfeiture, and exile without due process, would not "prevent the Legislature from passing all such laws for the government, regulation and disposition of the free colored population of the State as they may deem necessary."[58] The delegates went out of their way to be sure that the mass deportation of blacks out of the state was still possible, with persistent reference to the danger represented by blacks in their midst and the unnaturalness of the two races mixing together.[59]

Even those who seemed to be in favor of tempering the debate by insisting that blacks would have the protection of law while they remained in the state still insisted that such protection would be revoked should they fail to "conduct themselves peaceably."[60] Without legal protections afforded to "free Negroes," some delegates argued, the power of the law would not be able to constrain them, and they would surely reveal their innate criminal natures. "While they [free blacks] remain," argued Delegate Charles J. M. Gwinn, "let there be no inference even that their labor and property are placed without the shelter of law. For, although their physical power in the State is beneath apprehension, yet, as a class, if outlawed by our statutes, they would become a source of perpetual mischief; crowding our prisons with petty offenders, who seek their daily bread by thefts and violence."[61] The rationale for providing any legal protection was entirely based on self-preservation, rather than any recognition of equality between the races. "Free negroes" quite simply represented a tangible physical and moral danger to the white population. "We should at all times guard against the torch of the incendiary being applied to the magazine," argued Delegate Brent, "and here was a class of people, which at the some time, might become a moral magazine, fraught with our destruction."[62]

Over the next fifteen years, the end of slavery approached, and the "problem of free Negroes" became more pressing on delegates as a "reality." Confronting this "problem" required a way of "thinking" about the previously "unthinkable" category of such persons. That is, even if the *fact* of slavery was eroding in the years leading up to the war, the *category* of slave was still capable of doing an immense amount of discursive work in delimiting citizens from noncitizens. Both the fact and the category of "free Negroes" troubled this distinction, however, as they were neither slaves nor full members of the polity. If the project of removing them physically from the state failed (as it would), the delegates could turn to this second strategy: figuring them as criminals and associating them with categories of disqualification such as lunacy and idiocy. The ambiguous identity of "free Negroes" could be stabilized by figuring them as criminals, and in the Maryland debates, delegates specifically figured them as the kind of criminals that merit exclusion under criminal disenfranchisement provisions: as thieves and frauds. "Free Negroes" at best have an affinity with crime and at worst are, in and of themselves, purely criminal beings. They were posited as a source of danger in physical terms and also as a specific location of anxiety about criminal behavior.

REFORM AND LIBERALIZATION OF DISENFRANCHISEMENT
IN CONTEMPORARY MARYLAND

If the overt story of the nineteenth century is about maintaining the premises and goals of white supremacy while changing the tactics and strategies
through which it was maintained, the story of the late twentieth century is
importantly different. The long arc of political realignment, multiple international wars, and the varied phases of civil rights expansions and contractions would all lead us to generally expect the end of white supremacist
ideology as well as practice. As noted in Chapter 1, scholars of felon disenfranchisement have described the period beginning in the late 1960s as one
of "reform," gradually removing *lifetime* voting bans.[63] Nevertheless, even
as "ex-felon" disenfranchisement has disappeared from many states, there
has been an overall expansion of disenfranchisement for *currently* incarcerated persons as well as an overall explosion of incarceration rates across the
nation. The era of mass incarceration also has seen the solidification of the
principle of voting rights exclusion even if these exclusions have become
arguably less draconian. During the "reform" period, more people have become subject to collateral consequences and have had their voting rights
restricted.

These trends should not be surprising. What we saw during the twentieth
century was the reconfiguration of the understandings of penality and political membership that characterized the nineteenth century, yet the underlying relationship between punishment and political membership remained.
These reconfigurations are visible on multiple registers including public
policy, micro-level practices of policing, punishment, and constitutional
legal transformations. Throughout these transformations, we can track an
increasing concern that the domains of punishment and membership—so
intimately linked in the minds of nineteenth-century lawmakers—must be
held apart and at least articulated separately, even if they continue to work
in concert. Such a legal separation, especially important in the late twentieth
century, is in keeping with the neoliberalization of penality and criminal
subjectivity itself. The work of discursive subject formation at the boundaries between discourses of punishment and membership has not ceased in
the past century or in the contemporary moment. It has, however, changed
its tactics. Since the 1960s, we can observe a series of legal shifts in *how* disenfranchisement functions but largely not in whom it affects.

Following the adoption of the 1867 constitution, Maryland's criminal disenfranchisement provisions remained untouched for the next century. No specific alterations were made to the boundaries of the elective franchise in the state except for those imposed by federal authority. Over the past half century, however, we can track multiple discursive shifts that correspond to the national trend in disenfranchisement reform during these periods. First, in the late 1960s and early 1970s, the punishment/citizenship discourse was self-consciously split into distinct spheres by moving disenfranchisement provisions out of the constitution and into the election code. Second, during the past decade, the language of "infamous crimes" has been replaced with "felony conviction" as the basis for disenfranchisement. These discursive shifts reflect the rationalization and reform of disenfranchisement, but they achieve their ends by moving the work of differentiation between innocent citizens and guilty felons into other parts of law, into the legal shadows. Today, Maryland (like nearly every other state) continues to disenfranchise currently incarcerated felons in order to maintain citizenship through a display of innocence, relying on the punitive system to do this work. But it does so in the face of an active attempt to disavow the relationship between the discourses of punishment and membership.

That is, the story of disenfranchisement "reform" and "liberalization" also reflects a moment of shoring up the figuration of the white citizen through a rationalization of law and an administrative split between criminal and electoral law. The ultimate effect of these changes has been not to undo racialized or ableist conceptions of citizenship but rather to mask the continuing work of social and political differentiation performed by disenfranchisement: the maintenance of the ideal citizen as white, male, innocent, worthy, and mentally independent. While current suffrage restrictions might follow models of liberal and neoliberal universality (i.e., they are seemingly "gender-blind" and "color-blind"), such universalism is purchased expressly through the maintenance of an ideal citizen that continues to support masculinist, ableist, and white supremacist *norms* of work and labor. They insist on a legal system that is regulatory and environmental rather than focused on disciplinary logic. There is something decidedly liberal (rather than neoliberal) about the impulse to separate the domains of law and to insist that different parts of law operate on different aspects of human behavior. As is shown in the next section, the thought that drove the delegates in 1967 to insist on such a separation was driven by a lingering commitment to the rehabilitative ideal and nineteenth-century penological thinking. By the late 1990s and early 2000s, however, the transition to neoliberalism appeared largely complete, with legislators increasingly focused on a notion of disenfranchisement as a purely regulatory and technical policy.

FROM CONSTITUTIONAL TO ELECTORAL LAW

While the nineteenth-century convention delegates expressly understood disenfranchisement as a practice that reflected the mutual requirements of punishment and citizenship, the delegates to the 1967 constitutional convention refused such a discursive overlap. The draft constitution they produced removed the disenfranchisement provisions from the constitution itself. The delegates argued that disenfranchisement was acceptable only so long as it was *not* employed as a form of punishment. Delegate Addie J. Key introduced the committee report proposing that the criminal disenfranchisement provision be removed from the constitution and replaced it with a provision authorizing (and possibly requiring) the General Assembly to handle these restrictions in the election code. Key began by noting that the current Committee on Suffrage and Elections emphatically disagreed with the justification for disenfranchisement given by delegates at previous conventions:

> A look at the previous Constitutional Convention records clearly shows that the reason for such an item, appearing in the 1867 Constitution, as we know it, was to punish. It was stated by delegates then, during that Constitutional Convention, that people who commit crimes ought not have the right of good citizens, and this was the basis for including this article in our present Constitution. Now, our Committee on Suffrage and Elections admits that it does not feel the same as the 1867 Constitutional Convention delegates, *and would not like to punish twice those who commit serious crimes, would not like to punish forever people who do get involved in these misfortunes,* but they would continue this same kind of article. . . . Because of the changes going on in our society away from punishment to rehabilitation, the Committee admits . . . that if at some time in the future the penal institutions of the State became truly institutions for rehabilitation, that it might be desirable to restore the right to vote simultaneously with release from an institution. They admit that they believe that the legislature ought to be free to determine when that situation has arrived.[64]

This final clause became the central question for the 1967 delegates: empowering the legislature with the authority to handle criminal disenfranchisement. Even those who spoke out against any restriction framed the question largely as disenfranchisement's incompatibility with constitutional law but not necessarily its incompatibility with the law per se. Delegate Lloyd Taylor made a clear argument against disenfranchisement, noting that "a person who has been convicted and once served his term, should have all his civil rights restored," but then immediately followed by noting that "this is not a constitutional matter."[65] Even the few delegates opposed to criminal disenfranchisement entirely prioritized the removal of the restriction from the constitution itself as at least a partial solution.[66]

While the constitution drafted in 1967 was ultimately rejected by a statewide popular vote (although the provision removing the power to disenfranchise persons convicted of "serious crimes" was adopted by amendment to the existing constitution in 1972), the debate over the proper location of such a provision is nevertheless illustrative of the broader interest in splitting the discourses of punishment and citizenship. From the point of view of the 1967 delegates, the problem posed by the disenfranchisement provisions drafted in the nineteenth-century constitution was twofold: it inflicted disenfranchisement explicitly as a form of punishment and was excessive—that is, it was a form of "double punishment"—but more importantly, the imposition of punishment had no place within a constitutional document, which should be focused on providing a general framework for government. The solution they proposed to these problems was to move the provision to another body of law. That is, they identify the substantive problem of "double punishment" and the attendant "mistakes" of the previous century's delegates as a failure to distinguish between conceptual categories of law.

Disenfranchisement *as a part of constitutional law* reflected what became an unacceptable blurring of the demands, functions, and purposes of punishment and the boundaries of membership. Disenfranchisement, the delegates argued, was unacceptable as a form of punishment *precisely* because it was excessive, a form of "double punishment." The constitutional provision adopted in 1972 only authorized the General Assembly to enact restrictions based on a conviction for "infamous and serious" crimes. Criminal disenfranchisement was thus rendered, with respect to the law, as only a restriction on voting eligibility, a technical qualification for voting, determined by the power vested in the General Assembly to set voter qualifications.

The "success" of this move was to alter the terms on which disenfranchisement could be understood. It is a *discursive* success, operating on the level of meaning and understanding through a reliance on technical classifications. When legislative agitation to reform disenfranchisement policy began to emerge during the late 1990s and early 2000s, there was very little talk about disenfranchisement as a disproportionate punishment. Officially, it could no longer be regarded as punishment, in no small part because it had only a technical, rather than substantive, connection to criminal guilt. A 2002 report issued by the Maryland Office of Policy Analysis identifies four areas of concern regarding disenfranchisement provisions: (1) the disproportionate impact on African American men, (2) whether the provisions violate the Voting Rights Act of 1965, (3) whether felons should be excluded because they have "breached their 'social contract' with society," and (4) whether administrative difficulties might lead to inconsistent enforcement.[67] No mention was made in the report of disenfranchisement as a form of punishment, but the concern over inconsistent enforcement could be read as a concern over proportionality (i.e., like offenders should be treated in a like manner). The discussion over the "social contract" is remarkably brief, taking no explicit stance on whether felons have, in fact, breached such a contract or how exactly they might have done so, but it nevertheless quotes Locke's *Second Treatise*. The report focuses most of its attention on the impact of disenfranchisement on African American men. Despite this attention, nothing in the reforms that were to follow directly addressed the racial demographics of the disenfranchised population.

Each of the four areas of concern identified in the 2002 report fixates on the problem of disenfranchisement as purely a question of civil rights restrictions. Concern over its punitive character has dramatically diminished. The question of disenfranchisement, from the official point of view, is not at all a penological or criminological question, something the nineteenth-century delegates took for granted. When progressive reform finally passed in 2007, it was entirely in the terms of reform of voter qualifications. The 2007 bill was titled the "Voter Registration Protection Act" and had a stated purpose of "generally relating to voter registration eligibility requirements for individuals convicted of certain crimes."[68]

This is perhaps a positive movement, recognition that disenfranchisement fails any penological justification and that the delegates of the nineteenth-century conventions were emphatically wrong to support the practice on such terms. Yet Maryland—like all but two other states—continues to exclude currently incarcerated felons from the polls. The alterations of the election code made during the past decade certainly represent reform of disenfranchisement, but within a strictly limited set of terms. The "success" at hand is primarily the legal separation of the discourses of punishment and citizenship. It reflects an official denial that disenfranchisement sits at the intersection between punishment and citizenship, yet its punitive character remains, despite this separation in law. It is a successful move to alter the terms of the debate such that the overlap between punishment and citizenship becomes harder to see, an overlap that the nineteenth-century delegates had little problem seeing. Disenfranchisement was *both* a punishment and a regulation of the franchise, because citizenship was at least in part about being *innocent*, of being free from *infamy*.

FROM "INFAMY" TO "FELONY"

This second discursive shift is performed through the recent removal of the phrase "infamous crimes" from Maryland's disenfranchisement provision. The goal of this shift was expressly to strike what was taken to be a vague, confusing, and archaic term and to rely on a more precise technical distinction. It is true that as long as the term "infamous crimes" was used, there was confusion surrounding just what crimes fell under this classification. But the reason why "infamous crimes" were ground for exclusion can be seen in the nineteenth-century convention debates.

During both the 1851 and 1864 debates, delegates were concerned that broad categories of "infamous crimes" were too vague and that the "wrong kind" of crimes might be accidentally included or excluded from disenfranchisement. The crimes originally subject to disenfranchisement in the nineteenth century were those that signified a lack of truthfulness, reflecting beyond the character of the crime itself to the character of the criminal. What was in dispute during the nineteenth-century debates was not whether this was the wrong category of crime to target but the meaning of those terms. The concept of infamy as disenfranchiseable was deployed without question. Only what *counted* as infamy was subject to debate.

In 1851, Delegate George W. Weems expressed his own confusion with the term: "Now, he might consider it infamous, if a gentlemen were to spit in his face. And if he were to knock down the person who committed the outrage, that might be considered as infamous in him. He wanted something more definite in the phraseology, such as perjury, felon, &c."[69] Delegates responded that there was a precise definition in the legal scholarship that specifies the character of infamous crimes.[70] What defines an infamous crime is *not* that it leads to punishment in the penitentiary but that it is a crime characterized by deceit or fraud and that its history is linked to restrictions on who could give evidence in court. Delegate Benjamin C. Presstman explained that the term

> exists in the law books with a technical meaning, including treason, felony and all offences which come within the "*crimen falsi*" of the Roman Law. To avoid uncertainty, the committee had designated some offences by name, and then added the word "infamous" to cover the rest. Because the courts may commit errors, was not a sufficient reason for changing the language of the books.[71]

The confusion over which crimes would count as infamous and which would not reflects less a concern over the distinction the term attempts to draw between honest and deceitful persons and more a concern over what specific acts would indicate this character. In order to clear up this confusion, Delegate Albert Constable, who "objected to the phrase *infamous crimes*, because its meaning was uncertain," proposed that a more precise term be used to designate those crimes noxious to the demands of honest citizenship: felony.[72]

But finding a precise way to identify individuals who should carry this mark still vexed the delegates in the next convention in 1864. Delegate Richard H. Edelen (himself a strong proponent of disenfranchisement) also sought to move away from the language of infamy and to employ a more technical distinction: that disenfranchisement would follow any crime whose penalty included "confinement in the penitentiary."[73] For his definition, Edelen also turned to legal texts because, he said, "I am at a loss to understand the definition . . . of infamous crimes."[74] It is worth looking at the quotation in full:

> *Infamy*, in a general sense, is the condition of a person who is regarded with contempt and disapprobation by the generality of men on account of his vices. But in a legal sense, it is the state of one who has been lawfully convicted of a crime, followed by a judgment, by which he has lost his honor. The crimes which render a person infamous are, first, treason; second, felony; third, frauds; which come within the section of *crimen falsi* of the Roman law, as perjury and forgery, piracy, swindling and cheating,

barratry, and bribing a witness to keep away. The consequences of infamy, are the loss of political rights, and incapacity to testify as a witness. [75]

This conception of infamy focused squarely on the character of the *person* revealed through the crime. Even such a "precise" definition, however, was repeatedly referred to by the delegates as "vague and indeterminate," and they expressed a fear that the legislation would "have made and constituted [the] judges of election the judges of the term 'infamous crime.'"[76] Again, the delegates had no dispute over the notion that infamous crimes should be excluded; they were solely concerned with how this distinction could be defined and enforced. And while the stability of such a determination was in question, the use of what now seems like an archaic term reflects a better understanding during that period than we have today about the *kind* of exclusion being sought. It is less puzzling on this account that criminal disenfranchisement provisions were found (and continue to be found) alongside the disenfranchisement of persons under guardianship for insanity and lunacy. Taken together, both the insane and the criminal are *unfit* and *incapable* of participation in the same way that an unqualified person is barred from the vote. The question is whether one can determine a truly reformed character in the same way that one had previously determined an infamous character. As Delegate George W. Sands suggested, a person seeking restoration to the voter rolls should be required to "produce to the judges of the election . . . a certificate signed by six or more lawful voters, that since his discharge from the penitentiary, he has demeaned himself as a sober, honest, and law-abiding citizen."[77]

Delegate Samuel H. Berry, in direct response to this amendment, joked, "I would suggest to the gentleman to strike out the word 'sober.' It would be very unpopular in his section of the State."[78] The powerful connection between "sobriety" and voting rights has persisted. As reported on the front page of the *New York Times* in 2004, part of the state of Florida's rights restoration process required an audience before then-governor Jeb Bush, whose questioning of former convicts had virtually no boundaries:

> Gov. Jeb Bush looked out over a roomful of felons appealing to him for something they had lost, and tried to reassure them. "Don't be nervous; we're not mean people," the governor said as some fidgeted, prayed, hushed children or polished their handwritten statements. "You can just speak from the heart." And they did: convicted robbers, drunken drivers, drug traffickers and others, all finished with their sentences, standing up one by one in a basement room at the State Capitol and asking

Mr. Bush to restore their civil rights. Their files before him, Mr. Bush asked one man about his drinking, another about his temper, and so on. . . . "How's the anger situation going?" Mr. Bush asked one man after leafing through his file. . . . "You've stayed clean?" the governor asked another.[79]

The lingering concern over the vagueness of "infamous crimes" has long troubled the courts. In *State v. Bixler* (1884), the Maryland Court of Appeals ruled that perjury (although not a felony) was an infamous crime and thus subject to disenfranchisement. The opinion stated, "An 'infamous crime' is such crime as involved moral turpitude, or such as rendered the offender incompetent as a witness in Court, upon the theory that a person would not commit so heinous a crime unless he was so depraved as to be unworthy of credit."[80] Explaining the meaning of this distinction, the court expounds,

> The constitution in providing for exclusion from suffrage of persons
> whose character was too bad to be permitted to vote, could only have
> intended, by the language used, such crimes as were "infamous" at com-
> mon law, and are described as such in common law authorities. In the
> interest of citizenship and its incidental rights, the Constitution must be
> understood as confining the exclusion from suffrage, to such cases as fall
> under the common law understanding of the term, and not to include
> any offences of lower grade. Larceny is mentioned, and then follow the
> words "other *infamous* crime." It must be a *felony*, which larceny is, or
> that which is *infamous* though it be not a felony.[81]

All felonies are considered infamous crimes, but not all infamous crimes are felonies.[82] "Whether a crime is or is not punishable by confinement in the penitentiary," writes Niles in his 1915 commentary on the Maryland constitution, "is not a test of whether it is infamous. The test is, is it a felony, or a misdemeanor classified as infamous by common law authorities?"[83]

By the 1967 debates, the concern over the designation of infamy had not disappeared but rather had intensified. In those deliberations, Delegate Key reported that the variable and often changing designations of criminal classifications produced confusion and difficulty in enforcing the provisions equitably: "Repeatedly the state's attorneys have come to Annapolis as the people in the General Assembly know, to change different crimes from misdemeanors to felonies which further disenfranchise citizens who perhaps the day before the passage of a new bill permitting a crime to become a felony would have been permitted to vote."[84]

The delegates in 1967 seemed to have the same basic difficulty as their predecessors a century earlier: there existed no easily discernible way to know which crimes would trigger disenfranchisement and which would not. In reference to the proposed addition of the term "serious" to the disenfranchisement authorization given to the General Assembly, the following exchange is reported in the debates:

> Delegate (John R.) Hargrove: Could your Committee determine what a serious crime was? I do not think the courts have been able to do that.
>
> Delegate (Helen L.) Koss: Delegate Hargrove, if the courts have not, neither have we.[85]

Nevertheless, when the General Assembly amended the constitution in 1972, it followed the failed convention's recommended language and added "serious crimes" to "infamous crimes" and "felonies" as eligible for disenfranchisement. Interestingly, Delegate Taylor, insisting that the provision relies on an archaic definition of crime, points not to the term "infamous" but rather to "felony":

> I want to read from a text book on state government: "A felony at common law has been defined as 'any crime which occasioned a forfeiture of land and goods, and to which might be superadded capital or other punishment.' Forfeiture of lands and goods as a punishment for crime has been abolished in England and the United States so that the term no longer has its original meaning." So we have provided in this present draft of ours a concept that is outmoded and obsolete.[86]

The delegate was correct to note that "felony" is a term whose meaning has changed over time but completely missed that a central aspect of its meaning during the time that disenfranchisement provisions were enacted is that it signifies a moral failing that is *punished* by disenfranchisement. That is, as even a cursory reading of the nineteenth-century debates shows, the delegates saw disenfranchisement *as a form a punishment* that could correct the soul of the person. Not surprisingly, confusion over which specific offenses are "infamous crimes" persisted. The Maryland attorney general's office issued several clarification letters in 1973 that are referenced in a lengthy footnote in *Thiess v. State Administrative Board of Election Laws*.[87] In *Thiess*, the U.S. District Court for Maryland argued that the plaintiffs (a group of disenfranchised felons) could not support their claim that the phrase "infamous" was constitutionally vague, because it was possible to obtain a "laundry list" of infamous crimes from the attorney general so easily.[88]

The solution to all this confusion, introduced in the 2007 reforms, was to drop the terms "infamous and serious crimes" altogether from the disenfranchisement statute. As of this writing, disenfranchisement in Maryland occurs upon (1) a person's conviction of a felony and (2) while a person is currently serving a court-ordered sentence of imprisonment, probation, or parole.[89] The most recent reform in Maryland has only displaced the determination of which crimes trigger disenfranchisement from the election code to the sentencing judge. In trying to make disenfranchisement truly collateral, the reform has, in effect, only made disenfranchisement more directly an integral part of a punitive sentence of incarceration.

The move from "infamy" to "felony" is a discursive shift that reflects the transformation of criminological discourse from the nineteenth to the early twenty-first century. The nineteenth-century discourse, struggling with the rehabilitative ideal and the deep criminal subjectivity captured in categories such as delinquency, understood disenfranchisement in far more complex ways than it is today. This language crossed over neatly to the justifications for disenfranchisement on the basis of the qualifications of a citizen as a trustworthy and honest individual. Hence, it relied on "infamy" and an understanding of "felony" as indicative of moral character: persons who have demonstrated their affinity with falsity, deceit, and corruption and are assumed to be false, deceitful, and corrupt persons. But the use of the term "felony" continues to do the same work that "infamy" did previously: it identifies a source of the threat to the ballot box in the character of the criminal as deceitful and untrustworthy.

While the debates and confusion surrounding "infamy" were, at times, messy and contradictory, they were at least forthright in acknowledging what they were about: marking the boundaries of citizenship through punishment and punishing persons for not being worthy citizens. This is still what disenfranchisement does today, but it is displaced and hidden from view through separating the penal law from election law and disavowing the moral-differentiation work inherited by the classification of felony. The reforms of disenfranchisement provisions have only altered the *way* in which they operate. They have not altered the public standing conferred or the construction of the citizen as necessarily innocent.

Another way to put the question is to ask, why is it that the current Maryland election code refers to felonies when it establishes disenfranchisement? The term "felony" is historically and discursively indebted to the distinction between members and nonmembers. What infamy did then, felony does now: it distinguishes between the honest and the deceitful, between the innocent and the guilty. It carries with it the work of social and political differentiation. It marks the boundary between citizens and noncitizens, between full members and those whose membership is always in question. The nineteenth-century debates about what should and should not be considered infamous crimes, those reflecting moral turpitude, were messy debates. Yet, in at least one perverse way, they were preferable to the current state of affairs that hides both the messiness and the exercise of power. That is, the Maryland disenfranchisement provision continues to use the word "felony" because the exclusion of felons continues to be about drawing a distinction between those who are capable of being citizens and those who are not.

We continue to sort citizens according to their moral character, but we do it more quietly, through a decentralized system of criminal and civil law that supports rather than undermines a racial caste system. As such, it functions in a way similar to what Charles Mills calls "racial opacity," the "principled anti-transparency on matters related to race, the occultation and blocking from 'sunshine laws' of the racial 'partitioning' and 'secret reservations' of the 'first principles' on which the polity has actually been founded."[90] The reworking of these terms not only leaves the nineteenth-century thinking about moral and immoral subjects in place, but it does so while assuring that the racialized character of that thinking is more difficult to see, placing it under an epistemological block.

In the contemporary period, the seemingly technical term of "felony" does its work in the dark. The term draws a distinction between members and nonmembers without admitting to how it draws it, and worse, it claims to be a purely technical distinction between crimes that involve incarceration and those that do not. Yet, during the same period that Maryland has seemingly led the way as a reformer of criminal disenfranchisement, more than 70 percent of Maryland's current inmates are African American.[91] The reforms do not resolve the tension between citizenship and punishment because they are not meant to do so.

7

Civic Disabilities

This book has attempted to track a series of interrelated conceptual claims to help us understand the practice of felon disenfranchisement. First, punishment and political membership are deeply related discourses and have been throughout the history of the United States and in its broadly liberal tradition. Second, criminal disenfranchisement is a practice that sits at the intersection of these discourses, straddling them productively. Third, one of these "products" is the figure of the felon, who comes into being as a criminological figure to manage these discourses through a seemingly excessive and disproportionate punishment. Lastly, it is through attention to this figure and this practice that we can see how the American citizen *continues* to be figured as white, male, able, and innocent through the use of disenfranchisement.

This chapter turns to this last claim in particular, with an emphasis on how disenfranchisement's social and political *meaning* is mutually implicated in the production of racialized subjectivity. As I identified in the preceding chapter, the nineteenth-century convention delegates in Maryland sought to punish (and to thus produce) a specific moral character through disenfranchisement, and their conception of criminality itself was deeply tied to a pervasive set of assumptions about the racial character of criminality. This racial character, however, was in flux throughout this period, as it continues to be. As also noted, the provision that disenfranchised some criminals in the nineteenth century also included the disenfranchisement of persons *non compos mentis*, persons without the use of reason.

This link between mental disability and criminal disenfranchisement is anything but coincidental or archaic. Under current law, the exclusion of criminals from the franchise occurs within the same sentence as the exclusion of persons who are deemed mentally impaired. After establishing the grounds of membership in the elective franchise as any person over the age of eighteen who has registered to vote and proven residency, Article 1, Section 4 of the present-day Maryland constitution goes on to state that the General Assembly may "regulate or prohibit the right to vote of a person convicted of infamous or other serious crime or under care or guardianship for mental disability." In a single sentence, in the same breath, this link between criminality and mental disability is invoked to draw an internal boundary around those who can take part in the project of representative government. The disenfranchisement of criminals and persons under guardianship are specific *exceptions* to the franchise, exclusions applied to persons who would otherwise be eligible to cast a vote, whose status as full participatory citizens is unquestioned. Maryland's constitutional provision is exemplary of the remaining states. In the forty-eight other states with some form of criminal disenfranchisement, thirty-nine of these also have some form of cognitive-disability-related bar placed on the elective franchise.[1] And as in Maryland, most states authorize these two forms of disenfranchisement within the same provision, and often within the same sentence. Disenfranchisement is commonly referred to as a civic *disability*, and it is worth thinking through what that phrase means.

While the previous chapter works through broad trends and shifts in the discourse of disenfranchisement, this chapter focuses on the historical moment when these two exclusions were solidified in Maryland's disenfranchisement provisions. By exploring the connection between the dual exclusions for any "person convicted of larceny or other infamous crime" and for "lunatics and persons *non compos mentis*," I show how these restrictions maintained a white supremacist conception of citizenship. As shown in the previous chapter, delegates to Maryland's nineteenth-century constitutional conventions explicitly understood disenfranchisement as a practice that managed the boundaries of full citizenship through the courts' power to determine criminal guilt and mental competence. This chapter goes further, showing how the delegates were additionally shoring up the increasingly unstable conception of whiteness through defining a series of "exceptions" to the franchise. The figure of the "free Negro" was once again persistently invoked to do this work, marked through criminality *and insanity* as civically disabled in order both to reduce the threat that it posed to the standing of white workingmen and to shore up the purity of whiteness itself as innocent, able, and fit for self-rule as well as rule over others.

FIGURES OF DEPENDENCY: THE NEGRO, THE CRIMINAL, AND THE MORAL IDIOT

The exclusion of criminals and persons with mental impairments and disabilities has a clear historical parallel, and yet few scholars have questioned the *connection* between these two common exclusions. Most attention, scholarly or otherwise, has focused on one exclusion or the other. The majority of accounts of the disenfranchisement of "mentally incompetent" persons have centered on the voting rights of the elderly, and this issue has been treated as either a medical[2] or a legal question.[3] That there has been so little attention paid to the discursive connection between felon disenfranchisement and the disenfranchisement of "mentally incompetent" persons is surprising, not only because the exclusions are typically defined within the same sections of legal code but also because the exclusion of one group is often used to defend the exclusion of the other. For instance, in two lower-court decisions upholding disenfranchisement as legal, the courts bolstered their rulings with *explicit* comparisons between the two groups. In *Shepherd v. Trevino*, the U.S. Court of Appeals for the Fifth Circuit stated,

> A state properly has an interest in excluding from the franchise persons who have manifested a fundamental antipathy to the criminal laws of the state or of the nation by violating those laws sufficiently important to be classed as felonies. . . . Such persons have breached the social contract and, *like insane persons, have raised questions about their ability* to vote responsibly.[4]

And in *Kronlund v. Honstein*, the U.S. District Court for the Northern District of Georgia ruled,

A State has an interest in preserving the integrity of her electoral process by removing from the process those persons with proven anti-social behavior whose behavior can be said to be destructive of society's aims. For this reason, *a State may prohibit idiots and insane persons, as well as, those convicted of certain offenses* from participating in her elections. A State may also legitimately be concerned that persons convicted of certain types of crimes may have a greater tendency to commit election offenses.[5]

Beyond this obvious discursive connection, found both in constitutional and common law, the empirical connection between criminal punishment and the incidence of mental illness in the United States is striking. The highest rates of mental illness in the United States are found not inside hospitals but inside jails and prisons. As state-run mental institutions have lost funding, the criminal justice system has become the nation's de facto mental health institution. By 2006, the Department of Justice reported that more than half the country's inmates had reported mental health issues.[6] A report issued by the National Sheriffs' Association in May 2010 stated that there are now "three times more seriously mentally ill persons in jails and prisons than in hospitals."[7] In Arizona and Nevada, the odds of a seriously mentally ill person being in jail versus a hospital are nine to one.[8] The Sheriffs' Association report concluded that the country is in the same position as it was during the 1840s, when the poor treatment of mentally ill persons in jails and prisons helped launch a reform movement that eventually established a state hospital system.[9] It is perhaps fitting, therefore, to return our gaze momentarily to the nineteenth-century foundations of political exclusion of these groups to understand our present condition.

One notable exception to the general lack of theorizing about these exclusions *together* can be found in the work of Kay Schriner, along with Andrew Batavia, Lisa Ochs, and Todd Shields.[10] Their work provides a useful starting point, as they have focused attention on the exclusions for mental, emotional, and cognitive impairments, arguing that "the contemporary prohibitions against voting by some individuals with cognitive and emotional impairments are based, at least in part, on prejudicial attitudes that are like the attitudes that earlier kept women, blacks, and other devalued groups from the polls."[11] For these authors, the relationship between this form of disenfranchisement and other restrictions on the vote is *analogous*, and insofar as those other forms were based on unjustifiable assumptions about the ability of women, blacks, and other groups to take part in political life, they rightly argue that restrictions based on cognitive impairments are analogously unjustifiable. In a subsequent article, one of the only studies that attends both to the historical justification of disenfranchisement and to the interdependence between multiple forms of disenfranchisement, Schriner and Ochs clarify this account to show how the overarching logic of "guardianship" brings together multiple forms of exclusion in a triangular relationship of "dependency, disability, and deviance," which ultimately determines who counts as a member of "the people" in the United States.[12] Such an overarching framework, they argue, is necessary to understand American suffrage restrictions, the notion of guardianship, and the implication that any person under such guardianship does not (and by implication cannot) have independent standing as a full member of the political community.

Schriner and Ochs's historical argument draws from the exemplary case of Massachusetts's constitutional conventions in 1821 and 1853 but fails to account for the substantial way in which the concept of race itself was undergoing massive changes during this same period. As such, their otherwise compelling account falls short of identifying how disenfranchisement— specifically on the basis of dependency, disability, and deviance—did not simply mirror other exclusions from the ballot box. Suffrage restrictions have been an integral part of the formation and maintenance of the American citizen with *persistent reference* to categories of racial formation and by the policing of the boundaries of whiteness through deployments of biological development and processes of normalization. As the philosopher Ladelle McWhorter explains, trying to understand race without reference to the deployments of biopower and techniques of normalization that rely on multiple locations of power/knowledge "is like trying to understand a region's cuisine with no knowledge of its climate, terrain, economy, or agricultural technologies."[13]

There is a deeper and more prevalent connection to the formation and maintenance of racial categories marked expressly through mental disability and criminality than Schriner and Ochs account for. The suffrage restrictions put into place in the mid-nineteenth century must be read through the increasingly tight nexus established between these terms, made possible by the dramatic redefinition of race through discourses of criminality and disability that occurred in the nineteenth and early twentieth centuries.

Our understandings of race, ability, and criminality constitute a triangular relationship of meaning in which the specific "threat" posed by disability and criminality were threats of *racial* degeneration. That these groups were systematically marked for exclusion from the franchise is hardly surprising, given that they have each been figured as fundamentally and statically *unable* to care for themselves, to take part in collective rule, or to participate in self-government.

In *Racism and Sexual Oppression in Anglo-America*, McWhorter traces how the concept of "race" changed over the course of the nineteenth century from a marker of morphological difference to one of biological difference by linking race to rapidly changing theories of disability and criminality.[14] Whiteness, she demonstrates, was established through the ruthless identification of all forms of abnormality as instances of "arrested development." In an account developed by French medical and psychiatric authorities in the early 1820s, "idiocy" was no longer considered a disease or illness but instead reflected a stable and heritable lack of human development. Foucault locates this shift in the early nineteenth century in French medical theories of idiocy:

> At this point you see a completely new notion of idiocy emerging, which you would not be able to find in the eighteenth century. Esquirol defines it in this way: "Idiocy is not a disease, but a condition in which the intellectual faculties are never manifested, or have never been sufficiently developed. . . ." And, in 1824, Belhomme more or less textually summarizes this same definition; he says that "idiocy is . . . a constitutional condition in which the intellectual functions have never developed. . . ." This definition is important because it introduces the notion of development; it makes development, or rather the absence of development the [distinctive] criterion for distinguishing between madness and idiocy. Idiocy is not defined therefore with reference to truth or error, or with reference to the ability or inability to control oneself, or with reference to the intensity of the delirium, but with reference to development. . . . If idiocy is non-development, then it is stable and acquired once and for all: the idiot does not develop.[15]

This conception of development made its way to the United States at least by the middle of the nineteenth century by way of American physicians and social reformers who studied in France and relied extensively on

French authoritative accounts.[16] For instance, when Samuel Gridley Howe, a notable social reformer and strident abolitionist, delivered a report on "idiocy" to the Massachusetts legislature in 1848, he identified the French definitions of idiocy as forms of "under-development" to be among "the most acceptable definitions" available. His own definition went even further, defining idiocy as "that condition of a human being in which, from some morbid cause in the bodily organization, the faculties and sentiments remain dormant or underdeveloped, so that the person is incapable of self-guidance, and of approaching that degree of knowledge usual with others of his age."[17] The key terms of his definition—relative age, underdevelopment, an incapacity for self-guidance, and some undetermined "morbid cause"— all indicate persons as dependent and incapable of rule over their own lives. The bulk of his report focused on how "morbid causes" of idiocy were heritable, markers of an "idiot's" parents' "sins" against nature.[18] Howe identifies five specific causes in the 1848 report, all of which relate in some way to parentage: (1) the physical organization of one or both parents, (2) intemperance, (3) self-abuse, (4) intermarriage of relatives, and (5) attempts to procure abortion. In each case here, the sins (both as actions of their own or as signaled by the "low condition" of their bodies) of the parents are visited upon their children. The section of the report on "self-abuse" is emphatically an admonishment for parents to strictly observe their children to keep them from masturbation. Even self-abuse becomes a direct symptom of poor parenting and poor parental stock. An individual's arrested development was entirely transmittable, as a heritable trait, and therefore observable more generally as *racial* degeneration:

> So a race of men, abusing the power of procreation, may rush on in the path of deterioration until, arrived at a certain point, a new principle develops itself, the procreating power is exhausted, and that part of the human family must perish, or regain its power by admixture with a less degenerate race.[19]

By the end of the nineteenth century, the logic of arrested development and the dangers of hereditary pollution were easily transposed (if they needed to be) to the bodies of morphologically raced individuals as an *explanation* for their difference. The level of human development, as a stable and transmittable attribute, completely reorganized accounts of racial difference. According to McWhorter,

There were not only different kinds of living beings; there were advanced beings and arrested beings, more and less developed beings, higher and lower beings. Difference in morphology always indicated a difference in degree of development, which in turn always indicated a difference in value. And in the final analysis that meant that inferior races were inferior because they were less well developed.[20]

This account of race as a form of arrested development rested on the notion that there was a powerful logic of development, both *between* human races and *within* them, accounting for the seemingly infinite variations among persons on the basis of their relative degree of human faculties. As McWhorter argues, "Integrated into the science of biology . . . racial difference was, essentially, developmental difference. Appearance was simply a manifestation of a development process. Members of 'lower' races and subraces bore the stigma of arrested development just as criminals and mentally deficient individuals did."[21]

This link between cognitive disabilities and societal danger had already been well established by the middle of the nineteenth century in Isaac Kerlin's definition of the "moral idiot" as

the degenerate offspring of an intemperate or otherwise offending parent. His cognitive disability involved impairment of the moral faculty. . . . If not appropriately disciplined and trained, the moral idiot was likely to be a thief and a liar, an arsonist, and possibly even a murderer.[22]

Or, as Howe put it, such persons were destined to be criminals because they lacked a fundamental ability to follow any law or prohibition, stemming from their arrested cognitive development. Moral idiocy was "that condition in which the sentiments, the conscience, the religious feeling, the love of neighbor, the sense of beauty, and the like, are so far dormant or underdeveloped, as to incapacitate the person *from being a law unto himself,* in any thing like the degree which is usual with others of his age. . . . Idiots of this character are not to be found in our almshouses, but they are often found in our prisons."[23] Such moral idiots, the feebleminded, and countless other forms of abnormality were thus dangerous not only because they were certain to violate the law but because of the heritability of their "criminal" traits; they would pollute an otherwise healthy population with their "morbid conditions."

Connecting this fundamental criminality to blackness, therefore, required very little elaboration and was only "confirmed" by statistical evidence. As stated by the eminent sociologist Charles R. Henderson in his 1906 *Introduction to the Study of Dependent, Defective, and Delinquent Classes,*

> There can be no doubt that one of the most serious factors in crime statistics is found in the conditions of the freedmen of African descent, both North and South. . . . The primary factor is racial inheritance, physical and mental inferiority, barbarian and slave ancestry and culture, "two hundred and fifty years of unrequited toil" (Lincoln), sudden and unprepared change of economic and political status.[24]

Any statistical difference in crime rates between whites and blacks following the Civil War was explained through the heritable "race traits" that marked blacks as underdeveloped moral idiots, rather than the dramatic change in the application of a criminal justice system to a population that had previously been "policed" through the slave system.[25] The link between crime and blackness that had been supported largely by popular beliefs until Reconstruction, could now be "demonstrated" by statistical evidence, effectively "writing race into crime," as the historian Khalil Gibran Muhammad has described it. "At the dawn of the twentieth century," he notes, "in a rapidly industrializing, urbanizing, and demographically shifting America, blackness was refashioned through crime statistics. It became a more stable racial category in opposition to whiteness through racial criminalization."[26] As Muhammad documents, the deployment of crime statistics to support an image of inherent black criminality proceeded through the use of these statistics to support the respectability of whiteness. By constantly comparing "Negro" and "foreign-born" whites, he notes, "Progressive era social scientists used statistics and sociology to create a pathway for their [foreign-born whites'] redemption and rehabilitation."[27]

Again and again, throughout the nineteenth century and into the twentieth, by various techniques and modes of knowledge, the concepts of criminality, disability, and blackness were drawn together in mutually supportive discourses.[28] Indeed, these three groups were mutually implicated as fundamentally *dependent,* just as noted by Schriner and Ochs, but in a way that also always sought to manage whiteness as an unstable category of superiority and privilege. As seemingly "natural" forms of rule (parents over children, husbands over wives, masters over slaves—i.e., nonpolitical forms of rule)[29] were being challenged during the nineteenth century, retrenchment was required. As developmentally arrested and therefore naturally nonautonomous, persons marked as criminal, idiotic, or black were assumed to be unable to *work* or even *think* independently and therefore could not take part in the practice of self-government. Howe insists on this point, noting the absurdity of allowing "idiots" near the ballot box:

> The persons put down in this report, as simpletons, are those about whom there could be no doubt, even in this day and generation. They are persons the highest of whom should be considered unable to take any responsibility, to contract matrimony, or to vote. The latter tests, however, should never be applied by interested parties. . . . Politicians, too, are sometimes as blind as lovers to the demerits of a head which can command a hand. Several cases have occurred where the taxes were paid for *simpletons*, and they voted—until the opposite party showed that they had a greater number of *fools* whom they could qualify and bring to the polls, and then the poor creatures, who had been used to violate the purity of the ballot and to defraud an election, were thrown aside in contempt.[30]

These figures were identified as permanent children by virtue of their arrested development and were therefore fit not for political rule but for paternal rule. To return momentarily to John Locke's influential account of political authority, "Children," he notes, "are not born in this full state of *Equality*, though they are born to it. Their Parents have a sort of Rule and Jurisdiction over them when they come into the World, and for some time after, but 'tis a temporary one."[31] But what if the condition of childhood is permanent? Locke himself carves out the exception of those who, by virtue of "defects that may happen out of the ordinary course of nature," never reach the age of reason: "Lunaticks and Ideots," "Madmen," "Savages," "Slaves," and even criminals all fall, in one way or another, under this category for Locke.[32] It is telling that by 1879, Kerlin had redescribed his account of "moral idiocy" as "juvenile insanity": "I have described moral imbeciles as a class of children whose perversion or aberration is in the so-called moral sense; with either no deterioration of the intellect, or if slight, such as is secondary only. . . . *The condition is radically incurable*."[33] Here, we can find a near-perfect confluence between the theoretical limit cases of persons capable of political membership (by virtue of their ability to be contracting subjects) and the scientific certainty of who such persons are.

These tightly knit discourses of race, crime, and disability can easily be deployed to shore up the boundaries of the polity. We can see how these discourses play against and with each other in the 1864 Maryland constitutional convention debates, showing us how the figures of permanent, incurable, and heritable criminality and lunacy were embedded rhetorically in the body of the "free Negro," justifying a continuation of paternalistic and despotic rule. The delegates who drafted, debated, and adopted these qualifications and exclusions to the franchise were self-consciously deliberating on the notions of rule and equality.

As with the 1851 debates, the delegates in 1864 treated the question of the franchise and the problem of the "free Negro" separately, yet they nevertheless mutually informed and supported each other. In the end, we can see how these two questions worked in tandem, shedding light on how white citizenship, fundamentally questioned by the war itself and the end of chattel slavery, was stabilized as *capable* through the deployment of figures of criminality, blackness, and disability. The delegates, in restricting the franchise simultaneously through a series of uncontested qualifications (age, sex, race, and residency) and a set of specific disqualifications (criminality, lunacy, idiocy, and treason) were actively involved in producing the very categories of (dis)qualification in order to negatively define their own subjectivities. That is, the *meaning and stability* of the qualifiers could be produced through the disqualifications. Insofar as forms of these disqualifications continue to exist today in disenfranchisement provisions, they necessarily force us to reckon with the continuing work of these exclusions in producing and maintaining the *normal* American citizen.

THREE KEY EXCEPTIONS: REBELS, CRIMINALS, AND LUNATICS

The 1864 Maryland constitution did not introduce the exclusion of criminals and lunatics from the franchise—that happened in the previous convention—but it did maintain it with only minor alterations. The novel addition in 1864 was a restriction on suffrage for "rebels" who fought for the "so-called Confederate States of America," including all those who had given "aid, comfort, countenance or support to those engaged in hostility to the United States." The exclusion of rebels, criminals, and "lunatics" that was debated and subsequently adopted in the 1864 convention, it must be remembered, was debated based on the uncontested adoption of the basic grounds of qualification for voting, which had remained unchanged since 1810. The exceptions that were carved out, therefore, applied to persons already otherwise qualified to vote: free, white, male, over twenty-one, and an established resident of the state. Therefore, these three exclusions were on their face "color-blind" and "gender-blind" but only insofar as they were adopted consciously within already greatly restricted qualifications for voting. The question in turning to the debates is, how were the identities of rebels, criminals, and lunatics stabilized in order to establish them as excluded from the franchise? For each exception, the delegates produced a set of stable and essential markers that would demonstrate an otherwise qualified voter's incapacity to take part in collective self-government. In doing so, they established and secured whiteness as masculine, mentally able, and defined as the authority and the power to judge over one's own life and thereby the life of the polity.

"No Person Who Has at Any Time Been in Armed Hostility to the United States"

Only the first of these exceptions, rebel soldiers and sympathizers, was challenged wholesale by any of the delegates, chiefly by the vastly outnumbered Democrats (who were quite right to fear that they and their constituents were the targets of this exclusion). A general amnesty for rebels had been ordered by the governor for all soldiers who laid down their arms, which meant rebels could not be punished as criminals. Disenfranchisement, the minority opposition decried, was in fact one of the highest forms of punishment available. Delegate Richard H. Edelen asked, "Can you conceive of a higher degree of punishment, short of taking a man's life, than to declare him forever disqualified from holding any office of profit or trust in the State, and of closing against him forever the ballot box, making him a mere cypher in the community where he lives, stripping him of every political right?"[34] This did not, however, mean disenfranchisement was not a fitting punishment for *real* criminals who had been convicted as such. "The deprivation of the right to exercise the elective franchise," the same delegate continued, "is one of the punishments which you inflict upon a man by reason of having committed and been convicted of an infamous crime. It is a punishment. You proposed today to bar against a man the doors of every office, and to deprive him of the right to vote, without an opportunity of being heard in his defence."[35] The problem was not in restricting the franchise to punish offenders; it was over what was properly considered an offense.

To a certain degree, however, the amnesty that prevented convicting rebels as criminals declared their very criminality. Absent disenfranchisement, Delegate Henry Stockbridge asked, what would prevent these "unconvicted criminals" from "com[ing] back here to accomplish by his votes what he fails to accomplish in arms?"[36] These persons, the delegate insisted, have "committed a crime compared with which the men in your penitentiary are innocent and angels of light. They have not been convicted; yet the fact is as well known as if you had had the verdict of a thousand juries."[37]

At best, the act of rebellion signified a loss of reason and right thinking by the rebels, rendering them unable to exercise the franchise in their own interest. Stripping rebels of the franchise, Delegate David Scott stated, was an "act of kindness" toward them precisely because they had demonstrated an inability to care for themselves:

> We are acting kindly to these people. We are acting towards them the
> part of the considerate parent who keeps edge tools out of the hands of
> his children, and the public authorities who keep them out of the hands
> of lunatics and insane persons. . . . We are acting kindly towards these
> people in preventing them from the use of a franchise or privilege which
> they would use for their own destruction, and the destruction of others
> until they return to their reason.[38]

The act of rebellion marked the person either as thoroughly criminal or as childlike, insane, and underdeveloped in his use of reason. By virtue of these associations, the rebel soldier was professed to be unable to exercise the kind of judgment required of a full member of the polity—a fully free, white, male citizen of Maryland—despite the amnesty covering his specific transgression.

"Convicted of Larceny or Other Infamous Crime"

The second exclusion considered—namely, all "persons convicted of larceny or other infamous crime"—was taken for granted, and no delegate challenged it directly. The exclusion had been established in the previous 1851 constitution, and the only substantive question considered in reauthorizing it in the 1864 debates was over which crimes would be considered "infamous." If anything, the delegates to the 1864 convention reinforced the notion that disenfranchisement was punishment for a particularly criminal character. That is, the "infamy" of the "infamous crime" continued to be at the heart of the justification for disenfranchisement, because it marked an individual in a deep and persistent manner. As in the 1851 debates, disenfranchisement was considered a reasonable and fitting punishment because infamous crimes and larceny "revealed" the offender as morally deficient or underdeveloped, not because of the specific crime itself (which was punished separately by incarceration or fine). Only disenfranchisement could reach far enough to punish the character of the convict. Infamy, as interpreted by the delegates, was a condition of the person, not the crime.[39]

Offenders convicted of infamous crimes and larceny were marked by the specifically deceitful character of such crimes and were taken to be felonious in their very natures. This nature was independent of criminal conviction, apparently, as some delegates showed a particular concern over the number of "unconvicted felons" in the state casting votes. Delegate Joseph M. Cushing insisted there were "more unconvicted felons that vote at every election, two to one, than have ever been sent to the penitentiary."[40] "The fact," Delegate George A. Thruston agreed, "that unconvicted felons are allowed to vote is certainly no argument for adding to their number those who are convicted and known to be felons."[41] Under a conception of criminality that identifies felons and infamous criminals as criminal before a crime or absent judicial process, there was nothing nonsensical about such references to "unconvicted felons" who might successfully hide their criminal natures and cast a vote. Such a strong assumption, not surprisingly, could also imply that punishment might not change one's felonious character. As Delegate Archibald Stirling argued, "I should have no objection to an amendment to allow the legislature power to restore a man to the right of voting, *should he subsequently become a good man.* But I do not think he should be restored simply because he has served out his time in the penitentiary, without any alteration in his conduct."[42] Thus, the 1864 delegates echoed the claims of their colleagues at the previous 1851 convention, that even a "double penalty" of disenfranchisement is proportionate because the offender in question is *still an offender*—a person who, by virtue of his moral character, is not a "good man" even if he has been released from the penitentiary.[43] The fact of having served one's time in the penitentiary, while it might be able to discharge the *crime*, need not discharge one's *criminality*:

An infamous offence is the kind of felony which characterizes the party with entire turpitude. If a man is convicted and sent to the penitentiary he ought not to be allowed to associate at the ballot-box with those people who have not been legally convicted. I think the door ought to be held open to every such man to reform; but if he does reform let there be an act of equal solemnity with that which sent him to the penitentiary, to restore him.[44]

Of course, there is no such act, because "entire turpitude" was not something that could be removed. Criminals must be excluded from the franchise even after their sentences were over, as the completion of the sentence did not alter the criminal character of the man in question. The particular crimes selected for exclusion, the delegates insisted, demonstrated a fundamentally criminal character, undisputedly *known* through a legal conviction. Lacking a fundamental ability to act as judge in one's own case, an offender was excluded from taking part in political self-rule and therefore from membership in the polity. It is the central importance of such a *knowing* to which I want to draw attention. The production of a stable knowledge of the offender and, subsequently, the necessity of *knowing* if a person had in fact discharged (if he even could) his morally questionable character drove the debates throughout.

"*No Lunatic, or Person* Non compos mentis"

As in the previous two cases, the work of establishing lunacy was the work of stabilizing the identity of the lunatic so as to render him unfit to judge, in his own case and therefore for the polity. There was no doubt in the delegates' minds that a lunatic or person *non compos mentis* was unfit because "it is manifest that lunatics and idiots are incapable of determining how they shall vote, and will only be made tools of by interested persons."[45] As such, there was no controversy over the existing provision disenfranchising any persons presently "under guardianship," since guardianship, a legal determination, already indicated that a determination of mental incompetence had been made.

However, the extension of the franchise to all white workingmen made guardianship practically ineffective as a means of determining ballot-box competency, since mentally incompetent white men who did not own property were highly unlikely to have guardians or to have been declared a lunatic. As Delegate Samuel H. Berry explained,

It is very well known . . . that to apply for a writ *de lunatico inquirendo* requires a good deal of money. The cost is considerable to summon a jury and go through all the requirements of the law. Unless a party has property, or his friends have property to apply for him, it has never been done within my [legal] practice. But when there is no property, and when by common reputation they are regarded as lunatics, they have never been under guardianship in the experience I have had in the practice of the law.[46]

Mirroring the fear over "unconvicted felons," there was a widespread concern that "there are ten times as many lunatics not under guardianship as are under guardianship," meaning that "all lunatics will be entitled to vote who has not a guardian."[47] By removing the "under guardianship" clause from the provision, delegates sought to rely on "common reputation" to stabilize the character of white lunatics and exclude them from the ballot box, since a legal determination of guardianship could not possibly reach all the lunatics who threatened the purity of the polity.[48] However, who was to determine this common reputation at the moment of the vote? The question would necessarily have to be settled by election judges. Defenders of the "common reputation" standard insisted that determining lunacy was no more difficult than confirming a prospective voter's age or residency, and as such, if election judges were competent to establish these qualifications, they were surely competent to judge "all such questions equally affecting the right of a party to vote."[49] The question of lunacy, according to Delegate Berry, was categorically equivalent to other qualifications that judges were empowered to verify: "They [election judges] have the right to try the question of non-age or non-residence, and all such questions equally affecting the right of a party to vote."[50] Such an equivalence between one's sanity and one's residency or age was easily extended to all other qualifications, including race, gender, or criminality, each "equally affecting" one's capability. Mental disability was therefore figured expressly as a stable and essential and readily knowable fact of one's person.[51]

Other delegates countered that moving away from the certainty offered by the "guardianship" standard was a dangerous policy, not only because it would open the process to political abuse[52] but, moreover, because judges were insufficiently expert to determine mental competency and might be outright incompetent to do so.[53] First, even if they could accurately determine age or residency, these attributes were far more stable than something like insanity, because Delegate Stirling noted, "A man may be a lunatic and have sane intervals."[54] Second, because there are "different degrees of lunacy or insanity," it would be impossible to "fix a rule to exclude the insane or lunatics from voting. . . . One man would argue that a certain person was incapable of voting, because he was a lunatic, while others would insist that the person was sane. *It would be an endless question.*"[55] That the question could be given a definitive answer by a separate judicial proceeding in court, interestingly, was taken for granted, even by those who were most troubled by the power being vested in election judges. Under either standard, the goal—certainty with regard to mental incompetency—was not in and of itself achievable, and therefore the stability of the white, male voter was still in question.

DETERMINING "THE STATE OF FACT IN WHICH A MAN IS"

Insofar as the exclusion of rebel soldiers and of criminals relied in part on the same fundamental question of mental ability and thereby on the authority to decide in one's own case and for the polity, the inability to stabilize lunacy bleeds through these other categories and destabilizes them as knowable disqualifications. The boundary of the elective franchise was being drawn expressly based on a series of *certain knowledges* about the moral character of persons. The question of the franchise across these debates was decided in each case by varying levels of certainty about the knowledge of others, and this certainty depended on the kind of knowledge required (common, expert, judicial) and on the stability of that knowledge. At the level of general qualifications were markers taken to be both completely stable and perfectly knowable: those of race or gender. These exclusions were taken for granted and adopted with neither controversy nor discussion. And there were other markers taken to be knowable but less stable: residency and age. These qualifications required some degree of authority to determine, vested in election judges. Finally, the remaining exclusions, categorized as exceptions, were far less stable, as reflected by the specific concerns of the delegates.

For rebel soldiers and criminals, some mode of knowing was expressly invoked to establish a high degree of certainty about the person's fitness for the ballot box: a loyalty oath for soldiers, a legal conviction for larceny or other "infamous" crime. In both cases, this stability was necessarily purchased at some risk. The "real" rebel could make a false oath, willingly perjuring himself (itself a disenfranchiseable offense). The infamous criminal might avoid capture or leave the penitentiary without having "truly" reformed. The back-and-forth on the particulars of pardons, of how these rebels and these criminals might be able to remove the moral stain revealed by their past actions, shows these to be a central concern of the delegates. Yet in each and every exclusion and qualification, these markers are all reducible to a *knowledge of the person*, a knowledge that declares individuals, by virtue of their race, age, gender, or past actions, as categorically unfit to take part in political life, to hold office, and to take a turn in the practice of self-rule among equals. Or, as Delegate Stirling put it more bluntly,

> Suffrage implies acquiescence in the result of the ballot; and if a man
> simply wishes to use the ballot-box as a machine to aid an armed revolu-
> tion, he is not in a condition to vote, any more than the insane man in
> the hospital. If he does not hold himself amenable to the authority of
> the government, it does not concern him, and he is not in a condition
> to exercise the right of suffrage. *All these provisions are simply to ascertain,
> in this civil tumult, the state of fact in which a man is.*[56]

The case of lunatics and idiots, despite the brevity with which the delegates engaged the question, was more troubling on these terms, apparent in the hesitations of many delegates to rely on "common reputation" to determine lunacy. But there was no hesitation, from any quarter, to ban a white man placed under guardianship by the court, a man *known* through a judicial proceeding to be mentally incompetent, from casting a vote. The more confident a delegate was that one could securely know a lunatic or an idiot "by common reputation," the more insistent that delegate was in excluding lunatics and idiots not under guardianship, trusting that common knowledge could maintain the "purity" of the ballot box as a space of whiteness untainted by rebelliousness, criminality, or lunacy.

In the delegates' desire to maintain the boundary of a stable and knowable polity, to ensure that only those who they could be absolutely certain about could cast a vote, they grasped for strategies to manage the instability, insecurity, and unknowability of their fellow citizens as equals. And so they turned to common reputation, criminal convictions, the *de lunatic inquirendo*, and loyalty oaths. They sought "the state of fact" of those suspect white men in the hope that such facts could put an end to the "endless question." For there to be any semblance of an internal coherence between insanity, rebellion, and criminality, *each term had to be capable of doing the exclusionary work for the other.*

Rebels were disenfranchised because of their criminal character and their affinity with insanity, criminals for the permanent stain of felonious deceit, and lunatics because they, like the rebels and criminals they were tied to, could not rule over their own lives. But as was finally apparent in the case of lunacy, the "endless question" opened up again, sustainable only insofar as one could be certain, grounded in an empirical referent outside these exclusions. Elsewhere in the debates, the delegates deployed just such a referent, captured in their obsession with the problem of the "free Negro," a figure that was known, certain, and without doubt, indelibly connected in the delegates' minds to the specters of criminality, insanity, and as a result, civic dependency.[57]

Just as in the previous convention, only "free white men" made up the electorate, and as such, it is not surprising that there was little mention of race or slavery during the 1864 debates about the specific disenfranchisement of rebels, criminals, and lunatics. It was presumed that the specific exclusions for rebels, criminals, and lunatics were exceptions among free white men. The problem of the "free Negro," nevertheless, continued to pervade the debates.[58] While delegates differed in their assessments of the severity and origins of the "Negro problem," both pro- and antislavery factions at the 1864 convention took the fact of free blacks in the state to be a problem. The affinities between "free Negroes" and the established figures of moral, mental, and material dependency were invoked whenever the "Negro problem" was considered through specific references to the prevalence of insanity, idiocy, and criminality in "free Negroes."[59]

By establishing tight associations between blackness and these markers of "natural" dependency, even the previously unthinkable concept of "free Negroes" could maintain the distinction between those who were included and those who were excluded from the polity, reinforcing the categorical exclusion of nonwhites (because infamous criminals and lunatics were already well established as unfit for participation in political life) and simultaneously justifying the three exceptions to white suffrage carved out "separately" (by linking such exceptions to blackness). That is, through the deployment of a new conception of race, one that did not rely on chattel slavery as a fact, white, masculine, ablest supremacy could be maintained through new discursive practices.

The argument was simple: the delegates could establish either the inherent criminality of the "free Negro" or his inherent lunacy. They could do this by arguing that the criminality and the idiocy of the "free Negro" had directly increased the levels of crime and madness in the North, and therefore it had been slavery that kept these in check in the South. The criminal figurations that pervaded the 1851 debates returned with renewed force. As one delegate insisted, the relationship between "free Negroes" and crime had been well established by experience since the 1820s, as the state penitentiaries, courts, and juries had been "overrun" with manumitted slaves: "The people of the State began to be alarmed; they said they were tired of being taxed to support this degraded class who would not work, but would steal, who would go ragged, and idle their time away in squalid beggary, and necessarily become degraded, drunken, worthless criminals."[60] This firsthand experience was confirmed by the census results of 1860, proslavery delegates argued.[61] In the North, they argued, "free Negroes" had higher levels of crime, miscegenation, pauperism, and insanity than in the South.[62] The "mental condition of the negro" under slavery was offered as perhaps the strongest proof that slavery was a beneficent institution, as one delegate noted that the ratio of "insane free negroes" to "insane slaves" was seven to one.[63] Freedom, put simply, *caused* insanity in blacks. Slavery (or some slavelike condition), therefore, could constrain it. Slavery's ability to suppress both insanity and idiocy, and also physical impairments, was so striking to Delegate James U. Dennis that he placed the following tables into the record:

The effects of the fanatical, religious and political isms of the North may be seen in the returns of the insane and idiot:

	Free States.	Slave States.
Insane	17,864	6,135
Idiotic	11,160	7,705

The deaf and dumb and blind, afflictions arising from natural causes, are more nearly equalized still, with a Northern preponderance:

	Free States.	Slave States.
Deaf and dumb	9,722	5,355
Blind	7,293	5,342[64]

Even as Delegate Dennis seemed to note that physical impairments arise from "natural causes," his inclusion of these numbers still implied that emancipation would negatively affect the state. The differing levels of the "moral evils that usually afflict the human family" in the North and the South are taken to buttress the delegates' insistence that "Negroes" *required* slavery to contain their naturally degraded characters and their preponderance toward criminality and mental incompetence:

> Maryland is about to try the experiment of free labor. . . . I do not believe the change proposed will benefit the negro. I believe it will make his condition infinitely worse. Statistics show such to have been the result wherever it has been tried. A free negro population is a curse to themselves and to any community in which they reside.[65]

It is important to note that with only a few exceptions, the delegates relied almost entirely on aggregate counts of criminal convictions and cases of insanity/idiocy. Only occasionally did they provide rates or other population-adjusted measures. More obviously, these delegates seemingly ignored that differential rates and counts of criminal convictions and insanity can be readily accounted for by the simple fact that these measures would not actually include the vast majority of nonwhite persons in the South, since they would seldom be turned over to the courts. The slave system already held blacks under a form of completely despotic guardianship.

Yet this was essentially the delegates' point: without a slave system, these rates and counts would immediately skyrocket, because the "natural inclinations" of newly emancipated slaves would have no restraint. Quoting extensively from a pamphlet titled *Free Negroism, or Results of Emancipation in the North, and the West India Islands: with Statistics of the Decay of Commerce, Idleness of the Negro, His Return to Savagism, and the Effect of Emancipation upon the Farming, Mechanical and Laboring Classes*,[66] Delegate Jones emphatically endorsed its central thesis: "The first cause existing in society of the frequency and increase in crime is the degraded character of the colored population."[67] To free slaves would be to relegate them to their "natural inclinations," directly leading to a narrow set of outcomes: crime, pauperism, and even insanity. "Emancipation," Delegate Dr. Eli J. Henkle insisted, "is injurious to the negro and to the white races. The natural inclinations of the negro are to idleness, dissipation and vice, and where they are in large numbers, and suffered to follow their natural inclinations, they will relapse into barbarism, and even into idolatry."[68]

Given the problems that "free Negroes" represented, the immediate concern was to prevent "free Negroes" from Washington, D.C., and southern states from coming into Maryland, in order to protect the wages of white laborers.[69] Open borders would leave the state "overrun with free negroes," whose competition for work would drive down wages for white laborers. The problem was framed simply as "a question of political economy, and not at all as involved in the political question of their franchise."[70] But it was of course linked to the question of franchise, insofar as the "free Negro" represented a direct challenge to the standing of white workingmen. If "free Negroes" could not be physically removed from the state altogether, then the other strategy for marking their lower standing was to associate them with crimes that demonstrate their lack of standing: specifically, larceny and infamous crimes. Even as Delegate Edwin A. Abbot from Baltimore defended "free negro" laborers in the city as "some of the best laborers we have," he qualified his defense, saying, "it is true that they will steal a little at times, but then only a meal of victuals, a ham, or something of that kind."[71] A delegate from the countryside—Delegate Clarke—responded directly:

> In Baltimore city it is probable that they [free negroes] steal only a little
> ham and bacon. But then they have their clerks in their stores to watch
> their property, and they also have their police on the lookout. But in
> the country we are a little more unfortunate. They steal there something
> more than a little ham and bacon. They will go off to Washington city
> and take along with them 15 or 20 or more valuable sheep, and put
> themselves under the protection of the military authorities. They drive
> off your horses, and carry off wagon-loads of tobacco; they go into your
> corn-fields at night and pillage them, and if we are overrun with this
> class of people, the free negro will have an opportunity to destroy more
> in the night than the white man can make in the day.[72]

"Free Negro" laborers, therefore, represented two threats: they were dangerous *both* for being good workers and for being untrustworthy thieves. And if one believes that the "free Negro" laborer drives down the wages of white laborers (i.e., "steals" jobs and wages that rightfully belong to white laborers), then both dangers can be understood as one specific danger: larceny. Everything that the "free Negro" does outside the slave system becomes criminal by definition. Both working for a wage and robbing farms are, in this sense, forms of theft from white men. To the (soon to be) former slaveholders, the very fact of emancipation was a form of state-backed "theft" by their colleagues in the General Assembly who refused to compensate them for their "property." Such larcenies were easily embodied in the "free Negro laborer."

This is what Du Bois means by noting the connection between "free Negro labor" and criminality and its conceptual "impossibility," noted earlier.

The questions of color and crime, of course, underlie a far greater fear: that "Negroes" would be given more than just economic power and free movement. This fear, perfectly expressed by Delegate Clarke, was that they would claim political power:

> If this State shall be overrun by thousands and thousands of these
> people, you will not only have brought them into competition with
> the white man, but you may have men getting up before the people of
> this State, as is now done in the Senate of the United States, where it
> is proposed to give to negroes in Washington city the right of suffrage;
> you may have the same proposition made in the State of Maryland, and
> made an engine of political power. . . . If they are allowed to come here,
> and men, for party political purposes, succeed in giving them the elec-
> tive franchise, and the white men of Maryland become virtually enslaved
> by the negro voting for and supporting a particular class of white men,
> it will be one of my proudest memories that pending the consideration
> of the organic law of the State, I did what I could to preserve the rights
> and liberties of white men, to keep the rights and liberties of white men
> under the control of white men; and to keep the labor of white men at
> such a standard that it could not be brought into competition with free
> negro labor; and to prevent the bringing down of the white man, if not
> to a political equality, to at least an economical level with the negro,
> where, in order to sustain himself and his family, he will be compelled
> to work upon the same terms with the negro.[73]

Yet again, one can see in this delegate's remarks an echo of Judith Shklar's account of the relationship between labor and voting as markers of political standing, purchased necessarily at the expense of those who do not possess that standing. The delegates were in the process of extending basic "human" rights through emancipation, but they positively refused to extend the rights of citizenship to free blacks in the state, a process that, many of the delegates insisted, was downright dangerous. At every turn, however, even the most ardent emancipationists insisted that these persons would be ably handled by the existing forms of state management found in the orphan law, the criminal law, and other forms of legal and economic guardianship. The proslavery factions repeatedly pointed out that emancipation was a road to ruin, in which the political standing of the former slave would necessarily "degrade" that of whites and eventually lead to an open conflict, that is, a race war. "The effect," Delegate Henkle insisted, of allowing the black laborer and white laborer to "work side by side, in almost social and political equality . . . will be to pull down the white man, and there will finally be a struggle between the races."[74]

Even those who saw themselves fighting hardest on behalf of "the humanity of the negro" marked the limit of equality at the point of the political right of participation in self-government. As stated by an ardent abolitionist delegate, George W. Sands, the purpose of emancipation was to achieve the "complete separation of the races" by granting the "Negro" human rights but *never* political rights:

> I am sorry in all cases to see the unwillingness to acknowledge the humanity of the negro. . . . I believe if there ever comes about what I long for and pray for, a complete separation of the races, it is to come from emancipation and from colonization. Free them, give them equal human rights, the rights of husband and wife and parent. Give the negro the rights of a man, of a husband and father. Give him the right to labor and to receive an equivalent for that labor. Give him the right to educate himself, if he can, and his children. Bring him to the point where he will desire to take a part in the civil government of the land, and let him know that he can never do so; you will have brought him to the point where the emigration of this race will begin in a perfect flood-tide. *When he has become sufficiently educated to desire a voice in the government, and finds that there he can never be received as the equal of the white man, it is then that he will seek for himself a new country.*[75]

Emancipation opened the vast question of the status of black people relative to whites, and while whites may have been able to rely on some kind of abstract affirmation of the humanity of black people, what was unthinkable was (1) the equality of free black labor in relation to white labor and (2) the political equality of free black men. Therefore, both were managed through the production of an inherent black mental disability, either through criminality (managing labor) or lunacy (managing the franchise).

The difficulty of restricting suffrage of otherwise-qualified white men was in establishing the certainty that they were (despite being white, male, and free) incapable and unfit for participation in political rule among equals.

And while the delegates demonstrated occasional hesitations, they were at least certain that these attributes of criminality and lunacy provided such disqualifications. There was, after all, the constant threat and presence of these specters embodied all around the delegates in figures who carried with them those precise traits and whom they had no uncertainty whatsoever about: "free Negroes," whose exclusion was taken entirely for granted.

The project of emancipation was posited as an expression of white supremacy, of a strict separation between whites and blacks, and ultimately of blacks' removal from the state entirely. It was the emancipationists themselves who often turned out to be the strictest guardians of social and political distinction and who supported the most extensive restrictions on the franchise. They took for granted the proslavery delegates' assertions of blacks' innately criminal character, their powerful affinity with idiocy and lunacy, and above all, their generalized dependency, all of which unquestionably left them incapable of taking part in self-government. The emancipationists insisted on a foundational affinity between nonwhites, categorically excluded from the franchise by virtue of their "obvious" and established inferiority, and classes of white persons who, except by virtue of their revealed natures, likewise demanded political exclusion. Such whites were exceptions to the rule, falling away from the ideal, closer in kind to nonwhites. The object of the greatest instability, in the end, was of course whiteness itself, and it was in the most need of policing. As Charles Mills puts it, "To the extent that those phenotypically/genealogically/culturally categorized as white fail to live up to the civic and political responsibilities of Whiteness, they are in dereliction of their duties as citizens."[76]

"NOTHING STABILIZES LIKE INSTABILITY"

What is essential is to properly diagnose the problem, to understand it in a productive and accurate way. The thrust of this entire book has been to reformulate the "identity" of the felon as fabricated or produced in part through its exclusion from the polity, while remaining within its territorial and conceptual boundaries. This fabrication directly serves the interests of maintaining white supremacist notions of citizenship and does so through the application of a civic *disability* to some persons, deemed to be impaired, in order to mark those political members whose standing is beyond question, beyond reproach, and ultimately stable in their whiteness, their innocence, and their normality. That is, if we approach the practice of disenfranchise-

ment as a distinct form of civic disability, then the puzzle of disenfranchisement is also a problem of how the notion of such *disabilities* do the work of
stabilizing otherwise unstable identities, of allowing the "able" to be secure
in their self-conceptions. Moreover, the crux of this "puzzle" is that at each
and every moment when a disability appears to be a stable reference point, it
is possible to demonstrate how this stability is being purchased through the
disavowal of its own instability. As disability theorist and pedagogue Brenda
Brueggemann puts it succinctly, disability's power to do this work stems
from its *instability*: "Disability stabilizes most in its instability. The definition of disability always begins (and probably ends, too) in its ambiguity, in
its indeterminate boundaries."[77]

If we begin from the viewpoint of the discourses of civic disability, as well
as physical or mental, as being foundationally about the production of a
stable normative order purchased through the instability of disability itself,
then we are called to attend to recent work in the critical disabilities studies
movement as well as other poststructuralist approaches to social and political
practices. This tradition, which draws widely on queer theory, radical gender
theory, critical race theory, poststructuralist epistemology, and performance
studies, offers a powerful corrective to both medical and structuralist readings of social and political life.[78] As Robert McRuer puts it, the critical approach "emerges from cultural studies traditions that question the order of
things, considering how and why it [the order of things] is constructed and
naturalized; how it is embedded in complex economic, social, and cultural
relations; and how it might be changed."[79] As a self-conscious response to
the sociological approaches to disability that have come to characterize disability studies since the 1970s, the critical disabilities studies approach (and
its fellow travelers in queer theory, critical race theory, and critical legal studies)[80] focuses on how the production and maintenance of "stable" groups
marked as abnormal masks the instability of the norm.

Specifically, critical disability studies emerged as a response to the shortcomings of the "social model" of disability, which argued (counter to medical
and biological accounts of disability) that "it is society which disables people
with impairments, and therefore any meaningful solution must be directed
at social change rather than individual adjustment and rehabilitation."[81] The
social model rests on separating the fact of "impairment," a defect of an
organ or mechanism of the body, and the production of a "disability," the
disadvantage caused by social organization that ignores or is structured to
exclude impairments.[82] This distinction between a fact of "nature" and its

social and cultural form is directly analogous to the sex/gender distinction, frequently embraced in structuralist and "second-wave" feminist accounts of gender.[83] From the standpoint of the social model, "disability is not a medical or personal problem but a set of physical and social barriers that constrain, regulate and discriminate against people with impairments."[84] As such, disability is by definition a form of exclusion and unjust social oppression against persons who are impaired.[85]

As Iris Young notes, the social model has been incredibly powerful for grounding the civil rights claims of disabled persons, "because it shifts attention on issues of justice for people with disabilities from the 'needs' of people with disabilities to others who assume that a certain background of structures and practices is given."[86] Proponents of the social model therefore have focused their attention on the institutions and practices that have systematically excluded impaired persons from cultural, social, and political life, demanding that such persons should be *enabled* through inclusion, dismantling both formal and informal barriers to participation in all spheres of life. This has manifested itself in a broad endorsement of political inclusion of multiple forms of difference, drawing on the work of political theorists who have described how political commitments of equality can easily ignore, suppress, and marginalize difference to construct a "political space" devoid of the very pluralism that defines humanity.[87]

While the social model is surely correct to identify disability as a product of diverse social practices, it has nevertheless dangerously reified impairment as "some objective, transhistorical and transcultural entity which biomedicine accurately represents," according to Shelley Tremain.[88] In its very attempt to escape the determinism of medical and individualist models of disability, the social model's strict separation between impairment and disability subscribes to what Tremain calls a "realist ontology" that presumes the descriptions of impairments are value-neutral, in order to ground the claims for inclusion made by persons disabled by social, political, and economic institutions and practices. But as Tremain notes, "it seems politically naïve to suggest that the term 'impairment' is value-neutral, that is, 'merely descriptive,' as if there could ever be a description which was not also a *prescription* for the formulation of that to which it is claimed innocently to refer. Truth-discourses which purport to describe phenomena contribute to the construction of their objects."[89]

The critical disabilities studies movement challenges the return to essentialism that has so often characterized progressive social movements, which insist on the "biological," "natural," or "given" fact of difference as a ground for claiming greater social rights.[90] Nevertheless, a critical-theoretical approach to disability does not deny the materiality of the world and of bodies but instead tracks *how* the materiality of the world is always already interpreted through discursive regimes of power/knowledge. While the stuff of the world surely exists, including a wide variety of body types and mental forces, the meaning of that stuff is determined and those bodies and minds are known within an existing field of power. As Tremain describes the "foundational" quality of "impairment" under the social model, "The testimonials, acts, and enactments of the disabled subject are *performative* insofar as the allegedly 'natural' impairment that they are purported to disclose, or manifest, has no existence prior to or apart from those very constitutive performances."[91] Drawing on Foucault's nominalism and Judith Butler's account of performativity, this approach forces us to note that it is through discursive practices such as disenfranchisement that the meanings of lunacy, *non compos mentis*, idiocy, or mental impairment can be naturalized and fixed.

At one level, the restriction of voting rights for mentally impaired persons is a paradigmatic case for the social model, showing how an impairment (e.g., lunacy or idiocy) is transformed into a disability through formal exclusion (a specifically *civic* disability). At a deeper level, however, the social model risks inscribing difference as fixed rather than contingent or asserting lunacy or idiocy as natural facts rather than contingent deployments of power/knowledge.

If we accept the viewpoint of the social model, mental *disability* continues today to be produced in part by continuing exclusions for persons deemed mentally incompetent to vote and, as such, reveals the disenfranchisement of mentally *impaired* persons as a form of oppression. The social model thus pushes toward political inclusion, but it nevertheless fails to account for the ways in which impairments themselves are produced. From the point of view of the social model, the disenfranchisement of criminals and the mentally incompetent can be read as the moment when an impairment is converted into a disability. When constitutional delegates excluded these persons from the vote, they did so by identifying an essential character that marks them as lacking the *ability* to take part in government, marking them as *impaired*. This means these impairments are not themselves produced but instead are facts on which disability is produced. This could lead us to claim that the delegates simply misidentified some persons as impaired who are not, just as they also misidentified all women, blacks, and foreigners as impaired.

That is, the social model too easily displaces the difference it seeks to explain onto a form of difference taken to be "natural." This would be to assume, just as the delegates did, that all the disenfranchiseable impairments are empirical and natural facts about persons. This is why the social model is insufficient; because each and every one of these possible "impairments" was itself discursively produced concomitant with the civic "disability" of disenfranchisement. Insofar as the social model helps us understand disenfranchisement as a disability separate from—and laid out over—an underlying empirical impairment, it also leads us to understand a wide variety of political markers (criminality, race, gender, etc.) as impairments and risks ascribing foundational and essential qualities to these categories as well—precisely what proponents of the social model sought to avoid in their critique of the medical/individual models of disability. As Tremain puts it succinctly, "Impairment has been disability all along."[92]

To point to disenfranchisement—of any sort—as a civic disability directly risks ascribing a foundational or essential character to criminality. While perhaps providing a clean and neat distinction between "true" and "false" criminals—as Shklar does—such a distinction is made only through avoiding the more difficult question of how such truth or falsity has been produced. The nineteenth-century practice of disenfranchisement was not only embedded in a discursive milieu in which criminality, blackness, and lunacy supported and reinforced each other as related impairments, but disenfranchisement was also a crucial practice governing these same discourses, stabilizing whiteness as the political norm, and using suffrage as a technique to police those persons who failed to adhere to the norm. The categories of political impairment that were converted to civic disability were far from given, natural, or transhistorical, but they were made quite real as assemblages of power/knowledge deployed to stabilize, naturalize, and fix the contingency of human difference.

As a question of participation in democratic government, the franchise has hinged on establishing an *ability* to take part, signified first through age, whiteness, masculinity, and residency. But these categories, especially whiteness, were anything but stable: they required a policing not only along expressly racial boundaries but internally as well, through those markers of *disability* that were, through their affinity with blackness, able to produce and maintain the category of whiteness as *able*. The "success" of the delegates to the 1864 convention hinged on the ability to stabilize their exclusions, and it was within the context of the exclusion of "lunatics" and other persons under guardianship that they had the most trouble, where there was the greatest hesitation, because the very question of competency became a part of the problem. Their less-than-successful attempts to stabilize lunacy, criminality, and rebellion as forms of mental incompetence relied on the assumed fixity of blackness. At the time, this was enough to secure a "normal" (masculine) whiteness or at least to establish something like an ideal of mental ability that could in turn establish the limits of authority and the right to self-government. But this ideal, as a norm, is stable only in relation to the variation that produced it and, as such, is itself highly unstable, frail, and constantly under "threat." It is not at all surprising that by the early twentieth century, the security and durability of the "white race" had become a site of hysterical anxiety in the face of "degenerate races," ultimately underwriting state-backed eugenics programs throughout the country.[93]

At one level, therefore, the "problem" of disenfranchisement that is captured in the Maryland debates and that continues to plague us today is that it has been applied inappropriately, excluding from full political membership persons who should not have been excluded. Without doubt, as restrictions against women and nonwhites have been removed and the scope of disenfranchisement of criminals or mentally disabled persons has been "modernized," we have moved closer to some notion of "universal" suffrage. But insofar as the project of suffrage continues to focus on expanding the rights and obligations of citizenship *correctly*, that is, to the *right* persons, the logic of exclusion itself persists, and the work of subject formation performed by suffrage continues as well. If we are to move beyond treating disenfranchisement as this variety of "problem," then we must also be willing not only to move past it but also to recognize the limits of inclusion. Inclusion, even in an extreme form that draws no boundaries whatsoever about who is allowed to vote, is necessary but insufficient to address the deeper problem revealed by the 1864 debates in Maryland: an overarching desire to fix, stabilize, and essentialize identities in the name of producing a community of equals who are fit to rule over themselves and others. Insofar as restrictions on the franchise *and the franchise itself* support the construction of an idealized and normal citizen, and given the particular history of the franchise in the United States, how is it not the case that the "normal" and "ideal" citizen continues to be figured as white, innocent, and able-bodied? What we should know by now, at least, is that when we note the struggles for certainty that plagued the delegates to the 1864 convention, we are often not far away from them, continuing to ground and fix assumptions of the reasonableness, the goodness, and the ableness of our selves in order to solidify untenable positions of superiority that deny our own differences and vulnerabilities, our own rebelliousness and criminality, our own impairments and disabilities, and our own practices and selves.

8

(Re)figuring Justice

As I noted at the beginning of this book, there is no shortage of good reasons to condemn disenfranchisement and agitate for its end. It is pointless punishment, it is racist, it reproduces racial inequalities, it is excessive and cruel, it is an administrative nightmare, it undercuts the value we place on self-government, it skews electoral results, and on and on. At its core, it surely reflects an aberration of deeply held values and violates liberal and civic republican theories of justice. But it also performs discursively useful work by bringing into existence the very categories of thought and the normative terms that we use to condemn it (that it is disproportionate, that it is exclusionary, etc.).

My argument is that we must pause and reflect on *why* disenfranchisement has such a long and persistent history in the United States in order to be clear about what an "end" to disenfranchisement might look like. To be rid of it is far more difficult than simply realizing that it is a punitively pointless and unjust social policy. If it were that simple, would we not expect it to have already disappeared? But more people today, both in raw numbers and as a percentage of the voting-age population, are excluded from voting because of a criminal conviction than at any point in the nation's history. Our attachment to it is driven by practices of productive blindness and useful ignorance. The right to vote derives a considerable part of its value *because* of our refusal to let some persons vote. Moreover, it has been a powerful tool in the production and maintenance of white supremacy as a political system in the United States for nearly two centuries. Its ability to do this is directly linked to its role in the work of race-making, of policing the boundaries not simply of the polity but of the normatively *white* polity and of whiteness itself. In short, we must confront the fact that it does work for us and that this work may be deeply pernicious (the establishment and maintenance of white supremacy) as well as subtle (marking voting as a praiseworthy action of moral superiority).

Criminal disenfranchisement reveals how full citizenship is, perhaps contrary to popular ideals, not available to everyone born within the territorial boundaries of the nation. Its persistence is a reminder that we live our day-to-day lives constantly afraid of harm, either at the hands of others or, as I interpret Locke, from our own aggression. One response, shared by political theorists, legislators, and citizens alike, has been to erect boundaries between punishment and citizenship so we can avoid confronting the tenuous relationship between guilt and membership, so we can stabilize our sense of the political community and ourselves as members of that community. As a result, the satisfaction some of us feel when we exercise our political rights as citizens is purchased with the currency of exclusions, which we refuse to acknowledge as punitive exclusions, and as a result, the separation of punishment and citizenship causes those practices to become unintelligible. It is a practice that is very useful even as it is despicable.

One solution is to actually enforce the separation between the two spheres honestly and directly, to make punishment *only about* punishment and citizenship *only about* citizenship.[1] If we abolished all forms of criminal disenfranchisement tomorrow, this would be an excellent (and necessary) first step, but it would not be enough. As I have argued here, disenfranchisement is not the *cause* of the discursive relationship between punishment and political membership but more properly an *outcome* of that relationship and, in turn, reinforces that relationship. By slipping into a legal "background" of separate codes for criminal and electoral matters, it is more properly a *symptom* or *remainder* of an increasingly buried and invisible legal structure. Ending disenfranchisement would be a victory for sure, and I think we should end the practice without delay. The legitimacy of electoral politics in the United States on liberal grounds is directly put into question by its persistence. But insofar as the analysis here points to underlying tensions in whom and how we punish, to equality purchased at the expense of others, and to an increasingly depoliticized discourse about both citizenship and punishment, we have reason to worry that it would be a short-lived victory at best. If we abolish disenfranchisement today, it is likely that the work of moral, social, and political differentiation would continue, through a different abject figure and in a different location.

Disenfranchisement is, of course, just one among many phenomena that characterize the carceral landscape in the United States: mass incarceration and its collateral consequences; the normalization of indefinite detention; punitive immigration policy; the use of supermax prisons, life without parole, and solitary confinement for adults and juveniles; the registration and civil commitment of sex offenders; the trying of juveniles as adults. Such practices are routinely visited on felons in a milieu of governance and social order that exemplifies the abuses of juridical, rehabilitative, and biopolitical power. We do it all, and we do it all at once: punishing, confining, monitoring, managing, and producing. Analogous figures to the "felon" are easily identifiable at other discursive intersections: the "illegal immigrant," the "sex offender," or the "Muslim" in the post-9/11 United States could each be the object of a similar analysis to that of the "felon" as given here.[2] In these figures, when confronted with the interplay between these techniques of power and ways of knowing, we have erected brilliant structures of plausible theoretical deniability. The discursive shifts in the terms of such practices (away from overtly racist, sexist, ableist exclusions to seemingly "identity-blind" and "technical" versions) have further depoliticized spaces of contestation and resistance. It is harder to resist deployments of power in large part because it is hard to know where to look.

This is in part because the work of liberalism in the United States has an especially racialized effect on how we see the world. It presents an instance of what scholars have diagnosed as an "epistemology of ignorance": a way of knowing that is predicated on *not* knowing in specific ways.[3] The fight to end "ex-offender" disenfranchisement has rested on the assumption that individuals currently serving their sentences—a disproportionately black and Latino population—are worthy of exclusion.[4] If we take suffrage to be a mechanism of determining the interests or will of a population, we can see how disenfranchisement *and* the recent reform movement against ex-offender disenfranchisement are predicated on not knowing the interests or wills of incarcerated citizens. That this works so well is because the terms of race and other forms of difference are written into liberalism, not against or alongside it.

The deeper challenge presented by disenfranchisement is not simply to expand the boundaries of the polity by extending the right to vote to all but to rethink why suffrage so effectively does the work of normalizing, fixing, and stabilizing political activity itself. That is to say, how can we confront a white supremacist political system without also rethinking our approach to the self-definitions of the American polity and the citizen? This challenge pushes to the core of our notions of democracy and groupness that implicitly normalize forms of difference. Lennard Davis argues that the concept of the "normal" emerged during the nineteenth century in part as a solution to resolve a "paradox of representation" in democratic regimes.[5] Democratic representation, he argues, assumes both a set of unique individuals and a collective body that can be represented. It is the concept of the norm that bridges this gap between individuals and collectives, allowing a group of otherwise *different* persons to be aggregated and collapsed into a *unitary* collective by projecting the idea of a "normal citizen." Voting, therefore, becomes a way to elect a person who can represent the collective by "representing the normal," rather than a plurality of individual variations.[6] As a result, Davis argues, "representative democracy is normalcy, or, to try a neologism, normocracy."[7] Such a political constitution becomes predicated on the fungibility of human bodies, on the interchangeability of able-bodied citizens that necessarily suppresses difference even as difference is expressly included in the polity.

Disenfranchisement as a practice, it must be remembered, is an exclusion of those who would *otherwise have already been included* in the polity, whose full "citizenship" was assumed until they were otherwise demonstrated as deviating too far from the norm to be allowed near the ballot box. As the base qualifications for full citizenship have been dramatically extended to include nonwhites and women, for instance, the usage of disenfranchisement has become more important in maintaining the idea of the "normal citizen." But even if barriers to the vote continue to fall, there is no reason to assume *suffrage itself* will not continue to do this normalizing work of reducing variation to simplified choices, insofar as electoral representation may, as Davis argues, continue to normalize difference. "In the midst of this system," Davis notes, "the person with disabilities is only one casualty among many. Under normalcy, no one is or can be normal, just as no one is or can be equal. All have to work hard to make it seem that they conform, and so the person with disabilities is singled out as a dramatic case of not belonging. This identification makes it easier for the rest to think they fit the paradigm."[8] I would readily add "the felon" to the list of casualties, not simply because of this figure's similarly situated position to the "disabled" but also, as has been demonstrated in the previous chapter, because the two figures are so often one and the same. And given the racialized history of how abnormality, disability, and difference have functioned in the United States, the "normocracy" is deeply raced in a way that "inclusion" may be unable to address.

It is telling that Iris Young's own strident defense of democratic inclusion entails a move *away* from aggregative theories of democracy. We must instead, she insists, reshape the *kind* of democratic practices in which we engage. While I imagine she would surely support restoring the vote to persons who have been disenfranchised, her critique of aggregative theories of democracy implies that such inclusion would only be a prior condition toward moving to a mode of politics that looks less and less expectantly for answers from the ballot box.[9] We should be skeptical of the idea that by simply removing the barriers to the right to vote that continue to plague the United States, we will also move beyond the notions of criminality and ability that underlie and continue to enforce such barriers. We must confront a political moment in which the radical inclusion of the voices of those who are specifically thought to be *unfit* and *unable* becomes an opportunity to engage in new political deliberations, overturning fixed notions of subjectivity and ability. The point of including radical forms of difference must never be to suppress, normalize, or marginalize that difference but, rather, to create a kind of inclusion without aggregation or norm, an inclusion to a plurality within political subjects, an inclusion that refuses to allow oneself or others to be fixed or stabilized.

We must engage in political practice with an eye toward communication with others who are differently situated, even radically so, not for the limited sake of arriving at a consensus or aggregate decision but instead to open ourselves (even dangerously) to the wonder of new possibilities. As Young puts it,

A respectful stance of wonder toward other people is one of openness across, awaiting new insight about their needs, interests, perceptions, or values. Wonder also means being able to see one's own position, assumptions, perspectives as strange, because it has been put in relation to others. . . . I cannot assume that because last week I understood her standpoint, I can do so today. Respectful listening thus involves attentive and interested questioning. But answers are always gifts. The transcendence of the other person always means that she can remain silent, or tell only part of her story, for her own reasons.[10]

Inclusion is necessary but insufficient for this kind of politics. More than simply including others (be they criminals, mentally impaired, or even children and "foreigners") in the right to vote, we must *also* redirect our politics toward meaningful, respectful, and wondrous engagement with others, especially if we wish to address systemic injustice and recognize the dangers of relying on narratives of "fixed" and "given" basic structures of political life.[11]

If this book takes a step toward undoing the work of punitive political membership, it does so by bringing it outside the prevailing terms of political and social theory, penology, or criminology. Accordingly, action that challenges the work of punitive political membership must look beyond legislative reform, executive power, or judicial review but also to an alteration of our day-to-day practices of living with others. Rather than projecting fear and anxiety onto others, we must be willing to risk truly living, talking, and working with those around us. We must fully embrace the contingency of living in a world that cannot be controlled without exacting too high a price on our fellow citizens. We must *reinvent* and *refigure* citizenship and punishment on different terms, sharing the burdens of excess and marginality if they truly are unavoidable. If we want to remedy the cruelty of disenfranchisement, we also must commit ourselves to entirely new ways of being citizens and punishing criminals. We would have to, for lack of a better term, *get beyond* punishment and citizenship as they are practiced today. This is not to call for an escape from politics into the domain of ethics but rather to refuse that distinction and to insist on the *political* nature of our everyday existence and practices.

We should acknowledge the work these criminological figures do for us and with that acknowledgment refigure the normative terms of justice we apply to ourselves as agents, as (non)members, as criminals ourselves, and as people mutually implicated and indebted to each other. To this end, there remains a pragmatic need for a conception of "groupness" that does not rest on a facile notion of essentialism on one side or entirely amorphous selfhood on the other. In this final chapter, I turn to Young's account of the *series* (as a kind of social collectivity) as a helpful way to refigure criminals through their *situations* and ourselves as nonsovereign. This allows the distinction I have been using throughout this book—between "criminals" as an objectified other lacking subjectivity and "ourselves" as some authentic subject—to finally be rejected. Based on this conception of "groupness," I offer a political response, bringing together Beauvoirian and Foucauldian ethics alongside Young's account of justice, arguing that we must refigure ourselves, our practices, and our lives in order to *practice* justice as a simultaneously political and ethical project, deeply indebted to each other's freedom. In this way, any political response to disenfranchisement must reach beyond the logic of inclusion, must refuse the demands of color-blindness (as well as other forms of difference-blindness), and be directed toward the difficult task of dismantling the current racial order.[12]

CRIMINALITY AS SERIALITY

The kind of openness to others that Young points toward is difficult both practically and conceptually. One common criticism of taking up poststructuralist and genealogical approaches to thinking about the politics of disenfranchisement is to assert that there is no "there" there, that it reflects an evacuation of the terms of politics and replaces it with a simplistic and individualistic ethics. Noting that the stability of the "felon" as a kind of identity exists only through the ideological and tactical deployment of notions about race, sex, gender, and ability means, upon scrutiny, that this deployment fails to uphold the kind of stability required for the work of political membership. We are potentially left without any meaningful understanding of membership, let alone citizenship.

Of course, the criminal justice system has a ready-made answer to this problem: the "identity" of the felon is determined through a person's actions, marked and determined as felony status offenses of the criminal law. But, as should be apparent from the theoretical and historical work of this book, resorting to atomistic conceptions of action and identity disregards the historical and material contingency of illegality and the malleability of "identities" as the existing social and political environment of the world shapes them. The figure of the felon and the practice of disenfranchisement are, in a sense, less about one's "identity" and more about one's identification as a "member" of a social grouping.

What is necessary, from both practical and theoretical points of view, is a notion of belonging, membership, or groupness that can avoid the twin dangers of essentialist identities on the one hand and radically empty subjectivity on the other. To put it differently, we should ask if there is a way to *contingently* "stabilize" or "identify" persons for the purposes of conceiving of them collectively, but in a way that does not rely on either naive essentialism or strict normalization. This is necessary because, as Young notes, "oppression happens to social groups. But philosophy and social theory typically lack a viable conception of the social group."[13] If we are to adopt a framework that can identify "felons" or "criminals" as an oppressed group, then being able to talk about them as a "group" is necessary. My contention, however, is stronger: "felons" and "criminals" do constitute a social group, but not because they have an essential or fixed character but because they are *formed into* one.

A defining feature of being a felon is that one is *made* a felon through complicated intersections of existing identifications (e.g., racial, national, sexual), one's own actions, the actions of the state (e.g., identifying some actions as "criminal"), the actions of nonstate actors reproducing these identifications to demonstrate public standing (e.g., voting, working), and the broad set of collateral consequences of these intersections. That is, to "be" a felon is a complicated thing, and any critically informed analysis must proceed by troubling the idea that such an "identity" exists at all. Contrary to dismissive claims that identities are social productions and so have no reality, it is precisely because identities *are produced* that they are so real and so important. There are felons, and we can meaningfully refer to them as a group, but only if we have a clear sense of what we might mean by such a group. If we want to speak about justice from the viewpoint of groups—an important corrective to Rawlsian and other contemporary liberal conceptions of justice as inherently distributive questions—we need a conception of "group" that does not succumb to the same underlying assumptions about action and identity that underlie its more typical conceptions.

To do this, I turn to Young's reading of gender as *seriality*, itself based on Jean-Paul Sartre's analysis of serial collectives.[14] The scope in this section is rather narrow: to make a case for theorizing the so-called identity of the "felon" or the "criminal" and to show how this approach can help reveal how persons convicted of criminal offenses are similarly situated not primarily by their own actions or ascriptive attributes but by how those actions and attributes are essentialized through punitive and exclusionary practices, the *practico-inert* realities of living in the United States "on paper," that is, under state supervision by the criminal justice system.

Young's own interest in developing such an approach stems from her broader critique of theories of justice that are typically "methodologically individualist or atomist" and "assume that the individual is ontologically prior to the social."[15] Young's approach develops functional conceptions of justice and responsibility that neither rely on these untenable liberal assumptions of the autonomy, authenticity, and coherence of individualism nor limit themselves to legalist ways of thinking about responsibility. But the question of how to treat a group of persons who have already been found to be morally reprehensible and individually responsible through the criminal justice system is a place where we can and must work *with* Young to extend her account. Throughout her work, Young is routinely attentive to the role of the criminal justice system in larger questions of social and political justice. But to my knowledge, she never expressly took up the question of how to deal with criminals themselves *as a group*.[16] For my analysis, this is especially necessary, given that the kinds of treatment that fall on criminals and felons in particular do so *collectively* rather than individually and *collaterally* rather than directly.

While Young takes up the question of what constitutes a group, most notably in *Justice and Politics of Difference* and in *Democracy and Inclusion*, it is her 1994 article "Gender as Seriality" in which she most directly confronts the difficulty of dealing with the theoretical and pragmatic dilemma of how to think about persons who do not actively or self-consciously think of themselves as a group.[17] The specific "dilemma" she confronts there is how to reconcile a set of theoretical critiques and pragmatic demands faced by feminist politics. While affirming critical readings of sex and gender offered by theorists such as Judith Butler as "powerful and accurate," Young nevertheless concedes to the necessity of a "conception of women as a social collective" in order to ground feminist politics as a distinctive approach to political action.[18] While she fully rejects essentialist readings of sex and gender, Young worries that "the excessively critical orientation of such arguments" are "rather paralyzing" in terms of praxis.[19]

My own interest is not to evaluate the success or failure of Young's approach to gender (or justice, inclusion, democracy, responsibility, or any other of her objects of analysis) but rather to borrow from her *approach* and to embrace her "both/and" method of critical theory. In this case, I rely on her reading of Sartre's theory of social collectivities to navigate between these dangers: on one hand, the danger of essentialism that pervades theories of identity and group membership and, on the other hand, the potentially paralyzing effect of critical accounts—my own included.[20] Young argues that feminist politics can prevent theoretical paralysis by giving an account of gender that does not attempt to rise to the level of a total social theory. Instead, thinking of gender as seriality operates at a lower "level" of collectivity. This account can therefore remain attuned to the radical critiques of gender itself as a totalizing category, escaping, on the one hand, essentialist and individualist assumptions of personhood and, on the other, political practices that rely on normalizing or arbitrary qualifications for collective action.

Sartre's notion of the "social series" is a kind of social collective distinct from the "group." It is, Young notes, a "kind of social collectivity . . . that provides a way of thinking about women as a social collective without requiring that all women have common attributes or a common situation."[21] Nor does it "rely on identity or self-identity for understanding the social production and meaning of membership in collectives."[22] There are no consciously shared goals, collective actions, mutually acknowledged projects, pledges, contracts, constitutions, bylaws or statements of purpose that would otherwise mark a group, in the proper sense. In contrast to the "group," the social series is a kind of unity defined by what Sartre calls *practico-inert* reality. Young explains that *practico-inert* reality includes the "objects conditioned by a continuous material environment" and the "structures that have been created by the unintended collective results of past actions."[23] Such objects are practical in that they are the product of human action and inert in that they "constitute constraints on and resistances to action."[24] When persons pursue their individual ends in relation to the same *practico-inert* "objects" and "structures," they form a serial unity, linked together by those social objects.

We can summarize the features of a social series, as Young does, in roughly four points.[25] First, individuals are unified *passively* in relation to these objects. While they are actively related to a shared set of objects, they do not *relate to each other* intentionally but only as a byproduct of already-given material environments, habits, and social meanings. The kinds of actions in question are most likely habitual or routine in that actors engage in them without constant self-reflection as to their meanings; members are "unified passively by the relation their actions have to material objects and practico-inert histories."[26] Second, members of a series are members by virtue of these actions, however mundane, and not because of some common attribute that the members share. What members share is their relationship to the same *practico-inert* objects.[27] In this sense, membership in a series does not define something like one's "identity" and successfully moves the analysis away from essentialist claims of unity. Third, members of a series are related to each other "in isolation." They are functionally anonymous to each other and to themselves. They are "Other to the Others," and insofar as they are members of the series, they are "Other than themselves."[28] This means a central part of the experience of being a "member" of a series is the realization of oneself from the point of view of the series. This is to say that the series membership is always predicated on being both a subject and an object simultaneously. As Young puts it, "In seriality, a person not only experiences others but also himself or herself as an Other, that is, as an anonymous someone."[29] Last, Young asserts that what is perhaps most interesting or most useful about the notion of the series is that it is capable of resisting normalizing, essentializing, and naturalizing tendencies inherent in thicker notions of a group. It is a "blurry, shifting unity, an amorphous collective."[30]

The idea of the social series allows Young to successfully redeploy this conception of "woman" as a signifier that points to specific *practico-inert* objects, creating a unity that is grounded materially and yet that does not succumb to indefensible essentialism.[31] The relevant *practico-inert* objects that determine the series "women" include "physical facts" and "biological events" linked to female bodies (such as breasts, vaginas, menstruation, pregnancy, and lactation) and also the "social rules" governing these facts and events. Moreover, Young includes not only the built environment that structures the series (gender-segregated bathrooms, for example) but also the social and political environment, including the sexual divisions of labor, parenting, care, and compulsory heterosexuality.

Two specific benefits of thinking from the point of view of the series are especially important for my analysis. First, while individuals in a social series do not identify with one another or see themselves as engaged in a collective enterprise, there is nevertheless a "latent potential" for the series to become a group. For instance, in the event of a disturbance or an interruption in the otherwise everyday, routine, or habitual actions of the series members, the passive unity can give way to an active and self-conscious relation among members. A series of anonymous persons waiting for a bus that never arrives may organize themselves to address the chronic tardiness of the public transit system, for instance, and in doing so substantively alter their social and political relation. For Young, theorizing gender as a social series does not restrict the possibility that members of the series called "women" can (and very frequently do) begin to identify themselves as women, to organize themselves as groups as an active unity, and it can provide a basis for a coherent vision of feminist politics that does not relinquish the concept of "woman" or police gender boundaries and can avoid succumbing to naive essentialism. A series can serve as a contingent yet firm basis for a political body to constitute itself.

Second, individuals can find themselves members of multiple series at any given moment or over time. Young notes that Sartre's specific intent in developing the notion was to speak about unorganized class existence, and the idea can be easily applied to national or racial structures as well; and it can be applied differently at different moments in one's life. Young notes, "The same person may relate to [social positionings] in different ways in different social contexts or at different times in their lives."[32] Because the series resists being reduced to identity, it allows for a far more fluid, multiple, and contingent account of how persons move and live in the social world.[33]

On the basis of each of the four features of serial membership noted earlier, we can make the case that criminality generally and felony specifically are forms of seriality. Being known as a criminal reflects these criteria, at least under the present terms of the carceral regime and its collateral consequences in the United States. Criminals do not, by most definitions, qualify as an identity or a group, especially not a political one. Instead, as noted earlier, the standard story is that one is a criminal by virtue of a juridical conviction for specifically violating a settled, propagated, and (hopefully, one might add) democratically legitimate law.

On the contrary, it has been a purpose of this book to raise the possibility that felons, outlaws, bandits, thieves, highway robbers, convicts, ex-cons, and delinquents cannot be fully accounted for by such a limited story. The notion of the criminal is theoretically, if not functionally, more than a simple categorization or status applied to an otherwise isolated and independent individual. Thinking about criminality as seriality first and foremost helps avoid fetishizing one action—committing a crime—at the expense of the numerous other routine actions and habits that constitute the *practico-inert* reality of criminality. That is, while a criminal activity *might* be a necessary condition for membership in the series "criminals," it is not a sufficient one. I hesitate, however, to concede entirely that criminal activity is necessary, given the degree to which false accusations, coerced confessions, and the use of torture is endemic in U.S. policing practices.

Besides being disenfranchised, members of this series are also policed, arrested, tried, convicted, sentenced, possibly incarcerated, possibly paroled, monitored, barred from employment, barred from housing, barred from state benefits, and socially stigmatized. Even within varied criminological debates about inherent, biological, genetic, natural, or essential traits connected to criminality, there is nevertheless an ambivalence between, on the one hand, the ascription of a criminal "identity" and, on the other hand, a strong ideological attachment to a notion of free will that supports the justificatory language of liability and responsibility in criminal justice. As techniques of punishment, the nineteenth-century penitentiary forms, workhouses, the practice of convict leasing in the postbellum period, and nearly all contemporary forms of incarceration, detention, and supervision operate serially. To be a criminal in the United States is to be part of a passive unity of persons anonymously linked to each other as inmates, as "on paper," or as political and social degenerates.

Ultimately, the question turns on identifying the *practico-inert* objects that delimit the criminal series and that constrain our actions. That is, what specific historical objects are acted on by persons such that they become members of this amorphous unity? Obvious candidates include the criminal law itself, specific techniques of punishment, and the overwhelming regimes of collateral consequences attendant to conviction, not tied to a specific criminal action or judicial sentence but attendant to the status of felon, drug offender, sex offender, violent criminal, and so on. Insofar as these statutory collateral consequences presume to act on a settled "identity" or "class" of persons, they are part and parcel in the fabrication of the figure of the criminal as congealed legal structures that are both practical (existing in the world as human creations) and inert (objects resisting and constraining human actions of labor, dwelling, or suffrage).

The possible list is long, and obviously I take the restriction of voting rights to be an exemplary and important *practico-inert* object, but two other objects are worth noting for illustrative purposes: first, the likelihood of being "policed" and, second, the criminalization of some actions instead of others. Insofar as a criminal offense may or may not itself be a necessary condition for being a member of the criminal series, being policed surely is. Without detection, there might be a crime, but there can be no criminal. The history of the police and the modern ideas of police science are not my interest here, but it suffices to say that there is such a history; and as such, policing is an exemplary instance of a *practico-inert* object: produced in the world as an institution, with a set of techniques, and which, through a Weberian claim on the legitimate use of violence, is an object against which actions meet resistance. In the United States, the question thus turns on *who* is policed. Policing is not randomly or evenly distributed across populations in the United States. That is, the *practico-inert* structure of the police is not experienced by everyone in the same way in this country. Even in jurisdictions in which police presence is high, the distribution of this structure is far from random. The disproportionate presence of African Americans and Latinos in the criminal justice system, for instance, cannot be explained by disproportionate rates of offending by those groups. This is especially known to be true with drug offenses, as illegal drug usage is as prevalent, if not more prevalent, among whites.

Second, as Emile Durkheim and George Herbert Mead rightly insisted over a century ago, which actions are deemed criminal indicates the boundaries of social solidarity rather than the intrinsic or consequential evil of an action.[34] For instance, the historical criminalization of sodomy and abortion is a reflection of the reduced standing of homosexuals and women. The continued sentencing disparity between crack and powder cocaine, while recently improved, also continues to reflect the white supremacist legacies of criminalizing black autonomy itself. In general, the built environment of the criminal law directly generates the contingent but real structure against which some actions generate serial criminality and other do not.

The dramatic differences in *practico-inert* structures are starkly visible in the geographies of many elite universities in the United States, especially those situated in heavily policed cities in the United States and those that are within or adjacent to some of the most heavily policed neighborhoods in those cities. It is often a fruitful thought experiment for students to imagine what would happen to them if the police who patrol the streets of the surrounding neighborhoods applied the same level of enforcement and the same policing tactics to student dormitories that they do on the streets outside their windows. Even the most sheltered students quickly can think of how often their otherwise "criminal" actions have *not* left them exposed to the criminal justice system's powerful effect on their otherwise free actions.

From drug use to illegal downloading to tax evasion to sex, the *practico-inert* structures of their lives are predictably different from their neighbors. It is not simply their "law-abiding" natures that keep students out of jail. Their status, their normative whiteness, and their relative wealth each contribute partially to their abilities to often avoid policing altogether and to respond differently to it if they should encounter it.[35] Thinking about criminality as seriality promotes an understanding of criminality that can be no longer naively understood as a trait of the person or even as a reflection of only one's actions. Rather, criminality must always be thought of in relation to the *situation* at hand.

This approach has important practical and normative implications. First, a series always possess a latent capacity to become a group. For example, on December 9, 2010, prisoners simultaneously went on strike in seven prisons across the state of Georgia.[36] The general shock with which these strikes was met speaks to our habits of assuming that the criminal punishment system is effective in its ability to reduce inmates to passive collectives, isolated from their own political agency as well as from each other. Yet on that morning, the series of convicts in Georgia embraced their latent potential and began an active and self-reflective political action, identifying themselves as a coherent group with a specific list of demands, including a living wage, educational opportunities, improved living conditions, increased access to their families, and a reform of the state parole system. While this action was not triggered by some exogenous factor, the longstanding levels of abuse combined with a perniciously high corrections rate—one in thirteen Georgians are under state supervision—underscores the extent to which prisoners across Georgia were already in a coherent unity that could be converted into an organized group. The strike ended roughly ten days later, amid some concessions by the Georgia Department of Corrections but also amid renewed allegations of the use of brutal force to end the strike and to subject its leaders to harsh retribution.

Second, a critical feature of seriality is its blurry, shifting, and amorphous quality. If one were to alter the *practico-inert* structures, to change the milieu of habits and routine practices that build and support our present carceral regime, the membership of the serial collective would likewise change. An attention to seriality reminds us of how great our power is to alter criminal justice policy. By broadening our perspective beyond just legal statutes, policing policies, or sentencing guidelines, we can also attend to the everyday ways in which we are all necessarily involved in the production and maintenance of the milieu. One way that we may be able to reduce mass incarceration and end collateral consequences is by altering the way we view and respond to each other or, following Young's examples, the way we greet each other on the street and the way we move though the city.[37]

The scope and domain of actions, habits, and routines on which we *can* have agency to alter the milieu of *practico-inert* reality is far wider than we might otherwise think. By recognizing the ways in which those of us who are not presently incarcerated or under supervision nevertheless also act in relation to many of the same *practico-inert* structures of the law—that is, the degree to which we are criminals ourselves—might allow us to see ourselves as meaningfully in series with excessively policed neighbors who occasionally enjoy intoxicating substances as well. Or we might note how we are in series with inmates organizing for better living and working conditions. Tellingly, perhaps, the demands of striking inmates in Georgia reflect the way in which they, in addition to being members of the social series "criminal," are *also* members of the social series "workers," "brothers," "fathers," and citizens. This allows us to do two critical things: first, to locate ourselves in series with criminalized others as the basis for solidarity with the incarcerated and the disenfranchised and, second, to truly listen, with wonder and openness to those who have been exiled within the polity.

BAD FAITH AND DISENFRANCHISEMENT AS UNFREEDOM

One way to look at disenfranchisement, and at all suffrage restrictions for that matter, is through the notions of good and bad faith. If disenfranchisement, at its heart, is always about stabilizing the normative position of political membership, then it is necessarily an instance of what Jean-Paul Sartre and Simone de Beauvoir describe as political bad faith. As Sartre describes it in *Being and Nothingness*, bad faith is a specific form of a lie that we tell ourselves as a futile escape from the human condition of being "condemned to freedom."[38] This condition arises from what Sartre calls the "double property of the human being, who is at once a facticity and a transcendence."[39] Humans are both a thing in the world, an object, a "fact" of some kind, and yet always already beyond that facticity as a "transcendence." We are, Sartre famously asserts, caught in a bind by this double property: "If . . . freedom is defined as an escape from the given, from fact, then there is a fact of escape from fact. This is the facticity of freedom."[40]

To accept this seeming paradox, the facticity of freedom, would be to approach one's existence with good faith. Yet, far more commonly, we approach life in "bad faith," which "does not wish either to coordinate [these two aspects of human reality] nor to surmount them . . . [but] seeks to affirm their identity while preserving their differences."[41] Our bad faith reflects a refusal to acknowledge the contingency of the individual in the world or a refusal to acknowledge the facticity of the world. Rather than confront the double property of human existence, we seek refuge in one or the other, confronting the problem by refusing to properly confront it. Bad faith, on this account, is an attempt to escape from the self; it is a lie we knowingly tell ourselves. We are, by virtue of existing in the world, tied to, connected to, determined by, and formed by that world as it exists independently from ourselves. Its facticity reveals itself to us as an object, in Marxist overtones, that stands hostile and independent of ourselves. But we nevertheless exist in that world, conscious of that existence, and, as such, are capable of transcending it, of being free from facticity, *as a fact of our existence.* In the same moment, we are both radically determined by the world and radically free from it, simultaneously free and responsible.

Acting in bad faith has two paradigmatic forms at the extremes. On the one hand, it sees the world as driven by a facticity that denies the fact of freedom. It essentializes the self and others as objects, reduces everything to facticity. As Beauvoir describes the effect of bad faith in *The Second Sex*, each time "transcendence lapses into immanence, there is degradation of existence into 'in-itself,' of freedom into facticity."[42] When this form of bad faith occurs, she insists, it is an "absolute evil."[43] On the other hand, bad faith sees the world as driven by freedom, as transcendence, but at the expense of the world's facticity, its material and *practico-inert* existence. When this form of bad faith occurs, it is typically deployed to reject the claims of oppressed and dominated groups, refusing to take seriously their situations.[44] Beauvoir improves Sartre's account in a productive way, allowing for a more radical position on action and the facticity of the world in general, questioning Sartre's reliance on authenticity and an individualist emphasis on ethical action.[45]

If we look at the history of criminal disenfranchisement from this perspective, we can see these two forms of bad faith playing out differently across different periods. To those who think the felon is to be disenfranchised in response to a deep moral character of deceit or infamy, it is bad faith to think such persons themselves are immutable *practico-inert* objects in essence. This is the form bad faith took during the nineteenth-century debates over disenfranchisement. As an answer to the "Negro problem," it was the bad faith of overt oppression. Alternately, to those who think of disenfranchisement as a condition that only "temporarily" applies to felons or as a purely collateral consequence of the technical category of "felony," it is a form of bad faith to think that this practice withers away on its own; rather, it should be acknowledged as a *practico-inert* object, which forms and shapes the facticity of the world. This is the twentieth-century form of bad faith as it plays out under neoliberal terms.

To live in good faith is not to strategically switch between forms or to seek some moderate middle ground or to embrace a Sartrean notion of authentic personhood through freedom. Rather, following Beauvoir, living in good faith requires us to confront and acknowledge this dual property of human existence as a "fundamental ambiguity."[46] Such an acknowledgment is, in Beauvoir's terms, to think about the world and our freedom in deeply inter-subjective terms. Much as in the case of the series described earlier, Beauvoir breaks down the clear distinctions between subject and object, noting the ways in which we are always both subject and object in relation to ourselves and to others. Such acknowledgment forces us to recognize that "to will oneself free is also to will others free."[47] Bad faith, especially in its form as an absolute evil, occurs when one's freedom is purchased at the expense of the other, when one falsely thinks the other is irrelevant to one's own free-dom, or when one falsely believes oneself to stand independently from the world.[48] A form of one's own freedom, of course, *can indeed* be purchased on the backs of others, as the practice of disenfranchisement illustrates. The white workingman, the union loyalist, the sane and able-bodied, the in-nocent citizen are all in fact free, within liberal and republican terms. And they are free by virtue of the exclusion, the disavowal, and the abjection of the criminal, the lunatic, the rebel solider, the "free Negro" laborer, the slave, the child, or the woman.

What else is disenfranchisement (or any restriction on the franchise) in this regard than a form of concrete *unfreedom*, a choice of servitude for others in a hubristic attempt to free oneself through the other? What kind of freedom do I exercise through my vote in the absence of the criminal-ized other, barred from the ballot box in order to "purify" it? This form of freedom is productive, real, and an expression of bad faith, refusing to *acknowledge* the other and myself as both facticity *and* transcendence.[49] It is particularly pernicious in that it is a practice of freedom that *systematically depoliticizes its object*. In that disenfranchisement operates by restricting a form of distinctly political expression, it reduces the felon to an object *outside* the political realm, along with the attendant categories of difference (e.g., race and class) that were likely deployed to criminalize the person in the first place.

Acting in good faith requires that we necessarily confront the character of human existence as having both facticity and transcendence. Realizing that one is condemned to freedom implicitly requires us to ask if a particular "state of affairs must be perpetuated."[50] While Beauvoir is speaking here about the question of gender inferiority as a result of oppression, the demand is applicable more broadly. As she puts it, the question of "sex" and its relation to gender is necessarily one that calls for an existentialist account of ethics, where one's freedom is the central concern.[51] That the will to freedom *requires* others be free is, Beauvoir insists, "not an abstract formula. It points out to each person concrete action to be achieved."[52] This puts our practices squarely within the domain of ethics as well as politics in a new way. Beauvoir's existentialist ethics, by virtue of its deep intersubjectivity, requires freedom be a project of the self that is already in relation to the freedom of others and in relation to the facticity of the world, of its *contingent practico-inert* objects and structures. "One does not exist without doing something," she writes. "It is a matter of reconquering freedom on the contingent facticity of existence, that is, of taking the given, which, at the start, *is there* without reason, as something willed by man."[53] It is in this way that I read Beauvoir's ethics as deeply political, focused on action in a political context, and directed toward reshaping that context.

JUSTICE AS CONDITIONAL FAILURE

What would such action look like in terms of justice? And what does it mean to take "the given" in this way? To identify what actions we must take requires that we take stock of the current state of affairs in order to formulate our responses to it. For Foucault, this requires a genealogy of the subject and an account of the "rules of the game," given the "truth" of a particular milieu. One's actions must be self-reflective of this "given" in which freedom is practiced, including the fabrication of the self in relation to the fabrication of others. While Foucault's late work on the subject is often framed as a turn toward "ethics" at the expense of the continued analyses of power and politics, such a formulation misses the overtly political nature of Foucault's account of practices of freedom. The political nature of such projects is readily apparent in the nineteenth-century delegates' deployment of a set of "truth games" with regard to various excluded persons, seeking to determine "the state of fact a man is in" in order to shore up the boundaries of the polity. The whole history of disenfranchisement at its core can be read in a Foucauldian light as a "study [of] the games of truth in the relationship of self with self and the forming of oneself as a subject."[54]

Foucault writes, "The subject is constituted through practices of subjection, or, in a more anonymous way, through practices of liberation, of freedom, as in Antiquity, starting of course from a number of rules, styles and conventions that are found in the culture."[55] Freedom, therefore, is reformulated as a practice that is tailored to the "rules, styles and conventions" of a particular milieu. The "rules, styles and conventions" that allow a practice to be "free" require knowing the specific rules and practices of a specific *milieu*, of the truth games or regimes of veridiction that are in play, that is, as a subject that forms oneself, but *never* appearing to be "beyond the mechanism of power."[56] To be an ethical subject is to engage in practices that are self-conscious of their status as forming the self in relation to existing rules of conduct, or styles of existence. Foucault writes, "The task of testing oneself, examining oneself, monitoring oneself in a series of clearly defined exercises, makes the question of truth—the truth concerning what one is, what one does, and what one is capable of doing—central to the formation of the ethical subject."[57] These questions of the self are necessarily self-conscious of the rules of the truth game as a *game*, as a regime of veridiction under which they can be said to be true practices and, hence, contingent on the particular game one finds oneself in.[58] An awareness that practices of the self are practices of self-knowing is what links ethics to games of truth and, as such, to politics:

> One cannot care for the self without knowledge. The care for self is of course knowledge of self, . . . but it is also the knowledge of a certain number of rules of conduct or of principles which are at the same time truths and regulations. To care for self is to fit one's self out with these truths. That is where ethics is linked to the game of truth.[59]

Such an account of ethics, freedom, and the self brings us back to the importance of genealogy generally and its ability to expose the contingency of political membership shaped by practices of felon disenfranchisement.

In redescribing felon disenfranchisement as a productive practice—one that produces the subjects it takes as objects—we can see the contingency of this formation of knowledge (the figure of the felon) and the deeper injustice of the practice (which operates both within and against a liberal framework of justice). The outcome of such genealogical work, thus, is not to prove a particular formation as "good" or "bad" but instead to better understand the formation itself and the basis on which counterformations might be possible. As Ladelle McWhorter explains, "By marshaling over-looked evidence, a genealogy shows a community of believers that those claims are not fully justified according to their own standards of justification. The choice then is either to give up those discourses or claims or to give up the standards of justification that ground both those claims themselves and the counterclaims that genealogy makes."[60] To repeat this in Beauvoir's terms, the choice we face on the basis of genealogy "is whether this state of affairs must be perpetuated."[61] As Karen Vintges notes, "Beauvoir's emphasis on ethics as a way of life that demands constant exercise shows a remarkable similarity with the ethics of the later Foucault."[62] And taken together, these two compatible approaches bring us back to Young's conception of justice as both an ethical and a political project and as primarily concerned with *doing* rather than *holding*.

For Young, an account of justice that is attentive to difference, to groups rather than abstract individuals, and to what Beauvoir might call the "situation" requires a shift in focus away from an analytics of "distribution," which overly focuses us on "things" that can be "held" in various "patterns." The standard distributive approach to justice, Young notes, "must conceptualize all issues of justice in terms of patterns. It implies a static social ontology that ignores process."[63] Instead, questions of justice should attend to processes, practices, and actions. This is not to ignore the question of patterns or holdings, as these too can and should be addressed by any "adequate conception of justice"[64] Yet processes, practices, and actions are properly the stuff of "justice" in Young's account, driven by an attention to the demands and concerns of those who are the victims of *in*justice, dominated, and/or oppressed. "We act," she writes, "with knowledge of existing institutions, rules, and the structural consequences of a multiplicity of actions, and those structures are enacted and reproduced through the confluence of our actions."[65] For Young, this understanding of the self, the world, and the actions that connect the two underscores her commitment to critical theory, insisting that "good normative theorizing cannot avoid social and political description and explanation."[66] Likewise, description and explanation already include normative commitments and are driven by a stance that is "critical" in nature and normative in outcome. Justice, both in theory and in practice, cannot be left to either purely normative or positive theorizing but must reflect the "emancipatory interest" of the philosopher who lives, breathes, and wills to be free.

A series of specific historical figures has run throughout this book: the delinquent, the abnormal, the thief, the "free Negro laborer," the rebel solider, the mentally incompetent, the monster, the citizen, and above all, the felon. I turn to figures because we often think publicly in figures in place of arguments, and we make arguments through and on the behalf of figures. The same is easily said of justice, figured in many forms but commonly in the manner of the Roman goddess, holding a sword and a set of scales. The blindfold she wears is thought to have been introduced in the fifteenth century and is typical of depictions in the United States. I rely on figures not because they capture the truth of the matter but because figures ought to remind us of their histories of becoming. But they are also dangerous because once figured, they tend toward abstraction, finality, and stasis. We get accustomed to them, and we begin to rely on them for thinking. They begin to resist the processes of social, political, and material fabrication that brought them into being, and they begin to do the work for us. The only way they remain useful for us is if we constantly remind ourselves of their histories and ruthlessly question how they are figured and how they have become embodied. In the United States, *justice* has long been figured as for some white persons and in service of normative whiteness. Part of this comes through the willful blindness we impose on it, and part of it comes from our desire for justice to produce definitive ends, a static balance between simply opposing forces, weighed on a scale and enforced by the sword.

What we must seek is justice that is *continually refigured as a practice of freedom* always in relation to others. To will justice, like freedom, is to will it for others. We must read questions of justice as figures, and we must read figurations as always tied to practices of freedom in relation to others, situated contingently, and tied socially and politically as a debt to others. This will be difficult beyond measure, and it will be fraught with failure. But as Beauvoir rightly notes, a condition of ethics is failure:

> But it is also true that the most optimistic ethics have all begun by
> emphasizing the element of failure involved in the condition of man;

without failure, no ethics; for a being who, from the very start, would be an exact co-incidence with himself, in a perfect plenitude, the notion of having-to-be would have no meaning.[67]

The same should be said of justice, as a figure and a practice, as a kind of *conditional* failure.[68] As with Beauvoir's claim about ethics, we appeal to justice when something has typically gone wrong, when something has failed, and as such, it is intimately linked with some identifiable failing, some *injustice*. But part of the difficulty is what we expect from justice in terms of "success." That is, if what "justice" produces is a static state of affairs or if it reinforces a particular arrangement of the world's facticity and thus makes change more difficult, then this may be a success that we are better off without. Justice, rather, ought to be thought of as something with inexhaustible terms that *require* a lack of perfection or "success" and that are part of the production of a self in relation to others that starts from those debts and those contingencies.[69]

Failure is part of the facticity of the world, and yet we go to great philosophical, ethical, and political lengths to avoid confronting failure as part of existence, largely by condemning others to the static position of failure.[70] Rather than refuse the "fundamental ambiguity" of existence and the necessity of failure in that existence, Beauvoir insists, it is possible to "want this tension with the failure which it involves" and to approach failure as "assumed" rather than as something to be "surpassed."[71] This does not necessarily take failure as a strategy to be pursued (although there is radical potential in such proposals) but rather reflects a shift in what we might mean as a "success" in terms of justice.[72] Any kind of justice that forecloses rather than opens possibilities for action—especially for those who have been relegated to nonbeing, abjection, and dismissal—both refuses to acknowledge the conditions of living in the world and re-creates the world in that image: foreclosed, static, and in deadly bad faith. As McWhorter warns,

> Whatever presses for closure, finality, absolute assurance presses also for an end to vitality—that is, for a kind of death. Set opinions, fixed categories, unquestionable procedures and protocols rooted in theory and tradition that lie beyond critique are some of the main ingredients in a fascistic way of life, in a way of life that bears contempt for life. What we must realize is that the degree to which we leave things unexamined and undisturbed is the degree to which we diminish our lives and the life around us.[73]

What my account of disenfranchisement ultimately requires is a resistance to the kind of closure, finality, and absolute assurance that both disenfranchisement and its piecemeal reform call for.

Justice as conditional failure means that any success or progress will always be measured against the injustices that are constitutive with that success. Justice as conditional failure will disappoint us, but such disappointment should spurn us to act. Justice as conditional failure means that justice is conditioned on an explicit and unflinching statement of what must come next. In the case of disenfranchisement, this means that we must recognize the failure of "universal suffrage" even as it is achieved and take that tension with us as we build different political lives. It requires that we refuse to allow our political lives to be captured entirely by one practice (such as voting) but need not be a rejection of electoral politics (although such a possibility should always be open to debate). This way of thinking about justice and about politics requires us an embrace of the ambiguity and impurity of "both/and." We can and should be properly liberal and loudly denounce the restriction of voting rights for criminal offenders because it is surely a disproportionate punishment, because it subjects people to an unjustifiable cruelty, and because it is beneath even a nominally liberal democratic polity. Yet because disenfranchisement so effectively does the work of defining and managing the boundaries of that polity, we will not be rid of it unless we are also rid of the deeper and broader forms of marginalization that characterize even a radically inclusive political system. To put it differently, we *both* must be more inclusive in how we conceive of politics *and* must get beyond the logic of inclusion.

Disenfranchisement must be ended, the franchise must be expanded, *and* we must work to end the desire for closure, for certainty, the denial of ambiguity that enables the franchise to do its work.

Coda

Is not this the record of present America? Is not this its headlong progress? Are we not coming more and more, day by day, to making the statement, "I am white," the one fundamental tenet of our practical morality? Only when this basic, iron rule is involved is our defense of right nationwide and prompt. Murder may swagger, theft may rule and prostitution may flourish and the nation gives but spasmodic, intermittent and lukewarm attention. But let the murderer be black or the thief brown or the violator of womanhood have a drop of Negro blood, and the righteousness of the indignation sweeps the world. Nor would this fact make the indignation less justifiable did not we all know that it was blackness that was condemned and not crime.

—W. E. B. DU BOIS, "The Souls of White Folk," 1920[1]

On July 8, 2013, nearly thirty thousand inmates across the state of California began refusing meals as part of a coordinated hunger strike against deplorable prison conditions in the state. This hunger strike is a renewal of a 2011 hunger strike organized by inmates in the Security Housing Unit (SHU) at Pelican Bay State Prison in Northern California. The SHU is often referred to as "prison within a prison" by officials who insist that the twenty-three hours a day of solitary confinement imposed on inmates is reserved for the "worst of the worst." This can only be said to be true if what is meant by the claim is that the terms of confinement in the SHU have the effect of utterly dehumanizing the individuals confined there.

At the heart of the strike is the use of the state's "gang validation" process, which allows for inmates to be placed *indefinitely* in solitary confinement based on the secret testimony of another prisoner that they are affiliated with a gang. Some prisoners have been validated as "gang members" on the basis of reading material found in their cells, including copies of black power literature from the 1960s, such as George Jackson's prison memoir, *Soledad Brother*. The only way out of isolation is through a confessional practice called debriefing, a process that virtually guarantees false information—especially if an individual is not actually a gang member but only accused of being one, for instance, on the basis of another inmate's debrief—or reprisals against inmates once they are released back into the population. The strikers have thereby declared a moratorium on all gang and race-related divisions.

As I write this, the strike is continuing, but with far fewer persons. The California Department of Corrections and Rehabilitation (CDCR) continues to classify the action as an "illegal disruption" and insists that it is being controlled by gang leaders, or "shot-callers" as they are known. CDCR is reported to be punishing inmates taking part in the strike who are not already in solitary confinement by placing them in it. The strike is system-wide, although the CDCR will not release specific numbers for each prison in the state. Sympathy strikes have occurred throughout the country at other prisons, and protests and demonstrations have been held outside the prison walls. Much of the public support for the strike seems to be coming from activists in the prison abolition movement and from the more radical wings of leftist political organizers. The CDCR has clarified its medical guidelines to note that inmates will not be force-fed without consent. It is unclear what exactly this means, except that the CDCR is hoping to outlast the strikers. In at least one instance so far, it has. Billy "Guero" Sell, an inmate reported to be a part of the strike, died in late July.

A few days after the strike began, on July 13, 2013, George Zimmerman was acquitted of all charges in the shooting death of seventeen-year-old Trayvon Martin. As I write this, it is unclear how long the protests and rallies that have occurred since then will continue or what shape they will take in the future. At a rally in Oakland, protestors held signs that read, "The Whole System Is Guilty," "No Justice, No Peace," and "Jail Zimmerman."

It took the police department in Sanford, Florida, six long weeks following Zimmerman's lethal shooting of Martin to arrest and arraign him. During these six weeks, it was astonishing to many people that given the Sanford police department's failure to investigate the case properly and the possibility of applying Florida's "Stand Your Ground" defense, Zimmerman was apparently immune to prosecution (even as similar cases produced vastly different outcomes). Troubled not simply by this fact but also by the explicitly and implicitly racialized context of the case, I found myself deeply invested in seeing Zimmerman arrested, tried, and ultimately punished. I remain angry and disheartened by the verdict and by the prospect that Zimmerman would not be punished for killing Martin.

And yet at the same time, as the argument of this book should make clear, I hold a deep distrust in a broken criminal justice system that has historically been an instrument in the foundation and maintenance of white supremacy as a political system. Zimmerman's acquittal appears to be a failure of justice. And it is a restatement of what was already clear in the Sanford's police department's death investigation: the willful death of a person is not a crime when that person's very being is considered criminal or is always already presumed to be criminal. This is the same structure as lynch law. Yet a conviction would have been a failure of justice as well, and necessarily so, because the criminal punishment system in the United States appears incapable of providing justice and has never been able to adequately do so insofar as it is a foundational institution in the system of white supremacy. I think that I would prefer the former injustice over the latter in this case, but I also fear that the former injustice is less mobilizing than the latter one appears to be (so far). I am left angry and disheartened that I live in a world where these appear to be my only choices for justice.

If I have any hope that justice can be refigured to include the claims of hunger strikers, the family of Trayvon Martin, and the 5.3 million people disenfranchised for felony convictions in the United States, it is from the work of prison abolitionists. What I have tried to argue in this book is that any frank confrontation with the practice of disenfranchisement or punishment more generally requires that we imagine not simply a better world but a different one. And some of key impediments standing in the way of our imagination are the current state of the world, our willingness to understand it, and who we are as a product of that world. As I have said already, felon disenfranchisement should end today. But the harder and more important work is to destroy the structures, the ways of thinking, and the practices that gave rise to it. What will happen if felons are given the vote? I do not know. What will happen if we stop building prisons, tear down the ones we already have, and refuse to build any more? I do not know. What will happen if we work to not be color-blind, or difference blind, but to actively destroy the political system of white supremacy and whiteness itself? And who will we become as a result? I do not know.

Yet it is precisely the possibility opened up by such changes and by the uncertainty of the future absent the unjust structures of the present that gives me hope that another world is possible.

Notes

1. A PRODUCTIVE INJUSTICE

1. This estimate is based on data from 2008. See "*One in 100: Behind Bars in America 2008*" (Washington, DC: Pew Center on the States, 2008). For the first time since the 1970s, the incarceration rate in the United States appears to have declined modestly beginning in 2010. At the time of this writing, this decrease appears to be largely a result of contraction in the inmate populations in states such as California, Texas, and New York that have the highest incarceration rates in the nation. The reasons for this decline remain unclear. See Lauren E. Glaze and Erika Parks, "*Correctional Populations in the United States, 2011*," (Washington, DC: U.S. Department of Justice, Bureau of Justice Statistics, 2012).

2. Glaze and Parks, "Correctional Populations in the United States, 2011"; "*Trends in U.S. Corrections*" (Washington, DC: Sentencing Project, 2011).

3. The rest are either on parole or on probation, according to "conservative" estimates for 2004, drawn from Jeff Manza and Christopher Uggen, *Locked Out: Felon Disenfranchisement and American Democracy* (New York: Oxford University Press, 2006), 76–77. Alabama, Delaware, Florida, Kentucky, Mississippi, and Virginia each have disenfranchisement rates over 5 percent of the voting-eligible population.

4. The Sentencing Project maintains the most accurate and up-to-date information on state-by-state variations in disenfranchisement provisions. Throughout this book, I rely on its tracking of disenfranchisement provisions. See "*Felony Disenfranchisement Laws in the United States*" (Washington, DC: Sentencing Project, 2012).

5. The overwhelming majority of persons disenfranchised for a criminal conviction are male, but there is no reason to limit analysis by sex. Throughout this book, I have tried to maintain the use of gender-neutral language where

appropriate. Where an exclusive gender category is used, this is either to reflect (1) the gendered nature of the social phenomenon in question or (2) the gendered usage of the sources with which I am engaged.

6. *Farrakhan v. Gregoire*, 623 F.3d 990 (9th Cir. 2010).

7. For more detailed studies of these differences as well as accounts of the broader trends in disenfranchisement provisions, see Alec C. Ewald, "*A 'Crazy-Quilt' of Tiny Pieces: State and Local Administration of American Criminal Disenfranchisement Law*" (Washington, DC: Sentencing Project, 2005); Jamie Fellner and Marc Mauer, "*Losing the Vote: The Impact of Felony Disenfranchisement Laws in the United States*" (Washington, DC: Sentencing Project, Human Rights Watch, 1998); Steven Kalogeras, "*Legislative Changes on Felony Disenfranchisement, 1996–2003*" (Washington, DC: Sentencing Project, 2003); Alexander Keyssar, *The Right to Vote: The Contested History of Democracy in the United States* (New York: Basic Books, 2000); Manza and Uggen, *Locked Out*; Robert R. Preuhs, "*State Felon Disenfranchisement Policy*," *Social Science Quarterly* 82, no. 4 (2001): 733–748; Nkechi Taifa, "*Re-enfranchisement!: A Guide for Individual Restoration of Voting Rights in States That Permanently Disenfranchise Former Felons*" (Washington, DC: Advancement Project, 2002).

For variations in other forms of collateral consequences between states, see Kevin G. Buckler and Lawrence F. Travis III, "*Reanalyzing the Prevalence and Social Context of Collateral Consequence Statutes*," *Journal of Criminal Justice* 31 (2003): 435–453; Marc Mauer and Meda Chesney-Lind, *Invisible Punishment: The Collateral Consequences of Mass Imprisonment* (New York: New Press, 2002); Kathleen M. Olivares, Velmar S. Burton, and Francis Cullen, "*The Collateral Consequences of a Felony Conviction: A National Study of State Legal Code 10 Years Later*," *Federal Probation* 60 (1996): 10–17; Darren Wheelock, "*Collateral Consequences and Racial Inequality: Felon Status Restrictions as a System of Disadvantage*," *Journal of Contemporary Criminal Justice* 21, no. 1 (2005): 82–90.

8. It is only recently that disenfranchisement provisions have solidified around the classification of "felony," typically indicating a crime that calls for imprisonment for more than a year. The historical *meaning* of the terms "felony" and "felon" are rarely considered in studies of criminal disenfranchisement. These meanings, I argue later in Chapters 6 and 7, turn out to be important for understanding the *work* that the term "felony" does in determining the polity.

9. Ewald, "'Crazy-Quilt' of Tiny Pieces."

10. William Petroski, "*NAACP: Branstad's Voting Order Is Discriminatory 'Poll Tax*,'" *Des Moines Register*, January 19, 2011.

11. Michelle Alexander, *The New Jim Crow: Mass Incarceration in the Age of Colorblindness* (New York: New Press, 2010), 2. There are important limits to the "New Jim Crow" analysis, explored nicely in James Forman Jr., "*Racial*

Critiques of Mass Incarceration: Beyond the New Jim Crow," New York University *Law Review* 87 (2012): 101–146.

12. According to Manza and Uggen, "When African Americans make up a larger proportion of a state's prison population, that state is significantly more likely to adopt or extend felon disenfranchisement" (*Locked Out*, 67). See also Angela Behrens, Christopher Uggen, and Jeff Manza, *"Ballot Manipulation and the 'Menace of Negro Domination': Racial Threat and Felon Disenfranchisement in the United States, 1850–2002,"* American Journal of Sociology 109, no. 3 (2003): 559–605; Alec C. Ewald, *"Collateral Consequences in the American States,"* Social Science Quarterly 93, no. 1 (2012): 211–247.

13. There appears to be strong (but contested) evidence that multiple U.S. Senate races and the 2000 presidential election would have had different outcomes if felon disenfranchisement had not been in place. See Sasha Abramsky, *Conned: How Millions Went to Prison, Lost the Vote, and Helped Send George W. Bush to the White House* (New York: New Press, 2006); Audrey Chambers, *"Votes of Felons, Ex-Felons Would Have Changed Election Outcomes,"* Institute for Policy Research News 22 (2001): 1–2; Abby Goodnough, *"Disenfranchised Florida Felons Struggle to Regain Their Rights,"* New York Times, March 28, 2004; Manza and Uggen, *Locked Out*; Jeff Manza and Christopher Uggen, *"Punishment and Democracy: Disenfranchisement of Nonincarcerated Felons in the United States,"* Perspectives on Politics 2, no. 3 (2004): 491–505; Thomas J. Miles, *"Felon Disenfranchisement and Voter Turnout,"* Journal of Legal Studies 33, no. 1 (2004): 85–129; Miles, *"Three Empirical Essays in the Economics of Crime"* (Ph.D. diss., University of Chicago, 2000); Guy Stuart, *"Databases, Felons, and Voting: Bias and Partisanship of the Florida Felons List in the 2000 Elections,"* Political Science Quarterly 119, no. 3 (2004): 453–475; Christopher Uggen and Jeff Manza, *"Democratic Contraction? Political Consequences of Felon Disenfranchisement in the United States,"* American Sociological Review 67 (2002): 777–803. There is also evidence that felon disenfranchisement provisions reduce turnout among nonfelon populations; i.e. there are collateral effects to collateral consequences. See Melanie Bowers and Robert R. Preuhs, *"Collateral Consequences of a Collateral Penalty: The Negative Effect of Felon Disenfranchisement Laws on the Political Participation of Nonfelons,"* Social Science Quarterly 90, no. 3 (2009): 722–743.

14. These are, of course, all important questions, but they are well addressed in the existing empirical literature. For historical accounts of the roots of disenfranchisement with an emphasis on legislative and judicial history, see Behrens, Uggen, and Manza, *"Ballot Manipulation"*; Roger Clegg, *"Who Should Vote?,"* Texas Review of Law and Politics 6 (2002): 159–178; Alec C. Ewald, *" 'Civil Death': The Ideological Paradox of Criminal Disenfranchisement Law in the United States,"* Wisconsin Law Review 2002, no. 5 (2002): 1045–1138; Alec C. Ewald and Bran-

don Rottinghaus, eds., *Criminal Disenfranchisement in an International Perspective* (Cambridge: Cambridge University Press, 2009); Howard Itzkowitz and Lauren Oldak, "*Restoring the Ex-Offender's Right to Vote: Background and Developments*," *American Criminal Law Review* 11, no. 721 (1973): 721–770; Kalogeras, "Legislative Changes on Felony Disenfranchisement"; Katherine Irene Pettus, *Felony Disenfranchisement in America: Historical Origins, Institutional Racism, and Modern Consequences* (New York: LFB, 2005); Elizabeth Simson, "*Justice Denied: How Felony Disenfranchisement Laws Undermine American Democracy*" (Americans For Democratic Action Education Fund, 2002).

For public opinion data on support for disenfranchisement policies and public policy assessments, see Jeff Manza, Clem Brooks, and Christopher Uggen, "'*Civil Death' or Civil Rights? Public Attitudes towards Felon Disenfranchisement in the United States*," *Public Opinion Quarterly* 68, no. 2 (2004): 276–287; Michael Leo Owens and Adrienne R. Smith, "'*Deviants' and Democracy: Punitive Policy Designs and the Social Rights of Felons as Citizens*," *American Politics Research* 40, no. 3 (2012): 531–567; Brian Pinaire, Milton Heumann, and Laura Bilotta, "*Barred from the Vote: Public Attitudes toward the Disenfranchisement of Ex-Felons*," *Fordham Urban Law Journal* 30 (2003): 1519–1550.

15. My usage of the term "American" throughout this book is intentionally ambiguous. My analysis is both geographically and temporally specific, focusing on the experience of the United States over the life of its political self-consciousness as a primarily liberal project. There is something both troubling and revealing about the locution "American" in this context, and my analysis self-consciously reflects this ambivalence. On the one hand, because my analysis does not extend beyond the specific historical and political experience of the United States, I try to avoid saying "American" when I really mean "of the United States." Nevertheless, the term "American," especially as a modifier for the public ideology of "liberalism," does useful work distinguishing "American liberalism" from British and other European forms. Moreover, there is something revealing in the fact that we will speak, frequently, about "American citizenship," something that, legally speaking, does not exist. But as my argument in this book should make clear, there is a form of "American" citizenship arguably distinct from U.S. citizenship, at least in normative and cultural terms.

16. Charles W. Mills, *The Racial Contract* (Ithaca, NY: Cornell University Press, 1997), 3.

17. Manza and Uggen, *Locked Out*, chaps. 2 and 9.

18. Iris Marion Young, *Inclusion and Democracy* (Oxford: Oxford University Press, 2000).

19. On prison abolition, in particular, see CR-10 Publications Collective, ed., *Abolition Now! 10 Years of Strategy and Struggle against the Prison Industrial*

Complex (Oakland, CA: AK, 2008); Ryan Conrad, ed., *Prisons Will Not Protect You* (Lewiston, ME: Against Equality Publishing Collective, 2012); Angela Davis, *Abolition Democracy: Beyond Empire, Prisons, and Torture* (New York: Seven Stories, 2005); Davis, *Are Prisons Obsolete?* (New York: Seven Stories, 2003); Davis, "*Racialized Punishment and Prison Abolition*," in *A Companion to African-American Philosophy*, ed. Tommy Lott and John Pittman, 360–369 (Oxford, UK: Blackwell, 2003); Dorothy E. Roberts, "*Constructing a Criminal Justice System Free of Racial Bias: An Abolitionist Framework*," *Columbia Human Rights Law Review* 39 (2007): 261–285; Dean Spade, *Normal Life: Administrative Violence, Critical Trans Politics and the Limits of Law* (Cambridge, MA: South End, 2011); Eric A. Stanley and Nat Smith, eds., *Captive Genders: Trans Embodiment and the Prison Industrial Complex* (Oakland, CA: AK, 2011).

20. Ewald, "Civil Death," 1059–1061; Itzkowitz and Oldak, "Restoring the Ex-Offender's Right to Vote," 721–727. It is worth nothing that Itzkowitz and Oldak's article is the primary source for nearly all authors writing on the ancient and medieval roots of disenfranchisement. It is the standard (and usually the only) citation for any claims about disenfranchisement's historical roots. Also see Chapter 1 of Pettus, *Felony Disenfranchisement in America*.

21. Itzkowitz and Oldak, "Restoring the Ex-Offender's Right to Vote," 721–727; Manza and Uggen, *Locked Out*, 23. See also Giorgio Agamben, *Homo Sacer: Sovereign Power and Bare Life* (Stanford, CA: Stanford University Press, 1998).

22. Manza and Uggen, *Locked Out*, 25.

23. See, for instance, Constantin Fasolt's discussion of the ancient practice marking criminals as "enemies of Rome" and the process of *post-liminium*, which could reintegrate an offender back into the "people." Constantin Fasolt, *The Limits of History* (Chicago: University of Chicago Press, 2004), 167–173.

24. Keyssar, *Right to Vote*, 358–361. The Kentucky constitution only gave authority for the legislature to disenfranchise criminals. It was not until 1851 that it did so. In Vermont, the restriction in question was limited to election crimes.

25. Ibid., 63.

26. Manza and Uggen, *Locked Out*, 52.

27. Ibid., 51.

28. Ibid., 53–54.

29. Ibid., 55.

30. Ibid.

31. That voting rights were only extended to freed men (absent the Nineteenth Amendment) speaks to how the reconstitution of the polity in the years following the war was necessarily incomplete. The formal (if not yet actual) incorporation of adult black men into the *demos* was predicated on the continued

categorical exclusions of all women, children, and foreigners from the franchise and full citizenship. In this way, any analysis of white supremacy must always be thought in relation to the related axes of domination, especially heteropatriarchy. See Andrea Smith, "*Heteropatriarchy and the Three Pillars of White Supremacy,*" in *Color of Violence: The Incite! Anthology,* ed. Incite! Women of Color Against Violence, 66–73 (Cambridge, MA: South End, 2006).

32. Manza and Uggen, *Locked Out*, 67.

33. Keyssar notes, "The primary thrust of these reforms was the elimination of lifetime disfranchisement: more than fifteen states took this step between the late 1960s and 1998" (*Right to Vote*, 303).

34. Manza and Uggen, *Locked Out*, 59.

35. Keyssar, *Right to Vote*, 303.

36. See Lawrence D. Bobo and Victor Thompson, "*Unfair by Design: The War on Drugs, Race, and the Legitimacy of the Criminal Justice System,*" *Social Research* 73, no. 2 (2006): 445–472; Rose M. Brewer and Nancy A. Heitzeg, "*Criminal Justice, Color-Blind Racism, and the Political Economy of the Prison Industrial Complex,*" *American Behavioral Scientist* 51, no. 5 (2008): 625–644; Naomi Murakawa, "*The Origins of the Carceral Crisis: Racial Order as 'Law and Order' in Postwar American Politics,*" in *Race and American Political Development,* ed. Joseph E. Lowndes, Julie Novkov, and Dorian T. Warren, 234–255 (New York: Routledge, 2012); Doris Marie Provine, "*Race and Inequality in the War on Drugs,*" *Annual Review of Law and Social Science* 7, no. 1 (2011): 41–60; Michael H. Tonry, *Malign Neglect: Race, Crime, and Punishment in America* (New York: Oxford University Press, 1995); Vesla Weaver, "*Frontlash: Race and the Development of Punitive Crime Policy,*" *Studies in American Political Development* 21, no. 2 (2007): 230–265; Bruce Western, *Punishment and Inequality in America* (New York: Russell Sage Foundation, 2006).

37. For key works on the phenomenon of mass incarceration in the United States, see David Garland, ed., *Mass Imprisonment: Social Causes and Consequences* (London: Sage, 2001); Marc Mauer and Sentencing Project (U.S.), *Race to Incarcerate* (New York: New Press, 1999); "One in 100"; Mary E. Pattillo, David F. Weiman, and Bruce Western, *Imprisoning America: The Social Effects of Mass Incarceration* (New York: Russell Sage Foundation, 2004); Becky Pettit and Bruce Western, "*Mass Imprisonment and the Life Course: Race and Class Inequality in U.S. Incarceration,*" *American Sociological Review* 69 (April 2004): 151–169; Tonry, *Malign Neglect*; Western, *Punishment and Inequality in America*. For analyses on the collateral effects of mass incarceration, see Michael Jacobson, *Downsizing Prisons: How to Reduce Crime and End Mass Incarceration* (New York: New York University Press, 2005); Mauer and Chesney-Lind, *Invisible Punishment*; Devah Pager, *Marked: Race, Crime, and Finding Work in an Era of*

Mass Incarceration (Chicago: University of Chicago Press, 2007); Pattillo, Weiman, and Bruce Western, *Imprisoning America*; Beth E. Richie, "*The Social Impact of Mass Incarceration on Women,*" in *Invisible Punishment*, ed. Marc Mauer and Meda Chesney-Lind, 136–149 (New York: New Press, 2002).

38. David Garland, "*Introduction: The Meaning of Mass Imprisonment,*" in *Mass Imprisonment: Social Causes and Consequences*, ed. David Garland, 1–3 (London: Sage, 2001).

39. Ibid.

40. Keyssar, *Right to Vote*, 308.

41. Abramsky, *Conned*; Elizabeth Hull, *The Disenfranchisement of Ex-Felons* (Philadelphia: Temple University Press, 2006).

42. See Hull, *Disenfranchisement of Ex-Felons*, chaps. 6–7; Manza and Uggen, *Locked Out*, 222–225.

43. "These include three states that eliminated lifetime disenfranchisement provisions, four additional states that scaled back their lifetime disenfranchisement laws to apply to a narrower category of individuals, four states that simplified the restoration process for persons who have completed their sentence, and two states that reformed interagency data sharing procedures to address issues of accuracy in compiling the lists of persons to be removed or restored to voting eligibility." Ryan S. King, "*A Decade of Reform: Felony Disenfranchisement Policy in the United States*" (Washington, DC: Sentencing Project, 2006), 3. For more on the specific shape of recent reforms, see also Alec C. Ewald, "*Criminal Disenfranchisement and the Challenge of American Federalism,*" *Publius: The Journal of Federalism* 39, no. 3 (2009): 527–556.

44. Manza and Uggen, *Locked Out*, 286–287.

45. "Felony Disenfranchisement Laws in the United States."

46. Manza and Uggen note, "These restrictions [on currently incarcerated inmates] are the least anomalous in the international context, as many other nations disenfranchise prison inmates. Current public opinion clearly supports the continuing disenfranchisement of prison inmates. The wave of democratization since the 1960s has swept past inmates, without so much as a single state expanding their voting rights" (*Locked Out*, 230–231). Also see Chapter 12 of Hull, *Disenfranchisement of Ex-Felons*.

47. Alec C. Ewald, "*Collateral Consequences and the Perils of Categorical Ambiguity,*" in *Law as Punishment / Law as Regulation*, ed. Austin Sarat, Lawrence Douglas, and Martha Merrill Umphrey, 77–123 (Stanford, CA: Stanford Law Books, 2011), 103.

48. Keyssar, *Right to Vote*, 303.

49. For more on the racial impact of felon disenfranchisement policies, see Behrens, Uggen, and Manza, "Ballot Manipulation"; Khalilah Brown-Dean,

"Permanent Outsiders: Felon Disenfranchisement and the Breakdown of Black Politics," National Political Science Review 11 (2007): 103–119; Tanya Dugree-Pearson, *"Disenfranchisement: A Race Neutral Punishment for Felony Offenders or a Way to Diminish the Minority Vote?," Hamline Journal of Public Policy and Law* 23, no. 2 (2001): 359–402; Fellner and Mauer, "Losing the Vote"; Daniel Goldman, *"The Modern-Day Literacy Test? Felon Disenfranchisement and Race Discrimination," Stanford Law Review* 57, no. 2 (2004): 611–655; Manza and Uggen, *Locked Out*; Manza and Uggen, "Punishment and Democracy."; Marc Mauer, *"Disenfranchisement of Felons: The Modern-Day Voting Rights Challenge," Civil Rights Journal,* Winter 2002, 40–43; Keesha M. Middlemass, *"Rehabilitated but Not Fit to Vote: A Comparative Racial Analysis of Disenfranchisement Laws," Souls* 8, no. 2 (2006): 22–39; Miles S. Rapoport, *"Restoring the Vote," American Prospect* 12, no. 14 (2001); Simson, "Justice Denied"; Loïc Wacquant, *"Race as Civic Felony," International Social Science Journal* 57, no. 183 (2005): 127–142.

50. Caesare Beccaria, *On Crimes and Punishments,* trans. David Young (Indianapolis: Hackett, 1986); Jeremy Bentham, *The Principles of Morals and Legislation* (Amherst, NY: Prometheus Books, 1988); Georg Wilhelm Friedrich Hegel, *Elements of the Philosophy of Right,* ed. Allen W. Wood, trans. Hugh Barr Nisbet (Cambridge: Cambridge University Press, 1991); Thomas Hobbes, *A Dialogue between a Philosopher and a Student of the Common Laws of England,* ed. Joseph Cropsey (Chicago: University of Chicago Press, 1971); Hobbes, *Leviathan,* ed. Edwin Curley (Indianapolis: Hackett, 1994); Immanuel Kant, *The Metaphysics of Morals,* trans. Mary Gregor (Cambridge: Cambridge University Press, 1996); John Locke, *Two Treatises of Government,* ed. Peter Laslett (Cambridge: Cambridge University Press, 1988); John Stuart Mill, *On Liberty,* ed. Elizabeth Rapaport (Indianapolis: Hackett, 1978).

For contemporary commentary on these canonical works, see also J. Angelo Corlett, *Responsibility and Punishment,* 2nd ed. (Dordrecht, Netherlands: Kluwer, 2004); Jean Hampton, *"An Expressive Theory of Retribution,"* in *Retributivism and Its Critics,* ed. Wesley Cragg, 1–25 (Stuttgart, Germany: Franz Steiner, 1992); A. John Simmons, ed., *Punishment* (Princeton, NJ: Princeton University Press, 1995); Ronald J. Terchek and Stanley C. Brubaker, *"Punishing Liberals or Rehabilitating Liberalism?," American Political Science Review* 83, no. 4 (1989): 1309–1316; Mark Tunick, *Hegel's Political Philosophy: Interpreting the Practice of Legal Punishment* (Princeton, NJ: Princeton University Press, 1992); Tunick, *Punishment: Theory and Practice* (Berkeley: University of California Press, 1992); Barry Vaughan, *"Punishment and Conditional Citizenship," Punishment and Society* 2, no. 1 (2001): 23–39.

51. Sharon Dolovich, *"Legitimate Punishment in Liberal Democracy," Buffalo Criminal Law Review* 7, no. 2 (2004): 307–442; R. A. Duff, *Punishment, Com-*

munication, and Community (Oxford: Oxford University Press, 2001); Joel Feinberg, *Doing and Deserving: Essays in the Theory of Responsibility* (Princeton, NJ: Princeton University Press, 1970); H. L. A. Hart, *The Concept of Law*, 2nd ed. (Oxford: Oxford University Press, 1994); Hart, *Punishment and Responsibility: Essays in the Philosophy of Law* (New York: Oxford University Press, 1968).

52. See especially Feinberg, *Doing and Deserving*.

53. Disenfranchisement does have its defenders besides the Court. While the vast majority of theoretically oriented accounts reject the practice as ineffective, if not unjust, opposing viewpoints can be found. See Andrew Altman, "*Democratic Self-Determination and the Disenfranchisement of Felons*," *Journal of Applied Philosophy* 22, no. 3 (2005): 263–273; Clegg, "Who Should Vote?"; Christopher Manfredi, "*In Defense of Prisoner Disenfranchisement*," in *Criminal Disenfranchisement in an International Perspective*, ed. Alec C. Ewald and Brandon Rottinghaus, 259–280 (Cambridge: Cambridge University Press, 2009); Christopher Manfredi, "*Judicial Review and Criminal Disenfranchisement in the United States and Canada*," *Review of Politics* 60 (1998): 277–305.

54. See Itzkowitz and Oldak, "Restoring the Ex-Offender's Right to Vote"; "*Note: The Need for Reform of Ex-Felon Disenfranchisement Laws*," *Yale Law Journal* 83, no. 3 (1974): 580–601; Gary L. Reback, "*Disenfranchisement of Ex-Felons: A Reassessment*," *Stanford Law Review* 25, no. 6 (1973): 845–864; Peter Samson, "*Richardson v. Ramirez and the Constitutionality of Disenfranchising Ex-Felons*," *New England Law Review* 10 (1974): 477–492; Douglas R. Tims, "*The Disenfranchisement of Ex-Felons: A Cruelly Excessive Punishment*," *Southwestern University Law Review* 7, no. 1 (1975): 124–160.

55. See *Green v. Board of Election*, 380 F.2d 445 (2nd Cir. 1967) and *Richardson v. Ramirez*, 418 U.S. 24 (1974). For a discussion, see Gabriel J. Chin, "*Reconstruction, Felon Disenfranchisement, and the Right to Vote: Did the Fifteenth Amendment Repeal Section 2 of the Fourteenth Amendment?*," *Georgetown Law Journal* 92, no. 2 (2004): 259–316; Alice E. Harvey, "*Ex-Felon Disenfranchisement and Its Influence on the Black Vote: The Need for a Second Look*," *University of Pennsylvania Law Review* 142, no. 3 (1994): 1145–1189; Samson, "*Richardson v. Ramirez* and the Constitutionality of Disenfranchising Ex-Felons."; Andrew L. Shapiro, "*Challenging Criminal Disenfranchisement under the Voting Rights Act: A New Strategy*," *Yale Law Journal* 103 no. 2 (1993): 537–566.

For a broader overview of judicial interpretations in the United States and Canada, see Frank Askin, "*Disfranchising Felons (or, How William Rehnquist Earned His Stripes)*," *Rutgers Law Review* 59 (2006): 875–884; Gabriel J. Chin, "*Rehabilitating Unconstitutional Statutes: An Analysis of Cotton v. Fordice, 157 F.3d 388 (5th Cir. 1998)*," *University of Cincinnati Law Review* 71 (2002): 421–455; Itzkowitz and Oldak, "Restoring the Ex-Offender's Right to Vote"; Manfredi,

"Judicial Review and Criminal Disenfranchisement"; "Note: The Need for Reform of Ex-Felon Disenfranchisement Laws"; Andrew L. Shapiro, *"Note: The Disenfranchisement of Ex-Felons: Citizenship, Criminality, and 'the Purity of the Ballot Box,'"* Harvard Law Review 102 (1989): 1300–1317; Simson, "Justice Denied."

56. In *Hunter v. Underwood*, 471 U.S. 222 (1985), the Court ruled that while the loss of voting rights due to criminal activity was a viable exception to the Fourteenth Amendment's equal protection clause, as established earlier in *Richardson v. Ramirez*, 418 U.S. 24, if the intent of the legislation was to disenfranchise a group en masse, the exception was void.

57. *Hunter v. Underwood*, 471 U.S. 222. See also Hull, *Disenfranchisement of Ex-Felons*, 102.

58. In 2006, the U.S. Court of Appeals for the Second Circuit dismissed *Hayden v. Pataki*, 449 F.3d 305 (2nd Cir. 2006) and *Muntaqim v. Coombe*, 449 F.3d 371 (2nd Cir. 2006), both of which were Voting Rights Act–based challenges to New York State's felon disenfranchisement law. Additionally, the U.S. District Court, Eastern District of Washington, dismissed another Voting Rights Act–based claim of racially disproportionate effect, in *Farrakhan v. Gregoire* (CV-96-076-RHW), which was subsequently denied an en banc hearing in *Farrakhan v. Washington*, 359 F.3d 1116 (9th Cir. 2004) and then denied certiorari by the Supreme Court in *Locke v. Farrakhan*, 543 U.S. 984 (2004). In 2010, the Ninth Circuit in California ruled that there are no grounds for Voting Rights Act challenges without showing discriminatory intent in *Farrakhan v. Gregoire*, 623 F.3d 990.

59. See Everett S. Brown, *"The Restoration of Civil and Political Rights by Presidential Pardon,"* American Political Science Review 34, no. 2 (1940): 295–300; James A. Gathings, *"Loss of Citizenship and Civil Rights for Conviction of Crime,"* American Political Science Review 43, no. 6 (1949): 1228–1234; *Trop v. Dulles*, 356 U.S. 86 (1958). This problem is taken up nicely in Jesse Furman, *"Political Illiberalism: The Paradox of Disenfranchisement and the Ambivalences of Rawlsian Justice,"* Yale Law Journal 106, no. 4 (1997): 1197–1231.

60. See Harvey, "Ex-Felon Disenfranchisement"; Shapiro, "Challenging Criminal Disenfranchisement."

61. For example, see Furman, "Political Illiberalism"; Shapiro, "Note: The Disenfranchisement of Ex-Felons"; John R. Vile, *"The Right to Vote as Applied to Ex-Felons,"* Federal Probation 45, no. 1 (1981): 12–16.

62. To highlight just a few, see Saul Brenner and Nicholas J. Caste, *"Granting the Suffrage to Felons in Prison,"* Journal of Social Philosophy 34, no. 2 (2003): 228–243; Khalilah Brown-Dean, *"One Lens, Multiple Views: Felon Disenfran-*

chisement Laws and American Political Equality" (Ph.D. diss., Ohio State University, 2003); Traci Renee Burch, "*Punishment and Participation: How Criminal Convictions Threaten American Democracy*" (Ph.D. diss., Harvard University, 2007); Shawn D. Bushway and Gary Sweeten, "*Abolish Lifetime Bans for Ex-Felons*," *Criminology and Public Policy* 6, no. 4 (2007): 697–706; Sana Butler, "*2003: The 3rd Annual Year in Ideas: Give Felons the Vote*," *New York Times Magazine*, December 14, 2003, 70; Chin, "Reconstruction, Felon Disenfranchisement, and the Right to Vote"; Michael J. Cholbi, "*A Felon's Right to Vote*," *Law and Philosophy* 21, nos. 4–5 (2002): 543–565; Robert D. Crutchfield, "*Abandon Felon Disenfranchisement Policies*," *Criminology and Public Policy* 6, no. 4 (2007): 707–716; Alec C. Ewald, "*An 'Agenda for Demolition': The Fallacy and the Danger of the 'Subversive Voting' Argument for Felony Disenfranchisement*," *Columbia Human Rights Law Review* 36 (2004): 109–143; Ewald, "Civil Death"; Sarah C. Grady, "*Civil Death Is Different: An Examination of a Post-Graham Challenge to Felon Disenfranchisement under the Eighth Amendment*," *Journal of Criminal Law & Criminology* 102, no. 2 (2012): 441–470; Afi S. Johnson-Parris, "*Felon Disenfranchisement: The Unconscionable Social Contract Breached*," *Virginia Law Review* 89, no. 1 (2003): 109–138; Pamela Karlan, "*Convictions and Doubts: Retribution, Representation, and the Debate over Felon Disenfranchisement*," *Stanford Law Review* 56, no. 5 (2004): 1147–1170; Alexander Keyssar, "*Shoring Up the Right to Vote: A Modest Proposal*," *Political Science Quarterly* 118, no. 2 (2003): 181–190; John Kleinig and Kevin Murtagh, "*Disenfranchising Felons*," *Journal of Applied Philosophy* 22, no. 3 (2005): 217–239; Hugh Lafollette, "*Collateral Consequences of Punishment: Civil Penalties Accompanying Formal Punishment*," *Journal of Applied Philosophy* 22, no. 3 (2005): 241–261; Richard L. Lippke, "*The Disenfranchisement of Felons*," *Law and Philosophy* 20 (2001): 553–580; Mauer, "Disenfranchisement of Felons"; Rapoport, "Restoring the Vote"; Richard M. Re and Christopher M. Re, "*Voting and Vice: Criminal Disenfranchisement and the Reconstruction Amendments*," *Yale Law Journal* 121, no. 7 (2012): 1584–1670; Jeffrey H. Reiman, "*Liberal and Republican Arguments against the Disenfranchisement of Felons*," *Criminal Justice Ethics* 24, no. 1 (2005): 3–18; Wacquant, "Race as Civic Felony"; Wheelock, "Collateral Consequences and Racial Inequality."

63. *Green v. Board of Election*, 380 F.2d at 451.

64. *Washington v. State*, 75 Ala. 582, 585 (Ala. 1884)

65. Mary Fainsod Katzenstein, Leila Mohsen Ibrahim, and Katherine D. Rubin, "*The Dark Side of American Liberalism and Felony Disenfranchisement*," *Perspectives on Politics* 8, no. 4 (2010): 1042.

66. Hart, *Punishment and Responsibility*; Duff, *Punishment, Communication, and Community*, xi. It is important to note that Duff's account of justification

is nuanced, and he rightly notes that all normative theory must be immanent to practices and confront them in more complicated ways than as mere test cases. He writes, "A normative theory of punishment must be a *critical* theory. It must offer us not simply a comforting rationalization or justification of the status quo. . . . To say that normative theory must begin from actual practice is to say that it must begin as immanent or internal, rather than transcendent or external, critique. We cannot construct a wholly a priori account of punishment (or of any human practice) that we then bring to bear, from the outside, on our actual practice: for in what could such an account be grounded and why should it be relevant to existing practice?" (xv–xvi). Nevertheless, for Duff, the framework for the philosophy of punishment continues to be primarily one of justification rather than social or political meaning.

67. Particularly clear examples of this form can be seen in Cholbi, "Felon's Right to Vote"; Reiman, "Liberal and Republican Arguments against the Disenfranchisement of Felons." The Reiman article is a perfect example, as this approach is structured by looking at both liberal and civic republican justifications in turn and using both frameworks to deftly dismiss the acceptability of disenfranchisement. It is an illustrative article because (1) it perfects the form I have identified and (2) it is an excellent article. To be clear, it is not that theorists are unsuccessful in this approach. On the contrary, the problem is that they are very successful on extremely limited terms.

68. As will be demonstrated later, the representatives responsible for drafting disenfranchisement provisions routinely understood the two discourses as related. Delegates at the 1851 and 1864 Maryland Constitutional Conventions showed no hesitancy in seeing disenfranchisement in both the language of punishment and the language of citizenship, albeit with some confusing results. Recent archival work has begun to help ameliorate this problem. In particular, see John Dinan, "*The Adoption of Criminal Disenfranchisement Provisions in the United States: Lessons from the State Constitutional Convention Debates*," *Journal of Policy History* 19, no. 3 (2007): 282–312; Pippa Holloway, "*'A Chicken-Stealer Shall Lose His Vote': Disfranchisement for Larceny in the South, 1874–1890*," *Journal of Southern History* 75, no. 4 (2009): 931–962.

69. A notable exception to this trend is Brenner and Caste, "Granting the Suffrage to Felons in Prison."

70. There are only a few exceptions to this trend: Furman, "Political Illiberalism"; Holloway, "A Chicken-Stealer Shall Lose His Vote"; Katzenstein, Ibrahim, and Rubin, "Dark Side of American Liberalism"; Pettus, *Felony Disenfranchisement in America*; Jonathan Rothchild, "*Dispenser of the Mercy of the Government: Pardons, Justice, and Felony Disenfranchisement*," *Journal of Religious Ethics* 39, no. 1 (2011): 48–70; Shapiro, "Note: Disenfranchisement of Ex-Felons"; Loïc

Wacquant, "*Deadly Symbiosis: When Ghetto and Prison Meet and Mesh*," *Punishment & Society* 3, no. 1 (2001): 95–134.

71. Mills writes that *The Racial Contract* "is an attempt to redirect your vision, to make you see what, in a sense, has been there all along" (*Racial Contract*, 2). It is my hope that this book can work in a similar way.

72. Michel Foucault, *Discipline and Punish: The Birth of the Prison*, trans. Alan Sheridan (New York: Vintage Books, 1995), 265.

73. Ibid., 268.

74. Ibid., 272.

75. See Chapters 6 and 7 in this book and Dinan, "Adoption of Criminal Disenfranchisement Provisions."

76. As already noted, I use the term "American" ambiguously here. Nevertheless, it is entirely possible that this analysis reveals something more fundamental or generalizable about the relationship between citizenship, punishment, and *all* states (or perhaps liberal states), but I intentionally limit my analysis to the American context for several reasons. First, the United States is an outlier in the severity of suffrage restrictions imposed on convicted criminals and the sheer number of persons caught up in the criminal justice system. No country incarcerates a higher percentage of its citizens, and no democratic nation excludes so many convicted criminals from taking part in elections. At the time of writing, not only does the United States have the highest incarceration rate in the world, but in terms of sheer volume, the United States incarcerates more persons than the twenty-six European countries with the largest prison populations *combined*. Second, the institution of chattel slavery is integral to understanding American criminal justice and citizenship. Finally, and most importantly, it is imperative that analysis be grounded in a specific time and location. For analysis of disenfranchisement from expressly comparative and international perspectives, see Ewald and Rottinghaus, *Criminal Disenfranchisement in an International Perspective*.

77. Emile Durkheim, *The Division of Labor in Society*, trans. W. D. Halls (New York: Free Press, 1984); George H. Mead, "*The Psychology of Punitive Justice*," *American Journal of Sociology* 23, no. 5 (1918): 577–602; Friedrich Wilhelm Nietzsche, *On the Genealogy of Morality: A Polemic*, trans. Maudemarie Clark and Alan J. Swensen (Indianapolis: Hackett, 1998).

The "social analysis" of punishment has a long history, and has seen a resurgence among sociologists and legal theorists, articulated most eloquently by David Garland in a number of recent works: Garland, "*Frameworks of Inquiry in the Sociology of Punishment*," *British Journal of Sociology* 41, no. 1 (1990): 1–15; Garland, "The *Limits of the Sovereign State: Strategies of Crime Control in Contemporary Society*," *British Journal of Criminology* 1 (1996): 445–471; Garland, "*Penal Excess and Surplus Meaning: Public Torture Lynchings in Twentieth-Century America*," *Law & Society Review* 39, no. 4 (2005): 793–833; Garland, *Punishment and Modern Society: A Study in Social Theory* (Chicago: University of Chicago Press, 1990); Garland, "*Sociological Perspectives on Punishment*," *Crime and Justice* 14 (1991): 115–165; Garland and Peter Young, eds., *The Power to Punish* (Atlantic Heights, NJ: Humanities, 1983).

Other key works in this tradition include Malcolm M. Feeley and Jonathan Simon, "*The New Penology: Notes on the Emerging Strategy of Corrections and Its Implications*," *Criminology* 30, no. 4 (1992): 449–474; Ruth Wilson Gilmore, *Golden Gulag: Prisons, Surplus, Crisis, and Opposition in Globalizing California* (Berkeley: University of California Press, 2007); Erving Goffman, *Asylums: Essays on the Social Situation of Mental Patients and Other Inmates* (Garden City, NY: Anchor Books, 1961); Goffman, *Stigma: Notes on the Management of Spoiled Identity* (Englewood Cliffs, NJ: Prentice Hall, 1963); Steven Hutchinson, "*Countering Catastrophic Criminology: Reform, Punishment and the Modern Liberal Compromise*," *Punishment & Society* 8, no. 4 (2006): 443–467; Michael Ignatieff, "*State, Civil Society, and Total Institutions: A Critique of Recent Social Histories of Punishment*," *Crime and Justice* 3 (1981): 153–192; Joy James, *States of Confinement: Policing, Detention, and Prisons* (New York: Palgrave Macmillan, 2002); Jeffrey H. Reiman, *The Rich Get Richer and the Poor Get Prison: Ideology, Class, and Criminal Justice*, 7th ed. (Boston: Allyn and Bacon, 2004); Richie, "Social Impact of Mass Incarceration on Women"; Georg Rusche and Otto Kirchheimer, *Punishment and Social Structure* (New York: Russell & Russell, 1968); Jonathan Simon, *Governing through Crime: How the War on Crime Transformed American Democracy and Created a Culture of Fear* (New York: Oxford University Press, 2007); Wacquant, "Deadly Symbiosis"; Wacquant, "Race as Civic Felony"; Michael Welch, *Punishment in America: Social Control and the Ironies of Imprisonment* (Thousand Oaks, CA: Sage, 1999).

More recently, there has been a dramatic increase among critical theorists and philosophers concerned with the question of punishment, much of it centered around the work of Angela Davis: Davis, *Abolition Democracy*; Davis, *Are Prisons Obsolete?*; Davis, "*From the Prison of Slavery to the Slavery of Prison: Frederick Douglass and the Convict Lease System*," in *The Angela Y. Davis Reader*, ed. Joy James, 74–95 (Malden, MA: Blackwell, 1998); Davis, "*Race and Criminalization: Black Americans and the Punishment Industry*," in *The House That Race Built: Black Americas, U.S. Terrain*, ed. Wahneema Lubiano, 264–279 (New York: Pantheon, 1997); Davis, "Racialized Punishment and Prison Abolition"; Eduardo Mendieta, "*The Prison Contract and Surplus Punishment: On Angela Y. Davis's Abolitionism*," *Human Studies* 30 (2007); Jeffrey Paris, "*Decarceration and the Philosophies of Mass Imprisonment,"* *Human Studies* 30, no. 1 (2007): 291–309.

78. Young, *Inclusion and Democracy*, 10.

79. Iris Marion Young, *Justice and the Politics of Difference* (Princeton, NJ: Princeton University Press, 1990), 5.

80. Young, *Inclusion and Democracy*, 10.

81. In a way, I follow Rogers Smith's "multiple traditions" perspective as a critique of illiberal institutions and practice in American history, but I am more sympathetic to a line of its criticism that seeks to explore the ways in which individuals do not simply hold multiple (and potentially conflicting) ideological systems at the same time but that traditions might be linked together far more tightly than Smith allows, enabling and reinforcing each other despite their apparent inconsistencies. Rogers M. Smith, *"Beyond Tocqueville, Myrdal, and Hartz: The Multiple Traditions in America,"* *American Political Science Review* 87, no. 3 (1993): 549–566; Smith, *Civic Ideals: Conflicting Visions of Citizenship in U.S. History* (New Haven, CT: Yale University Press, 1997); Jacqueline Stevens and Rogers Smith, *"Beyond Tocqueville, Please!,"* *American Political Science Review* 89, no. 4 (1995): 987–995.

82. Wacquant, "Deadly Symbiosis"; Wacquant, "Race as Civic Felony"; Loïc Wacquant, *"From Slavery to Mass Incarceration,"* *New Left Review* 13 (2002): 41–60.

83. For excellent accounts of the deep connections between race and punishment in the United States, see A. Davis, *Abolition Democracy*; A. Davis, *Are Prisons Obsolete?*; A. Davis, "Race and Criminalization"; A. Davis, "Racialized Punishment and Prison Abolition"; Gilmore, *Golden Gulag*; James, *States of Confinement*.

84. See Corey Brettschneider, *"The Rights of the Guilty: Punishment and Political Legitimacy,"* *Political Theory* 35, no. 2 (2007): 175–199; Peter Ramsey, *"The Responsible Subject as Citizen: Criminal Law, Democracy, and the Welfare State,"* *Modern Law Review* 69, no. 1 (2006): 29–58.

85. Michael Sandel, *Democracy's Discontent: America in Search of a Public Philosophy* (Cambridge, MA: Harvard University Press, 1996).

86. Katzenstein, Ibrahim, and Rubin, "Dark Side of American Liberalism."

87. Ibid., 1045–1046. Cf. R. Smith, *Civic Ideals*.

88. See Charles W. Mills, *"Liberalism and the Racial State,"* in *State of White Supremacy: Racism, Governance, and the United States*, ed. Moon-Kue Jung, João H. Costa Vargas, and Eduardo Bonilla-Silva, 27–46 (Stanford, CA: Stanford University Press, 2011); Mills, *Racial Contract*. See also David Colander, Robert E. Prasch, and Falguni A. Sheth, eds., *Race, Liberalism, and Econom-*

ics (Ann Arbor: University of Michigan Press, 2004); Falguni A. Sheth, *Toward a Political Philosophy of Race* (Albany: State University of New York Press, 2009).

89. See Duff's account of the unavoidable connection between punishment, exclusion/inclusion, and liberal political community. Duff, *Punishment, Communication, and Community*, 75–79.

90. Furman, "Political Illiberalism," 1198.

91. This position echoes Bonnie Honig's critique of Rawls's attempt to develop liberalism as a totalizing system. What emerges, she argues, are "remainders" which continue to assert themselves in the system but which have no place within that system. Interestingly, the "remainder" which haunts Rawls, Honig argues, is the "bad character" of the criminal. See Bonnie Honig, *Political Theory and the Displacement of Politics* (Ithaca, NY: Cornell University Press, 1993); Honig, "*Rawls on Politics and Punishment*," *Political Research Quarterly* 46, no. 1 (1993): 99–125.

92. See Giorgio Agamben, *The Signature of All Things: On Method* (New York: Zone Books, 2009); Hubert L. Dreyfus, Paul Rabinow, and Michel Foucault, *Michel Foucault: Beyond Structuralism and Hermeneutics*, 2nd ed. (Chicago: University of Chicago Press, 1983).

93. Colin Koopman, *Genealogy as Critique: Foucault and the Problems of Modernity* (Bloomington: Indiana University Press, 2013); Jacqueline Stevens, "*On the Morals of Genealogy*," *Political Theory* 31, no. 4 (2003): 558–588.

94. I have come to believe that the best way to be faithful to Foucault is to not worry too much about being faithful.

95. Michel Foucault, "*Nietzsche, Genealogy, History*," in *Language, Counter-Memory, Practice*, ed. Donald F. Bouchard, 139–164 (Ithaca, NY: Cornell University Press, 1977), 146.

96. Ladelle McWhorter, *Bodies and Pleasures: Foucault and the Politics of Sexual Normalization* (Bloomington: Indiana University Press, 1999), 43.

97. Thank you to Colin Koopman and his colleagues in the Critical Genealogies Collaboratory at the University of Oregon for helping me articulate this point.

98. Koopman, *Genealogy as Critique*, 129.

99. Ibid.

100. When I began teaching courses about race and politics, I would typically have to spend time convincing my students that race is a social and political construct. Today, my students *begin* by stating that this is an obvious fact about race, its constructed nature having become something like a truism. What continues to happen, however, is either (1) the obviousness of this truth allows them to dismiss claims based on racial difference as mere "social con-

structions," or (2) they do not see their own actions in any way a part of how race is socially constructed. Part of the work of genealogy, as I understand it, is to address both of these problems.

101. Koopman, *Genealogy as Critique*, 44.

2. FABRICATING FIGURES

1. I do not mean to imply that Foucault is the only theorist of punishment who takes seriously the "constructed" nature of criminalized persons. Besides working in the footsteps of Nietzsche (in particular, the second essay of *On the Genealogy of Morality*), Foucault's analysis is complemented in particular by Durkheim's numerous writings on crime and social structure, Mead's work on "punitive psychology," and numerous other social theorists. In particular, it is important to note the work of Erving Goffman, Greshem Sykes, and John Irwin. What limits their projects, however, is that their interest in felons, the stigmatized, or the "society of captives" is largely limited to the figures found exclusively behind the prison walls. While Goffman steps outside the institutional setting, his sociological concerns about stigma are far broader than explicitly criminalized forms. Durkheim, *Division of Labor in Society*; Goffman, *Asylums*; Goffman, *Stigma*; John Irwin, *The Felon* (Englewood Cliffs, NJ: Prentice Hall, 1970); John Irwin, *The Jail: Managing the Underclass in American Society* (Berkeley: University of California Press, 1985); Mead, "Psychology of Punitive Justice"; Gresham M. Sykes, *The Society of Captives: A Study of a Maximum Security Prison* (Princeton, NJ: Princeton University Press, 1958).

2. A remarkable exception is an anonymous note in the 1989 *Harvard Law Review* authored by Andrew H. Shapiro: "Note: Disenfranchisement of Ex-Felons."

3. For a broad overview of the question of the subject in Foucault's work, see Roger Alan Deacon, *Fabricating Foucault: Rationalising the Management of Individuals* (Milwaukee: Marquette University Press, 2003).

4. Michel Foucault, *Abnormal: Lectures at the Collège de France, 1974–1975*, trans. Graham Burchell (New York: Picador, 2003); Foucault, *Discipline and Punish*; Foucault, *Les anormaux*, ed. François Ewald, Alessandro Fontana, Valerio Marchetti, and Antonella Salomoni (Paris: Gallimard, 1999); Foucault, *Surveiller et punir: Naissance de la prison* (Paris: Gallimard, 1975). All subsequent references to *Discipline and Punish* are given in English and French, abbreviated as EDP and FSP, respectively. References to *Abnormal* follow the same convention and are cited as EAB and FAN, respectively.

5. Foucault's 1972 and 1973 lectures at the Collège de France also focused on prisons, punishment, and imprisoned persons, given under the titles *Théories et institutions pénales* (Penal Theories and Institutions) and *La société punitive*

(The Punitive Society). Transcripts of these lectures remain unavailable in either French or English at the time of this writing, but course summaries are widely available and indicate substantive overlap with the themes found in *Discipline and Punish*. See pp. 17–37 in Michel Foucault, *Ethics: Subjectivity and Truth*, vol. 1 of *The Essential Works of Michel Foucault, 1954–1984* (New York: New Press, 1997). Foucault returned to explicitly criminological questions in a series of 1981 lectures at the Catholic University of Louvain, titled *Mal faire, dire vrai: Fonction de l'aveu en justice* (*Wrong-Doing, Truth-Telling: The Function of Avowal in Justice*). These lectures have only been recently transcribed, published, and translated. Foucault, *Mal faire, dire vrai: Fonction de l'aveu en justice—Cours de Louvain, 1981* (Louvain: Presses Universitaires de Louvain, 2012); Foucault, *Wrong-Doing, Truth-Telling: The Function of Avowal in Justice*, trans. Stephen W. Sawyer (Chicago: University of Chicago Press, 2014).

6. See Chapters 11 and 12 of Macey's *The Lives of Michel Foucault* for an account of Foucault's involvement in the GIP as well as Chapter 6 of Miller's *The Passion of Michel Foucault*. David Macey, *The Lives of Michel Foucault* (London: Hutchinson, 1993); Jim Miller, *The Passion of Michel Foucault* (New York: Simon & Schuster, 1993). The bulk of the archival material associated with the GIP can be found in a folio published by IMEC. Philippe Artières, Laurent Quéro, and Michelle Zancarini-Fournet, eds., *Le Groupe d'information sur les prisons: Archives d'une lutte, 1970–1972* (Paris: Éditions de L'IMEC, 2003). For critical work on Foucault and the GIP, see Cecile Brich, "*The Groupe d'information sur les prisons: The Voice of Prisoners? Or Foucault's?*," *Foucault Studies*, no. 5 (2008): 26–47; Brady Heiner, "*Foucault and the Black Panthers*," *City: Analysis of Urban Trends, Culture, Theory, Policy, Action* 11, no. 3 (2007): 313–356; Marcello Hoffman, "Foucault and the 'Lesson' of the Prisoner Support Movement," *New Political Science* 34 (2012): 21–36; Kevin Thompson, "*To Judge the Intolerable*," *Philosophy Today* 54 (2010): 169–176; Michael Welch, "*Counterveillance: How Foucault and the Groupe d'information sur les prisons Reversed the Optics*," *Theoretical Criminology* 15 (2011): 301–313; Welch, "*Pastoral Power as Penal Resistance: Foucault and the Groupe d'information sur les prisons*," *Punishment & Society* 12, no. 1 (2010): 47–63.

7. EDP, 255 / FSP, 258.
8. EDP, 255 / FSP, 259.
9. Ibid.
10. EDP, 251 / FSP, 255.
11. EDP, 254 / FSP, 258.
12. EDP, 251 / FSP, 255.
13. EDP, 252 / FSP, 255.
14. EDP, 253 / FSP, 256.

15. EDP, 254 / FSP, 258.

16. EDP, 254–255 / FSP, 258.

17. Garland, *Punishment and Modern Society*, 148. I do not contest Garland's reading of Foucault, but whereas he is interested in describing the connection between the delinquent and the power/knowledge regime of criminology, I am more interested in the possibility of fabrication of subjects and the process through which this happens.

18. EDP, 255 / FSP, 258.

19. EDP, 265 / FSP 270.

20. EDP, 267 / FSP 272; EDP, 268 / FSP, 273.

21. EDP, 255 / FSP, 258.

22. The figure of the "monster" runs throughout *Abnormal*. For the importance of this figuration, see Stuart Elden, "*The Constitution of the Normal: Monsters and Masturbation at the Collège de France*," *boundary 2* 28, no. 1 (2001): 91–105; Andrew N. Sharpe, *Foucault's Monsters and the Challenge of Law* (New York: Routledge, 2010).

23. EDP, 255 / FSP, 259.

24. EDP, 251–252 / FSP, 255.

25. EDP, 252 / FSP, 255–256.

26. EAB, 323 / FAN, 307.

27. See Arnold I. Davidson, introduction to *EAB*, xvii–xxvi.

28. Article 64 states, "There is neither crime nor offense when the defendant was in a state of dementia at the time of the action, or when he was constrained by a force that he could not resist" (quoted in EAB, 29 / FAN, 27, note 29).

29. EAB, 15 / FAN, 15.

30. EAB, 16 / FAN, 16.

31. Ibid.

32. Ibid.

33. Ibid.

34. EAB, 18 / FAN, 18.

35. This logic is apparent in the practice of racial profiling generally, and it is at the heart of racially loaded "stop-and-frisk" policies specifically. By ascribing criminality in the absence of criminal activity, nearly any action can become criminal or an indicator of criminal activity (e.g., "furtive movements" as grounds for arrest).

36. EDP, 256 / FSP, 259.

37. EAB, 18 / FAN, 18.

38. EAB, 19 / FAN, 19.

39. As will be noted in Chapter 7, the paradoxical language of "unconvicted criminals" is not my own invention.

40. EAB, 22 / FAN, 21.

41. EAB, 21 / FAN, 20.

42. EAB, 23 / FAN, 22.

43. EDP, 252 / FSP, 255.

44. EAB, 25 / FAN, 24.

45. EAB, 31 / FAN, 29.

46. EAB, 33 / FAN, 31.

47. Ibid.

48. EDP, 278–279 / FSP, 283–284.

49. EDP, 272 / FSP, 277.

50. EDP, 232 / FSP, 234.

51. EDP, 276 / FSP, 280–281.

52. EDP, 277 / FSP, 281–282.

53. EDP, 277 / FSP, 281.

54. Shapiro, "Note: Disenfranchisement of Ex-Felons," 1311.

55. The scope of collateral consequences to a felony conviction has been well documented, but it is still sometimes surprising to see the extent of some bans. A 2002 report by the Safer Foundation in Chicago documented that in Illinois alone, persons convicted of a felony at any time in their lives were barred from sixty-five different jobs or professions ranging from medical care to livestock handling. *"A Review of the State of Illinois Professional and Occupational Licensure Policies as Related to Employment for Ex-Offenders"* (Chicago: Safer Foundation, 2002). See also Buckler and Travis, "Reanalyzing the Prevalence and Social Context"; Ewald, "Collateral Consequences and the Perils of Categorical Ambiguity"; Lafollette, "Collateral Consequences of Punishment"; Mauer and Chesney-Lind, *Invisible Punishment.*

56. "Felony Disenfranchisement Laws in the United States"; "One in 100."

57. The political standing conferred by suffrage is taken up at greater length in Chapter 5.

58. Shapiro, "Note: Disenfranchisement of Ex-Felons," 1310.

59. There are important exceptions, such as Foucault's attention in *Discipline and Punish* to the Auburn System and his use of a photograph of Statesville Penitentiary in Illinois.

60. Michel Foucault, *Naissance de la biopolitique: Cours au Collège de France, 1978–1979,* ed. François Ewald, Alessandro Fontana, and Michel Senellart (Paris: Gallimard, 2004); Foucault, *Sécurité, territoire, population: Cours au Collège de France, 1977–1978,* ed. Michel Senellart, François Ewald, and Alessandro Fontana (Paris: Gallimard, 2004); Foucault, *Security, Territory, Population: Lectures at the Collège de France, 1977–1978,* trans. Graham Burchell (New York: Palgrave Macmillan, 2007).

3. NEOLIBERAL PENALITY AND THE BIOPOLITICS
OF *HOMO ŒCONOMICUS*

1. This is not to say that prisons today are simply "warehouses" for unproductive workers or failed citizens. On the contrary, prison labor is a massive component of the contemporary carceral regime, operating through state-granted monopolies, paying inmates wages typically below a dollar per hour, and typically reaping massive profits for state-run industries and private contractors that exploit prison labor. In California, twenty-four state prisons have manufacturing facilities operating under the auspices of the California Prison Industry (CALPIA). State law requires all state agencies (including public hospitals and schools) to purchase goods produced by CALPIA unless they can be found cheaper elsewhere. Top wages for inmate workers are ninety-five cents per hour.

2. Michel Foucault, *The Birth of Biopolitics: Lectures at the Collège de France, 1978–79,* trans. Graham Burchell (New York: Palgrave Macmillan, 2008); Foucault, *Naissance de la biopolitique*; Foucault, *Sécurité, territoire, population*; Foucault, *Security, Territory, Population.* All subsequent references to *Security, Territory, Population* are given in English and French, abbreviated as ESTP and FSTP, respectively. References to *Birth of Biopolitics* follow the same convention and are cited as EBB and FNB, respectively.

3. In a May 2008 e-mail correspondence, Becker confirmed that he never met or had any correspondence with Foucault. Nor did the editors of Foucault's lectures contact him. He has since been made aware of them, in part by the work of his colleague at the University of Chicago Bernard Harcourt. Harcourt's critical book on the "Chicago School" and Foucault's analysis of neoliberal economic theory was dedicated, in part, to Becker. See Bernard E. Harcourt, *The Illusion of Free Markets: Punishment and the Myth of Natural Order* (Cambridge, MA: Harvard University Press, 2011).

4. On this point more generally, see Andrew Dilts, *"From 'Entrepreneur of the Self' to 'Care of the Self': Neo-liberal Governmentality and Foucault's Ethics,"* *Foucault Studies,* no. 12 (2011): 130–146; Nicholas J. Kiersey, *"Neoliberal Political Economy and the Subjectivity of Crisis: Why Governmentality Is Not Hollow,"* *Global Society* 23, no. 4 (2009): 363–386; Jason Read, *"A Genealogy of Homo-Economicus: Neoliberalism and the Production of Subjectivity,"* *Foucault Studies,* no. 6 (2009): 25–36.

5. See, for instance, Taylor C. Boas and Jordan Gans-Morse, *"Neoliberalism: From New Liberal Philosophy to Anti-liberal Slogan,"* *Studies in Comparative International Development* 44, no. 2 (2009): 137–161; James Ferguson, *"The Uses of Neoliberalism,"* *Antipode* 41, no. S1 (2009): 166–184; Stuart Hall, *"The Neo-*

liberal Revolution," *Cultural Studies* 25, no. 6 (2011): 705–728; Carolyn Hardin, *"Finding the 'Neo' in Neoliberalism,"* *Cultural Studies,* December 5, 2012, doi: 10.1080/09502386.2012.748815; Jamie Peck, *Constructions of Neoliberal Reason* (Oxford: Oxford University Press, 2010); Jamie Peck and Adam Tickell, *"Conceptualizing Neoliberalism, Thinking Thatcherism,"* in *Contesting Neoliberalism: Urban Frontiers,* ed. Helga Leitner, Jamie Peck, and Eric S. Sheppard (New York: Guilford, 2007); Loïc Wacquant, *"Three Steps to a Historical Anthropology of Actually Existing Neoliberalism,"* *Social Anthropology* 20, no. 1 (2012): 66–79.

6. David Harvey, *A Brief History of Neoliberalism* (Oxford: Oxford University Press, 2007), 7.

7. Peck and Tickell, "Conceptualizing Neoliberalism," 28.

8. For relatively early engagements with the idea of a distinctive form of "neo-" liberalism, see Victor Ferkiss, *" 'Neoliberalism: How New? How Liberal? How Significant?': A Review Essay,"* *Western Political Quarterly* 39, no. 1 (1986): 165–179; Carl Friedrich, *"Review: The Political Thought of Neo-liberalism,"* *American Political Science Review* 49, no. 2 (1955): 509–525; Lewis Hill, *"On Laissez-Faire Capitalism and 'Liberalism,'"* *American Journal of Economics and Sociology* 23, no. 4 (1964): 393–396; Charles Peters, *"A Neoliberal's Manifesto,"* *Washington Monthly,* May 1983, 1–10; Morton Schoolman, *"The Moral Sentiments of Neoliberalism,"* *Political Theory* 15, no. 2 (1987): 205–224.

9. Wendy Brown, *"American Nightmare: Neoliberalism, Neoconservatism, and De-Democratization,"* *Political Theory* 34, no. 6 (2006): 690–714.

10. Wendy Brown, *"Neo-liberalism and the End of Liberal Democracy,"* *Theory & Event* 7, no. 1 (2003), doi:10.1353/tae.2003.0020.

11. Ibid.

12. See Lisa Duggan, *The Twilight of Equality? Neoliberalism, Cultural Politics, and the Attack on Democracy* (Boston: Beacon, 2003); Ferguson, "Uses of Neoliberalism."

13. Joe Soss, Richard C. Fording, and Sanford Schram, *Disciplining the Poor: Neoliberal Paternalism and the Persistent Power of Race* (Chicago: University of Chicago Press, 2011), 20.

14. Pierre Bourdieu, *"The Essence of Neoliberalism,"* trans. Jeremy J. Shapiro, *Le monde diplomatique,* December 1998, http://mondediplo.com/1998/12/08bourdieu.

15. Harcourt, *Illusion of Free Markets;* Loïc Wacquant, *"The Penalisation of Poverty and the Rise of Neo-liberalism,"* *European Journal on Criminal Policy and Research* 9, no. 4 (2001): 401–412; Wacquant, *Prisons of Poverty,* exp. ed. (Minneapolis: University of Minnesota Press, 2009); Wacquant, *Punishing the Poor: The Neoliberal Government of Social Insecurity* (Durham, NC: Duke University Press, 2009).

16. See, in particular, Leonard Feldman, *Citizens without Shelter: Homelessness, Democracy, and Political Exclusion* (Ithaca, NY: Cornell University Press, 2004); Bernard E. Harcourt, *Illusion of Order: The False Promise of Broken Windows Policing* (Cambridge, MA: Harvard University Press, 2005); Soss, Fording, and Schram, *Disciplining the Poor*.

17. Wacquant, *Punishing the Poor*, xviii.

18. Peck and Tickell, "Conceptualizing Neoliberalism," 33.

19. Wacquant, *Prisons of Poverty*, 1.

20. Lester K. Spence, "*The Neoliberal Turn in Black Politics*," *Souls* 14, nos. 3–4 (2013): 156.

21. Wacquant, *Prisons of Poverty*, 37.

22. Ibid., 79.

23. Ibid., 88.

24. Soss, Fording, and Schram, *Disciplining the Poor*, 13. In particular, see Chapters 2 and 3 of their work.

25. See Michael C. Dawson, *Not in Our Lifetimes: The Future of Black Politics* (Chicago: University of Chicago Press, 2011); Spence, "Neoliberal Turn in Black Politics."

26. Thomas Lemke, *Biopolitics: An Advanced Introduction*, trans. Eric Frederick Trump (New York: New York University Press, 2011), 5.

27. EBB, 186 / FNB, 192. The pioneering volume on governmentality is *The Foucault Effect*, which included the fourth lecture of *Security, Territory, Population* in English for the first time under the title "Governmentality" and a collection of essays, many written by Foucault's students. For surveys of recent work in governmentality, see the February 2009 special issue of *Foucault Studies* titled "Neoliberal Governmentality," as well as Maris Bonnafous-Boucher, "*From Government to Governance*," *Ethical Perspectives: Journal of the European Ethics Network* 12, no. 4 (2005): 521–534; Ulrich Bröckling, Susanne Krasmann, and Thomas Lemke, eds., *Governmentality: Current Issues and Future Challenges* (New York: Routledge, 2011); Jacques Donzelot and Colin Gordon, "*Governing Liberal Societies: The Foucault Effect In The English-Speaking World*," *Foucault Studies*, no. 5 (2008): 48–62; Stuart Elden, "*Governmentality, Calculation, Territory*," *Environment and Planning D: Society and Space* 25, no. 3 (2007): 562–580; Elden, "*Rethinking Governmentality*," *Political Geography* 26, no. 1 (2007): 29–33; Jeffrey T. Nealon, *Foucault beyond Foucault: Power and Its Intensifications since 1984* (Stanford, CA: Stanford University Press, 2008); Judith Revel, *Le vocabulaire de Foucault* (Paris: Ellipses, 2002), 13–15, 38–40; Nikolas Rose, Pat O'Malley, and Mariana Valverde, "*Governmentality*," *Annual Review of Law and Social Science* 2 (2006): 83–104.

28. Lemke, *Biopolitics*, 34. Foucault appears to use the terms "biopolitics" and "biopower" synonymously: in the 1976 lectures, he writes, "What does this

new technology of power, this biopolitics, this biopower that is beginning to establish itself, involve?" Michel Foucault, *Society Must Be Defended: Lectures at the Collège de France, 1975–1976*, trans. David Macey (New York: Picador, 2003), 243. For more on the terms "biopower," "biopolitics," and "governmentality," see Michel Senellart's *course context*, found at the end of *Sécurité, territoire, population*, and Lemke, *Biopolitics*; Mariana Valverde, "*Genealogies of European States: Foucauldian Reflections*," *Economy and Society* 36, no. 1 (2007): 159–178. On the various schools of biopower that have arisen since the 1970s, see Paul Rabinow and Nikolas Rose, "*Biopower Today*," *BioSocieties* 1 (2006): 195–217.

29. On the relationship between the 1976 lectures and *The History of Sexuality*, see Stuart Elden, "*The War of Races and the Constitution of the State: Foucault's 'Il faut défendre la société' and the Politics of Calculation*," *boundary 2* 29, no. 2 (2002): 125–151.

30. Foucault, *Society Must Be Defended*, 239–240.

31. See Michel Foucault, *The History of Sexuality, Vol. 1: An Introduction* (New York: Vintage Books, 1990), part 4. On the specific relation between law and power, see Ben Golder and Peter Fitzpatrick, *Foucault's Law* (London: Routledge, 2009).

32. Foucault, *History of Sexuality, Vol. 1*, 102. See also Foucault, *Society Must Be Defended*, 240–242.

33. Foucault, *History of Sexuality, Vol. 1*, 136.

34. Ibid.

35. Ibid., 138.

36. Ibid., 137–138.

37. Ibid.

38. Ibid., 139.

39. Lemke, *Biopolitics*, 37.

40. Foucault, *Society Must Be Defended*, 242.

41. Ibid., 243, 245.

42. Ibid., 246.

43. Foucault, *History of Sexuality, Vol. 1*, 143.

44. The analyses of biopolitics, governmentality, and subjectivity continued in the years following 1976 until Foucault's death in 1984. While the scope of these analyses shifted over those years, the 1978 and 1979 lectures, *Security, Territory, Population* and *Birth of Biopolitics*, were directly focused on explication of these terms. The 1980 lectures, *Subjectivity and Truth* (which remain unavailable in French or English), carry on the question of governmentality but also mark the important shift in Foucault's interest toward ancient philosophy and practices. His interest in the ancient world continued through his remaining lecture courses and in the final published volumes of *The History of Sexuality*.

45. Foucault, *Security, Territory, Population*, 1.
46. Valverde, "Genealogies of European States," 172.
47. Foucault, *Security, Territory, Population*, 4.
48. Ibid.
49. Ibid., 4–5.
50. Foucault takes up multiple examples besides theft throughout the lectures, many coming back to questions of disease, space, surveillance, and government management. See Elden's essay on the deep connections between these examples: Stuart Elden, *"Plague, Panopticon, Police," Surveillance & Society* 1, no. 3 (2003): 240–253.
51. Foucault, *Security, Territory, Population*, 47.
52. Ibid., 66.
53. Lemke, *Biopolitics*, 42.
54. See the lecture of April 5, 1978, in *Security, Territory, Population*.
55. Ibid., 108–109.
56. Valverde confirms this emphasis, writing, "It is the practices that are regarded as primary objects of analysis, with the state and related institutions being regarded as 'coagulations' of practices" ("Genealogies of European States," 162).
57. EBB, 319 / FNB, 323.
58. EBB, 317 / FNB, 323.
59. Colin Gordon and Lemke both provide excellent syntheses of the entire lecture course. Michael Peters, in particular, covers the analysis of German *ordo*-liberalism. Colin Gordon, *"Governmental Rationality: An Introduction,"* in *The Foucault Effect: Studies in Governmentality*, ed. Graham Burchell, Colin Gordon, and Peter Miller, 1–51 (Chicago: University of Chicago Press, 1991); Thomas Lemke, *"'The Birth of Bio-politics': Michel Foucault's Lecture at the Collège de France on Neo-liberal Governmentality," Economy and Society* 20, no. 2 (2001): 190–207; Michael A. Peters, *"Foucault, Biopolitics and the Birth of Neo-liberalism," Critical Studies in Education* 48, no. 2 (2007): 165–178.
60. Duncan Ivison, *The Self at Liberty: Political Argument and the Arts of Government* (Ithaca, NY: Cornell University Press, 1997), 36.
61. Lemke, "Birth of Bio-politics," 197.
62. EBB, 217 / FNB, 223.
63. Lemke, "Birth of Bio-politics," 200.
64. EBB, 247 / FNB, 253.
65. Ibid.
66. EBB, 225 / FNB, 231.
67. The key texts are Gary S. Becker, *"Investment in Human Capital: A Theoretical Analysis," Journal of Political Economy* 70, no. 5, Part 2: Investment in

Human Beings (1962): 9–49; Becker, *"Irrational Behavior and Economic Theory,"* *Journal of Political Economy* 70, no. 1 (1962): 1–13; Gary S. Becker, *"Rational Action and Economic Theory: A Reply to I. Kirzner," Journal of Political Economy* 71, no. 1 (1963): 82–83; Becker, *"A Theory of the Allocation of Time," Economic Journal* 75, no. 299 (1965): 493–517. For a fuller account of Foucault's reading of human capital theory, see Dilts, "From 'Entrepreneur of the Self' to 'Care of the Self.'"

68. EBB, 226 / FNB, 232.

69. Lemke, "Birth of Bio-politics," 199.

70. EBB, 226 / FNB, 232.

71. EBB, 240 / FNB, 245.

72. EBB, 249 / FNB, 254.

73. Ibid.

74. EBB, 249 / FNB, 254–255.

75. Gary S. Becker, *"Crime and Punishment: An Economic Approach," Journal of Political Economy* 76, no. 2 (1968): 169–217.

76. Although Foucault makes no explicit mention of it here, he must have been conscious of the striking similarity between Nietzsche's analysis of punishment in *On the Genealogy of Morality* (the creditor-debtor relationship) and Becker's definition (as a purely economic relationship).

77. EBB, 252 / FNB, 257.

78. EBB, 253 / FNB, 258.

79. Becker, "Crime and Punishment," 176, 201.

80. EBB, 253 / FNB, 258.

81. EBB, 253 / FNB, 258.

82. EBB 254 / FNB, 259, emphasis in original.

83. George J. Stigler, *"The Optimum Enforcement of Laws," Journal of Political Economy* 78, no. 3 (1970): 526–527.

84. EBB, 256 / FNB, 261–262.

85. See Bernard E. Harcourt, *Against Prediction: Profiling, Policing, and Punishing in an Actuarial Age* (Chicago: University of Chicago Press, 2007); Harcourt, *Illusion of Free Markets.*

86. EBB, 258–259 / FNB, 264.

87. EBB, 259 / FNB, 264.

88. Isaac Ehrlich, *"The Deterrent Effect of Capital Punishment: A Question of Life and Death," American Economic Review* 65, no. 3 (1975): 399, quoted with Foucault's emphasis.

89. EBB, 259 / FNB, 264.

90. Lemke, "Birth of Bio-politics," 200.

91. EBB, 259–260 / FNB, 265.

92. Michel Foucault, "On the Genealogy of Ethics: An Overview of Work in Progress," in *The Essential Foucault: Selections from Essential Works of Foucault, 1954–1984*, ed. Paul Rabinow and Nikolas S. Rose (New York: New Press, 2003), 104.

93. Becker, "Crime and Punishment," 209.

94. Lemke notes, "The [neo-liberal] strategy of rendering individual subjects 'responsible' . . . entails shifting the responsibility for social risks such as illness, unemployment, poverty, etc., and for life in society into the domain for which the individual is responsible and transforming it into a problem of 'self-care.' The key feature of the neo-liberal rationality is the congruence it endeavors to achieve between a responsible and moral individual and an economic-rational actor." Lemke, "Birth of Bio-politics," 201.

95. EBB, 253, 270–271 / FNB, 258, 274.

96. Gordon, "Governmental Rationality," 43.

97. See Dilts, "From 'Entrepreneur of the Self' to 'Care of the Self.'"

98. This quality of punishment is captured nicely in Chapter 2, "The Desire to Punish," of William E. Connolly, *The Ethos of Pluralization* (Minneapolis: University of Minnesota Press, 1995).

99. For examples of how this works in both theoretical and historical terms, see Robert Castel, "*From Dangerousness to Risk*," in *The Foucault Effect: Studies in Governmentality*, ed. Graham Burchell, Colin Gordon, and Peter Miller, 281–298 (Chicago: University of Chicago Press, 1991); Harcourt, *Against Prediction*.

100. EBB, 42–43 / FNB, 44.

101. Foucault, "*Politics and the Study of Discourse*," in *The Foucault Effect: Studies in Governmentality*, ed. Graham Burchell, Colin Gordon, and Peter Miller, 53–72 (Chicago: University of Chicago Press, 1991), 58.

102. This problem can be seen in the co-optation of "color-blindness" to discount the lived experiences of people of color. A similar process is at work in the effect of the 1993 "Don't Ask, Don't Tell" military policy: an increase in the expulsion of homosexuals from the armed forces. See Lani Guinier, *The Tyranny of the Majority: Fundamental Fairness in Representative Democracy* (New York: Free Press, 1994); Janet E. Halley, *Don't: A Reader's Guide to the Military's Antigay Policy* (Durham, NC: Duke University Press, 1999).

103. Karl Marx, "*On the Jewish Question*," in *The Marx-Engels Reader*, ed. Robert C. Tucker, 26–52 (New York: Norton, 1978), 33.

104. See Dilts, "From 'Entrepreneur of the Self' to 'Care of the Self.'"

105. Spence, "Neoliberal Turn in Black Politics," 144.

106. I take the term "constitutive exclusion" from Sina Kramer, who defines it as the "structure and process by which a political body is constituted through the exclusion of some form of difference intolerable to it" (478). As Kramer

notes, the bearers of this difference are not radically displaced or exiled but remain within the political body under an "epistemological block," unintelligible as full political agents. Sina Kramer, "*On Negativity in Revolution in Poetic Language*," *Continental Philosophy Review* 46, no. 3 (2013): 465–479.

107. Among others, this is roughly the line of thought taken by Louis Hartz, *The Liberal Tradition in America: An Interpretation of American Political Thought since the Revolution* (San Diego: Harcourt Brace Jovanovich, 1991); and Gunnar Myrdal, *An American Dilemma: The Negro Problem and Modern Democracy* (New York: Harper & Row, 1962).

108. For example, see Mills, *Racial Contract*; Carol Pateman, *The Sexual Contract* (Stanford, CA: Stanford University Press, 1988); R. Smith, "*Beyond Tocqueville, Myrdal, and Hartz*"; R. Smith, *Civic Ideals*; Stevens and Smith, "Beyond Tocqueville, Please!"

109. See also Pateman, *Sexual Contract*.

4. TO KILL A THIEF

1. Charles II, "By the King: A Proclamation for Discovery of Robberies and Burglaries, and for a Reward to the Discoverers" (London, 1661).

2. Sandel, *Democracy's Discontent*.

3. See Cholbi, "Felon's Right to Vote"; Ewald, "Civil Death"; Johnson-Parris, "Felon Disenfranchisement"; Kleinig and Murtagh, "Disenfranchising Felons"; Reiman, "Liberal and Republican Arguments against the Disenfranchisement of Felons"; Jason Schall, "*The Consistency of Felon Disenfranchisement with Citizenship Theory*" (Washington, DC: Sentencing Project, 2004).

4. Reiman, "Liberal and Republican Arguments against the Disenfranchisement of Felons," 13.

5. *Baily v. Baronian*, 120 R.I. 389 (R.I. 1978); *Farrakhan v. Locke*, 987 F. Supp. 1304 (E.D. Wash. 1997); *Green v. Board of Election*, 380 F.2d 445 (2nd Cir. 1967).

6. *Farrakhan v. Locke*, 987 F. Supp. at 1312.

7. Keally McBride, *Punishment and Political Order* (Ann Arbor: University of Michigan Press, 2007), 122. I am deeply indebted to McBride's work both in its method and its object.

8. See, for instance, Richard Ashcraft, "*Locke's State of Nature: Historical Fact or Moral Fiction?*," *American Political Science Review* 62, no. 3 (1968): 898–915; Patrick Coby, "*The Law of Nature in Locke's Second Treatise: Is Locke a Hobbesian?*," *Review of Politics* 49, no. 1 (1987): 3–28; John Dunn, *The Political Thought of John Locke* (Cambridge: Cambridge University Press, 1969); Eldon J. Eisenach, "*Crime, Death and Loyalty in English Liberalism*," *Political Theory* 6, no. 2 (1978): 213–232; Daniel M. Farrell, "*Punishment without the State*," *Nous* 22,

no. 3 (1988): 437–453; Robert A. Goldwin, *"Locke's State of Nature in Political Society,"* *Western Political Quarterly* 29, no. 1 (1976): 126–135; A. John Simmons, *"Locke's State of Nature,"* *Political Theory* 17, no. 3 (1989): 449–470; Leo Strauss, *Natural Right and History* (Chicago: University of Chicago Press, 1965); Strauss, *"On Locke's Doctrine of Natural Right,"* *Philosophical Review* 61, no. 4 (1952): 475–502; Richard Tuck, *The Rights of War and Peace: Political Thought and the International Order from Grotius to Kant* (Oxford: Oxford University Press, 1999); James Tully, *"Political Freedom,"* *Journal of Philosophy* 87, no. 10 (1990): 517–523; John W. Yolton, *"Locke on the Law of Nature,"* *Philosophical Review* 67, no. 4 (1958): 477–498.

9. For instance, see Jeffrie G. Murphy, *"A Paradox in Locke's Theory of Natural Rights,"* *Dialogue* 8 (1969–1970): 256–271.

10. The most notable Locke scholars who give punishment a place of priority in their analyses include Simmons, Von Leyden, and Ashcraft. According to Simmons, "Locke's defense of a natural executive right . . . lies at the very heart of his political philosophy." A. John Simmons, *The Lockean Theory of Rights* (Princeton, NJ: Princeton University Press, 1992), 127. See also Richard Ashcraft, *Locke's Two Treatises of Government* (London: Allen & Unwin, 1987); Ashcraft, *Revolutionary Politics and Locke's "Two Treatises of Government"* (Princeton, NJ: Princeton University Press, 1986); Simmons, *"Locke and the Right to Punish,"* *Philosophy & Public Affairs* 20, no. 4 (1991): 311–349; Simmons, *On the Edge of Anarchy: Locke, Consent, and the Limits of Society* (Princeton, NJ: Princeton University Press, 1993); Wolfgang Von Leyden, *"Locke's Strange Doctrine of Punishment,"* in *John Locke: Symposium, Wolfenbüttel 1979*, ed. Reinhard Brandt, 113–127 (Berlin: Walter du Gruyter, 1981).

11. For instance, see Larry Alexander, *"Consent, Punishment, and Proportionality,"* *Philosophy & Public Affairs* 15, no. 2 (1986): 178–182; Brian Calvert, *"Locke on Punishment and the Death Penalty,"* *Philosophy* 68, no. 264 (1993): 211–229; Carlos Nino, *"A Consensual Theory of Punishment,"* *Philosophy & Public Affairs* 12, no. 4 (1983): 289–306; Carlos Nino, *"Does Consent Override Proportionality?,"* *Philosophy & Public Affairs* 15, no. 2 (1986): 183–187; A. John Simmons, *"Locke on the Death Penalty,"* *Philosophy* 69, no. 270 (1994): 471–477.

There are several important exceptions both to these ways of thinking about Locke's account of punishment and to the lack of attention to the "thief" in how that account functions. Rebecca Kingston, *"Locke, Waldron and the Moral Status of 'Crooks,'"* *European Journal of Political Theory* 7, no. 2 (2008): 203–221; Jeremy Waldron, *God, Locke, and Equality: Christian Foundations of John Locke's Political Thought* (New York: Cambridge University Press, 2002). In particular, see David Bates, *States of War: Enlightenment Origins of the Political* (New York: Columbia University Press, 2011). In Chapter 3 of Bates's book, he offers a similar reading of the thief to explain the conceptual differences between war and peace for Locke and liberal theory, emphasizing the importance of this figure to Locke's conception of the political community.

12. I borrow the term "degenerates" explicitly from Darrell Moore's account of subject formation in Locke. Moore carefully accounts for the construction of savages and subjects at the intersection between the social contract and Locke's account of human reason. Darrell Moore, *"Epidermal Capital: Formations of (Black) Subjectivity in Political Philosophy and Culture"* (Ph.D. diss., Northwestern University, 1997).

13. Shannon Winnubst, *Queering Freedom* (Bloomington: Indiana University Press, 2006), 38–43.

14. Ibid., 44.

15. Mills, *Racial Contract.*

16. All passages of the *Second Treatise* are cited in the text by section/paragraph numbers and are drawn from Locke, *Two Treatises of Government.*

17. In 2.28.6 of *An Essay Concerning Human Understanding,* Locke states that punishment is necessarily a part of law. John Locke, *An Essay Concerning Human Understanding,* ed. Peter H. Nidditch (Oxford: Oxford University Press, 1975).

18. Waldron, *God, Locke, and Equality,* 143.

19. I follow Locke's usage of the masculine-gendered pronoun in describing thieves, despite the fact that, as Terrell Carver has noted, Locke's narrative alternates between "covert" and "overt" gendered language throughout the text. Carver notes that use of "man," "mankind," and the thief used in Chapters 2–5 is seemingly "de-gendered" for Locke, as opposed to the overtly gendered account he uses elsewhere. See Terrell Carver, *"Gender and Narrative in Locke's Two Treatises of Government,"* in *Feminist Interpretations of John Locke,* ed. Nancy Hirschmann and Kirstie McClure, 187–212 (University Park: Pennsylvania State University Press, 2007).

20. Waldron, *God, Locke, and Equality,* 144. Waldron, however, seems overly confident that the status of "violator" is knowable prior to the institution of state punishment.

21. In §6 of the *Second Treatise,* Locke seems to conflate reason and the Law of Nature. This articulation seems to be partially at odds with his the "Fourth Essay on the Law of Nature," where he states that through reason mankind "arrives at the knowledge of natural law." John Locke, *"Essays on the Law of Nature,"* in *Political Essays,* ed. Mark Goldie, 79–133 (Cambridge: Cambridge University Press, 1997), 101.

22. This right is also stated explicitly in §§182 and 207. In §§172, 186, 202, and 228, further reference is made to thieves, robbers, and pirates, and in each

case Locke connects such persons to the exercise of unjust force calling for a response.

23. I agree with both A. John Simmons and Nathan Tarcov that the State of Nature and the State of War are not, as John Dunn has argued, mutually exclusive. See Dunn, *Political Thought of John Locke*, 96–119; Simmons, *On the Edge of Anarchy*, 43n. 7; Nathan Tarcov, *"Locke's Second Treatise and 'the Best Fence against Rebellion,'" Review of Politics* 43, no. 2 (1981): 198–217.

24. The figure of the highwayman was common in seventeenth-century English popular culture. See Michael Billett, *Highwaymen and Outlaws* (London: Arms and Armour, 1997); Christopher Hill, *Liberty against the Law: Some Seventeenth-Century Controversies* (London: Penguin, 1996); Gillian Spraggs, *Outlaws and Highwaymen: The Cult of the Robber in England from the Middle Ages to the Nineteenth Century* (London: Pimlico, 2001).

25. Simmons insists that the States of Nature, War, and civil society are relational between persons, meaning that a single person can be in a State of Nature with one person while at the same time in a State of War or peace with another. See Simmons, *On the Edge of Anarchy*, 16–17. Alternately, an individual may be in a State of War with another person while also in a state of civil society. See Ashcraft, *Locke's Two Treatises of Government*, 202–205.

26. See Locke, *Two Treatises*, §§176, 181, and 186.

27. James Farr, *"Locke, Natural Law, and New World Slavery," Political Theory* 36, no. 4 (2008): 495–522; Farr, *" 'So Vile and Miserable an Estate': The Problem of Slavery in Locke's Political Thought," Political Theory* 14, no. 2 (1986): 263–289. The difficulty, in particular, of squaring Locke's ideal theory with historical slavery is significant. See, especially, Mills, *Racial Contract*. This need not limit the utility of Locke's lexicon, however, even in the context of specifically "American" slavery; see Chapter 4 of Howard McGary and Bill E. Lawson, *Between Slavery and Freedom: Philosophy and American Slavery* (Bloomington: Indiana University Press, 1992). Moreover, there is ample evidence that Locke's ideal theory was connected to the material conditions of the African slave trade. Most recently, see Brad Hinshelwood, *"The Carolinian Context of John Locke's Theory of Slavery," Political Theory* 41, no. 4 (2013): 562–590.

28. Farr, *"So Vile and Miserable an Estate,"* 271.

29. Andrew Norris, *"The Exemplary Exception: Philosophical and Political Decisions in Giorgio Agamben's Homo Sacer,"* in *Politics, Metaphysics, and Death: Essays on Giorgio Agamben's "Homo Sacer,"* ed. Andrew Norris, 262–283 (Durham, NC: Duke University Press, 2005), 272–273.

30. Jean-Jacques Rousseau, *Of the Social Contract,* in *"The Social Contract" and Other Later Political Writings,* ed. Victor Gourevitch, 39–152 (Cambridge: Cambridge University Press, 1997), I.4.12, 48. Rousseau rejects the Lockean ac-

count of slavery as well as any confusion between what I have described as "war" and "crime." It is telling, however, that the one location in *The Social Contract* where Rousseau troubles this distinction is in his account of the death penalty in II.5.4.

31. In part, Norris argues that the same account of sovereignty that Agamben locates in Hobbes's *Leviathan* can also be seen in Locke's work as well: "Even a writer as profoundly out of temper with Agamben as Locke, and one who seeks to identify human life with a substantive vision of law-governed free activity, can become entangled in . . . the logic of execution. Indeed, it is because Locke is loath to identify human beings with their bare life in an Hobbesian manner that he in the end reduces a class of people to that life." Norris, "Exemplary Exception," 273. See also Agamben, *Homo Sacer.*

32. Orlando Patterson, *Slavery and Social Death: A Comparative Study* (Cambridge, MA: Harvard University Press, 1982). The idea of slavery as a condition of living death, or of being dead already, was (as Patterson notes) a common understanding of ancient slave systems and an apt characterization of the "experience" of slavery (8).

33. Waldron argues that Locke cannot possibly extend the right of punishment to a right of slavery, as this would be to misunderstand when "actual force" is over. The problem in the State of Nature is that "actual" force cannot cease where there is no common judge. Waldron is right, however, to note that under Locke's account, there is no reason to expect slavery in any form to be a "stable or regularized system." Waldron, *God, Locke, and Equality,* 148–149.

34. Bates, *States of War,* 104.

35. My reading plays with the slippage between a commonsense notion of proportionality and excess. In part, my point is that Locke also plays with this slippage in order to demonstrate the distinction between states of war and peace, introducing the requirement of proportionality within a context in which it has no seeming ability to constrain the natural punitive right.

36. Some commentators insist the problem is that punishment itself is not possible in the State of Nature. But this seems to be an untenable textual conclusion, given the time Locke devotes to making it clear that punishment, rightly called, does exist outside civil society. See Farrell, "Punishment without the State."

37. David Bates implies that the victim may punish the offender but leaves open the question of if the victim *must* or *should* punish the thief. It is my contention that the possibility of being able to choose to punish (or not) is what is at stake in joining civil society. In the Sate of Nature, where the State of War *cannot* end without an offer of peace or punishment, the choice to extend mercy is taken off the table. If punishment is to be avoided, it appears to be entirely

in the hands of the offender's choice to offer peace, as unlikely (and dangerous) as that may be. The implication of this reading is to underscore how *unfree* the punisher becomes in the absence of civil society in Locke's system. See Bates, *States of War*, 107.

38. Von Leyden, "Locke's Strange Doctrine of Punishment," 118. By Locke's own account in §9, the "strangeness" of his doctrine seems to be that it is "unusual" but nevertheless is one that must already be agreed to by those who think it right that a state can "put to death, or punish an Alien." In §13, the strangeness of the doctrine is more central to my point: to give such a right will surely be to give too much power to persons who are least able to execute that right. The idea of punishment as a natural right of individuals, rather than simply of the state, however, is less novel than Locke thinks. As Richard Tuck shows, Grotius had already articulated nearly the same position. See Richard Tuck, *Natural Rights Theories: Their Origin and Development* (Cambridge: Cambridge University Press, 1979), 63; Tuck, *Rights of War and Peace*, 171. See also Strauss, *Natural Right and History*, 214.

39. Von Leyden, "Locke's Strange Doctrine of Punishment," 118.

40. Ibid.

41. As Kirstie McClure puts it, "By Locke's own account it is the 'inconveniences' attending the exercise of natural rights, especially the executive right of punishment, that necessitate the creation of civil government." Kirstie McClure, *Judging Rights: Lockean Politics and the Limits of Consent* (Ithaca, NY: Cornell University Press, 1996), 134.

42. Ashcraft, *Locke's Two Treatises of Government*, 196–230; Ashcraft, *Revolutionary Politics and Locke's "Two Treatises of Government,"* esp. 329–336; Dunn, *Political Thought of John Locke*, 165–186.

43. Ashcraft, *Locke's Two Treatises of Government*, 210.

44. Ibid., 202.

45. Ashcraft, *Revolutionary Politics and Locke's "Two Treatises of Government,"* 331.

46. Ashcraft, *Locke's Two Treatises of Government*, 201, 202.

47. I draw here on Darrell Moore's argument that Locke develops an account of "subjects-as-individuals" who come into existence through their capacity to internalize the natural law, "defined against the existence of individuals who cannot or refuse to act in accord with the natural law and are, consequently, considered dangerous to a well-ordered society" ("Epidermal Capital," 14). These other subjects are "degenerate or irrational" and necessarily excluded from membership (20). A similar process is at work with the thief and the member, but in a way that generates greater instability between transgressors and punishers.

48. This understanding of the thief as unable (or unwilling) to consult reason to know the natural law is not limited to Locke's political theory but figures as a central proof in his epistemology as to why there are not innate principles of truth or justice, since they must be acquired through reason. See Locke, *An Essay Concerning Human Understanding*, 66. See also James Martel's excellent and comprehensive account of the "reasonable subject" in Locke's epistemological thought and its connection to his political thought. James R. Martel, *Love Is a Sweet Chain: Desire, Autonomy, and Friendship in Liberal Political Theory* (London: Routledge, 2001).

49. McClure, *Judging Rights*, 209.

50. McBride, *Punishment and Political Order*, 104.

51. See also James Tully's articulation of the "penalized self" as the ontological Lockean subject, relying on the *Essay*. James Tully, *An Approach to Political Philosophy: Locke in Contexts* (Cambridge: Cambridge University Press, 1993), 239–241.

52. I do not mean that such distinctions are impossible, but Locke's depictions of conquest employ criminal figures. In §176, Locke insists that the difference between an "unjust conqueror" and a "petty villain" is one of size, reputation, and power but is not a categorical difference. See Ashcraft on this point in particular: Ashcraft, *Locke's Two Treatises of Government*, 207; Ashcraft, *Revolutionary Politics and Locke's "Two Treatises of Government*," 399–401. In §181, Locke underscores the centrality of force to the definition of war, again using the image of breaking into a house to make his point, echoing the images of "beasts" used in Chapters 2 and 3 to describe thieves and murderers. In §186, Locke specifically uses the example of highway robbery to explain the inability to make binding promises under the threat of force. See also Tuck, *Rights of War and Peace*, 166–172.

53. For instance, see Bruce Ackerman, "*The Emergency Constitution*," *Yale Law Journal* 113, no. 5 (2004): 1029–1091; Ackerman, "*This Is Not a War*," *Yale Law Journal* 113, no. 8 (2004): 1871–1907.

54. Nor should this account be limited to the question of chattel slavery specifically, as Bill Lawson shows in his own reading of Locke on the relation between slavery and citizenship in McGary and Lawson, *Between Slavery and Freedom*, 55–70.

55. See Kramer, "On Negativity in *Revolution in Poetic Language*."

5. INNOCENT CITIZENS, GUILTY SUBJECTS

1. Frederick Douglass, "*Farewell Speech to the British People*," March 30, 1847, in *The Life and Writings of Frederick Douglass*, ed. Philip Sheldon Foner, 5 vols. (New York: International, 1950), 1:209.

2. Davis, *Abolition Democracy*, 38.

3. A notable exception is Marek Steedman's excellent study of postbellum black citizenship in the South. Marek D. Steedman, *Jim Crow Citizenship: Liberalism and the Southern Defense of Racial Hierarchy* (New York: Routledge, 2012).

4. Judith N. Shklar, *American Citizenship: The Quest for Inclusion* (Cambridge, MA: Harvard University Press, 1991).

5. Ibid., 1.

6. Ibid., 2.

7. Ibid., 3.

8. Ibid., 15.

9. Ibid.

10. Ibid., 16, emphasis added.

11. Ibid.

12. Ibid., 39.

13. Ibid., 39–40.

14. See ibid., 47–52. On the question of dignity of labor itself, see 79–85 as well.

15. Ibid., 52.

16. Ibid., 57, emphasis added.

17. Ibid., 57.

18. Ibid.

19. Ibid., 58.

20. Ibid., 20.

21. Ibid.

22. While Shklar's historical narrative is brief, it is accurate; Keyssar's history of voting rights confirms the centrality of slavery in suffrage discourses (*Right to Vote*).

23. Shklar, *American Citizenship*, 17.

24. Ibid., 38.

25. Ibid., 57.

26. Ibid., 28–29.

27. Ibid., 27, emphasis added.

28. Ibid., 55–56.

29. Seyla Benhabib, *"Judith Shklar's Dystopic Liberalism,"* *Social Research* 61, no. 2 (1994): 480.

30. Ibid., 481.

31. Joel Olson, *The Abolition of White Democracy* (Minneapolis: University of Minnesota Press, 2004).

32. Ibid., 43.

33. Here, Olson quotes Shklar from "Obligation, Loyalty, Exile," where she writes, "And whether or not you choose your nationality is a very tricky question, but you are stuck with your race." Judith N. Shklar, *"Obligation, Loyalty, Exile," Political Theory* 21, no. 2 (1993): 185. Interestingly, in an earlier version of this chapter in Olson's book, the footnote uses the term "essentialist" instead of "biological." Joel Olson, *"The Democratic Problem of the White Citizen," Constellations* 8, no. 2 (2001): 182n. 41.

34. Shklar, *American Citizenship*, 49.

35. It is true that she returns to some of these themes elsewhere, but not specifically within the context of suffrage or of the boundaries of membership. Her concern is more specifically focused on the central question of preventing cruelty as an organizing principle of liberalism.

36. Olson, *Abolition of White Democracy*, 44.

37. Ibid., 45.

38. Ibid.

39. Judith N. Shklar, *"Democracy and the Past: Jefferson and His Heirs,"* in *Redeeming American Political Thought*, ed. Stanley Hoffmann and Dennis F. Thompson, 173–186 (Chicago: University of Chicago Press, 1998), 179.

40. Olson relies primarily on Noel Ignatiev's history of the Irish immigrant experience to explain how formal rights of citizenship were a pathway to whiteness, given that his primary interest is in exposing the hidden importance of race in the construction of American citizenship and democracy. Olson prioritizes whiteness as more important (at least materially) than political membership. What Olson primarily wants to point out is Shklar's inattention to how the *manner* in which claims to citizenship were expressed (through explicitly racist actions and expressions) leaves the abstract citizen as necessarily white. It is this realization, he contends, that necessarily changes the terms of philosophical debates of inclusion and multiculturalism. Olson's interest in Shklar is, I think, instrumental to his larger argument, that two of the most central debates in political theory, which he terms the participation-inclusion debate and the multiculturalism debate, are inadequate on their own terms because they fail to take account of the fact that citizenship and democracy in the United States are constructed as *white*. See Chapters 3 and 4 of *Abolition of White Democracy*.

41. Davis, "Racialized Punishment and Prison Abolition," 363.

42. Barbara Esposito, Lee Wood, and Kathryn Bardsley, *Prison Slavery* (Washington, DC: Committee to Abolish Prison Slavery, 1982).

43. Douglas A. Blackmon, *Slavery by Another Name: The Re-enslavement of Black Americans from the Civil War to World War II* (New York: Anchor Books, 2008); Davis, "From the Prison of Slavery to the Slavery of Prison"; Milfred C.

Fierce, *Slavery Revisited: Blacks and the Southern Convict Lease System, 1865–1933* (Brooklyn, NY: Africana Studies Research Center, Brooklyn College, City University of New York, 1994); Alex Lichtenstein, *Twice the Work of Free Labor: The Political Economy of Convict Labor in the New South* (London: Verso, 1996); Matthew J. Mancini, *One Dies, Get Another: Convict Leasing in the American South, 1866–1928* (Columbia: University of South Carolina Press, 1996); D. E. Tobias, "*A Negro on the Position of the Negro in America*," *Nineteenth Century: A Monthly Review* 46, no. 274 (1899): 957–973; Ida B. Wells, Frederick Douglass, Irvine Garland Penn, and Ferdinand L. Barnett, *The Reason Why the Colored American Is Not in the World's Columbian Exposition* (Urbana: University of Illinois Press, 1999).

44. Davis, "Racialized Punishment and Prison Abolition," 363.

45. McBride, *Punishment and Political Order*, 128. See, especially, the entirety of Chapter 6 of *Punishment and Political Order* for McBride's careful analysis of the continuing connections between prison labor and neoliberal forms of property.

46. Ibid., 129.

47. Davis, *Are Prisons Obsolete?*, 27. See also Adam Jay Hirsch, *The Rise of the Penitentiary: Prisons and Punishment in Early America* (New Haven, CT: Yale University Press, 1992).

48. Davis, *Are Prisons Obsolete?*, 28–29.

49. Lichtenstein, *Twice the Work of Free Labor*, 3.

50. Davis, *Are Prisons Obsolete?*, 31.

51. Ibid.

52. Ida B. Wells, "*The Convict Lease System*," in *The Reason Why the Colored American Is Not in the World's Columbian Exposition*, 23.

53. Ibid., 24.

54. Ibid.

55. Ibid., 27.

56. Quoted in Helen Taylor Greene and Shaun L. Gabbidon, *African American Criminological Thought* (Albany: State University of New York Press, 2000), 33. This analysis first appeared in the 1901 article "The Negro as He Really Is," which was reworked into Chapters 7 and 8 of *The Souls of Black Folk*. W. E. B. Du Bois, "*The Negro as He Really Is*," *World's Work* 2 (1901): 848–866. I focus on Du Bois's analysis here because he, more than other analysts of the period, saw convict leasing within broader questions of Reconstruction and criminology. See Gabbidon and Greene, who argue that Du Bois should rightly be considered part of the early American criminological school of thought. Shaun L. Gabbidon, "*An Argument for Including W. E. B. Du Bois in the Criminology/Criminal*

Justice Literature," Journal of Criminal Justice Education 7, no. 1 (1996): 99–112; Greene and Gabbidon, *African American Criminological Thought*; Gabbidon, "*W. E. B. Du Bois: Pioneering American Criminologist," Journal of Black Studies* 31, no. 5 (2001): 581–599.

57. Greene and Gabbidon, *African American Criminological Thought*, 39.

58. W. E. B. Du Bois, *The Souls of Black Folk*, ed. Robert Gooding-Williams (Boston: Bedford Books, 1997), 141.

59. Ibid.

60. Ibid., 141–142.

61. W. E. B. Du Bois, *Black Reconstruction in America*, ed. David L. Lewis (New York: Simon & Schuster, 1995), 506.

62. Ibid.

63. Anonymous "English Traveler" quoted in ibid., 698.

64. Ibid.

65. Wacquant, "Deadly Symbiosis," 99.

66. Ibid., 95.

67. Ibid., 120.

68. Ibid., 119. See also Wacquant, "Race as Civic Felony."

69. Asatar P. Bair, *Prison Labor in the United States: An Economic Analysis* (New York: Routledge, 2008), 109.

70. Ibid., 30–33.

71. See Jeannine Marie DeLombard, *In the Shadows of the Gallows: Race, Crime, and American Civic Identity* (Philadelphia: University of Pennsylvania Press, 2012); Khalil Gibran Muhammad, *The Condemnation of Blackness: Race, Crime, and the Making of Modern Urban America* (Cambridge, MA: Harvard University Press, 2010).

72. While Shklar is careful to note the fact of indentured servitude, she makes no mention in her work of either convict leasing or sharecropping. See Shklar, *American Citizenship*, 40.

73. Ibid., 46

74. Ibid., 61–62.

75. Ibid., 18.

76. This is, perhaps, an overly sympathetic reading, given the long historical struggle and movement of physically, emotionally, and mentally disabled persons for the right to earn, to work, and to have access to public accommodations. Given that the entire second half of *American Citizenship* is dedicated to such struggles, Shklar is remiss in ignoring the diminished political standing of disabled persons. This is extremely problematic, however, as the link between disability and voting rights has a similarly deep connection. I take up this connection conceptually and historically in Chapter 7.

77. Ibid., 35, emphasis added.

78. Ibid., 101, emphasis added.

79. I use the terms "blindness," "blind," and "blind spot" cautiously, in that visual blindness is taken to be a disabling impairment. Given the term's usage in frequent liberal ideals of public life (e.g., color-blind, gender-blind, etc.), it is important to think critically about what we mean when we deploy such terms. As should be clear in my subsequent usage, however, I use the term with this tension in mind, noting the way in which the blind spots in question are *produced* through willful and accidental practices of thought.

80. Judith N. Shklar, "*The Liberalism of Fear*," in *Liberalism and the Moral Life*, ed. Nancy L. Rosenblum, 21–38 (Cambridge, MA: Harvard University Press, 1989), 37.

81. Ibid.

82. Ibid

83. Ibid.

84. Judith N. Shklar, "*Obligation, Loyalty, Exile*," *Political Theory* 21, no. 2 (1993): 196.

85. Ibid.

86. I draw here on Judith Butler's conception of gender (and sexual difference itself) as performative, based on a "*stylized repetition of acts.*" Butler draws our attention primarily to the specific practices in which one must repeatedly engage to generate the social content of gender. Additionally, she draws our attention to the discursive conditions under which these practices take place, typically those that articulate an essentialist discourse about the content of the identity in question and that presume those essentialized attributes as the justificatory basis of continued domination, subjugation, and outright oppression. See Judith Butler, *Gender Trouble: Feminism and the Subversion of Identity* (New York: Routledge, 1990), 140.

87. Paterson's characterization of slavery as "human parasitism" comes to mind here. Patterson, *Slavery and Social Death*.

88. I use the term "fetish" here in keeping with a generally Marxist understanding of the term rather than an anthropological or psychoanalytic usage.

6. PUNISHING AT THE BALLOT BOX

1. Maryland Constitutional Convention (1851), *Debates and Proceedings of the Maryland Reform Convention to Revise the State Constitution* (Annapolis: W. M'Neir, 1851), 96.

2. Davis, "Racialized Punishment and Prison Abolition." See also Amy Allen, "*Justice and Reconciliation: The Death of the Prison?*," *Human Studies* 30, no. 4 (2007): 311–321.

3. By exemplary and paradigmatic, I mean roughly what Giorgio Agamben describes as that which "entails a movement that goes from singularity to singularity and, without ever leaving singularity, transforms every singular case into an *exemplar* of a general rule that can never be stated a priori" (*Signature of All Things*, 22).

4. Brenda Jo Brueggemann and James A. Fredal, "*Studying Disability Rhetorically*," in *Disability Discourse*, ed. Mairian Corker and Sally French, 130–135 (Buckingham, UK: Open University Press, 1999).

5. Additionally, records from the 1774–1776 convention are not available, and transcripts were not kept during the 1867 debates, only daily reports on discussion, amendments, and votes. This necessarily limits my archive.

6. There are many excellent sources tracing the constitutional changes in Maryland's history. See Dan Friedman, *The Maryland State Constitution: A Reference Guide* (Westport, CT: Praeger, 2006); James Warner Harry, *The Maryland Constitution of 1851* (Baltimore: John Hopkins University Press, 1902); Maryland Constitutional Convention Commission, *Report of the Constitutional Convention Commission: To His Excellency, Spiro T. Agnew, Governor of Maryland, the Honorable, the General Assembly of Maryland, the Delegates to the Constitutional Convention of Maryland and to the People of Maryland* (Annapolis: State of Maryland, 1967); Alfred Salem Niles, *Maryland Constitutional Law* (Baltimore: Hepbron & Haydon, 1915).

7. Upon a third public-drunkenness conviction, "the Offender shal be adjudged a Person infamous, and thereby made vncapable of giving vote [*sic*]." See Act of 1658, in Archives of Maryland, Vol. 1, 375. See also Raphael Semmes, *Crime and Punishment in Early Maryland* (Baltimore: Johns Hopkins University Press, 1996), 146. The colonial period of constitutionalism in Maryland is itself a fascinating study of the tensions between proprietary law, discretion, and more formal constitutional order. See Vicki Hsueh's excellent study of the Maryland Charter in Vicki Hsueh, *Hybrid Constitutions: Challenging Legacies of Law, Privilege, and Culture in Colonial America* (Durham, NC: Duke University Press, 2010).

8. Maryland Constitutional Convention Commission, *Report of the Constitutional Convention Commission*, 28.

9. Section 5 of the Declaration of Rights of 1776 states that "every man having property in, a common interest with, and attachment to the community, ought to have a right of suffrage." This is restricted in Section 2 of the constitution to "all freemen above twenty-one years of age, having a freehold of fifty acres of land . . . or having thirty pounds current money, and having resided in the county in which they offer to vote one whole year."

10. Act of 1801, Chapter 90.

11. Act of 1809, Chapters 83 and 198, both ratified 1810.

12. Alexis de Tocqueville, *Democracy in America* (New York: HarperPerennial, 2006), 59.

13. Duggan, *Twilight of Equality?*, 5.

14. Section 54 of Maryland Constitution of 1776.

15. James Warner Harry's 1902 study of the 1851 convention states that "Maryland, since the framing of the Constitution of 1776 had become a government of the minority." Harry, *Maryland Constitution of 1851*, 13.

16. Ibid.

17. Maryland Constitutional Convention Commission, *Report of the Constitutional Convention Commission*, 44.

18. The sections were renumbered in 1864. Article 1, Section 2, of 1851 became Article 1, Section 5, in 1864, and Article 1, Section 5, of 1851 becomes Article 1, Section 3, in 1864.

19. Friedman, *Maryland State Constitution*, 50, 380.

20. Niles, *Maryland Constitutional Law*, 87. See *Neal v. Delaware*, 103 U.S. 370 (1880).

21. Maryland Constitutional Convention Commission, *Constitutional Revision Study Documents of the Constitutional Convention of Maryland* (Annapolis, 1968), 602.

22. Maryland Constitutional Convention Commission, *Report of the Constitutional Convention Commission*, 62.

23. See Friedman, *Maryland State Constitution*, 50.

24. Maryland Session Laws, 1972, Chapter 368. Article 1, Section 2 was later renumbered as Section 4 in 1977.

25. Friedman, *Maryland State Constitution*, 53.

26. Election bribery is currently defined as a misdemeanor under Maryland Election Code §16-201 but a disqualification for registering to vote under §3-102 (i.e., persons convicted of buying or selling votes).

27. HB 25 in 1999 would have allowed felons to vote after probation. HB 438 of 2000 would have allowed felons to vote after a five-year waiting period. SB 83 of 2001 had a three-year waiting period for persons with one conviction and permanently disenfranchised persons with two convictions.

28. "*Task Force to Study Repealing the Disenfranchisement of Convicted Felons in Maryland*" (Annapolis, MD: Department of Legislative Services, Office of Policy Analysis, 2002), 7. While the report only makes scant mention of the 2000 presidential election, it was one of many produced in the wake of the contested Florida election, resulting in new scrutiny placed on the preparation of voter lists.

29. The bill (SB 184) was virtually identical to the one proposed in 2001 (SB 83).

30. Hull, *Disenfranchisement of Ex-Felons*, 74.

31. In 1851, the debate largely centered on the comments of four delegates: William D. Merrick, Levin L. Dirickson, John S. Sellman, and Robert J. Brent. Maryland Constitutional Convention (1851), *Debates*, 88–94.

32. Conviction for voter bribery is in a separate provision from the other exclusions and receives far greater attention during the 1851 convention. During the 1864 debates, attention shifts to the "larceny and other infamous crimes" provision.

33. Maryland Constitutional Convention (1851), *Debates*, 92.

34. Ibid., 88–89.

35. Several delegates objected to permanent disenfranchisement on pragmatic grounds, stating that it is ineffective because juries will be hesitant to impose such a punishment. Delegate Dirickson stated, "If, then, you desire to destroy bribery, let the punishment be modified and made proportionate to the offence. . . . No jury . . . could be induced to convict; the penalty absolutely victimized—and therefore defeated the very object sought to be obtained by its extreme and most disproportionate severity" (ibid., 93–94). This same point was echoed by Delegates Brent, Sellman, and Charles J. M. Gwinn. None of them, however, questioned the logic of imposing disenfranchisement as a form of punishment. They only attempted to limit it to a fixed period of time rather than imposing a lifetime ban.

36. I use the term "ideally" here because it is certainly arguable that the ballot box only has such a meaning in an abstract sense, given that (1) American elections are characterized by low turnout rates and (2) they are typically only reflections of candidate preferences. Nevertheless, the strong ideological support for elections and voting reflects a belief that this is the purpose they serve: to communicate popular sentiment in an aggregate way.

37. The importance of capability for voting rights is thoroughly demonstrated by Alexander Keyssar in *The Right to Vote* and is explained in Jacob Katz Cogan, "*The Look Within: Property, Capacity, and Suffrage in Nineteenth-Century America*," *Yale Law Journal* 107, no. 2 (1997): 473–498.

38. I take up the specific discursive relationship between criminal exclusions and *non compos mentis* exclusions in the next chapter.

39. Maryland Constitutional Convention (1851), *Debates*, 95.

40. Ibid., 93.

41. The nineteenth-century polling place was a far different kind of place from what contemporary U.S. voters have come to expect in terms of "order" and "chaos." Alec Ewald's careful study of the "local texture" of elections in the United States is illustrative here. Alec C. Ewald, *The Way We Vote: The Local*

Dimension of American Suffrage (Nashville, TN: Vanderbilt University Press, 2009).

42. Maryland Constitutional Convention (1851), *Debates*, 93.

43. Ibid., 87.

44. This is entirely true in 1851. During the 1864 debates, the one expressly racialized reference in the debates about criminal disenfranchisement in the Maryland convention records was a concern expressed by Delegate David Scott that a person who had been convicted in another state for having a copy of *Uncle Tom's Cabin* would be subject to disenfranchisement. In 1857, there was a case in Maryland of a free black person receiving a ten-year prison sentence for owning that book. See Charles Wagandt, *The Mighty Revolution: Negro Emancipation in Maryland, 1862–1864* (Baltimore: Maryland Historical Society, 2004), 46n. 26.

45. Dinan, "Adoption of Criminal Disenfranchisement Provisions." This was in Alabama's 1901 convention. See *Hunter v. Underwood*, 471 U.S. 222 (1985).

46. Dinan, "Adoption of Criminal Disenfranchisement Provisions," 297.

47. Ibid., 298.

48. Holloway, "Chicken-Stealer Shall Lose His Vote."

49. Ibid., 956–957.

50. Harry, *Maryland Constitution of 1851*, 59–63.

51. Ibid., 33–34.

52. It was state policy from the 1830s on to promote the removal of "free negroes" to Liberia, and land was purchased there with state funds in 1834. Ibid., 60–61.

53. Carl N. Everstine, *The General Assembly of Maryland 1850–1920* (Charlottesville, VA: Michie, 1984), 80–81.

54. Manumission was eventually banned by the General Assembly in 1860. Wagandt, *Mighty Revolution*, 8.

55. See Article 3, Section 43, of the constitution of 1851 as well as the Action 1836, Chapter 148, which amended the 1776 constitution to prohibit the legislature from abolishing "the relation of Master and Slave in this state." Even before the 1850 convention began proper deliberations, a committee was appointed to write a series of resolutions condemning the recent federal compromises on slavery, with its being banned in the new state of California, the territories of Utah and New Mexico, and Washington, D.C., for not meeting "the just demands of the South." The federal fugitive slave law was praised but seen as a "tardy and meager measure of compliance with the clear, explicit, and imperative injunction of the constitution." Harry, *Maryland Constitution of 1851*, 37–38.

56. Wagandt, *Mighty Revolution*, 223.

57. Maryland Constitutional Convention Commission, *Report of the Constitutional Convention Commission*, 62.

58. Declaration of Rights of 1851, Article 21.

59. Maryland Constitutional Convention (1851), *Debates*, 194–199.

60. Ibid., 198.

61. Ibid., 196.

62. Ibid., 198.

63. See Manza and Uggen, *Locked Out*.

64. Maryland Constitutional Convention Commission, *Debates of the Constitutional Convention of 1967–1968* (Annapolis: Hall of Records Commission, 1982), 1971, emphasis added. I believe that the delegate is mistaken in citing the 1867 debates, as a verbatim record of those debates was not kept. To the best of my knowledge, all that exists in the Maryland Archives is a daily summary of proposed amendments, motions, and votes cast. Perhaps the delegate is referring to the earlier debates but is confused since it is the 1867 constitution that was in effect at the time. The delegate is, however, quite correct to characterize the nineteenth-century understanding of disenfranchisement as a form of punishment.

65. Ibid., 1972.

66. The only exception is Delegate Elizabeth Levy Bothe, who alone among delegates speaking on the issue in any year of any convention attempts to strike the entire disenfranchisement provision from the constitution and not give the General Assembly the authority to restrict the franchise at all: "It is my belief . . . that the General Assembly should have no authority of any sort to disenfranchise anyone otherwise qualified to vote. . . . The automatic disenfranchisement of anybody because of his acts is an extremely dangerous precedent. . . . I think that we ought to allow every citizen who meets the minimal qualifications the opportunity, if he sees fit, to take advantage of voting. We should not tamper with this sacred right." She even goes so far as to insist that there be no exclusion for currently incarcerated individuals and that currently incarcerated individuals not be barred from holding office: "As to the question of whether a felon or insane person would run for office, I am not at all concerned about that. I do not see any reason why a convict cannot file for office. If the voters want to elect him, that is their affair. If these same people want to put him in office, I suppose that is the way it will have to be." Her proposal was voted down by a 2–1 margin. Ibid., 2024–2028.

67. "Task Force to Study Repealing the Disenfranchisement of Convicted Felons in Maryland," 4.

68. SB 488 / HB 554.

69. Maryland Constitutional Convention (1851), *Debates*, 381–382.

70. Delegate Benjamin B. Chambers states, "The words used were technical words in common law, and in common law treatises; and to strike them out might involve us in difficulty. It depended on the punishment affixed by law to a crime." Ibid., 382.

71. Ibid., 383.

72. Delegate Constable "objected to the phrase *infamous crimes*, because its meaning was uncertain, and there might be a want of uniformity in its application, arising from a diversity of opinion as to import, which would operate injustice. . . . Whatever might have been the *crimes* known as *infamous* at common law, he believed there were none below the grade of felony, it was obvious that they might be multiplied indefinitely by statute. Thus *forgery*, which was not a *felony* at common law, and hence not embraced in the class of offences that it denounced as *infamous*, had been made so by act of parliament. In the same manner, assault and battery and other trivial *misdemeanors*, may be made *infamous crimes*; and those who commit them be subjected to the harsh disabilities imposed by this section. This phrase then, was liable to be extended both by *legislation* and *construction*, and if done by the *latter*, the same crime when committed by different persons might not always be visited with these disabilities. [In order to avoid this confusion] . . . he would move to substitute the word, *felony*, for the phrase, *infamous crimes*." Ibid.

73. Maryland Constitutional Convention (1864), Wm. Blair Lord, and Henry M. Parkhurst, *The Debates of the Constitutional Convention of the State of Maryland* (Annapolis: R. P. Bayly, 1864), 1295.

74. Ibid.

75. The text Edelen quotes from is from volume 1 of John Bouvier, *Institutes of American Law*, 4 vols. (Philadelphia: R. E. Peterson, 1851). It is also probably the case that this is same text which was referred to during the 1851 debates by Delegate Presstman, given the specific reference to "Roman Law."

76. Maryland Constitutional Convention (1864), Lord, and Parkhurst, *Debates*, 1298.

77. Ibid., 1296.

78. Ibid.

79. Goodnough, "Disenfranchised Florida Felons Struggle to Regain Their Rights."

80. *State v. Bixler*, 62 Md. 354, 360 (Md. 1884).

81. Ibid.

82. Niles, *Maryland Constitutional Law*, 94.

83. Ibid.

84. Maryland Constitutional Convention Commission, *Debates of the Constitutional Convention of 1967–1968*, 1971.

85. Ibid., 1973.

86. Ibid., 2266.

87. *Thiess v. State Administrative Board of Election Laws*, 387 F. Supp. 1038 (D. Md. 1974).

88. The easy availability of such a "laundry list" of infamous crimes did not diminish the difficulty of enforcing the restrictions, as county election officials reported as recently as 2004 that they were unaware that such a list even existed. Ewald's excellent report on state-by-state variations in disenfranchisement policies includes this interesting note about local election officials in Maryland: "For county registrars, the infamous crimes list adds difficulty to administering the law. Nine of ten local officials interviewed knew the eligibility basics, though three did not mention the concept of infamous crimes at all." Ewald, "'Crazy-Quilt' of Tiny Pieces," 24.

89. See Md. Ann. Code, art. EL, §3-102 and §16-202.

90. Mills, "Liberalism and the Racial State," 33.

91. "*The New Jim Crow?*," *Baltimore Sun*, June 18, 2012.

7. CIVIC DISABILITIES

1. The single best resource documenting the state-by-state differences and current standards for "mental competency" challenges is "*Vote. It's Your Right: A Guide to the Voting Rights of People with Mental Disabilities*" (Washington, DC: Bazelon Center for Mental Health Law and National Disability Rights Network, 2008).

2. P. S. Appelbaum, "*Law & Psychiatry: 'I Vote. I Count': Mental Disability and the Right to Vote*," *Psychiatric Services* 51, no. 7 (2000): 849–863; Jason Karlawish et al., "*Addressing the Ethical, Legal, and Social Issues Raised by Voting by Persons with Dementia*," *Journal of the American Medical Association* 292, no. 11 (2004): 1345–1350; Morris M. Klein and Saul A. Grossman, "*Voting Competence and Mental Illness*," *American Journal of Psychiatry* 127, no. 11 (1971): 1562–1565.

3. Pamela Karlan, "*Framing the Voting Rights Claims of Cognitively Impaired Individuals*," *McGeorge Law Review* 38 (2007): 917–930; Jason Karlawish and Richard Bonnie, "*Voting by Elderly Persons with Cognitive Impairment: Lessons from Other Domestic Nations*," *McGeorge Law Review* 38 (2007): 879–916; Nina A. Kohn, "*Preserving Voting Rights in Long-Term Care Institutions: Facilitating Resident Voting While Maintaining Election Integrity*," *McGeorge Law Review* 38 (2007): 1065–1111; Paul Felix Lazarsfeld, Bernard Berelson, and Hazel Gaudet, *The People's Choice: How the Voter Makes Up His Mind in a Presidential Campaign* (New York: Duell Sloan and Pearce, 1944); Deborah Markowitz, "*Voting and Cognitive Impairments: An Election Administrator's Perspective*," *Mc-*

George Law Review 38 (2007): 871–878; Steven K. Metcalf, "The *Right to Vote of the Mentally Disabled in Oklahoma: A Case Study in Overinclusive Language and Fundamental Rights*," *Tulsa Law Journal* 25 (1989): 171–194; "*Note: Mental Disability and the Right to Vote*," *Yale Law Journal* 88 (1979): 1644–1664; Charles Sabatino and Edward Spurgeon, "*Facilitating Voting as People Age: Implications of Cognitive Impairment*," *McGeorge Law Review* 38 (2007): 843–860; Kay Schriner, Lisa Ochs, and Todd Shields, "*Democratic Dilemmas: Notes on the ADA and Voting Rights of People with Cognitive and Emotional Impairments*," *Berkeley Journal of Employment & Labor Law* 21 (2000): 437–472; Schriner, Ochs, and Shields, "*The Last Suffrage Movement: Voting Rights for Persons with Cognitive and Emotional Disabilities*," *Publius: The Journal of Federalism* 27, no. 3 (1997): 75–96; Daniel P. Tokaji and Ruth Colker, "*Absentee Voting by People with Disabilities: Promoting Access and Integrity*," *McGeorge Law Review* 38 (2007): 1015–1064.

4. *Shepherd v. Trevino*, 757 F.2d 1110, 1115 (5th Cir. 1978), emphasis added.

5. *Kronlund v. Honstein*, 327 F. Supp. 71, 73 (N.D. Ga. 1971), emphasis added.

6. Erik Eckholm, "*Inmates Report Mental Illness at High Levels*," *New York Times*, September 7, 2006. See also Pam Belluck, "*Life, with Dementia*," *New York Times*, February 25, 2012.

7. E. Fuller Torrey et al., "*More Mentally Ill Persons Are in Jails and Prisons Than Hospitals: A Survey of the States*" (Alexandria, VA: National Sheriffs' Association, 2010), 1.

8. Ibid., 19.

9. Ibid., 14–15.

10. Andrew Batavia and Kay Schriner, "*The Americans with Disabilities Act as Engine of Social Change: Models of Disability and the Potential of a Civil Rights Approach*," *Policy Studies Journal* 29, no. 4 (2001): 690–702; Kay Schriner and Andrew Batavia, "*The Americans with Disabilities Act: Does It Secure the Fundamental Right to Vote?*," *Policy Studies Journal* 29, no. 4 (2001): 663–673; Kay Schriner and Lisa Ochs, "*Creating the Disabled Citizen: How Massachusetts Disenfranchised People under Guardianship*," *Ohio State Law Journal* 62 (2001): 481–533; Schriner, Ochs, and Shields, "Democratic Dilemmas"; Schriner, Ochs, and Shields, "Last Suffrage Movement"; Lisa Schur et al., "*Enabling Democracy: Disability and Voter Turnout*," *Political Research Quarterly* 55, no. 1 (2002): 167–190.

11. Schriner, Ochs, and Shields, "Democratic Dilemmas," 453.

12. Schriner and Ochs, "Creating the Disabled Citizen."

13. Ladelle McWhorter, "*Where Do White People Come From? A Foucaultian Critique of Whiteness Studies*," *Philosophy & Social Criticism* 31, nos. 5–6 (2005): 540.

14. Ladelle McWhorter, *Racism and Sexual Oppression in Anglo-America: A Genealogy* (Bloomington: Indiana University Press, 2009).

15. Michel Foucault, *Psychiatric Power: Lectures at the Collège de France, 1973–1974*, trans. Graham Burchell (New York: Palgrave Macmillan, 2006), 206.

16. For an account of the transmission of French medical theories to the United States, see Chapter 3 of McWhorter, *Racism and Sexual Oppression in Anglo-America*. See also the extended discussion of Edward Seguin in Chapter 2 of James Trent, *Inventing the Feeble Mind: A History of Mental Retardation in the United States* (Berkeley: University of California Press, 1994).

17. Samuel Gridley Howe, *Report Made to the Legislature of Massachusetts, upon Idiocy* (Boston: Coolidge & Wiley, 1848), 16–17, 20.

18. Ibid.

19. Ibid., 80.

20. McWhorter, *Racism and Sexual Oppression in Anglo-America*, 123.

21. Ibid., 139.

22. Ibid., 134. McWhorter locates the emergence of this figure in Isaac Kerlin, *The Mind Unveiled; or, A Brief History of Twenty-Two Imbecile Children* (Philadelphia: U. Hunt and Son, 1858). See also Trent, *Inventing the Feeble Mind*, 84–88.

23. Howe, *Report Made to the Legislature of Massachusetts, upon Idiocy*, 20, emphasis added. Note the constant reference to age and the expressly Kantian language in the definition.

24. Charles R. Henderson, *Introduction to the Study of Dependent, Defective, and Delinquent Classes and of Their Social Treatment* (Boston: D. C. Heath, 1906), 247.

25. Du Bois, *Souls of Black Folk*, 141–142. See also his account of black crime in *Black Reconstruction in America*, especially the final chapter.

26. Muhammad, *Condemnation of Blackness*, 5.

27. Ibid., 6–7. See Chapter 3 of *Condemnation of Blackness* in particular for a compelling account of how criminal statistics were put so effectively to use to allow European immigrants to become white. See also Chapter 5 of DeLombard, *In the Shadows of the Gallows*.

28. For instance, a discourse around risk and death had already emerged in the antebellum period to set insurance premiums on slaves as property. As Michael Ralph documents, postbellum life insurance premiums reconfigured these connections by linking blackness, debility, and criminality. See Michael Ralph, " 'Life . . . in the Midst of Death': Notes on the Relationship between Slave Insurance, Life Insurance and Disability," *Disability Studies Quarterly* 32, no. 3 (2012), http://dsq-sds.org/article/view/3267.

29. See Book I of Aristotle's *Politics* for the account of these forms of rule as "natural." It is worth noting that Locke too distinguishes *political* power from

these same three forms in §2 of the *Second Treatise*. See Aristotle, *Politics*, trans. Benjamin Jowett (New York: Modern Library, 1943); Locke, *Two Treatises of Government*.

30. Howe, *Report Made to the Legislature of Massachusetts, upon Idiocy*, 73–74.

31. Locke, *Two Treatises of Government*, §55.

32. Ibid., §60. Locke mentions lunatics, idiots, and madmen specifically here. Elsewhere in the text, it is clear that "reason" is not held by those who would refuse to recognize property (e.g., "Savages") and those who have declared war on another unlawfully (e.g., thieves and pirates, who can rightfully be killed or enslaved).

33. Quoted in Trent, *Inventing the Feeble Mind*, 85, emphasis added.

34. Maryland Constitutional Convention (1864), Lord, and Parkhurst, *Debates*, 1273.

35. Ibid.

36. Ibid., 1274.

37. Ibid., 1274–1275.

38. Ibid., 1278.

39. See Delegate Edelen's comments at ibid., 1295.

40. Ibid., 1294.

41. Ibid., 1295.

42. Ibid., 1289, emphasis added.

43. The effectiveness of the penitentiary was a matter of some contention in 1864. Delegate Thruston stated, "Persons convicted of theft or other infamous offences certainly are not entitled to vote. Men convicted of crime and sent to the penitentiary rarely reform. I think it is much better therefore to obviate all danger of such persons being allowed to vote, than to leave the door open to the few who may be disposed to reform" (ibid., 1291). The same position was echoed by Delegate Oliver Miller: "I think the criminal statistics show that very few who come out of the penitentiary ever reform. They go on pretty much the same way again" (1292). This position was rejected emphatically by Delegate Cushing: "A man in the penitentiary is not forced to herd with other felons. He is kept at hard work, and is not allowed to speak to the people that are near him. It is mainly a reformatory power. It gives him time for reflection; and under the present system tends to his improvement" (1294).

44. Delegate Stirling, ibid., 1290.

45. Delegate Thruston, ibid., 1297.

46. Ibid., 1297.

47. Delegates Thruston and Berry, respectively, ibid., 1297, 1296.

48. Interestingly (and ironically given the delegates' obsession over competence), the entire debate over removing the "under guardianship" clause was prompted by a transcription error in the proposed text, leaving it initially un-

clear if the exclusion was intended to only apply to persons under legally imposed guardianship as "lunatics" or as "persons *non compos mentis*" or if persons under guardianship would be excluded in addition to "lunatics" and "persons *non compos mentis*" who might not be under guardianship. Even after correcting the mistake, the delegates used this as an opening to attack the "under guardianship" clause as providing insufficient protection of the franchise. In the end, the amendment to remove the "under guardianship" clause was adopted by so wide a margin that the "nays" were not even recorded in the record. The final reading of the 1864 constitution removed the language of "guardianship," disenfranchising all "lunatics" and persons "*non compos mentis*," regardless of a legal determination.

49. Delegate Berry, ibid., 1298.

50. Ibid.

51. Delegate Thruston even went so far as to assert that questions of age and residency were "far more difficult than this [question] will be" (ibid., 1298).

52. Delegate Jones of Somerset insisted this was "an uncertain and dangerous power" to give to election judges. If it were "left to the judges of election to say that any man is a lunatic and not entitled to vote," he worried, "I doubt whether a sane man can be found in the State" (ibid., 1296).

53. Delegate Jones stated, "No question of judicial construction shall be left open for litigation," continuing, "especially before a tribunal evidently and confessedly incompetent practically to decide such a question" (ibid., 1297).

54. Ibid., 1296. Driven by this concern, Delegate Stirling turns out to be an advocate for a comparatively inclusive definition of the elective franchise on this question, insisting that the test should be in the activity of voting itself: "If a man is able actually to offer his vote, it is sufficient" (1297). Yet he nevertheless accepts exclusion of persons "absolutely under guardianship either as a lunatic, or as a person *non compos mentis*" (1297).

55. Delegate Scott, ibid., 1298, emphasis added.

56. Ibid., 1743, emphasis added.

57. The other key referent for this stabilization, and for which my own account is admittedly and woefully inadequate, is the gender category of "woman." There are numerous references to women throughout the debates, but there is no sustained discussion of women as a "problem," as there was with "free Negroes." When women were invoked, it was (1) in a rare moment of "inclusive" rhetorical flourish (e.g., "the men and women of this state" rather than just "men"), (2) to emphasize the logic of being counted for representation without being given the vote, or (3) to note the extremity of the dependency of black women. In limiting my discussion here to the particular referent of the "free Negro," I do not mean to at all imply that it was the only referent to do this

work but that it was the one most pressing on the minds of the delegates in 1864. Given my own theoretical approach, I readily concede that this omission here limits the reach of my conclusions, as my reading of the debates is clearly a gendered one and, as such, demands further attention.

58. While the "Negro problem" pervades the entire debates, it was taken up in 1864 explicitly in five related questions: (1) the effects of emancipation itself, (2) support for manumitted slaves, (3) forced apprenticeship for "Negro youth," (4) immigration of blacks into the state, and (5) the basis of representation for free blacks in the General Assembly. On the immigration of "free Negroes," see the debates of May 20–21 (ibid., 109–112; 122–127); on apprenticeship of black youth, see June 11, August 26, and September 2 (391–393; 1576–1602; 1795–1800); on the support of manumitted slaves, see July 26 (945–961); on emancipation, see June 17–24 (538–744); and on basis of representation for "free Negroes" in the General Assembly, see July 28 (1032–1059).

59. See also Steedman's discussion of dependency in Chapter 3 of *Jim Crow Citizenship*.

60. Delegate Jones of Somerset, Maryland Constitutional Convention (1864), Lord, and Parkhurst, *Debates*, 599.

61. The biopolitical importance of census data cannot be overstated. On the use of census data and racial formation, see Patricia Cline Cohen, *A Calculating People: The Spread of Numeracy in Early America* (New York: Routledge, 1999); DeLombard, *In the Shadows of the Gallows*; Melissa Nobles, *Shades of Citizenship: Race and the Census in Modern Politics* (Stanford, CA: Stanford University Press, 2000).

62. Maryland Constitutional Convention (1864), Lord, and Parkhurst, *Debates*, 620.

63. Ibid., 624.

64. Ibid., 641.

65. Delegate Dennis, ibid., 644.

66. The thirty-two-page pamphlet, published in 1863 by Van Evrie, Horton in New York, is described in an advertisement: "This is a brief history of the Results of Emancipation, showing its wretched and miserable failure, and that Negro Freedom is simply a tax upon White Labor. The facts in relation to the real condition of the Freed Negroes in Hayti, Jamaica, &c., have been carefully suppressed by the Abolition papers, but they ought to be laid before the public, so that the evils which now afflict Mexico, Hayti and all countries where the Negro-equalizing doctrines have been tried, may be known and understood." Advertisement quoted in John H. Van Evrie, *White Supremacy and Negro Subordination: or, Negroes a Subordinate Race, and (So-Called) Slavery Its Normal Condition* (New York: Van Evrie, Horton, 1868), n.p.

67. Maryland Constitutional Convention (1864), Lord, and Parkhurst, *Debates*, 598.

68. Ibid., 625.

69. In the early days of the convention, a committee formed to deal specifically with the question of "free Negroes" proposed that "no free negro or free mulatto shall come into or settle in this State after the adoption of this Constitution" (ibid., 110). While this proposal ultimately never made it into the constitution, a desire to simply be rid of "free Negroes" pervaded the debate.

70. Delegate Daniel Clarke, ibid., 112.

71. Ibid., 122.

72. Ibid.

73. Ibid., 123.

74. Ibid., 627.

75. Ibid., 111, emphasis added.

76. Mills, *Racial Contract*, 14.

77. Brenda Jo Brueggemann, *"Enabling Pedagogy,"* in *Disability Studies: Enabling the Humanities*, ed. Sharon L. Snyder, Brenda Jo Brueggemann, and Rosemarie Garland Thomson, 317–336 (New York: Modern Language Association of America, 2002), 319.

78. See Fiona Kumari Campbell, *Contours of Ableism: The Production of Disability and Abledness* (New York: Palgrave Macmillan, 2009); Mairian Corker and Sally French, eds., *Disability Discourse* (Buckingham, UK: Open University Press, 1999); Mairian Corker and Tom Shakespeare, eds., *Disability/Postmodernity: Embodying Disability Theory* (London: Continuum, 2002); Lennard Davis, *Enforcing Normalcy: Disability, Deafness and the Body* (London: Verso, 1995); Kim Q. Hall, ed., *Feminist Disability Studies* (Bloomington: Indiana University Press, 2011); Simi Linton, *Claiming Disability: Knowledge and Identity* (New York: New York University Press, 1998); Robert McRuer, *Crip Theory: Cultural Signs of Queerness and Disability* (New York: New York University Press, 2006); Margrit Shildrick, *Dangerous Discourses of Disability, Subjectivity and Sexuality* (New York: Palgrave Macmillan, 2009); Sharon L. Snyder, Brenda Jo Brueggemann, and Rosemarie Garland-Thomson, eds., *Disability Studies: Enabling the Humanities* (New York: Modern Language Association of America, 2002); Shelley Tremain, *"On the Government of Disability,"* *Social Theory and Practice* 27, no. 4 (2001): 617–636; Tremain, *"On the Subject of Impairment,"* in *Disability/Postmodernity*, ed. Mairian Corker and Tom Shakespeare, 32–45 (London: Continuum, 2002); Tremain, ed., *Foucault and the Government of Disability* (Ann Arbor: University of Michigan Press, 2005); Anne Wilson and Peter Beresford, *"Madness, Distress and Postmodernity: Putting the Record Straight,"* in *Disability/Postmodernity*, ed. Mairian Corker and Tom Shakespeare, 143–158 (London: Continuum, 2002).

79. McRuer, *Crip Theory*, 2.

80. For particularly effective instances of such work, see Butler, *Gender Trouble*; Janet E. Halley, *"Reasoning about Sodomy: Act and Identity in and after Bowers v. Hardwick," Virginia Law Review* 79, no. 7 (1993): 1721–1780; *Dorothy E. Roberts, "Punishing Drug Addicts Who Have Babies: Women of Color, Equality, and the Right of Privacy," Harvard Law Review* 104 no. 7 (1990): 1419–1482.

81. Colin Barnes, Geof Mercer, and Tom Shakespeare, *Exploring Disability: A Sociological Introduction* (Cambridge, UK: Polity, 1999), 27. For useful overviews of the history of disability studies, see more generally David L. Braddock and Susan L. Parish, *"An Institutional History of Disability,"* in *Handbook of Disability Studies*, ed. Gary L. Albrecht, Katherine D. Seelman, and Michael Bury, 11–68 (Thousand Oaks, CA: Sage, 2000); Bill Hughes, *"Disability and the Body,"* in *Disability Studies Today*, ed. Colin Barnes, Mike Oliver, and Len Barton, 58–76 (Cambridge, UK: Polity, 2002); Carol Thomas, *"Disability Theory: Key Ideas, Issues and Thinkers,"* in *Disability Studies Today*, ed. Colin Barnes, Mike Oliver, and Len Barton, 38–57 (Cambridge, UK: Polity, 2002).

82. Barnes, Mercer, and Shakespeare, *Exploring Disability*, 28.

83. Tremain, "On the Government of Disability," 623–630.

84. Hughes, "Disability and the Body," 63.

85. See, for instance, Martha Minnow, *Making All the Difference: Inclusion, Exclusion, and American Law* (Ithaca, NY: Cornell University Press, 1991); Anita Silvers, David Wasserman, and Mary B. Mahowald, *Disability, Difference, Discrimination: Perspectives on Justice Bioethics and Public Policy* (Lanham, MD: Rowman & Littlefield, 1998); Young, *Justice and the Politics of Difference*.

86. Iris Marion Young, *foreword* to *Disability/Postmodernity: Embodying Disability Theory*, ed. Mairian Corker and Tom Shakespeare, xii–xiv (London: Continuum, 2002), xiii.

87. In particular, proponents of the social model routinely point to Iris Young's work. For instance, see Barnes, Mercer, and Shakespeare, *Exploring Disability*, 80–83, 94.

88. Tremain, "On the Subject of Impairment," 34.

89. Ibid.

90. As McRuer notes, "Although crip theory . . . should be understood as having a similar contestatory relationship to disability studies and identity that queer theory has to LGBT studies and identity, crip theory does not—perhaps paradoxically—seek to dematerialize disability identity" (*Crip Theory*, 35).

91. Tremain, "On the Government of Disability," 632.

92. Tremain, "On the Subject of Impairment," 42. Alternatively, Hughes puts it this way: "The political radicalism of disability studies was underpinned by a theoretical conservatism that conceded impairment to medical hegemony.

Thus the social model, conceived as the intractable opponent of all things associated with the medical model of disability, came to share with it a common conception of the body as a domain of corporeality untouched by culture" ("Disability and the Body," 67).

93. McWhorter, *Racism and Sexual Oppression in Anglo-America*.

8. (RE)FIGURING JUSTICE

1. Cf. Bernard E. Harcourt, "*Post-modern Meditations on Punishment: On the Limits of Reason and the Virtues of Randomization (a Polemic and Manifesto for the Twenty-First Century),*" *Social Research* 74, no. 2 (2007): 307–346.

2. This work, of course, is already being done. For especially excellent examples see Natalie Cisneros, "*The 'Illegal Alien': A Genealogical and Intersectional Approach*" (Ph.D. diss., Vanderbilt University, 2012); Joseph Fischel, "*Sex and Harm in the Age of Consent*" (Ph.D. diss., University of Chicago, 2011); Nicholas De Genova, "*The Legal Production of Mexican/Migrant 'Illegality,'*" *Latino Studies* 2 (2004): 160–185; Sheth, *Toward a Political Philosophy of Race*; Chris Zepeda-Millán, "*Dignity's Revolt: Threat, Identity, and Immigrant Mass Mobilization*" (Ph.D. diss., Cornell University, 2012).

3. See Shannon Sullivan and Nancy Tuana, eds., *Race and Epistemologies of Ignorance* (Albany: State University of New York Press, 2007).

4. This is similar to how campaigns to reduce sentences and mandatory minimums for drug offenders and other nonviolent offenders can lead to increased punitiveness for violent offenders. See Jonathan Simon, "*Drugs Are Not the (Only) Problem: Structural Racism, Mass Imprisonment, and the Overpunishment of Violent Crime,*" in *Race, Crime, and Punishment: Breaking the Connection in America*, ed. Keith O. Lawrence, 133–148 (Washington, DC: Aspen Institute, 2011).

5. Lennard Davis, "*Bodies of Difference: Politics, Disability, and Representation,*" in *Disability Studies: Enabling the Humanities*, ed. Sharon L. Snyder, Brenda Jo Brueggemann, and Rosemarie Garland-Thomson, 100–108 (New York: Modern Language Association of America, 2002); L. Davis, *Enforcing Normalcy*.

6. Davis's critique of representation echoes Rousseau's insistence that the general will (distinct from the aggregation of individual wills) cannot be represented. See Rousseau, *Of the Social Contract*, III.15.

7. Davis, "Bodies of Difference," 103–104.

8. Ibid., 105.

9. See Young, *Inclusion and Democracy*, Chapter 2 especially. It is also notable that Young endorses a "both/and" position toward the social model of disability and the critical disability studies approach described in the previous chapter, challenging presumptions of a fixed bodily identity. "I would propose,"

she writes, "that the assertion of a 'postmodern' approach to disability studies not be concerned as a displacement of the social model of disability. . . . The social model of disability seems necessary for activists to maintain in their arguments with employers, educators, legislators, and judges" (foreword to *Disability/Postmodernity*, xiv). But, she also notes, we should embrace a "skeptical attitude towards any assumptions about persons positioned as disabled as obvious or given, and a determination to fashion a genealogy of such assumptions that will change the way we all look at the social constraints and particular capacities of many people relatively ignored in theories of subjectivity" (xiii–xiv). Young carefully (and I think rightly) places "postmodern" in scare quotes, drawing attention to the questionable use of this adjective to modify these approaches.

10. Iris Marion Young, "*Asymmetrical Reciprocity: On Moral Respect, Wonder, and Enlarged Thought*," *Constellations* 3, no. 3 (1997): 358.

11. On this point, see Young's critique of the Rawlsian "basic structure" in Iris Marion Young, "*Taking the Basic Structure Seriously*," *Perspectives on Politics* 4, no. 1 (2006): 91–97. In her critique of Rawls's exclusion of persons with "mental disorders" as capable of taking part in political decision making, Young notes that the "usual sense" in which persons are unable to take part in society "harbors for many societies both a prejudice that people with differing physical or mental impairments cannot contribute to the same degree as others, and often presupposes contingent physical structures and social expectations that make some people appear less capable than they would appear within altered structures or expectations" (95–96).

12. Joel Olson is said to have kept a note on his desk that read, "What is the most damage I can do, given my biography, abilities, and commitments, to the racial order and rule of capital?" This powerful question is enshrined on a plaque in an outdoor memorial classroom in his honor at Northern Arizona University, where he taught at the time of his death. It is a question worth asking every day for those of us so situated.

13. Young, *Justice and the Politics of Difference*, 9.

14. Jean-Paul Sartre, *Critique of Dialectical Reason*, vol. 1, trans. Alan Sheridan-Smith (London: Verso, 2004), 256–269; Iris Marion Young, "*Gender as Seriality: Thinking About Women as a Social Collective*," *Signs* 19, no. 3 (1994): 713–738.

15. Young, *Justice and the Politics of Difference*, 45.

16. Young does write directly on the question of criminalized mothers in Iris Marion Young, "*Punishment, Treatment, Empowerment: Three Approaches to Policy for Pregnant Addicts*," *Feminist Studies* 20, no. 1 (1994): 32–57.

17. Young, "Gender as Seriality"; Young, *Inclusion and Democracy*; Young, *Justice and the Politics of Difference*.

18. Young, "Gender as Seriality," 716, 719.

19. Ibid., 717.

20. This was something that Young directly warned me about personally, prior to her untimely passing in 2006. Young wrote that she approaches Sartre's philosophy in the spirit of the "Bandita" who "raids the texts of male philosophers and steals from them what she finds pretty or useful, leaving the rest behind": "In doing so I need not drag all of Sartre with me, and I may be 'disloyal' to him" ("Gender as Seriality," 723). I turn to Young's account in the same spirit and hope to act as a fellow traveler, a feminist criminal, and a bandit myself, to steal from Young's stealing from Sartre. However, I do hope to be "loyal" to Young and respect her sharp analysis and generous spirit. At the least, I want to be faithful to her insistence that critical theory should promote rather than prevent political practice by questioning assumptions about the fluidity and permanence that marks our notions of criminal subjectivity, identity, and identification.

21. Young, "Gender as Seriality," 723.

22. Ibid.

23. Ibid., 724. Young goes on to state that the series is a "less organized and unself-conscious collective" than the group and is "unified passively by the objects around which their actions are oriented or by the objectified results of the material effects of the actions of the others" (724).

24. Ibid., 725–726.

25. For Young's summary, see ibid., 727–728.

26. Ibid.

27. Ibid., 727.

28. Ibid.

29. Ibid., 725.

30. Ibid., 728.

31. Young's turn to seriality reflects her attachment to a critical form of materialism. "Material" must be read to include discursive structures, and her account of "routine practices and habits" surely includes the conditions of practice and habit, the ways of thinking, and epistemological and ontological assumptions about the world. It is a sophisticated conception of materiality, to be sure, but one that is in keeping with Young's project of theorizing justice from the point of view of difference and her attention to the techniques of normalization that characterized her entire body of work.

32. Ibid., 732–733.

33. See also Young's account of the specific mistake of reducing difference into "identity" in Chapter 3 of *Inclusion and Democracy*.

34. Durkheim, *Division of Labor in Society*; Mead, "Psychology of Punitive Justice."

35. I would frequently ask students at the University of Chicago to reflect on this fact. It was often telling the degree to which students who had been otherwise quite comfortable speaking about the "pathologies" of criminality of the impoverished neighborhoods of Woodlawn and Englewood would sometimes reconsider their claims following this thought experiment.

36. Sarah Wheaton, *"Inmates in Georgia Prisons Use Contraband Phones to Coordinate Protest,"* New York Times, December 12, 2010; Wheaton, *"Prisoners Strike in Georgia,"* New York Times, December 12, 2010.

37. I draw these examples of city life to echo Young's own insistence that cities are ideal spaces from which to theorize justice from the point of view of difference rather than homogeneity. See Young, *Justice and the Politics of Difference*, 226–256. On the idea of greeting as a form of political activity, see Young, *Inclusion and Democracy*, 57–62. See also Danielle S. Allen, *Talking to Strangers: Anxieties of Citizenship since Brown v. Board of Education* (Chicago: University of Chicago Press, 2006).

38. Jean-Paul Sartre, *Being and Nothingness: An Essay on Phenomenological Ontology*, trans. Hazel Barns (New York: Philosophical Library, 1956), 49, 485.

39. Ibid., 56.

40. Ibid., 485.

41. Ibid., 56.

42. Simone de Beauvoir, *The Second Sex*, trans. Constance Borde and Shelia Malovany-Chevallier (New York: Vintage, 2011), 16.

43. Ibid.

44. This is, on my reading of Young, one way of understanding the marginalization of historically oppressed and marginalized groups from the theorizing of justice in the Western tradition. See Chapter 6 of Young, *Justice and the Politics of Difference*.

45. See Judith Butler, *"Sex and Gender in Simone de Beauvoir's Second Sex,"* Yale French Studies 72 (1986): 35–49.

46. Simone de Beauvoir, *The Ethics of Ambiguity*, trans. Bernard Frechtman (Secaucus, NJ: Citadel, 1948).

47. Ibid., 73.

48. Beauvoir explores a broader sweep of paradigmatic forms of bad faith in the section "Personal Freedom and Others" of *The Ethics of Ambiguity* through her accounts of the sub-man, the serious man, the adventurer, the passionate man, the critic, and the artist. See ibid., 35–73.

49. I use the term "acknowledge" rather than "recognize" intentionally here, to note the important difference between the two, as explained in detail in Patchen Markell, *Bound by Recognition* (Princeton, NJ: Princeton University Press, 2003). Recognition, on Markell's account, need not take into account the finitude of human action and remains attached to the notion of a sovereign

subject. Acknowledgment, on the other hand, self-consciously accounts for the way in which one's actions are always beyond oneself and implicated in an inter-subjective account of the self. To choose "acknowledgment" over "recognition" as a term of analysis is not to imply that one can simply replace one term with the other, but rather this distinction requires a different approach to agency and the self.

50. Beauvoir, *Second Sex*, 13.

51. Ibid., 17.

52. Beauvoir, *Ethics of Ambiguity*, 73.

53. Ibid., 156.

54. Michel Foucault, *The History of Sexuality, Vol. 2: The Use of Pleasure*, trans. Robert Hurley (New York: Vintage Books, 1990), 6.

55. Michel Foucault, "*An Aesthetics of Existence*," in *Foucault: Live*, 450–454 (New York: Semiotext(e), 1996), 452.

56. Ibid. I take up this analysis more broadly in Dilts, "From 'Entrepreneur of the Self' to 'Care of the Self.'"

57. Michel Foucault, *The History of Sexuality, Vol. 3: The Care of the Self*, trans. Robert Hurley (New York: Vintage Books, 1988), 68.

58. On this point, see Part III of Béatrice Han, *Foucault's Critical Project: Between the Transcendental and the Historical*, trans. Edward Pile (Stanford, CA: Stanford University Press, 2002).

59. Michel Foucault, "*The Ethic of Care for the Self as a Practice of Freedom: An Interview with Michel Foucault on January 20, 1984*," *Philosophy Social Criticism* 12 (1987): 116, emphasis added.

60. McWhorter, *Bodies and Pleasures*, 49.

61. Beauvoir, *Second Sex*, 13.

62. Karen Vintges, "*Simone de Beauvoir: A Feminist Thinker for the Twenty-First Century*," in *The Philosophy of Simone De Beauvoir*, ed. Margaret Simons, 214–227 (Bloomington: Indiana University Press, 2006), 226n. 227. It is true that Foucault and Beauvoir are typically read as being in tension with each other. I think this tension is present but is not evidence that their accounts are incompatible, especially at the level of action and the contingency of present conditions. Moreover, as Judith Butler rightly notes, we can read Foucault's analysis of sex and the body as a "radicalization" of Beauvoir's analysis. See Butler, "Sex and Gender in Simone de Beauvoir's *Second Sex*," 46–47.

63. Young, *Justice and the Politics of Difference*, 28.

64. Ibid., 29.

65. Ibid., 28–29.

66. Ibid., 5.

67. Beauvoir, *Ethics of Ambiguity*, 10.

68. See Jacques Derrida, "*Force of Law: The 'Mystical Foundation of Authority,*'" in *Deconstruction and the Possibility of Justice*, ed. Drucilla Cornell, Michel Rosenfeld, and David Gray Carlson, 3–67 (New York: Routledge, 1992).

69. I am necessarily and intentionally blurring Rawls's distinction between the "concept" of justice (as something whose principles assign rights, duties, and the division of social advantages) and "conceptions" of justice that are contestable instances of this concept. See John Rawls, *A Theory of Justice*, rev. ed. (Cambridge, MA: Harvard University Press, 1999), 9.

70. See especially, Beauvoir, *Ethics of Ambiguity*, 7–34. My gratitude to Robin James for always reminding me of the importance of Beauvoir's critique of philosophical ethics in these pages.

71. Ibid., 13.

72. On some of the possibilities of embracing the idea of "failure" rather than "success," see Judith/Jack Halberstam, *The Queer Art of Failure* (Durham, NC: Duke University Press, 2011).

73. Ladelle McWhorter, *foreword* to *Foucault and the Government of Disability*, ed. Shelley Tremain, xiii–xvii (Ann Arbor: University of Michigan Press, 2005), xvi.

CODA

1. W. E. B. Du Bois, "*The Souls of White Folk*," *Monthly Review* 55, no. 6 (November 2003): 48.

Bibliography

Abramsky, Sasha. *Conned: How Millions Went to Prison, Lost the Vote, and Helped Send George W. Bush to the White House.* New York: New Press, 2006.

Ackerman, Bruce. "*The Emergency Constitution.*" *Yale Law Journal* 113, no. 5 (2004): 1029–1091.

———. "*This Is Not a War.*" *Yale Law Journal* 113, no. 8 (2004): 1871–1907.

Agamben, Giorgio. *Homo Sacer: Sovereign Power and Bare Life.* Stanford, CA: Stanford University Press, 1998.

———. *The Signature of All Things: On Method.* New York: Zone Books, 2009.

Alexander, Larry. "*Consent, Punishment, and Proportionality.*" *Philosophy & Public Affairs* 15, no. 2 (1986): 178–182.

Alexander, Michelle. *The New Jim Crow: Mass Incarceration in the Age of Colorblindness.* New York: New Press, 2010.

Allen, Amy. "*Justice and Reconciliation: The Death of the Prison?*" *Human Studies* 30, no. 4 (2007): 311–321.

Allen, Danielle S. *Talking to Strangers: Anxieties of Citizenship since Brown v. Board of Education.* Chicago: University of Chicago Press, 2006.

Altman, Andrew. "*Democratic Self-Determination and the Disenfranchisement of Felons.*" *Journal of Applied Philosophy* 22, no. 3 (2005): 263–273.

Appelbaum, P. S. "*Law & Psychiatry: 'I Vote. I Count': Mental Disability and the Right to Vote.*" *Psychiatric Services* 51, no. 7 (2000): 849–863.

Aristotle. *Politics.* Translated by Benjamin Jowett. New York: Modern Library, 1943.

Artières, Philippe, Laurent Quéro, and Michelle Zancarini-Fournet, eds. *Le Groupe d'information sur les prisons: Archives d'une luttle, 1970–1972.* Paris: Éditions de L'IMEC, 2003.

Ashcraft, Richard. "*Locke's State of Nature: Historical Fact or Moral Fiction?*" *American Political Science Review* 62, no. 3 (1968): 898–915.

———. *Locke's Two Treatises of Government.* London: Allen & Unwin, 1987.

———. *Revolutionary Politics and Locke's "Two Treatises of Government."* Princeton, NJ: Princeton University Press, 1986.

Askin, Frank. "*Disfranchising Felons (or, How William Rehnquist Earned His Stripes)*." *Rutgers Law Review* 59 (2006): 875–884.

Baily v. Baronian, 120 R.I. 389 (R.I. 1978).

Bair, Asatar P. *Prison Labor in the United States: An Economic Analysis.* New York: Routledge, 2008.

Barnes, Colin, Geof Mercer, and Tom Shakespeare. *Exploring Disability: A Sociological Introduction.* Cambridge, UK: Polity, 1999.

Batavia, Andrew, and Kay Schriner. "*The Americans with Disabilities Act as Engine of Social Change: Models of Disability and the Potential of a Civil Rights Approach.*" *Policy Studies Journal* 29, no. 4 (2001): 690–702.

Bates, David. *States of War: Enlightenment Origins of the Political.* New York: Columbia University Press, 2011.

Beauvoir, Simone de. *The Ethics of Ambiguity.* Translated by Bernard Frechtman. Secaucus, NJ: Citadel, 1948.

———. *The Second Sex.* Translated by Constance Borde and Shelia Malovany-Chevallier. New York: Vintage, 2011.

Beccaria, Caesare. *On Crimes and Punishments.* Translated by David Young. Indianapolis: Hackett, 1986.

Becker, Gary S. "*Crime and Punishment: An Economic Approach.*" *Journal of Political Economy* 76, no. 2 (1968): 169–217.

———. "*Investment in Human Capital: A Theoretical Analysis.*" *Journal of Political Economy* 70, no. 5, Part 2: Investment in Human Beings (1962): 9–49.

———. "*Irrational Behavior and Economic Theory.*" *Journal of Political Economy* 70, no. 1 (1962): 1–13.

———. "*Rational Action and Economic Theory: A Reply to I. Kirzner.*" *Journal of Political Economy* 71, no. 1 (1963): 82–83.

———. "*A Theory of the Allocation of Time.*" *Economic Journal* 75, no. 299 (1965): 493–517.

Behrens, Angela, Christopher Uggen, and Jeff Manza. "*Ballot Manipulation and the 'Menace of Negro Domination': Racial Threat and Felon Disenfranchisement in the United States, 1850–2002.*" *American Journal of Sociology* 109, no. 3 (2003): 559–605.

Belluck, Pam. "*Life, with Dementia.*" *New York Times*, February 25, 2012.

Benhabib, Seyla. "*Judith Shklar's Dystopic Liberalism.*" *Social Research* 61, no. 2 (1994): 477–488.

Bentham, Jeremy. *The Principles of Morals and Legislation*. Amherst, NY: Prometheus Books, 1988.

Billett, Michael. *Highwaymen and Outlaws*. London: Arms and Armour, 1997.

Blackmon, Douglas A. *Slavery by Another Name: The Re-enslavement of Black Americans from the Civil War to World War II*. New York: Anchor Books, 2008.

Boas, Taylor C., and Jordan Gans-Morse. "*Neoliberalism: From New Liberal Philosophy to Anti-liberal Slogan*." *Studies in Comparative International Development* 44, no. 2 (2009): 137–161.

Bobo, Lawrence D., and Victor Thompson. "*Unfair by Design: The War on Drugs, Race, and the Legitimacy of the Criminal Justice System*." *Social Research* 73, no. 2 (2006): 445–472.

Bonnafous-Boucher, Maris. "*From Government to Governance*." *Ethical Perspectives: Journal of the European Ethics Network* 12, no. 4 (2005): 521–534.

Bourdieu, Pierre. "*The Essence of Neoliberalism*." Translated by Jeremy J. Shapiro. *Le monde diplomatique*, December 1998. http://mondediplo.com/1998/12/08bourdieu.

Bouvier, John. *Institutes of American Law*. 4 vols. Philadelphia: R. E. Peterson, 1851.

Bowers, Melanie, and Robert R. Preuhs. "*Collateral Consequences of a Collateral Penalty: The Negative Effect of Felon Disenfranchisement Laws on the Political Participation of Nonfelons*." *Social Science Quarterly* 90, no. 3 (2009): 722–743.

Braddock, David L., and Susan L. Parish. "*An Institutional History of Disability*." In *Handbook of Disability Studies*, edited by Gary L. Albrecht, Katherine D. Seelman, and Michael Bury, 11–68. Thousand Oaks, CA: Sage, 2000.

Brenner, Saul, and Nicholas J. Caste. "*Granting the Suffrage to Felons in Prison*." *Journal of Social Philosophy* 34, no. 2 (2003): 228–243.

Brettschneider, Corey. "*The Rights of the Guilty: Punishment and Political Legitimacy*." *Political Theory* 35, no. 2 (2007): 175–199.

Brewer, Rose M., and Nancy A. Heitzeg. "*Criminal Justice, Color-Blind Racism, and the Political Economy of the Prison Industrial Complex*." *American Behavioral Scientist* 51, no. 5 (2008): 625–644.

Brich, Cecile. "*The Groupe d'information sur les prisons: The Voice of Prisoners? Or Foucault's?*" *Foucault Studies*, no. 5 (2008): 26–47.

Bröckling, Ulrich, Susanne Krasmann, and Thomas Lemke, eds. *Governmentality: Current Issues and Future Challenges*. New York: Routledge, 2011.

Brown, Everett S. "*The Restoration of Civil and Political Rights by Presidential Pardon*." *American Political Science Review* 34, no. 2 (1940): 295–300.

Brown, Wendy. "*American Nightmare: Neoliberalism, Neoconservatism, and De-democratization.*" *Political Theory* 34, no. 6 (2006): 690–714.

———. "*Neo-liberalism and the End of Liberal Democracy.*" *Theory & Event* 7, no. 1 (2003). doi:10.1353/tae.2003.0020.

Brown-Dean, Khalilah. "*One Lens, Multiple Views: Felon Disenfranchisement Laws and American Political Equality.*" Ph.D. diss., Ohio State University, 2003.

———. "*Permanent Outsiders: Felon Disenfranchisement and the Breakdown of Black Politics.*" *National Political Science Review* 11 (2007): 103–119.

Brueggemann, Brenda Jo. "*Enabling Pedagogy.*" In *Disability Studies: Enabling the Humanities*, edited by Sharon L. Snyder, Brenda Jo Brueggemann, and Rosemarie Garland Thomson, 317–336. New York: Modern Language Association of America, 2002.

Brueggemann, Brenda Jo, and James A. Fredal. "*Studying Disability Rhetorically.*" In *Disability Discourse*, edited by Mairian Corker and Sally French, 130–135. Buckingham, UK: Open University Press, 1999.

Buckler, Kevin G., and Lawrence F. Travis III. "*Reanalyzing the Prevalence and Social Context of Collateral Consequence Statutes.*" *Journal of Criminal Justice* 31 (2003): 435–453.

Burch, Traci Renee. "*Punishment and Participation: How Criminal Convictions Threaten American Democracy.*" Ph.D. diss., Harvard University, 2007.

Burchell, Graham, Colin Gordon, and Peter Miller, eds. *The Foucault Effect: Studies in Governmentality*. Chicago: University of Chicago Press, 1991.

Bushway, Shawn D., and Gary Sweeten. "*Abolish Lifetime Bans for Ex-Felons.*" *Criminology and Public Policy* 6, no. 4 (2007): 697–706.

Butler, Judith. *Gender Trouble: Feminism and the Subversion of Identity*. New York: Routledge, 1990.

———. "*Sex and Gender in Simone de Beauvoir's Second Sex.*" *Yale French Studies* 72 (1986): 35–49.

Butler, Sana. "*2003: The 3rd Annual Year in Ideas; Give Felons the Vote.*" *New York Times Magazine*, December 14, 2003, 70.

Calvert, Brian. "*Locke on Punishment and the Death Penalty.*" *Philosophy* 68, no. 264 (1993): 211–229.

Campbell, Fiona Kumari. *Contours of Ableism: The Production of Disability and Abledness*. New York: Palgrave Macmillan, 2009.

Carver, Terrell. "*Gender and Narrative in Locke's Two Treatises of Government.*" In *Feminist Interpretations of John Locke*, edited by Nancy Hirschmann and Kirstie McClure, 187–212. University Park: Pennsylvania State University Press, 2007.

Castel, Robert. "*From Dangerousness to Risk.*" In *The Foucault Effect: Studies in Governmentality*, edited by Graham Burchell, Colin Gordon, and Peter Miller, 281–298. Chicago: University of Chicago Press, 1991.

Chambers, Audrey. "*Votes of Felons, Ex-Felons Would Have Changed Election Outcomes.*" *Institute for Policy Research News* 22 (2001): 1–2.

Charles II. "*By the King: A Proclamation for Discovery of Robberies and Burglaries, and for a Reward to the Discoverers.*" London, 1661.

Chin, Gabriel J. "*Reconstruction, Felon Disenfranchisement, and the Right to Vote: Did the Fifteenth Amendment Repeal Section 2 of the Fourteenth Amendment?*" *Georgetown Law Journal* 92, no. 2 (2004): 259–316.

———. "*Rehabilitating Unconstitutional Statutes: An Analysis of Cotton v. Fordice, 157 F.3d 388 (5th Cir. 1998).*" *University of Cincinnati Law Review* 71 (2002): 421–455.

Cholbi, Michael J. "*A Felon's Right to Vote.*" *Law and Philosophy* 21, nos. 4–5 (2002): 543–565.

Cisneros, Natalie. "*The 'Illegal Alien': A Genealogical and Intersectional Approach.*" Ph.D. diss., Vanderbilt University, 2012.

Clegg, Roger. "*Who Should Vote?*" *Texas Review of Law and Politics* 6 (2002): 159–178.

Coby, Patrick. "*The Law of Nature in Locke's Second Treatise: Is Locke a Hobbesian?*" *Review of Politics* 49, no. 1 (1987): 3–28.

Cogan, Jacob Katz. "*The Look Within: Property, Capacity, and Suffrage in Nineteenth-Century America.*" *Yale Law Journal* 107, no. 2 (1997): 473–498.

Cohen, Patricia Cline. *A Calculating People: The Spread of Numeracy in Early America*. New York: Routledge, 1999.

Colander, David, Robert E. Prasch, and Falguni A. Sheth, eds. *Race, Liberalism, and Economics*. Ann Arbor: University of Michigan Press, 2004.

Connolly, William E. *The Ethos of Pluralization*. Minneapolis: University of Minnesota Press, 1995.

Conrad, Ryan, ed. *Prisons Will Not Protect You*. Lewiston, ME: Against Equality Publishing Collective, 2012.

Corker, Mairian, and Sally French, eds. *Disability Discourse*. Buckingham, UK: Open University Press, 1999.

Corker, Mairian, and Tom Shakespeare, eds. *Disability/Postmodernity: Embodying Disability Theory*. London: Continuum, 2002.

Corlett, J. Angelo. *Responsibility and Punishment*. 2nd ed. Dordrecht, Netherlands: Kluwer, 2004.

CR-10 Publications Collective, ed. *Abolition Now! 10 Years of Strategy and Struggle against the Prison Industrial Complex*. Oakland, CA: AK, 2008.

Crutchfield, Robert D. "*Abandon Felon Disenfranchisement Policies.*" *Criminology and Public Policy* 6, no. 4 (2007): 707–716.

Davidson, Arnold I. Introduction to *Abnormal: Lectures at the Collège de France, 1974–1975*, by Michel Foucault, xvii–xxvi. New York: Picador, 2003.

Davis, Angela. *Abolition Democracy: Beyond Empire, Prisons, and Torture.* New York: Seven Stories, 2005.

———. *Are Prisons Obsolete?* New York: Seven Stories, 2003.

———. "*From the Prison of Slavery to the Slavery of Prison: Frederick Douglass and the Convict Lease System.*" In *The Angela Y. Davis Reader*, edited by Joy James, 74–95. Malden, MA: Blackwell, 1998.

———. "*Race and Criminalization: Black Americans and the Punishment Industry.*" In *The House That Race Built: Black Americas, U.S. Terrain*, edited by Wahneema Lubiano, 264–279. New York: Pantheon, 1997.

———. "*Racialized Punishment and Prison Abolition.*" In *A Companion to African-American Philosophy*, edited by Tommy Lott and John Pittman, 360–369. Oxford, UK: Blackwell, 2003.

Davis, Lennard. "*Bodies of Difference: Politics, Disability, and Representation.*" In *Disability Studies: Enabling the Humanities*, edited by Sharon L. Snyder, Brenda Jo Brueggemann, and Rosemarie Garland-Thomson, 100–108. New York: Modern Language Association of America, 2002.

———. *Enforcing Normalcy: Disability, Deafness and the Body.* London: Verso, 1995.

Dawson, Michael C. *Not in Our Lifetimes: The Future of Black Politics.* Chicago: University of Chicago Press, 2011.

Deacon, Roger Alan. *Fabricating Foucault: Rationalising the Management of Individuals.* Milwaukee: Marquette University Press, 2003.

DeLombard, Jeannine Marie. *In the Shadows of the Gallows: Race, Crime, and American Civic Identity.* Philadelphia: University of Pennsylvania Press, 2012.

Derrida, Jacques. "*Force of Law: The 'Mystical Foundation of Authority.'*" In *Deconstruction and the Possibility of Justice*, edited by Drucilla Cornell, Michel Rosenfeld, and David Gray Carlson, 3–67. New York: Routledge, 1992.

Dilts, Andrew. "*From 'Entrepreneur of the Self' to 'Care of the Self': Neo-liberal Governmentality and Foucault's Ethics.*" *Foucault Studies*, no. 12 (2011): 130–146.

Dinan, John. "*The Adoption of Criminal Disenfranchisement Provisions in the United States: Lessons from the State Constitutional Convention Debates.*" *Journal of Policy History* 19, no. 3 (2007): 282–312.

Dolovich, Sharon. "*Legitimate Punishment in Liberal Democracy.*" *Buffalo Criminal Law Review* 7, no. 2 (2004): 307–442.

Donzelot, Jacques, and Colin Gordon. "*Governing Liberal Societies: The Foucault Effect in the English-Speaking World.*" *Foucault Studies*, no. 5 (2008): 48–62.

Douglass, Frederick. *The Life and Writings of Frederick Douglass.* Edited by Philip Sheldon Foner. 5 vols. New York: International, 1950.

Dreyfus, Hubert L., Paul Rabinow, and Michel Foucault. *Michel Foucault: Beyond Structuralism and Hermeneutics.* 2nd ed. Chicago: University of Chicago Press, 1983.

Du Bois, W. E. B. *Black Reconstruction in America.* Edited by David L. Lewis. New York: Simon & Schuster, 1995.

———. "*The Negro as He Really Is.*" *World's Work* 2 (1901): 848–866.

———. *The Souls of Black Folk.* Edited by Robert Gooding-Williams. Boston: Bedford Books, 1997.

———. "*The Souls of White Folk.*" *Monthly Review* 55, no. 6 (November 2003): 44–58.

Duff, R. A. *Punishment, Communication, and Community.* Oxford: Oxford University Press, 2001.

Duggan, Lisa. *The Twilight of Equality? Neoliberalism, Cultural Politics, and the Attack on Democracy.* Boston: Beacon, 2003.

Dugree-Pearson, Tanya. "*Disenfranchisement: A Race Neutral Punishment for Felony Offenders or a Way to Diminish the Minority Vote?*" *Hamline Journal of Public Policy and Law* 23, no. 2 (2001): 359–402.

Dunn, John. *The Political Thought of John Locke.* Cambridge: Cambridge University Press, 1969.

Durkheim, Emile. *The Division of Labor in Society.* Translated by W. D. Halls. New York: Free Press, 1984.

Eckholm, Erik. "*Inmates Report Mental Illness at High Levels.*" *New York Times*, September 7, 2006.

Ehrlich, Isaac. "*The Deterrent Effect of Capital Punishment: A Question of Life and Death.*" *American Economic Review* 65, no. 3 (1975): 397–417.

Eisenach, Eldon J. "*Crime, Death and Loyalty in English Liberalism.*" *Political Theory* 6, no. 2 (1978): 213–232.

Elden, Stuart. "*The Constitution of the Normal: Monsters and Masturbation at the Collège de France.*" *boundary 2* 28, no. 1 (2001): 91–105.

———. "*Governmentality, Calculation, Territory.*" *Environment and Planning D: Society and Space* 25, no. 3 (2007): 562–580.

———. "*Plague, Panopticon, Police.*" *Surveillance & Society* 1, no. 3 (2003): 240–253.

———. "*Rethinking Governmentality.*" *Political Geography* 26, no. 1 (2007): 29–33.

———. *"The War of Races and the Constitution of the State: Foucault's 'Il faut défendre la société' and the Politics of Calculation."* boundary 2 29, no. 2 (2002): 125–151.

Esposito, Barbara, Lee Wood, and Kathryn Bardsley. *Prison Slavery.* Washington, DC: Committee to Abolish Prison Slavery, 1982.

Everstine, Carl N. *The General Assembly of Maryland, 1850–1920.* Charlottesville, VA: Michie, 1984.

Ewald, Alec C. *"An 'Agenda for Demolition': The Fallacy and the Danger of the 'Subversive Voting' Argument for Felony Disenfranchisement."* Columbia Human Rights Law Review 36 (2004): 109–143.

———. *"'Civil Death': The Ideological Paradox of Criminal Disenfranchisement Law in the United States."* Wisconsin Law Review 2002, no. 5 (2002): 1045–1138.

———. *"Collateral Consequences and the Perils of Categorical Ambiguity."* In *Law as Punishment / Law as Regulation,* edited by Austin Sarat, Lawrence Douglas, and Martha Merrill Umphrey, 77–123. Stanford, CA: Stanford Law Books, 2011.

———. *"Collateral Consequences in the American States."* Social Science Quarterly 93, no. 1 (2012): 211–247.

———. *"A 'Crazy-Quilt' of Tiny Pieces: State and Local Administration of American Criminal Disenfranchisement Law."* Washington, DC: Sentencing Project, 2005.

———. *"Criminal Disenfranchisement and the Challenge of American Federalism."* Publius: The Journal of Federalism 39, no. 3 (2009): 527–556.

———. *The Way We Vote: The Local Dimension of American Suffrage.* Nashville, TN: Vanderbilt University Press, 2009.

Ewald, Alec C., and Brandon Rottinghaus, eds. *Criminal Disenfranchisement in an International Perspective.* Cambridge: Cambridge University Press, 2009.

Farr, James. *"Locke, Natural Law, and New World Slavery."* Political Theory 36, no. 4 (2008): 495–522.

———. *"'So Vile and Miserable an Estate': The Problem of Slavery in Locke's Political Thought."* Political Theory 14, no. 2 (1986): 263–289.

Farrakhan v. Gregoire, 623 F.3d 990 (9th Cir. 2010).

Farrakhan v. Locke, 987 F. Supp. 1304 (E.D. Wash. 1997).

Farrakhan v. Washington, 359 F.3d 1116 (9th Cir. 2004).

Farrell, Daniel M. *"Punishment without the State."* Nous 22, no. 3 (1988): 437–453.

Fasolt, Constantin. *The Limits of History.* Chicago: University of Chicago Press, 2004.

Feeley, Malcolm M., and Jonathan Simon. "*The New Penology: Notes on the Emerging Strategy of Corrections and Its Implications.*" *Criminology* 30, no. 4 (1992): 449–474.

Feinberg, Joel. *Doing and Deserving: Essays in the Theory of Responsibility.* Princeton, NJ: Princeton University Press, 1970.

Feldman, Leonard. *Citizens without Shelter: Homelessness, Democracy, and Political Exclusion.* Ithaca, NY: Cornell University Press, 2004.

Fellner, Jamie, and Marc Mauer. "*Losing the Vote: The Impact of Felony Disenfranchisement Laws in the United States.*" Washington, DC: Sentencing Project, Human Rights Watch, 1998.

"*Felony Disenfranchisement Laws in the United States.*" Washington, DC: Sentencing Project, 2012.

Ferguson, James. "*The Uses of Neoliberalism.*" *Antipode* 41, no. S1 (2009): 166–184.

Ferkiss, Victor. "*'Neoliberalism: How New? How Liberal? How Significant?': A Review Essay.*" *Western Political Quarterly* 39, no. 1 (1986): 165–179.

Fierce, Milfred C. *Slavery Revisited: Blacks and the Southern Convict Lease System, 1865–1933.* Brooklyn, NY: Africana Studies Research Center, Brooklyn College, City University of New York, 1994.

Fischel, Joseph. "*Sex and Harm in the Age of Consent.*" Ph.D. diss., University of Chicago, 2011.

Forman, James, Jr. "*Racial Critiques of Mass Incarceration: Beyond the New Jim Crow.*" *New York University Law Review* 87 (2012): 101–146.

Foucault, Michel. *Abnormal: Lectures at the Collège de France, 1974–1975.* Translated by Graham Burchell. New York: Picador, 2003.

———. "*An Aesthetics of Existence.*" In *Foucault: Live,* 450–454. New York: Semiotext(e), 1996.

———. *The Birth of Biopolitics: Lectures at the Collège de France, 1978–79.* Translated by Graham Burchell. New York: Palgrave Macmillan, 2008.

———. *Discipline and Punish: The Birth of the Prison.* Translated by Alan Sheridan. New York: Vintage Books, 1995.

———. *The Essential Foucault: Selections from Essential Works of Foucault, 1954–1984.* Edited by Paul Rabinow and Nikolas S. Rose. New York: New Press, 2003.

———. "*The Ethic of Care for the Self as a Practice of Freedom: An Interview with Michel Foucault on January 20, 1984.*" *Philosophy Social Criticism* 12 (1987): 112–131.

———. *Ethics: Subjectivity and Truth.* Vol. 1 of *The Essential Works of Michel Foucault, 1954–1984.* New York: New Press, 1997.

———. *The History of Sexuality, Vol. 1: An Introduction.* New York: Vintage Books, 1990.

———. *The History of Sexuality, Vol. 2: The Use of Pleasure.* Translated by Robert Hurley. New York: Vintage Books, 1990.

———. *The History of Sexuality, Vol. 3: The Care of the Self.* Translated by Robert Hurley. New York: Vintage Books, 1988.

———. *Les anormaux.* Edited by François Ewald, Alessandro Fontana, Valerio Marchetti, and Antonella Salomoni. Paris: Gallimard, 1999.

———. *Mal faire, dire vrai: Fonction de l'aveu en justice—Cours de Louvain, 1981.* Louvain: Presses universitaires de Louvain, 2012.

———. *Naissance de la biopolitique: Cours au Collège de France, 1978–1979.* Edited by François Ewald, Alessandro Fontana, and Michel Senellart. Paris: Gallimard, 2004.

———. "*Nietzsche, Genealogy, History.*" In *Language, Counter-Memory, Practice*, edited by Donald F. Bouchard, 139–164. Ithaca, NY: Cornell University Press, 1977.

———. "*Politics and the Study of Discourse.*" In *The Foucault Effect: Studies in Governmentality*, edited by Graham Burchell, Colin Gordon, and Peter Miller, 53–72. Chicago: University of Chicago Press, 1991.

———. *Psychiatric Power: Lectures at the Collège de France, 1973–1974.* Translated by Graham Burchell. New York: Palgrave Macmillan, 2006.

———. *Sécurité, territoire, population: Cours au Collège de France, 1977–1978.* Edited by Michel Senellart, François Ewald, and Alessandro Fontana. Paris: Gallimard, 2004.

———. *Security, Territory, Population: Lectures at the Collège de France, 1977–1978.* Translated by Graham Burchell. New York: Palgrave Macmillan, 2007.

———. *Society Must Be Defended: Lectures at the Collège de France, 1975–1976.* Translated by David Macey. New York: Picador, 2003.

———. *Surveiller et punir: Naissance de la prison.* Paris: Gallimard, 1975.

———. *Wrong-Doing, Truth-Telling: The Function of Avowal in Justice.* Translated by Stephen W. Sawyer. Chicago: University of Chicago Press, 2014.

Friedman, Dan. *The Maryland State Constitution: A Reference Guide.* Westport, CT: Praeger, 2006.

Friedrich, Carl. "*Review: The Political Thought of Neo-liberalism.*" *American Political Science Review* 49, no. 2 (1955): 509–525.

Furman, Jesse. "*Political Illiberalism: The Paradox of Disenfranchisement and the Ambivalences of Rawlsian Justice.*" *Yale Law Journal* 106, no. 4 (1997): 1197–1231.

Gabbidon, Shaun L. "*An Argument for Including W. E. B. Du Bois in the Criminology/Criminal Justice Literature.*" *Journal of Criminal Justice Education* 7, no. 1 (1996): 99–112.

———. "*W. E. B. Du Bois: Pioneering American Criminologist.*" *Journal of Black Studies* 31, no. 5 (2001): 581–599.

Garland, David. "*Frameworks of Inquiry in the Sociology of Punishment.*" *British Journal of Sociology* 41, no. 1 (1990): 1–15.

———. "*Introduction: The Meaning of Mass Imprisonment.*" In *Mass Imprisonment: Social Causes and Consequences*, edited by David Garland, 1–3. London: Sage, 2001.

———. "*The Limits of the Sovereign State: Strategies of Crime Control in Contemporary Society.*" *British Journal of Criminology* 1 (1996): 445–471.

———, ed. *Mass Imprisonment: Social Causes and Consequences*. London: Sage, 2001.

———. "*Penal Excess and Surplus Meaning: Public Torture Lynchings in Twentieth-Century America.*" *Law & Society Review* 39, no. 4 (2005): 793–833.

———. *Punishment and Modern Society: A Study in Social Theory*. Chicago: University of Chicago Press, 1990.

———. "*Sociological Perspectives on Punishment.*" *Crime and Justice* 14 (1991): 115–165.

Garland, David, and Peter Young, eds. *The Power to Punish*. Atlantic Heights, NJ: Humanities, 1983.

Gathings, James A. "*Loss of Citizenship and Civil Rights for Conviction of Crime.*" *American Political Science Review* 43, no. 6 (1949): 1228–1234.

Genova, Nicholas De. "*The Legal Production of Mexican/Migrant 'Illegality.'*" *Latino Studies* 2 (2004): 160–185.

Gilmore, Ruth Wilson. *Golden Gulag: Prisons, Surplus, Crisis, and Opposition in Globalizing California*. Berkeley: University of California Press, 2007.

Glaze, Lauren E., and Erika Parks. "*Correctional Populations in the United States, 2011.*" Washington, DC: U.S. Department of Justice, Bureau of Justice Statistics, 2012.

Goffman, Erving. *Asylums: Essays on the Social Situation of Mental Patients and Other Inmates*. Garden City, NY: Anchor Books, 1961.

———. *Stigma: Notes on the Management of Spoiled Identity*. Englewood Cliffs, NJ: Prentice Hall, 1963.

Golder, Ben, and Peter Fitzpatrick. *Foucault's Law*. London: Routledge, 2009.

Goldman, Daniel. "*The Modern-Day Literacy Test? Felon Disenfranchisement and Race Discrimination.*" *Stanford Law Review* 57, no. 2 (2004): 611–655.

Goldwin, Robert A. "*Locke's State of Nature in Political Society.*" *Western Political Quarterly* 29, no. 1 (1976): 126–135.

Goodnough, Abby. "*Disenfranchised Florida Felons Struggle to Regain Their Rights.*" *New York Times*, March 28, 2004.

Gordon, Colin. "*Governmental Rationality: An Introduction.*" In *The Foucault Effect: Studies in Governmentality*, edited by Graham Burchell, Colin Gordon, and Peter Miller, 1–51. Chicago: University of Chicago Press, 1991.

Grady, Sarah C. "*Civil Death Is Different: An Examination of a Post-Graham Challenge to Felon Disenfranchisement under the Eighth Amendment.*" *Journal of Criminal Law & Criminology* 102, no. 2 (2012): 441–470.

Green v. Board of Election, 380 F.2d 445 (2nd Cir. 1967).

Greene, Helen Taylor, and Shaun L. Gabbidon. *African American Criminological Thought.* Albany: State University of New York Press, 2000.

Guinier, Lani. *The Tyranny of the Majority: Fundamental Fairness in Representative Democracy.* New York: Free Press, 1994.

Halberstam, Judith/Jack. *The Queer Art of Failure.* Durham, NC: Duke University Press, 2011.

Hall, Kim Q., ed. *Feminist Disability Studies.* Bloomington: Indiana University Press, 2011.

Hall, Stuart. "*The Neo-liberal Revolution.*" *Cultural Studies* 25, no. 6 (2011): 705–728.

Halley, Janet E. *Don't: A Reader's Guide to the Military's Anti-gay Policy.* Durham, NC: Duke University Press, 1999.

———. "*Reasoning about Sodomy: Act and Identity in and after Bowers v. Hardwick.*" *Virginia Law Review* 79, no. 7 (1993): 1721–1780.

Hampton, Jean. "*An Expressive Theory of Retribution.*" In *Retributivism and Its Critics*, edited by Wesley Cragg, 1–25. Stuttgart, Germany: Franz Steiner, 1992.

Han, Béatrice. *Foucault's Critical Project: Between the Transcendental and the Historical.* Translated by Edward Pile. Stanford, CA: Stanford University Press, 2002.

Harcourt, Bernard E. *Against Prediction: Profiling, Policing, and Punishing in an Actuarial Age.* Chicago: University of Chicago Press, 2007.

———. *The Illusion of Free Markets: Punishment and the Myth of Natural Order.* Cambridge, MA: Harvard University Press, 2011.

———. *Illusion of Order: The False Promise of Broken Windows Policing.* Cambridge, MA: Harvard University Press, 2005.

———. "*Post-modern Meditations on Punishment: On the Limits of Reason and the Virtues of Randomization (a Polemic and Manifesto for the Twenty-First Century).*" *Social Research* 74, no. 2 (2007): 307–346.

Hardin, Carolyn. "*Finding the 'Neo' in Neoliberalism.*" *Cultural Studies*, December 5, 2012. doi:10.1080/09502386.2012.748815.

Harry, James Warner. *The Maryland Constitution of 1851.* Baltimore: John Hopkins University Press, 1902.

Hart, H. L. A. *The Concept of Law.* 2nd ed. Oxford: Oxford University Press, 1994.

————. *Punishment and Responsibility: Essays in the Philosophy of Law.* New York: Oxford University Press, 1968.

Hartz, Louis. *The Liberal Tradition in America: An Interpretation of American Political Thought since the Revolution.* San Diego: Harcourt Brace Jovanovich, 1991.

Harvey, Alice E. *"Ex-Felon Disenfranchisement and Its Influence on the Black Vote: The Need for a Second Look." University of Pennsylvania Law Review* 142, no. 3 (1994): 1145–1189.

Harvey, David. *A Brief History of Neoliberalism.* Oxford: Oxford University Press, 2007.

Hayden v. Pataki, 449 F.3d 305 (2nd Cir. 2006).

Hegel, Georg Wilhelm Friedrich. *Elements of the Philosophy of Right.* Edited by Allen W. Wood. Translated by Hugh Barr Nisbet. Cambridge: Cambridge University Press, 1991.

Heiner, Brady. *"Foucault and the Black Panthers." City: Analysis of Urban Trends, Culture, Theory, Policy, Action* 11, no. 3 (2007): 313–356.

Henderson, Charles R. *Introduction to the Study of Dependent, Defective, and Delinquent Classes and of Their Social Treatment.* Boston: D. C. Heath, 1906.

Hill, Christopher. *Liberty against the Law: Some Seventeenth-Century Controversies.* London: Penguin, 1996.

Hill, Lewis. *"On Laissez-Faire Capitalism and 'Liberalism.'" American Journal of Economics and Sociology* 23, no. 4 (1964): 393–396.

Hinshelwood, Brad. *"The Carolinian Context of John Locke's Theory of Slavery." Political Theory* 41, no. 4 (2013): 562–590.

Hirsch, Adam Jay. *The Rise of the Penitentiary: Prisons and Punishment in Early America.* New Haven, CT: Yale University Press, 1992.

Hobbes, Thomas. *A Dialogue between a Philosopher and a Student of the Common Laws of England.* Edited by Joseph Cropsey. Chicago: University of Chicago Press, 1971.

————. *Leviathan.* Edited by Edwin Curley. Indianapolis: Hackett, 1994.

Hoffman, Marcello. *"Foucault and the 'Lesson' of the Prisoner Support Movement." New Political Science* 34 (2012): 21–36.

Holloway, Pippa. *"'A Chicken-Stealer Shall Lose His Vote': Disfranchisement for Larceny in the South, 1874–1890." Journal of Southern History* 75, no. 4 (2009): 931–962.

Honig, Bonnie. *Political Theory and the Displacement of Politics.* Ithaca, NY: Cornell University Press, 1993.

————. *"Rawls on Politics and Punishment." Political Research Quarterly* 46, no. 1 (1993): 99–125.

Howe, Samuel Gridley. *Report Made to the Legislature of Massachusetts, upon Idiocy.* Boston: Coolidge & Wiley, 1848.

Hsueh, Vicki. *Hybrid Constitutions: Challenging Legacies of Law, Privilege, and Culture in Colonial America.* Durham, NC: Duke University Press, 2010.

Hughes, Bill. "*Disability and the Body.*" In *Disability Studies Today,* edited by Colin Barnes, Mike Oliver, and Len Barton, 58–76. Cambridge, UK: Polity, 2002.

Hull, Elizabeth. *The Disenfranchisement of Ex-Felons.* Philadelphia: Temple University Press, 2006.

Hunter v. Underwood, 471 U.S. 222 (1985).

Hutchinson, Steven. "*Countering Catastrophic Criminology: Reform, Punishment and the Modern Liberal Compromise.*" *Punishment & Society* 8, no. 4 (2006): 443–467.

Ignatieff, Michael. "*State, Civil Society, and Total Institutions: A Critique of Recent Social Histories of Punishment.*" *Crime and Justice* 3 (1981): 153–192.

Irwin, John. *The Felon.* Englewood Cliffs, NJ: Prentice Hall, 1970.

———. *The Jail: Managing the Underclass in American Society.* Berkeley: University of California Press, 1985.

Itzkowitz, Howard, and Lauren Oldak. "*Restoring the Ex-Offender's Right to Vote: Background and Developments.*" *American Criminal Law Review* 11, no. 721 (1973): 721–770.

Ivison, Duncan. *The Self at Liberty: Political Argument and the Arts of Government.* Ithaca, NY: Cornell University Press, 1997.

Jacobson, Michael. *Downsizing Prisons: How to Reduce Crime and End Mass Incarceration.* New York: New York University Press, 2005.

James, Joy. *States of Confinement: Policing, Detention, and Prisons.* New York: Palgrave Macmillan, 2002.

Johnson-Parris, Afi S. "*Felon Disenfranchisement: The Unconscionable Social Contract Breached.*" *Virginia Law Review* 89, no. 1 (2003): 109–138.

Kalogeras, Steven. "*Legislative Changes on Felony Disenfranchisement, 1996–2003.*" Washington, DC: Sentencing Project, 2003.

Kant, Immanuel. *The Metaphysics of Morals.* Translated by Mary Gregor. Cambridge: Cambridge University Press, 1996.

Karlan, Pamela. "*Convictions and Doubts: Retribution, Representation, and the Debate over Felon Disenfranchisement.*" *Stanford Law Review* 56, no. 5 (2004): 1147–1170.

———. "*Framing the Voting Rights Claims of Cognitively Impaired Individuals.*" *McGeorge Law Review* 38 (2007): 917–930.

Karlawish, Jason, and Richard Bonnie. "*Voting by Elderly Persons with Cognitive Impairment: Lessons from Other Domestic Nations.*" *McGeorge Law Review* 38 (2007): 879–916.

Karlawish, Jason, Richard Bonnie, Paul Appelbaum, Constantine Lyketsos, Bryan James, David Knopman, Christopher Patusky, Rosalie Kane, and Pamela Karlan. "*Addressing the Ethical, Legal, and Social Issues Raised by Vot-*

ing by Persons with Dementia." *Journal of the American Medical Association* 292, no. 11 (2004): 1345–1350.

Katzenstein, Mary Fainsod, Leila Mohsen Ibrahim, and Katherine D. Rubin. "*The Dark Side of American Liberalism and Felony Disenfranchisement.*" *Perspectives on Politics* 8, no. 4 (2010): 1035–1054.

Kerlin, Isaac. *The Mind Unveiled; or, A Brief History of Twenty-Two Imbecile Children.* Philadelphia: U. Hunt and Son, 1858.

Keyssar, Alexander. *The Right to Vote: The Contested History of Democracy in the United States.* New York: Basic Books, 2000.

———. "*Shoring Up the Right to Vote: A Modest Proposal.*" *Political Science Quarterly* 118, no. 2 (2003): 181–190.

Kiersey, Nicholas J. "*Neoliberal Political Economy and the Subjectivity of Crisis: Why Governmentality Is Not Hollow.*" *Global Society* 23, no. 4 (2009): 363–386.

King, Ryan S. "*A Decade of Reform: Felony Disenfranchisement Policy in the United States.*" Washington, DC: Sentencing Project, 2006.

Kingston, Rebecca. "*Locke, Waldron and the Moral Status of 'Crooks.'*" *European Journal of Political Theory* 7, no. 2 (2008): 203–221.

Klein, Morris M., and Saul A. Grossman. "*Voting Competence and Mental Illness.*" *American Journal of Psychiatry* 127, no. 11 (1971): 1562–1565.

Kleinig, John, and Kevin Murtagh. "*Disenfranchising Felons.*" *Journal of Applied Philosophy* 22, no. 3 (2005): 217–239.

Kohn, Nina A. "*Preserving Voting Rights in Long-Term Care Institutions: Facilitating Resident Voting While Maintaining Election Integrity.*" *McGeorge Law Review* 38 (2007): 1065–1111.

Koopman, Colin. *Genealogy as Critique: Foucault and the Problems of Modernity.* Bloomington: Indiana University Press, 2013.

Kramer, Sina. "*On Negativity in Revolution in Poetic Language.*" *Continental Philosophy Review* 46, no. 3 (2013): 465–479.

Kronlund v. Honstein, 327 F. Supp. 71 (N.D. Ga. 1971).

Lafollette, Hugh. "*Collateral Consequences of Punishment: Civil Penalties Accompanying Formal Punishment.*" *Journal of Applied Philosophy* 22, no. 3 (2005): 241–261.

Lazarsfeld, Paul Felix, Bernard Berelson, and Hazel Gaudet. *The People's Choice: How the Voter Makes Up His Mind in a Presidential Campaign.* New York: Duell Sloan and Pearce, 1944.

Lemke, Thomas. *Biopolitics: An Advanced Introduction.* Translated by Eric Frederick Trump. New York: New York University Press, 2011.

———. "*'The Birth of Bio-politics': Michel Foucault's Lecture at the Collège de France on Neo-liberal Governmentality.*" *Economy and Society* 20, no. 2 (2001): 190–207.

Lichtenstein, Alex. *Twice the Work of Free Labor: The Political Economy of Convict Labor in the New South*. London: Verso, 1996.

Linton, Simi. *Claiming Disability: Knowledge and Identity*. New York: New York University Press, 1998.

Lippke, Richard L. "*The Disenfranchisement of Felons*." *Law and Philosophy* 20 (2001): 553–580.

Locke, John. *An Essay Concerning Human Understanding*. Edited by Peter H. Nidditch. Oxford: Oxford University Press, 1975.

———. "*Essays on the Law of Nature*." In *Political Essays*, edited by Mark Goldie, 79–133. Cambridge: Cambridge University Press, 1997.

———. *Two Treatises of Government*. Edited by Peter Laslett. Cambridge: Cambridge University Press, 1988.

Locke v. Farrakhan, 543 U.S. 984 (2004).

Macey, David. *The Lives of Michel Foucault*. London: Hutchinson, 1993.

Mancini, Matthew J. *One Dies, Get Another: Convict Leasing in the American South, 1866–1928*. Columbia: University of South Carolina Press, 1996.

Manfredi, Christopher. "*In Defense of Prisoner Disenfranchisement*." In *Criminal Disenfranchisement in an International Perspective*, edited by Alec C. Ewald and Brandon Rottinghaus, 259–280. Cambridge: Cambridge University Press, 2009.

———. "*Judicial Review and Criminal Disenfranchisement in the United States and Canada*." *Review of Politics* 60 (1998): 277–305.

Manza, Jeff, Clem Brooks, and Christopher Uggen. " '*Civil Death' or Civil Rights? Public Attitudes towards Felon Disenfranchisement in the United States*." *Public Opinion Quarterly* 68, no. 2 (2004): 276–287.

Manza, Jeff, and Christopher Uggen. *Locked Out: Felon Disenfranchisement and American Democracy*. New York: Oxford University Press, 2006.

———. "*Punishment and Democracy: Disenfranchisement of Nonincarcerated Felons in the United States*." *Perspectives on Politics* 2, no. 3 (2004): 491–505.

Markell, Patchen. *Bound by Recognition*. Princeton, NJ: Princeton University Press, 2003.

Markowitz, Deborah. "*Voting and Cognitive Impairments: An Election Administrator's Perspective*." *McGeorge Law Review* 38 (2007): 871–878.

Martel, James R. *Love Is a Sweet Chain: Desire, Autonomy, and Friendship in Liberal Political Theory*. London: Routledge, 2001.

Marx, Karl. "*On the Jewish Question*." In *The Marx-Engels Reader*, edited by Robert C. Tucker, 26–52. New York: Norton, 1978.

Maryland Constitutional Convention (1851). *Debates and Proceedings of the Maryland Reform Convention to Revise the State Constitution*. Annapolis: W. M'Neir, 1851.

Maryland Constitutional Convention (1864), Wm. Blair Lord, and Henry M. Parkhurst. *The Debates of the Constitutional Convention of the State of Maryland.* Annapolis: R. P. Bayly, 1864.

Maryland Constitutional Convention Commission. *Constitutional Revision Study Documents of the Constitutional Convention of Maryland.* Annapolis, 1968.

————. *Debates of the Constitutional Convention of 1967–1968.* Annapolis: Hall of Records Commission, 1982.

————. *Report of the Constitutional Convention Commission: To His Excellency, Spiro T. Agnew, Governor of Maryland, the Honorable, the General Assembly of Maryland, the Delegates to the Constitutional Convention of Maryland and to the People of Maryland.* Annapolis: State of Maryland, 1967.

Mauer, Marc. "*Disenfranchisement of Felons: The Modern-Day Voting Rights Challenge.*" *Civil Rights Journal,* Winter 2002, 40–43.

Mauer, Marc, and Meda Chesney-Lind. *Invisible Punishment: The Collateral Consequences of Mass Imprisonment.* New York: New Press, 2002.

Mauer, Marc, and Sentencing Project (U.S.). *Race to Incarcerate.* New York: New Press, 1999.

McBride, Keally. *Punishment and Political Order.* Ann Arbor: University of Michigan Press, 2007.

McClure, Kirstie. *Judging Rights: Lockean Politics and the Limits of Consent.* Ithaca, NY: Cornell University Press, 1996.

McGary, Howard, and Bill E. Lawson. *Between Slavery and Freedom: Philosophy and American Slavery.* Bloomington: Indiana University Press, 1992.

McRuer, Robert. *Crip Theory: Cultural Signs of Queerness and Disability.* New York: New York University Press, 2006.

McWhorter, Ladelle. *Bodies and Pleasures: Foucault and the Politics of Sexual Normalization.* Bloomington: Indiana University Press, 1999.

————. Foreword to *Foucault and the Government of Disability,* edited by Shelley Tremain, xiii–xvii. Ann Arbor: University of Michigan Press, 2005.

————. *Racism and Sexual Oppression in Anglo-America: A Genealogy.* Bloomington: Indiana University Press, 2009.

————. "*Where Do White People Come From? A Foucaultian Critique of Whiteness Studies.*" *Philosophy & Social Criticism* 31, nos. 5–6 (2005): 533–556.

Mead, George H. "*The Psychology of Punitive Justice.*" *American Journal of Sociology* 23, no. 5 (1918): 577–602.

Mendieta, Eduardo. "*The Prison Contract and Surplus Punishment: On Angela Y. Davis's Abolitionism.*" *Human Studies* 30 (2007): 291–309.

Metcalf, Steven K. "*The Right to Vote of the Mentally Disabled in Oklahoma: A Case Study in Overinclusive Language and Fundamental Rights.*" *Tulsa Law Journal* 25 (1989): 171–194.

Middlemass, Keesha M. "*Rehabilitated but Not Fit to Vote: A Comparative Racial Analysis of Disenfranchisement Laws.*" *Souls* 8, no. 2 (2006): 22–39.

Miles, Thomas J. "*Felon Disenfranchisement and Voter Turnout.*" *Journal of Legal Studies* 33, no. 1 (2004): 85–129.

———. "*Three Empirical Essays in the Economics of Crime.*" Ph.D. diss., University of Chicago, 2000.

Mill, John Stuart. *On Liberty.* Edited by Elizabeth Rapaport. Indianapolis: Hackett, 1978.

Miller, Jim. *The Passion of Michel Foucault.* New York: Simon & Schuster, 1993.

Mills, Charles W. "*Liberalism and the Racial State.*" In *State of White Supremacy: Racism, Governance, and the United States*, edited by Moon-Kue Jung, João H. Costa Vargas, and Eduardo Bonilla-Silva, 27–46. Stanford, CA: Stanford University Press, 2011.

———. *The Racial Contract.* Ithaca, NY: Cornell University Press, 1997.

Minnow, Martha. *Making All the Difference: Inclusion, Exclusion, and American Law.* Ithaca, NY: Cornell University Press, 1991.

Moore, Darrell. "*Epidermal Capital: Formations of (Black) Subjectivity in Political Philosophy and Culture.*" Ph.D. diss., Northwestern University, 1997.

Muhammad, Khalil Gibran. *The Condemnation of Blackness: Race, Crime, and the Making of Modern Urban America.* Cambridge, MA: Harvard University Press, 2010.

Muntaqim v. Coombe, 449 F.3d 371 (2nd Cir. 2006).

Murakawa, Naomi. "*The Origins of the Carceral Crisis: Racial Order as 'Law and Order' in Postwar American Politics.*" In *Race and American Political Development*, edited by Joseph E. Lowndes, Julie Novkov, and Dorian T. Warren, 234–255. New York: Routledge, 2012.

Murphy, Jeffrie G. "*A Paradox in Locke's Theory of Natural Rights.*" *Dialogue* 8 (1969–1970): 256–271.

Myrdal, Gunnar. *An American Dilemma: The Negro Problem and Modern Democracy.* New York: Harper & Row, 1962.

Nealon, Jeffrey T. *Foucault beyond Foucault: Power and Its Intensifications since 1984.* Stanford, CA: Stanford University Press, 2008.

Neal v. Delaware, 103 U.S. 370 (1880).

"*The New Jim Crow?*" *Baltimore Sun*, June 18, 2012.

Nietzsche, Friedrich Wilhelm. *On the Genealogy of Morality: A Polemic.* Translated by Maudemarie Clark and Alan J. Swensen. Indianapolis: Hackett, 1998.

Niles, Alfred Salem. *Maryland Constitutional Law.* Baltimore: Hepbron & Haydon, 1915.

Nino, Carlos. "*A Consensual Theory of Punishment.*" *Philosophy & Public Affairs* 12, no. 4 (1983): 289–306.

————. *"Does Consent Override Proportionality?" Philosophy & Public Affairs* 15, no. 2 (1986): 183–187.

Nobles, Melissa. *Shades of Citizenship: Race and the Census in Modern Politics.* Stanford, CA: Stanford University Press, 2000.

Norris, Andrew. *"The Exemplary Exception: Philosophical and Political Decisions in Giorgio Agamben's Homo Sacer."* In *Politics, Metaphysics, and Death: Essays on Giorgio Agamben's "Homo Sacer,"* edited by Andrew Norris, 262–283. Durham, NC: Duke University Press, 2005.

"Note: Mental Disability and the Right to Vote." Yale Law Journal 88 (1979): 1644–1664.

"Note: The Need for Reform of Ex-Felon Disenfranchisement Laws." Yale Law Journal 83, no. 3 (1974): 580–601.

Olivares, Kathleen M., Velmar S. Burton, and Francis Cullen. *"The Collateral Consequences of a Felony Conviction: A National Study of State Legal Code 10 Years Later." Federal Probation* 60 (1996): 10–17.

Olson, Joel. *The Abolition of White Democracy.* Minneapolis: University of Minnesota Press, 2004.

————. *"The Democratic Problem of the White Citizen." Constellations* 8, no. 2 (2001): 163–183.

"One in 100: Behind Bars in America 2008." Washington, DC: Pew Center on the States, 2008.

Owens, Michael Leo, and Adrienne R. Smith. *"'Deviants' and Democracy: Punitive Policy Designs and the Social Rights of Felons as Citizens." American Politics Research* 40, no. 3 (2012): 531–567.

Pager, Devah. *Marked: Race, Crime, and Finding Work in an Era of Mass Incarceration.* Chicago: University of Chicago Press, 2007.

Paris, Jeffrey. *"Decarceration and the Philosophies of Mass Imprisonment." Human Studies* 30, no. 1 (2007): 323–343.

Pateman, Carol. *The Sexual Contract.* Stanford, CA: Stanford University Press, 1988.

Patterson, Orlando. *Slavery and Social Death: A Comparative Study.* Cambridge, MA: Harvard University Press, 1982.

Pattillo, Mary E., David F. Weiman, and Bruce Western. *Imprisoning America: The Social Effects of Mass Incarceration.* New York: Russell Sage Foundation, 2004.

Peck, Jamie. *Constructions of Neoliberal Reason.* Oxford: Oxford University Press, 2010.

Peck, Jamie, and Adam Tickell. *"Conceptualizing Neoliberalism, Thinking Thatcherism."* In *Contesting Neoliberalism: Urban Frontiers,* edited by Helga Leitner, Jamie Peck, and Eric S. Sheppard, 26–50. New York: Guilford, 2007.

Peters, Charles. *"A Neoliberal's Manifesto." Washington Monthly,* May 1983, 1–10.

Peters, Michael A. "*Foucault, Biopolitics and the Birth of Neoliberalism*." *Critical Studies in Education* 48, no. 2 (2007): 165–178.

Petroski, William. "*NAACP: Branstad's Voting Order Is Discriminatory 'Poll Tax.'*" *Des Moines Register*, January 19, 2011.

Pettit, Becky, and Bruce Western. "*Mass Imprisonment and the Life Course: Race and Class Inequality in U.S. Incarceration*." *American Sociological Review* 69 (April 2004): 151–169.

Pettus, Katherine Irene. *Felony Disenfranchisement in America: Historical Origins, Institutional Racism, and Modern Consequences*. New York: LFB, 2005.

Pinaire, Brian, Milton Heumann, and Laura Bilotta. "*Barred from the Vote: Public Attitudes toward the Disenfranchisement of Ex-Felons*." *Fordham Urban Law Journal* 30 (2003): 1519–1550.

Preuhs, Robert R. "*State Felon Disenfranchisement Policy*." *Social Science Quarterly* 82, no. 4 (2001): 733–748.

Provine, Doris Marie. "*Race and Inequality in the War on Drugs*." *Annual Review of Law and Social Science* 7, no. 1 (2011): 41–60.

Rabinow, Paul, and Nikolas Rose. "*Biopower Today*." *BioSocieties* 1 (2006): 195–217.

Ralph, Michael. "*'Life . . . in the Midst of Death': Notes on the Relationship between Slave Insurance, Life Insurance and Disability*." *Disability Studies Quarterly* 32, no. 3 (2012). http://dsq-sds.org/article/view/3267.

Ramsey, Peter. "*The Responsible Subject as Citizen: Criminal Law, Democracy, and the Welfare State*." *Modern Law Review* 69, no. 1 (2006): 29–58.

Rapoport, Miles S. "*Restoring the Vote*." *American Prospect* 12, no. 14 (2001).

Rawls, John. *A Theory of Justice*. Rev. ed. Cambridge, MA: Harvard University Press, 1999.

Re, Richard M., and Christopher M. Re. "*Voting and Vice: Criminal Disenfranchisement and the Reconstruction Amendments*." *Yale Law Journal* 121, no. 7 (2012): 1584–1670.

Read, Jason. "*A Genealogy of Homo-Economicus: Neoliberalism and the Production of Subjectivity*." *Foucault Studies*, no. 6 (2009): 25–36.

Reback, Gary L. "*Disenfranchisement of Ex-Felons: A Reassessment*." *Stanford Law Review* 25, no. 6 (1973): 845–864.

Reiman, Jeffrey H. "*Liberal and Republican Arguments against the Disenfranchisement of Felons*." *Criminal Justice Ethics* 24, no. 1 (2005): 3–18.

———. *The Rich Get Richer and the Poor Get Prison: Ideology, Class, and Criminal Justice*. 7th ed. Boston: Allyn and Bacon, 2004.

Revel, Judith. *Le vocabulaire de Foucault*. Paris: Ellipses, 2002.

"*Review of the State of Illinois Professional and Occupational Licensure Policies as Related to Employment for Ex-Offenders, A*." Chicago: Safer Foundation, 2002.

Richardson v. Ramirez, 418 U.S. 24 (1974).

Richie, Beth E. *"The Social Impact of Mass Incarceration on Women."* In *Invisible Punishment*, edited by Marc Mauer and Meda Chesney-Lind, 136–149. New York: New Press, 2002.

Roberts, Dorothy E. *"Constructing a Criminal Justice System Free of Racial Bias: An Abolitionist Framework."* *Columbia Human Rights Law Review* 39 (2007): 261–285.

———. *"Punishing Drug Addicts Who Have Babies: Women of Color, Equality, and the Right of Privacy."* *Harvard Law Review* 104, no. 7 (1990): 1419–1482.

Rose, Nikolas, Pat O'Malley, and Mariana Valverde. *"Governmentality."* *Annual Review of Law and Social Science* 2 (2006): 83–104.

Rothchild, Jonathan. *"Dispenser of the Mercy of the Government: Pardons, Justice, and Felony Disenfranchisement."* *Journal of Religious Ethics* 39, no. 1 (2011): 48–70.

Rousseau, Jean-Jacques. *Of the Social Contract.* In *"The Social Contract" and Other Later Political Writings*, edited by Victor Gourevitch, 39–152. Cambridge: Cambridge University Press, 1997.

Rusche, Georg, and Otto Kirchheimer. *Punishment and Social Structure.* New York: Russell & Russell, 1968.

Sabatino, Charles, and Edward Spurgeon. *"Facilitating Voting as People Age: Implications of Cognitive Impairment."* *McGeorge Law Review* 38 (2007): 843–860.

Samson, Peter. *"Richardson v. Ramirez and the Constitutionality of Disenfranchising Ex-Felons."* *New England Law Review* 10 (1974): 477–492.

Sandel, Michael. *Democracy's Discontent: America in Search of a Public Philosophy.* Cambridge, MA: Harvard University Press, 1996.

Sartre, Jean-Paul. *Being and Nothingness: An Essay on Phenomenological Ontology.* Translated by Hazel Barns. New York: Philosophical Library, 1956.

———. *Critique of Dialectical Reason.* Vol. 1. Translated by Alan Sheridan-Smith. London: Verso, 2004.

Schall, Jason. *"The Consistency of Felon Disenfranchisement with Citizenship Theory."* Washington, DC: Sentencing Project, 2004.

Schoolman, Morton. *"The Moral Sentiments of Neoliberalism."* *Political Theory* 15, no. 2 (1987): 205–224.

Schriner, Kay, and Andrew Batavia. *"The Americans with Disabilities Act: Does It Secure the Fundamental Right to Vote?"* *Policy Studies Journal* 29, no. 4 (2001): 663–673.

Schriner, Kay, and Lisa Ochs. *"Creating the Disabled Citizen: How Massachusetts Disenfranchised People under Guardianship."* *Ohio State Law Journal* 62 (2001): 481–533.

Schriner, Kay, Lisa Ochs, and Todd Shields. "*Democratic Dilemmas: Notes on the ADA and Voting Rights of People with Cognitive and Emotional Impairments.*" *Berkeley Journal of Employment & Labor Law* 21 (2000): 437–472.

———. "*The Last Suffrage Movement: Voting Rights for Persons with Cognitive and Emotional Disabilities.*" *Publius: The Journal of Federalism* 27, no. 3 (1997): 75–96.

Schur, Lisa, Todd Shields, Douglas Kruse, and Kay Schriner. "*Enabling Democracy: Disability and Voter Turnout.*" *Political Research Quarterly* 55, no. 1 (2002): 167–190.

Semmes, Raphael. *Crime and Punishment in Early Maryland.* Baltimore: Johns Hopkins University Press, 1996.

Shapiro, Andrew L. "*Challenging Criminal Disenfranchisement under the Voting Rights Act: A New Strategy.*" *Yale Law Journal* 103, no. 2 (1993): 537–566.

———. "*Note: The Disenfranchisement of Ex-Felons: Citizenship, Criminality, and 'the Purity of the Ballot Box.'*" *Harvard Law Review* 102 (1989): 1300–1317.

Sharpe, Andrew N. *Foucault's Monsters and the Challenge of Law.* New York: Routledge, 2010.

Shepherd v. Trevino, 757 F.2d 1110 (5th Cir. 1978).

Sheth, Falguni A. *Toward a Political Philosophy of Race.* Albany: State University of New York Press, 2009.

Shildrick, Margrit. *Dangerous Discourses of Disability, Subjectivity and Sexuality.* New York: Palgrave Macmillan, 2009.

Shklar, Judith N. *American Citizenship: The Quest for Inclusion.* Cambridge, MA: Harvard University Press, 1991.

———. "*Democracy and the Past: Jefferson and His Heirs.*" In *Redeeming American Political Thought,* edited by Stanley Hoffmann and Dennis F. Thompson, 173–186. Chicago: University of Chicago Press, 1998.

———. "*The Liberalism of Fear.*" In *Liberalism and the Moral Life,* edited by Nancy L. Rosenblum, 21–38. Cambridge, MA: Harvard University Press, 1989.

———. "*Obligation, Loyalty, Exile.*" *Political Theory* 21, no. 2 (1993): 181–197.

Silvers, Anita, David Wasserman, and Mary B. Mahowald. *Disability, Difference, Discrimination: Perspectives on Justice Bioethics and Public Policy.* Lanham, MD: Rowman & Littlefield, 1998.

Simmons, A. John. "*Locke and the Right to Punish.*" *Philosophy & Public Affairs* 20, no. 4 (1991): 311–349.

———. *The Lockean Theory of Rights.* Princeton, NJ: Princeton University Press, 1992.

———. "*Locke on the Death Penalty.*" *Philosophy* 69, no. 270 (1994): 471–477.

———. "*Locke's State of Nature.*" *Political Theory* 17, no. 3 (1989): 449–470.

———. *On the Edge of Anarchy: Locke, Consent, and the Limits of Society*. Princeton, NJ: Princeton University Press, 1993.

———, ed. *Punishment*. Princeton, NJ: Princeton University Press, 1995.

Simon, Jonathan. *"Drugs Are Not the (Only) Problem: Structural Racism, Mass Imprisonment, and the Overpunishment of Violent Crime."* In *Race, Crime, and Punishment: Breaking the Connection in America*, edited by Keith O. Lawrence, 133–148. Washington, DC: Aspen Institute, 2011.

———. *Governing through Crime: How the War on Crime Transformed American Democracy and Created a Culture of Fear*. New York: Oxford University Press, 2007.

Simson, Elizabeth. *"Justice Denied: How Felony Disenfranchisement Laws Undermine American Democracy."* Americans For Democratic Action Education Fund, 2002.

Smith, Andrea. *"Heteropatriarchy and the Three Pillars of White Supremacy."* In *Color of Violence: The Incite! Anthology*, edited by Incite! Women of Color Against Violence, 66–73. Cambridge, MA: South End, 2006.

Smith, Rogers M. *"Beyond Tocqueville, Myrdal, and Hartz: The Multiple Traditions in America."* *American Political Science Review* 87, no. 3 (1993): 549–566.

———. *Civic Ideals: Conflicting Visions of Citizenship in U.S. History*. New Haven, CT: Yale University Press, 1997.

Snyder, Sharon L., Brenda Jo Brueggemann, and Rosemarie Garland-Thomson, eds. *Disability Studies: Enabling the Humanities*. New York: Modern Language Association of America, 2002.

Soss, Joe, Richard C. Fording, and Sanford Schram. *Disciplining the Poor: Neoliberal Paternalism and the Persistent Power of Race*. Chicago: University of Chicago Press, 2011.

Spade, Dean. *Normal Life: Administrative Violence, Critical Trans Politics and the Limits of Law*. Cambridge, MA: South End, 2011.

Spence, Lester K. *"The Neoliberal Turn in Black Politics."* *Souls* 14, nos. 3–4 (2013): 139–159.

Spraggs, Gillian. *Outlaws and Highwaymen: The Cult of the Robber in England from the Middle Ages to the Nineteenth Century*. London: Pimlico, 2001.

Stanley, Eric A., and Nat Smith, eds. *Captive Genders: Trans Embodiment and the Prison Industrial Complex*. Oakland, CA: AK, 2011.

State v. Bixler, 62 Md. 354 (Md. 1884).

Steedman, Marek D. *Jim Crow Citizenship: Liberalism and the Southern Defense of Racial Hierarchy*. New York: Routledge, 2012.

Stevens, Jacqueline. *"On the Morals of Genealogy."* *Political Theory* 31, no. 4 (2003): 558–588.

Stevens, Jacqueline, and Rogers Smith. "*Beyond Tocqueville, Please!*" *American Political Science Review* 89, no. 4 (1995): 987–995.

Stigler, George J. "*The Optimum Enforcement of Laws.*" *Journal of Political Economy* 78, no. 3 (1970): 526–536.

Strauss, Leo. *Natural Right and History*. Chicago: University of Chicago Press, 1965.

———. "*On Locke's Doctrine of Natural Right.*" *Philosophical Review* 61, no. 4 (1952): 475–502.

Stuart, Guy. "*Databases, Felons, and Voting: Bias and Partisanship of the Florida Felons List in the 2000 Elections.*" *Political Science Quarterly* 119, no. 3 (2004): 453–475.

Sullivan, Shannon, and Nancy Tuana, eds. *Race and Epistemologies of Ignorance*. Albany: State University of New York Press, 2007.

Sykes, Gresham M. *The Society of Captives: A Study of a Maximum Security Prison*. Princeton, NJ: Princeton University Press, 1958.

Taifa, Nkechi. "*Re-enfranchisement! A Guide for Individual Restoration of Voting Rights in States That Permanently Disenfranchise Former Felons.*" Washington, DC: Advancement Project, 2002.

Tarcov, Nathan. "*Locke's Second Treatise and 'the Best Fence against Rebellion.'*" *Review of Politics* 43, no. 2 (1981): 198–217.

"*Task Force to Study Repealing the Disenfranchisement of Convicted Felons in Maryland.*" Annapolis, MD: Department of Legislative Services, Office of Policy Analysis, 2002.

Terchek, Ronald J., and Stanley C. Brubaker. "*Punishing Liberals or Rehabilitating Liberalism?*" *American Political Science Review* 83, no. 4 (1989): 1309–1316.

Thiess v. State Administrative Board of Election Laws, 387 F. Supp. 1038 (D. Md. 1974).

Thomas, Carol. "*Disability Theory: Key Ideas, Issues and Thinkers.*" In *Disability Studies Today*, edited by Colin Barnes, Mike Oliver, and Len Barton, 38–57. Cambridge, UK: Polity, 2002.

Thompson, Kevin. "*To Judge the Intolerable.*" *Philosophy Today* 54 (2010): 169–176.

Tims, Douglas R. "*The Disenfranchisement of Ex-Felons: A Cruelly Excessive Punishment.*" *Southwestern University Law Review* 7, no. 1 (1975): 124–160.

Tobias, D. E. "*A Negro on the Position of the Negro in America.*" *Nineteenth Century: A Monthly Review* 46, no. 274 (1899): 957–973.

Tocqueville, Alexis de. *Democracy in America*. New York: HarperPerennial, 2006.

Tokaji, Daniel P., and Ruth Colker. "*Absentee Voting by People with Disabilities: Promoting Access and Integrity.*" *McGeorge Law Review* 38 (2007): 1015–1064.

Tonry, Michael H. *Malign Neglect: Race, Crime, and Punishment in America.* New York: Oxford University Press, 1995.

Torrey, E. Fuller, Aaron D. Kennard, Don Eslinger, Richard Lamb, and James Pavle. *"More Mentally Ill Persons Are in Jails and Prisons Than Hospitals: A Survey of the States."* Alexandria, VA: National Sheriffs' Association, 2010.

Tremain, Shelley, ed. *Foucault and the Government of Disability.* Ann Arbor: University of Michigan Press, 2005.

———. *"On the Government of Disability."* *Social Theory and Practice* 27, no. 4 (2001): 617–636.

———. *"On the Subject of Impairment."* In *Disability/Postmodernity*, edited by Mairian Corker and Tom Shakespeare, 32–45. London: Continuum, 2002.

"Trends in U.S. Corrections." Washington, DC: Sentencing Project, 2011.

Trent, James. *Inventing the Feeble Mind: A History of Mental Retardation in the United States.* Berkeley: University of California Press, 1994.

Trop v. Dulles, 356 U.S. 86 (1958).

Tuck, Richard. *Natural Rights Theories: Their Origin and Development.* Cambridge: Cambridge University Press, 1979.

———. *The Rights of War and Peace: Political Thought and the International Order from Grotius to Kant.* Oxford: Oxford University Press, 1999.

Tully, James. *An Approach to Political Philosophy: Locke in Contexts.* Cambridge: Cambridge University Press, 1993.

———. *"Political Freedom."* *Journal of Philosophy* 87, no. 10 (1990): 517–523.

Tunick, Mark. *Hegel's Political Philosophy: Interpreting the Practice of Legal Punishment.* Princeton, NJ: Princeton University Press, 1992.

———. *Punishment: Theory and Practice.* Berkeley: University of California Press, 1992.

Uggen, Christopher, and Jeff Manza. *"Democratic Contraction? Political Consequences of Felon Disenfranchisement in the United States."* *American Sociological Review* 67 (2002): 777–803.

Valverde, Mariana. *"Genealogies of European States: Foucauldian Reflections."* *Economy and Society* 36, no. 1 (2007): 159–178.

Van Evrie, John H. *White Supremacy and Negro Subordination; or, Negroes a Subordinate Race, and (So-Called) Slavery Its Normal Condition.* New York: Van Evrie, Horton, 1868.

Vaughan, Barry. *"Punishment and Conditional Citizenship."* *Punishment and Society* 2, no. 1 (2001): 23–39.

Vile, John R. *"The Right to Vote as Applied to Ex-Felons."* *Federal Probation* 45, no. 1 (1981): 12–16.

Vintges, Karen. *"Simone de Beauvoir: A Feminist Thinker for the Twenty-First Century."* In *The Philosophy of Simone de Beauvoir*, edited by Margaret Simons, 214–227. Bloomington: Indiana University Press, 2006.

Von Leyden, Wolfgang. "*Locke's Strange Doctrine of Punishment*." In *John Locke: Symposium, Wolfenbüttel 1979*, edited by Reinhard Brandt, 113–127. Berlin: Walter du Gruyter, 1981.

"*Vote. It's Your Right: A Guide to the Voting Rights of People with Mental Disabilities.*" Washington, DC: Bazelon Center for Mental Health Law and National Disability Rights Network, 2008.

Wacquant, Loïc. "*Deadly Symbiosis: When Ghetto and Prison Meet and Mesh.*" *Punishment & Society* 3, no. 1 (2001): 95–134.

———. "*From Slavery to Mass Incarceration.*" *New Left Review* 13 (2002): 41–60.

———. "*The Penalisation of Poverty and the Rise of Neo-liberalism.*" *European Journal on Criminal Policy and Research* 9, no. 4 (2001): 401–412.

———. *Prisons of Poverty*. Exp. ed. Minneapolis: University of Minnesota Press, 2009.

———. *Punishing the Poor: The Neoliberal Government of Social Insecurity*. Durham, NC: Duke University Press, 2009.

———. "*Race as Civic Felony.*" *International Social Science Journal* 57, no. 183 (2005): 127–142.

———. "*Three Steps to a Historical Anthropology of Actually Existing Neoliberalism.*" *Social Anthropology* 20, no. 1 (2012): 66–79.

Wagandt, Charles. *The Mighty Revolution: Negro Emancipation in Maryland, 1862–1864*. Baltimore: Maryland Historical Society, 2004.

Waldron, Jeremy. *God, Locke, and Equality: Christian Foundations of John Locke's Political Thought*. New York: Cambridge University Press, 2002.

Washington v. State, 75 Ala. 582 (Ala. 1884).

Weaver, Vesla. "*Frontlash: Race and the Development of Punitive Crime Policy.*" *Studies in American Political Development* 21, no. 2 (2007): 230–265.

Welch, Michael. "*Counterveillance: How Foucault and the Groupe d'information sur les prisons Reversed the Optics.*" *Theoretical Criminology* 15 (2011): 301–313.

———. "*Pastoral Power as Penal Resistance: Foucault and the Groupe d'Information sur les Prisons.*" *Punishment & Society* 12, no. 1 (2010): 47–63.

———. *Punishment in America: Social Control and the Ironies of Imprisonment*. Thousand Oaks, CA: Sage, 1999.

Wells, Ida B., Frederick Douglass, Irvine Garland Penn, and Ferdinand L. Barnett. *The Reason Why the Colored American Is Not in the World's Columbian Exposition*. Urbana: University of Illinois Press, 1999.

Western, Bruce. *Punishment and Inequality in America*. New York: Russell Sage Foundation, 2006.

Wheaton, Sarah. "*Inmates in Georgia Prisons Use Contraband Phones to Coordinate Protest.*" *New York Times*, December 12, 2010.

———. "*Prisoners Strike in Georgia.*" *New York Times*, December 12, 2010.

Wheelock, Darren. "*Collateral Consequences and Racial Inequality: Felon Status Restrictions as a System of Disadvantage.*" *Journal of Contemporary Criminal Justice* 21, no. 1 (2005): 82–90.

Wilson, Anne, and Peter Beresford. "*Madness, Distress and Postmodernity: Putting the Record Straight.*" In *Disability/Postmodernity*, edited by Mairian Corker and Tom Shakespeare, 143–158. London: Continuum, 2002.

Winnubst, Shannon. *Queering Freedom*. Bloomington: Indiana University Press, 2006.

Yolton, John W. "*Locke on the Law of Nature.*" *Philosophical Review* 67, no. 4 (1958): 477–498.

Young, Iris Marion. "*Asymmetrical Reciprocity: On Moral Respect, Wonder, and Enlarged Thought.*" *Constellations* 3, no. 3 (1997): 340–363.

———. *Foreword* to *Disability/Postmodernity: Embodying Disability Theory*, edited by Mairian Corker and Tom Shakespeare, xii–xiv. London: Continuum, 2002.

———. "*Gender as Seriality: Thinking about Women as a Social Collective.*" *Signs* 19, no. 3 (1994): 713–738.

———. *Inclusion and Democracy*. Oxford: Oxford University Press, 2000.

———. *Justice and the Politics of Difference*. Princeton, NJ: Princeton University Press, 1990.

———. "*Punishment, Treatment, Empowerment: Three Approaches to Policy for Pregnant Addicts.*" *Feminist Studies* 20, no. 1 (1994): 32–57.

———. "*Taking the Basic Structure Seriously.*" *Perspectives on Politics* 4, no. 1 (2006): 91–97.

Zepeda-Millán, Chris. "*Dignity's Revolt: Threat, Identity, and Immigrant Mass Mobilization.*" Ph.D. diss., Cornell University, 2012.

Index